LightWave 3D® 8 Lighting

Nicholas Boughen

Wordware Publishing, Inc.

Library of Congress Cataloging-in-Publication Data

Boughen, Nicholas.
   LightWave 3D 8 lighting / by Nicholas Boughen.
      p.   cm.
   Includes index.
   ISBN 1-55622-094-4 (pbk., companion cd-rom)
   1. Computer animation. 2. Computer graphics. 3. LightWave 3D. I. Title.
   TR897.7.B675 2004
   006.6'96—dc22   2004000201
                                    CIP

ISBN 1-55622-094-4

10 9 8 7 6 5 4 3 2 1
0402

All inquiries for volume purchases of this book should be addressed to Wordware
Publishing, Inc., at the above address. Telephone inquiries may be made by calling:

(972) 423-0090

This work is dedicated

To my wife, Victoria,
And my son, Michael,
And to my beautiful new daughter, Princess Katherine

And also to every artist who wishes to learn;
Who, for some reason or another,
Has discovered that we will never be the best
Until we pursue excellence
In a race against ourselves

Contents

Part I
Lighting Theory

Part II

Introduction to LightWave's Lighting Toolkit

Part III

Creating Lighting

Foreword

Education is not the filling of a pail, but the lighting of a fire.
— W. B. Yeats

Years ago when I was in college preparing for My Future — is it the Future already? — I learned some valuable information that has been the foundation on which I have built my skill set. I learned about design, layout, and other visual communication skills. Oh yeah, and lighting. I learned lighting by accident.

My last year in school I had a few credits to burn, so I signed up for a photography class thinking it would be a great way to capture images and create my own reference material from which to paint. I thought I would spend most of my time learning about developing film and operating the camera. Instead, we spent the entire semester learning about lighting for photography. Little did I know that I was about to learn the most valuable information about working in 3D. I was convinced that all I needed to do was point and click the camera, and I would have a perfect picture. If there is one thing that I took away from that class, is to always pay attention to lighting conditions when creating a photo — lighting plays a key role in getting a quality shot.

Unfortunately, most young 3D artists approach lighting the same way I approached photography before that class. Many artists spend days working on a model and countless hours texturing it — only to spend just a few minutes lighting it. For many, lighting is a second thought. The three steps of 3D for most people are Model, Animate, Render. What many people forget is that without great lighting, even the best models and textures won't give you a great final product.

As a member of the 3D community, I spend many hours of my free time in community forums talking about LightWave®, sharing tips and tricks, and visiting the many online image galleries. Common replys to gallery posts are "great model," "awesome textures," "killer animation," and other praise for every area of 3D, but very few replies mention lighting. What would those "killer" images be without "killer" lighting?

Throughout the years I have had the honor of meeting many talented artists, but I have never met someone more passionate about lighting than Nicholas Boughen. Who better to teach you the skills of lighting than someone who has over 20 years of experience, and puts it to use on a daily basis? Remember that you are learning from someone who not only has the ability and knowledge to apply it in a real-world production environment but also has the unique talents required to pass that knowledge on to others.

Get ready to attend lighting school.

LightWave 3D 8 Lighting will teach you how to work with lights inside of LightWave and how to break down real-world lighting so that you can recreate it in your virtual world. This book will take your lighting to a whole new level and give your work that edge you've been looking for. I'm sure you will be left with the same impression I had when I finished this book — "Priceless."

— William Vaughan

Freedom is just chaos, with better lighting.
— Alan Dean Foster, *To the Vanishing Point*

. . .

William "Proton" Vaughan is a seasoned LightWave veteran who currently is NewTek's LightWave 3D evangelist. Not only does he love working in LightWave and promoting it around the globe for NewTek, he is also the recipient of several New Media Addy awards.

William Vaughan brings broad-based experience to his position at NewTek, having done 3D work for print, web, multimedia, games, and broadcast. Over the past ten years, Vaughan has established a strong reputation for his award-winning work for clients such as Compaq, New Line Cinema, Halliburton, and many others. He has also worked in the LightWave community as an instructor at North Harris Community College.

Vaughan's other activities in LightWave user education include training entire companies to use LightWave, such as NASA, Fulbright & Jaworski, and KHOU Channel 11, the CBS affiliate in Houston.

Acknowledgments

First and foremost, I must offer my gratitude to the readers of *LightWave 3D 7.5 Lighting* who provided generous praise of that first book as well as encouragement and suggestions to update the work and keep it current.

Secondly, I wish to thank my publisher, Wes Beckwith, for his endless encouragement, support, and enthusiasm for both the writing project and for LightWave. I am grateful for the confidence he placed in me to complete this project to a high standard and on schedule. Thanks to all the Wordware folks for their contributions and efforts on this book, especially the ever-vigilant Beth Kohler who sifts through the text to find and squash the smallest errors.

I'd also like to acknowledge the contributions of William "Proton" Vaughan, NewTek's LightWave evangelist, who served as technical editor on this book, scanning through all the hundreds of pages of text seeking technical imperfection or unclarity in the work. His effort also served to bring you a better, more informative final product. A few of his models have been included in this edition — both in the images on the pages and also on the companion CD.

I wish to mention the tireless support from the rest of the NewTek family. Specifically I wish to acknowledge Chuck Baker, Deuce Bennett, Andrew Cross, and Art Howe who provided me with everything I needed to complete the book.

Thanks to Erkki Halkka and Steve Worley for their respective contributions to the plug-ins section of this book, as well as their great lighting tools, Overcaster and G2, respectively.

I'd like to acknowledge the contributions of Jessica Chambers, Technical Director at the Shadbolt Centre for the Arts in Burnaby, British Columbia, Canada. Thanks to Jessica for the use of her head in Chapter 1 and the use of her theatre facilities to photograph some of the lighting concepts I attempt to describe herein.

Thanks to Rainmaker's Brian Moylan, Director of Digital Imaging and Jason Dowdeswell, VFX Supervisor, for endless support and enthusiasm for the job, for keeping it real, and for encouraging personal projects such as this that sometimes take time and focus away from the pressure cooker of daily production work.

No such acknowledgment would be complete without mentioning my friend and personal Yoda, James Hebb, Director of The Embassy

Visual Effects in Vancouver, who got me started down this road in the first place way back in the olden days.

There are numerous others who have contributed in some part to this book. From some hyper-talented lighting designers and college professors back in the mists of time to the LightWave artists of the world, some with whom I work every day, some who I know only by reputation. All from whom I constantly learn new tricks and techniques. Every step down the path has lead to this book and so here it is. I hope you enjoy it. I hope, especially though, that this book brings you some new skill or understanding and helps improve your lighting in some small way.

Introduction

This book is divided into three main parts: theory, tools, and practice. Part I covers the fundamentals of what light is, how it acts and reacts in our world, and what those reactions look like. Part II covers the virtual lighting equipment available to achieve your LightWave lighting goals. Part III deals with how to use those tools to create the lighting we desire. Theory is first in this book because it is fundamental to using the tools. In fact, any artist using any toolkit can make good use of the theoretical section of this book. The qualities of light do not change, regardless of what software you are using.

While reading this book you will find many areas where overlapping and repetition occurs. Lighting a scene involves the application of numerous tools, methods, and properties that are all interlinked. Although I have endeavored to separate each element into chapters for easy comprehension, they nonetheless overlap here and there. I found that a small measure of repetition is preferable to constantly referring the reader to other chapters.

Why Write This Book?

I have had the privilege of working with some incredibly talented artists, yet some of them have not grasped the simplest lighting principles. The final scene is beautiful to be sure, but many artists run into two main problems lighting those scenes. One is that even though the lighting is perfect and beautiful, it may have taken hours to accomplish through a system of trial and error. The other problem is that the lighting is imperfect, perhaps disobeying the laws of physics. It just looks wrong. The artist and viewer may not be able to put their finger exactly on the problem, but even an untrained eye has spent a lifetime experiencing the properties and qualities of light. You can't fool the audience. Understanding a few principles can solve this problem for the artist.

I have a 20-year background in practical lighting for stage and video. My studies derive from those of artists throughout history who have labored to understand the properties and qualities of light so they might incorporate those qualities into their own works. It seems natural that 3D artists should begin from the same point as painters, sculptors, and photographers, especially since 3D art embodies all three of these disciplines.

Good lighting can make the difference between a good shot and a great one. I would like to see more artists equipped with a strong enough understanding of lighting to make them masters of their art. To that end, I wish to share the knowledge and experience I have acquired over the years.

Why Read This Book?

If you have ever looked at a photograph and been unable to decipher the light sources, direction, and color, or if you have been unable to replicate this lighting within LightWave 3D, then this book will help you. If you have ever thought your lighting looked flat, boring, meaningless, inane, incomprehensible, stale, cliché (stop me any time), overused, cheesy, CG, fake, or derivative, then reading this book might be a good move. If you have ever wondered how to make objects stand out from the background, how to demonstrate all the minute detail you have spent weeks modeling, or want to make a shot feel sad, angry, or joyous, then you might take some time to look through these pages. If you have seen the work of some great 3D artists and marveled at how photo-real everything looks and wished you could add that sense of realism to your work, then read on.

Good lighting is crucial to the final look of your shot. Even a poorly designed, marginally textured object can still look as if it really exists in the scene if the lighting is good. On the other hand, a beautifully designed, painstakingly modeled and textured object, if lit poorly, will be easily identified as computer generated.

Screw Physics!

Physics nitpickers, beware. This section may offend some readers.

Lighting can be a very contentious issue. That is not to say that it is very complex or difficult to learn. It is not. But it can be difficult to talk about. This is mainly because there is a certain breed of people who just can't let reality go. I teach that a shadow may have a certain color based on a number of different environmental factors. Someone nitpicks that shadows don't actually have any color, being, themselves, the simple absence of light. (This is technically true, but quite unimportant to CG lighting.) I teach that certain light types behave a particular way. Some physics snob claims it's all wrong and lectures me about angstroms, electromagnetic wavelengths, photons, and wave theory.

It comes down to a few simple arguments. First, computer-generated imagery is fake. It is therefore not real and subsequently is not obliged to live by real laws of physics.

Second, it is unimportant what hacks and tricks you had to pull, what physics you had to ignore, as long as things turned out the way you intended and the final render looks great.

Third, did you really purchase this book for a lecture on angstroms, electromagnetism, and the behavior of up quarks and down quarks? Or is it the art of computer-generated lighting we're talking about?

Hopefully by the time you have reached this paragraph, you have either tossed this book in the bin because you are a nit-picking physics snob and I have deeply offended your sense of reality (yay!), or you have come to the conclusion that there will be some "bending" of the laws of physics here. As a matter of fact, I plan to outright break, smash, and stomp some physics simply to amuse myself. Does it matter so long as the final render looks photo-real? Well, does it?

Physics is important to lighting for a number of reasons, not least of which is that it explains why light and shadow behave the way they do, but it is not there to fetter our artistic endeavors, our tastes, or even our baser need to get a render done quickly. Let's face it: If we were constrained to using lighting tools that only obeyed the laws of physics, frames would take days, weeks, or months to render instead of minutes.

Physics helps us understand how real things work so that we know how to build tools and techniques that approximate those realities. Of course, the goal is to approximate them so well that they look completely photo-real. This approximation is likely to be a big compromise that is made up of completely impossible tools and techniques, cheats, fakes, hidden truths, and some seriously great compositing work post-render consisting of motion blur, film grain, smoke, dust, nasty edge-work, rotoscoping, and probably shaking a live chicken over the tablet about five minutes before delivery deadline.

Take lights, for example. In the real world, there is only one basic light type. All light sources fall into this one category and can be described using one set of rules. (Argue if you will; I'm not listening.) LightWave, on the other hand, is equipped with five different light types. Each different light is characterized by specific light properties which may or may not exist in real lighting but have been designed to make your frames render much, much more quickly. None of the lights available in LightWave behave exactly as real light does. Those brainiacs who have coded our lighting tools have split up various light properties into separate lighting instruments and controls, giving us the ability to create lighting looks without having to go through all the hassle of using real physics to render.

For example, in the real world, if you turn up the intensity of a light, the specular highlight and reflection on a surface will also increase. That is because they are all part of the same property. In the virtual world, however, these properties can all be manipulated individually, completely disobeying the law. Shame!

So to begin with, we are going to ignore physics except in our observations of real-world light. When it comes to lighting in the virtual world, we need to understand the laws so we can make something that *appears* to work like them, but we do not need to obey them. In this way, we are gods and make our own physical laws. Light behaves the way we desire it to in our virtual worlds because we wish it.

There, now don't you feel like tossing a lightning bolt or something?

Some Notes about Observation

Observation of the real world is the backbone upon which all of your artwork, including lighting, rests. You will never, ever learn good lighting, animation, texturing, or much of anything else by simply sitting in front of a computer monitor, clicking keys and scrolling your mouse wheel. If it is your desire to become a truly world-class artist, it is your obligation to yourself to get out there and study the world that you are striving to copy.

Painters perform many painting and drawing studies before attempting a large work. If they need to work out just how a human hand lies or just how cotton fabric crumples, they will draw hands in many different positions and they will get cotton and lay it out, drawing it over and over until they fully understand its properties and behaviors. Lighting is just like this.

If you expect to create realistic lighting, you absolutely must get out there and observe lighting conditions. See the properties of light and shadow under as many different environmental conditions as possible. Analyze and study both lighting and shadow. Understand how different textures react to specific lighting conditions. Know what a reflection is before you attempt to alter the reflectivity, specularity, and glossiness of a texture at the workstation. As a lighting artist, it is your duty to reach a Zen understanding of lighting. Be one with the light, young pixel samurai, and you shall reap the rewards.

Rules of the Road

The first rule any artist learns is that there are no rules. This book demonstrates how light works, how to look at it, and and how certain tools in LightWave's toolkit can be used to approximate or replicate it. There are also a number of lighting techniques covered, including some that are commonly used in film and television. These are not rules. They are principles and techniques. Once you understand lighting, you will discover that you do not need rules or techniques described for you, that you can create your own techniques, and that you can make up your own rules. Simply put, you can light a scene any way you wish, if it pleases you. Your best bet for learning how to gain complete control over your lights is to experiment, ignore standard practices, and investigate exactly how your lighting instruments perform and react. Anyone who tries to tell you about rules is mistaken.

What is "good lighting"? That's a loaded question. If I had to define it I would say good lighting is what occurs when the results are what the artists set out to create. I have met directors who believe that good lighting means everything in the scene is brightly lit so you can see every detail. What if the scene is in a dark alley at night with a couple of small overhead street lamps, just barely bright enough to create two dim pools on the asphalt? Should I throw in a nice bright distant light at 100% so everything is brightly lit? Of course I shouldn't. This is a pretty obvious example, but it demonstrates the point. Good lighting looks and feels right. Believe it or not, you are already an expert on what light should look like. You've been observing the effects and qualities of light since you first opened your eyes. Trust what your eyes tell you. My job is to dissect and define all those things you already know and present them to you in a way that will allow you to manipulate them like old, familiar hand tools.

Note: A note about art: There is little that can replace a traditional art background. You have probably heard or read this a hundred times and rolled your eyes, but it remains fundamentally true. It is not about whether you can draw, paint, or sculpt; it is about learning how to look at your subject and dissect it into forms, colors, and intersections so they can be recreated on your own canvas, or in this case your computer. If you do not have any art training, do not dismay; this book will still help you improve your lighting. I would be remiss, however, if I did not recommend that you take a couple of evenings a week to attend a class at your local arts institute. Most community centers have art classes of some sort. If your desire is to become a world-class artist, you really should study art.

All right, enough of that soapbox.

Lighting, Both Beautiful and Accurate

Pleasing lighting is not mutually exclusive from accurate lighting.

This may seem to be an obvious statement, but you would be surprised how many artists throw lights into a scene to highlight an item when there is no lighting source to justify the illumination. Accuracy is key to good-looking lighting. If you really need to highlight something and there are no light sources to justify it, there are other steps you can take to achieve a good look. Altering the background to create contrast is one such solution, although it's not always possible. Find a way to add a light source to justify the light you need. If nothing else works, at least try to make the offending effect subtle enough to pass notice. You might even get away with making alterations to the subject or its textures.

Creativity is not just about building, painting, and lighting. It is also about finding creative solutions to problems just like this. They pop up every day and part of your job is to fix them. And speaking of finding solutions to problems, the final chapter in this book, Chapter 27, is called "Anatomy of a Production Lighting Rig," where I spend some time describing the problems and requirements that led to the creation of a special feature film lighting rig. There were a number of unique problems, and this rig solved most of them, while maintaining flexibility, accuracy, and beauty of light.

In your career as a lighting artist, you will probably encounter situations where you are ordered to highlight something and denied permission to make any alterations that would justify that highlight. This does happen, especially when the budget is tight, time is short, and/or the director or VFX supervisor may be inexperienced. This is where the VFX supervisor has a job trying to coordinate between director, gaffer, and CG department to try to make the final composition seamless and real. You should try to argue your point, but sometimes they don't want to hear it. Just smile, nod, do the work, and don't put it on your reel. Sometimes you just have to walk away.

Note: Some filmmakers are euphemistically referred to as "guerilla filmmakers." This evokes a mental image of hurried, hit-and-miss operations that spawn marginal results. If you are very lucky, you will never end up trying to light shots for these "guerilla" filmmakers whose favorite expression at the end of a long day seems to be "They'll fix it in post." That means it is up to you and the rest of the VFX team to fix whatever mistakes they can't be bothered to fix themselves. I have seen some pretty incredible expectations come from set regarding post fixes:

- A chair is accidentally left in frame for a shot. Instead of reshooting, the crew wraps for the day and requires a compositor to paint out the chair.
- A scene is in the can. Later the production team decides it doesn't like the round neckline on a dress. A compositor is ordered to make it square.
- Green-screen shots come back with completely improper lighting angles for the CG environment that is to be added by the VFX team. Green light spills all over the talent. Many hours of rotoscoping are required; lighting must be altered to accommodate the plate.

All these are due to lack of planning and laziness. Unfortunately it adds a massive workload to the VFX department, which would like to be spending its time making the shots world class but instead spend time cleaning up other people's messes and do not then have enough time to properly finish its own shots.

Don't despair. There are also many filmmakers who plan carefully and who care about the results.

If you are lucky, the shots are carefully planned, the CG department is included in the planning process, and the shots come back as expected. What is more likely is that one or all of these events will not occur. This is where your creativity is really going to come into play — where you will really need to know your lighting to pull off a miracle.

You will discover that there are many ways to skin a cat. Regardless of whether the shots you receive are manna from heaven or guerilla crap, you will find that stunning results can be achieved with the slightest planning.

About Trial and Error

Many CG artists rely on trial and error as a prime lighting technique. This is not the same as experimentation. Since rendering a frame is hardly real-time feedback, there will be some amount of tweaking and rendering to achieve the right levels, colors, and balance; however, most aspects of lighting do not, and should not, require trial and error. Properties such as instrument choice, position and direction, basic intensity, and color should require marginal adjustment, especially in visual effects shots where these properties have already been established by the film crew or where visual references are available in the plate and your job is simply to recreate the lighting environment. The VFX artist should be able to look at a plate, identify exactly how many light sources there are, roughly what their position and direction are, roughly what the colors are, what light types are required, then plan out a lighting kit and proceed with placement.

Designing your own lighting is a slightly different matter and may require more experimentation, especially considering this may be part of the creative process for some artists. This process, however, should not be mistaken for "trial and error." Trial and error is best illustrated by the artist who does not know what he wants and does not know exactly how to achieve it, and adds lights, colors, direction, and intensity, hoping that sooner or later he will accidentally hit on a pleasing combination. Once again, the artist should be able to look at the scenic requirements, plan out lighting type, placement, angle, and color, and then proceed with placement.

Visual Effects vs. CG Lighting Design

There are two main reasons to light a scene or an element in LightWave. One reason is that you are adding a CG element to a background plate that has come from set. You usually have few options but to replicate the on-set lighting so that your element will blend into the plate. This is visual effects (VFX) lighting. The other reason is that you are working on an all-CG shot and you must create the entire lighting environment. This is CG lighting design.

The skill set required to produce competent visual effects lighting is primarily technical, requiring an understanding of the real light sources and techniques used in the plate and how to replicate those sources and techniques using specific tools available in LightWave. Lighting design requires these technical skills and also calls on the artist's knowledge of such qualities as intensity, direction, color, shadow, and contrast. The artist is now making an artistic interpretation and converting that interpretation into a lighting environment. Do you want to know how to do this? All these things are covered in the pages that follow.

> **Note:** As this is a book about lighting, it helps to see the results of applying different effects that aren't as apparent in the black and white illustrations. Dozens of these figures are also printed in a color insert. Additionally, all the figures in the book are included on the CD.

What's New in LightWave [8]

- The first thing you will notice when you fire up Layout (after you get over the tonal changes in the interface) is that the camera and lights have all been redesigned, sporting more detail and more graphical hints as to their actual use and properties. Kudos to NewTek for braving the territory of *change*. Check out Chapter 7 for images of the new light graphics if you don't have a workstation in front of you.

- Light quality is now envelopable. This only applies to linear and area lights, but that's enough, since these two are the render hogs. This is a great new feature because it means that with the application of a simple expression, you can alter the quality of the light based on the distance from camera. If the camera is far away, why bother with the high-quality render settings anyway? But if the camera gets extremely close, you'll want the light quality as high as possible. With the envelope, you can either keyframe the quality change as the camera gets closer or you can make it automatic based on distance to camera. Cool! Anything that saves render time is a good thing in my book. More on this in Chapter 7.

- Light exclusion in the Object Properties panel Lights tab (and object exclusion in the Light Properties panel Objects tab) can now be right-clicked at the top to get the options Select All, Clear All, and Invert Selection. If you have ever needed to select every light except one or two in a list of 75 lights, you will really appreciate this simple new addition.

- Projection images are now visible in the Light View of the light that is projecting the images. This great new feature enables you to more quickly line up the projection image so you can have it fall precisely where you want it to. This may seem like a little tool, but anything that improves your work flow is very good.

- OpenGL now displays the eight brightest lights first instead of the first eight lights in scene order. In past versions, the Layout OpenGL display showed up to eight lights but only the first eight in the scene. This didn't make sense, especially if you wanted specific lights visible in OpenGL, but they were numbers 32 and 33. Now you can turn on and off whichever lights you want to display, or LightWave will automatically display the eight brightest.

- The ability to change the properties of multiple selected lights has been added. The following properties can be changed on multiple selected lights:

SaveLight
DistantLight
PointLight
Spotlight
LinearLight
AreaLight
LightFalloffType
LightRange
LightConeAngle
LightEdgeAngle
LightQuality
ShadowMapSize
ShadowMapFuzziness
ShadowMapFitCone
ShadowMapAngle
FlareIntensity

These are a few of the things awaiting you in the latest, greatest version of our favorite 3D software. Go forth and illuminate!

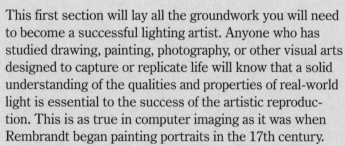

Part I

Lighting Theory

This first section will lay all the groundwork you will need to become a successful lighting artist. Anyone who has studied drawing, painting, photography, or other visual arts designed to capture or replicate life will know that a solid understanding of the qualities and properties of real-world light is essential to the success of the artistic reproduction. This is as true in computer imaging as it was when Rembrandt began painting portraits in the 17th century.

Lighting cannot be learned at a computer terminal. It can only be learned by observing and understanding real light in a real environment. Expect to spend time outdoors examining the quality of a shadow from a nearby tree. Look not only at the color of the sunlight, but the hue of the shadow. Note how the colored light from one source mixes with the colored light from another source to produce an entirely new effect.

To be a successful lighting artist, the properties of light must interest you enough to study them. This section will help you with that.

Chapter 1

Properties of Light

This chapter deals with the properties of light in the real world, specifically intensity, color, direction, diffuseness, shadow, shape, contrast, movement, and size. By the time you finish this chapter you should be able to identify and explain each of these properties in a lighting environment

Understanding light is not difficult. Just as an automobile mechanic understands how to build, repair, and operate a vehicle — not by seeing the vehicle as a single system but as a complex interaction of individual systems — understanding light is as simple as understanding each of the individual properties that are part of the whole. Once the following concepts are grasped, you will be able to look at any lighting situation and clearly identify the direction of the source, its intensity or luminosity, the light color, the diffuseness of the light, the movement (if any), the shadow qualities, the shape, and the contrast. Actually, you are already an expert in observing light. These terms and definitions will simply allow you to manipulate them effectively.

Intensity/Luminosity

Intensity and luminosity are similar concepts. The following two images illustrate the difference. Figure 1.1 shows intensity, while Figure 1.2 demonstrates luminosity.

Figure 1.1: Intensity refers to the brightness of a light source.

Figure 1.2: Luminosity refers to the brightness of a surface.

The difference is this: In CG art, we use *intensity* to refer to the brightness of a light source — an actual lighting instrument within the CG environment such as a spotlight or point light. In other words, when we say intensity, we are talking about *direct* lighting from a hot lightbulb filament or a candle flame. When we say *luminosity*, we are talking about *indirect* lighting such as when direct light is diffused through a frosted glass bulb or the colored glass in a neon sign. LightWave's Global Illumination (radiosity) allows us to make polygonal objects luminous. So if we model a frosted white lightbulb, we can have the actual polygons of the object emitting light without adding any lights to the scene. When object surfaces have a luminosity setting higher than 0%, they contribute light to the scene if radiosity is enabled. The higher the luminosity, the more light is emitted. So in the case of radiosity, luminosity means the same as intensity but refers to the light emission from surfaces as opposed to lights.

Take our lightbulb example. In the old days of CG, we would have to create the effect in LightWave by putting a point light in or near the lightbulb object and letting it shine its rays out into the scene. Nowadays, we have another option. Instead of adding a point light, we can turn up the luminosity value on the actual lightbulb surface and enable radiosity. The render will take considerably longer, but the resulting light will be far more accurate. Most of the time, the easy method of adding a point light will work fine, but sometimes detail is everything and nothing else will look as good.

> **Note:** Either Monte Carlo or Interpolated Global Illumination must be enabled for this to work. Luminous surfaces will not emit light into the scene if you have Backdrop Only Global Illumination selected.

Intensity or luminosity is one of the first things you may notice about a light source's quality. Is it very bright or very dim? Is it somewhere in the middle? Is it so blindingly bright that it can only be the sun or a nuclear blast? Or is it so gentle that it must be a candle? The intensity of a light source will often signal to the viewer what the light source is, even if the source itself is not visible in frame.

> **Note:** It is easy to let the audience know what and where your light source is without being obtrusive or obvious. As you read through these light properties, imagine how you might use each one to let your audience know just how the scene is illuminated.

Color

Perhaps the second quality you may notice in a light source is the color. Take the sun, for example. On a midsummer's day, the sun can be very close to white and on the yellowish side. On an autumn afternoon, it can be a fiery orange. Look in the shadows on a clear, bright sunny day. Don't they look blue? What about the living room with the fireplace burning? Here you see orange, red, and yellow all spilling across the room. Or check out those mercury vapor lamps used for street lights. These are sort of a light orange.

Take a look at the photograph on the following page.

There are three main light sources in this shot, resulting in three distinct color ranges. In a few places, you can see direct sunlight, mainly along the top of the image and at the bottom right. The sun is the key light. It is nearly white, on the amber side of the spectrum. But the most obvious light sources and colors are the fill sources. On the left of the image, rock faces that angle upward are a deep blue. This is because they are facing the blue sky on a bright, sunny day. The sky is highly luminous and is emitting a blue-tinted diffuse light. On the right half of the image, the cliff face is undercut, making it face downward toward the road where sunlight is reflecting off the dirt and creating an amber fill.

Figure 1.3: (See color image.)

Note: This image is a great example not only of contrasting color in a lighting environment, but also of fill lighting and of diffuse lighting sources.

Note: After the LightWave 7.5 version of this book was released, there was heated debate over the color of shadows on a sunny, clear, blue-skied day. Some argue that shadows have no color, being by nature the absence of light. On the other hand, it can be argued that on earth shadows are never completely devoid of light. I suppose for the picky physicists in the room, the question should be "What color of illumination fills the shadowed area?" I won't address the doubt, incredulity, debates, insults, or downright crying that was involved, and I stand by my analysis of the lighting conditions. I urge you, the incredulous reader, to simply go outside and do some careful, thoughtful observation. Come to your own conclusions.

There are as many colors for lights as there are colors in the visible spectrum. In fact, you can divide up the visible spectrum of light into many more wavelengths than can be discerned by the human eye. Your computer monitor is probably capable of displaying about 16 million colors, and that's only some of the available ones!

Color can be a visual key to what is going on in your scene. If you see a back alley scene, and there's a pink light source out of frame that's blinking on and off, you will subconsciously know that this probably represents a neon sign flashing "Tattoos" or something. If you want to create a somber, depressing mood, you might choose cool colors — steels and blues, colors that seem cold and dead. If you wish to make the viewer ill at ease, you may choose eerie, unnatural colors in the green portion of the spectrum. Or perhaps pinks and ambers may be your choice for a bright, happy setting. Keep in mind that these examples are merely the most common uses for these color ranges. Why are they common? Most people have specific emotional reactions to certain colors. You can use this knowledge to get your audience into a specific frame of mind.

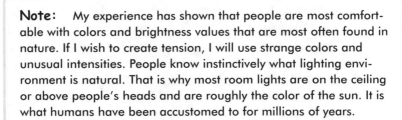

Note: My experience has shown that people are most comfortable with colors and brightness values that are most often found in nature. If I wish to create tension, I will use strange colors and unusual intensities. People know instinctively what lighting environment is natural. That is why most room lights are on the ceiling or above people's heads and are roughly the color of the sun. It is what humans have been accustomed to for millions of years.

Direction

Light direction is another powerful tool in establishing light source and setting. If the shot is outdoors and the angle is very steep, very bright, and amber-white, we might assume that the light source is the sun. If the shot is outdoors and the light is very bright, amber-white, and coming from below, we are certain that it cannot be the sun. It must be something else. Everything is the same except for the angle.

In a living room, all the lights are out, but there is a light source out of frame. It is coming from floor level and is colored red, orange, and yellow. We guess this is a fireplace. If we look again and see by the angle of the shadows that the source is above us rather than below, we will probably think that the house is on fire.

Take the classic example of the spooky story told on a camping trip. The storyteller places a flashlight below the chin causing deep, strange shadows that make the face appear frightening and unnatural. This is referred to as "dramatic lighting." The same flashlight pointed straight at the face or from above will elicit no such reaction.

From the earliest days when theater moved indoors, footlights were used to illuminate the stage. Why footlights? Well, the earliest lights were candles floating in a moat of water in front of the stage. These were followed by gas lights. The nature of these lights required them to be within easy access of the operators, especially considering how many theaters burned down during the phases of these technologies. When electric lights were introduced, they were placed in footlight positions mainly due to tradition. The villains of the old melodramas made use of the footlights by leaning close over them, producing the same frightening and unnatural shadows of the campers telling the ghost story. Footlights can still be found in theatrical productions where a lighting designer seeks that melodramatic feeling of the old theater, or where strange, unnatural lighting effects are desired.

The following three images illustrate the use of direction in lighting a subject. Figure 1.4 uses a natural lighting angle high and to the subject's left. The lighting angle is similar to one that may be found on a sunny day. The subject appears normal and familiar. Figure 1.5 uses a low-angular direction. We still recognize the subject as familiar, but the lighting is obviously strange, especially considering the lack of a fill source. Figure 1.6 uses the "spooky flashlight" dramatic lighting effect. It makes the viewer ill at ease because of the subject's unnatural appearance.

Figure 1.4: A normal lighting angle like the sun or a ceiling light.

Figure 1.5: A side lighting angle. Unusual, but seen during sunrises and sunsets.

Figure 1.6: A low lighting angle. Very unnatural and strange.

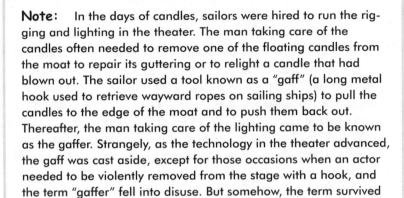

Note: In the days of candles, sailors were hired to run the rigging and lighting in the theater. The man taking care of the candles often needed to remove one of the floating candles from the moat to repair its guttering or to relight a candle that had blown out. The sailor used a tool known as a "gaff" (a long metal hook used to retrieve wayward ropes on sailing ships) to pull the candles to the edge of the moat and to push them back out. Thereafter, the man taking care of the lighting came to be known as the gaffer. Strangely, as the technology in the theater advanced, the gaff was cast aside, except for those occasions when an actor needed to be violently removed from the stage with a hook, and the term "gaffer" fell into disuse. But somehow, the term survived in the film industry and today the head of the lighting department is known as the gaffer.

Diffuseness

In general, *diffuse light* is any light that has been scattered after leaving the light source, or any light source that has a varying area of luminosity or intensity. Scattering can be caused by atmospheric gases or by reflection, or bounce, off an uneven or rough surface. Any material that causes parallel light rays to be scattered, bent, or reflected into non-parallel paths is creating diffuseness in the light.

Figure 1.3 is an example of an image that is lit primarily by two diffuse light sources.

Here on earth, all light has some measure of diffuseness. This is because the light rays (or particles or waves if you wish to be picky) pass through atmospheric gases, colliding with the gas molecules and shooting in all directions. The most obvious example of this is the sky. Blue light is scattered in the atmosphere much more than light at the red end of the spectrum. This is because blue light has a much shorter wavelength than red light and is, therefore, scattered throughout the atmosphere about ten times as much as red light. This scattering is what makes the sky appear blue. Subsequently, the scattered blue light continues omnidirectionally, some of which reaches the ground as diffuse light. This bluish, diffused light can be seen in shadows on clear days. Direct sunlight can also be diffused through clouds, colliding with water droplets and continuing omnidirectionally. Cloudy days provide an excellent example of white diffused light. All the shadows on cloudy days are soft and diffused. Only the deepest crevices are likely to be very dark since light is approaching from most directions but may not reach into them.

Diffuseness can tell us much about the light source and the environment. Direct light sources such as the sun, a candle flame, or a bare, clear lightbulb produce parallel light rays and hard shadows. But put a curtain, a lampshade, or frosted glass in front of the source and the light becomes diffuse, making shadows softer. Fluorescent sources are all diffuse sources. They all have a wide area of luminosity that creates soft shadows because the light appears to "wrap around" objects, creating an area of shadow "falloff."

The following two images are the same except that one is directly lit and the other is diffusely lit. There is diffuse lighting in both images but direct lighting in only one of them.

Figure 1.7: Sharp shadows and higher contrast are visible in this image, which has both diffuse and direct lighting sources. The direct light is overpowering the diffuse light and diffused shadows.

Figure 1.8: This image is nearly identical to the previous one, except for the absence of direct lighting. As the contrast is lower, the softer illumination and softer shadows are clearly visible.

Shadow

Shadows are not technically a quality of light. While some may teach that lights cast shadows, in fact it is objects that cast shadows. A shadow is the absence of light and therefore cannot generally be considered a light quality. Rather we think of it as a "lighting" quality. In other words, shadows are one of the things we think about when creating our lighting, although it is not actually a part of light.

The images shown in Figures 1.4, 1.5, and 1.6 demonstrate that shadow is linked to the direction of the light source. They help us see the subtleties of form in the subject, and can be used to evoke an emotional response from the viewer.

Shadows are as crucial to lighting as beer is to pizza. Without one, the other is rather plain. It is shadows that give all objects their form and shape. Shadows play a large part in helping us define what plane we are looking at when we see a wall or the ground. Look at a wall near you and notice the shadow gradient that occurs as the wall recedes farther from the light source. Notice the intersection with the floor and see where the deepest shadows lie. Imagine if there were no shadows. In a white room with a white door frame and a white door, you would never be able to find the door. All that really defines the door and frame is the shadows.

We are all experts at seeing shadows. We have grown up our entire lives honing our expertise in this area. It is because of this expertise that each of us can look at a visual effects or other computer-generated shot in a movie and know instantly that it is not real if the lighting is not quite right. We may not be able to verbalize exactly what the problem is or even that it is with the lighting, but nonetheless it will look wrong.

This is why shadow is one of the most subtle and most crucial of lighting qualities. As lighting artists, we must understand exactly what happens to create shadows of all types in all situations. Chapter 5 deals with shadows in detail. For now, suffice it to say that there are two main types of shadows: hard and soft. *Hard shadows* are the sort you see from small light sources like the sun or a clear, bare lightbulb. (I know the sun is very large, but it acts small most of the time as far as lighting is concerned, mainly because it is extremely far away and only a small amount of the sun's light reaches us. See Chapter 5.) *Soft shadows* are the kind you usually see in the absence of hard shadows. That is not to say that they cannot exist together; they usually do, but hard shadows are scene stealers. People tend not to notice the gentler soft shadows when the bully hard shadows are around — this is an important point. Because we live on a planet with a gaseous atmosphere, soft shadows are everywhere, under every lighting condition. Failing to add them to your scene is like forgetting the cheese on your pizza. Soft shadows exist in situations where there is a diffuse lighting source such as the sky, clouds, a computer monitor, or sunlight reflecting off a wall. In reality, there is always a diffuse lighting source.

Shape

The shape of a light can tell you a great deal about the light source. Shape is very similar to shadow in some ways. For example, the shadow cast by palm leaves may actually be palm leaves, or in the case of LightWave, it may actually be geometry casting a shadow. Lighting designers long ago invented a device for changing the shape of the light before it leaves a lighting instrument so that you don't actually have to place a palm tree in front of the light in order to get the effect. Earlier, I mentioned that you don't always need to see the light source to know what it is. This is true of shadows as well. You don't need to see a palm tree to know it is casting the shadow. This shaping device is called a *gobo* or *lighting template*. Simply put, it is a small sheet of metal with a shape cut out. The sheet is placed at the focal point of the light, and the cut-out shape is projected. So if that shape were to be some palm leaves, it might appear that the light source is the sun and that it is shining down through some palm leaves. Technically, the gobo is casting a shadow inside the lighting instrument, only allowing some of the light to shine through. That is what alters the shape of the light. There are also *moving gobos*, which can be as simple as a disc rotating in front of the light or as complex as a movie projector. Lighting designers also use shutters and barn doors to alter the shape of their lights. *Shutters* are metal plates, also at the focal point, that can be slid inward to create straight edges on the normally round beam of a spotlight. *Barn doors* are placed at the lens end of the light some distance past the focal point and are usually used to cut down on *spill* (undesirable light diffusing out of the lens housing in all directions), although they can also shape a light somewhat or assist in sharpening the gobo image. All of these tools and more are available in the LightWave toolset, as we will discover in later chapters.

Figure 1.9: Even if the wire fence were not visible in the scene, you would know the shape and proximity of the object casting the shadow on the child. Shape is a great tool for setting the scene.

So you see that shape and shadow are very similar. For the purposes of CG lighting, we will consider shadow to be cast by geometry in the scene and shape to be the light that is coming from the light source before touching any geometry.

Contrast

Contrast refers to the range of difference between the lightest parts of the image and the darkest parts. An image in which the lightest parts are much lighter than the darkest parts is considered to have high contrast. On the other hand, a frame in which the lightest parts and the darkest parts are similar is considered to have low contrast. For example, on a bright sunny day, the sunlight shines on a white table. It is nearly blinding to look at and the shadows below it seem to be pitch black. There is a great difference between the table and the shadow below. This is high contrast. If, on the other hand, it is a cloudy day and you look at the table, you will notice that the white of the table and the light gray of the concrete below do not seem to be so different. This is low contrast.

The following images demonstrate the difference between low-contrast and high-contrast imagery.

Figure 1.10: This image demonstrates low contrast. All the illumination and texture values fall within the middle range of grays.

Figure 1.11: This image demonstrates high contrast. All the illumination and texture values range from highest (white) to lowest (black).

Some of this effect is caused by the dilation of your pupils. When it is very bright outside, your pupils get smaller, blocking out much of the light and protecting the retina. When this happens, only the brightest light gets through. The concrete under the table is lit even more than it is on a cloudy, low-contrast day, but your eye is not registering the light. It has been filtered out by the pupil. This creates a high-contrast situation. When the sun is obscured by clouds, there is much less light available. The pupils dilate, allowing more light in. The concrete beneath the table becomes more easily visible and more similar in contrast to the table. Essentially what is happening is that as the pupil opens and closes, the eye's light *range* is changing. It is that light range that determines high or low contrast.

Why the anatomy lesson? It is important to understand not how the eye works, but what light is actually there and what situations create the lighting quality known as contrast so that these can be accurately recreated (or at least butchered, cheated, and faked) in a CG environment.

Movement

Movement may not be the first thing you consider when you think about light, but it is a powerful tool. Movement refers to the qualities of light that change over time. Take a fireplace, for example. Each bit of flame is a light source. As the fuel is spent, the flame rises and flickers, changing color and intensity. This is a moving light source. So often I have seen artists attempting to create realistic light from a flame by applying variations in intensity but not in motion or color. Motion, especially, is crucial to this look.

Check out the scene "Fireplace" on the companion CD. This gives a quick-and-dirty example of how you might set up fireplace lighting.

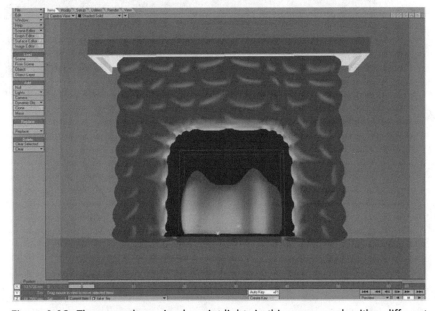

Figure 1.12: There are three simple point lights in this scene, each with a different motion path, intensity variation, and red color channel variation. This took me about five minutes to set up. If you wanted to do a really beautiful, elaborate setup, it would probably only take a couple of hours.

15

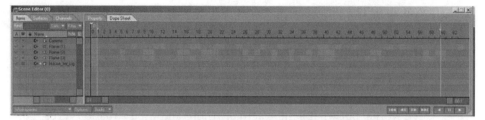

Figure 1.13: You can see in the Scene Editor how the keyframes are irregularly spaced to create unique behaviors for each point light. Each point light is behaving as a spark or a lick of flame. You can also repeat the motion of each light to "regenerate" them if you have a long scene, but if you do this, vary the length of each light's motion path so that the repeats don't happen together. You'll get a more interesting mix of motions that way and your viewer will be less likely to spot a repeating motion.

Similarly, the motion paths for intensity and color create great variation.

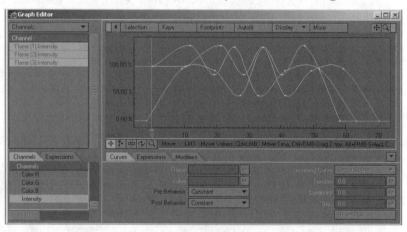

Figure 1.14: Intensity motion channels for all three lights in the Graph Editor.

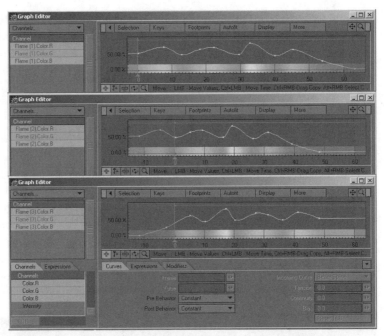

Figure 1.15: Color channels for all three lights in the Graph Editor. When you load up the example scene, you'll see the actual light color in the Graph Editor as well. It's in the image shown in Figure 1.12, but of course it's a grayscale image.

There are many other examples of light in motion, such as a mirror ball in a club, headlights on a car, someone carrying a flashlight, or even the sun passing overhead. Movement can also apply to changes in the beam angle of a spotlight or changes in intensity or color. One could argue that a change over time of any of the other light qualities constitutes movement. Just imagine how you could use some of these moving qualities to help convey your intentions. Moving intensity might mean an explosion has occurred or someone has turned down a gas lamp. Moving color might mean the sun is rising or a neon sign is flashing outside. Moving direction might mean a car headlight flashing by in the night or a spinning orange beacon on top of a construction vehicle. Moving diffuseness could show that a light source is getting closer or the sun is coming out from behind the clouds. Moving shadow might be palm leaves swaying in the breeze or it could be your shadow sweeping across the ground as car headlights flash past. Moving shape could be a film projection on a screen or window shutters being closed. Moving contrast could mean a supernova is occurring or a nearby rocket is blasting off. These examples came to mind in a moment. There are infinite other combinations that you can use to create a lighting environment that is true to the setting, conveys the mood you wish, and carries the desired emotional impact.

Size

Size matters.

The size of a light source, like most of the other properties, often will not matter in shots, but can occasionally be crucial to lending reality to your lighting environment. What difference does size make? Mainly the difference is in the shadows. Shadow shape and behavior will vary depending on the size of the light source. A very large source like the sun will result in hard shadows near the object and softer shadows farther away. A very small light source such as a light-emitting diode will result in very hard shadows that only become soft very far away, if the light transmits that far. The net effect is that tiny light sources appear to result exclusively in hard shadows.

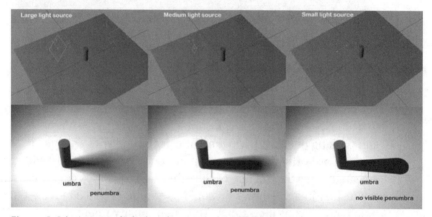

Figure 1.16: An area light has been used in all three images to demonstrate the varying size of a light source. The rendered images below them show the corresponding result of each size difference. Nothing is changed except the size of the area light. A very small area light acts as though it were a point source. This image uses a grid size of 1 meter.

On the other hand, a very small light source is more likely to result in areas of highlight on specular surfaces, while very large lights are more diffused and are therefore less likely to result in bright specular highlights.

· · ·

This chapter has demonstrated the basic properties of light. The physicists among you will, no doubt, care to argue the physical accuracy of several points; however, this is not a physics handbook. The understanding of the properties as described will enable you to light your scenes so they appear to obey the laws of physics (which is very important) without actually having to obey every principle and law (which is not very important).

The final render matters. Whether or not you obeyed the letter of physical law does not.

You should now be able to examine any lighting environment and define the properties of intensity, color, direction, diffuseness, shadow, shape, contrast, movement, and size.

Chapter 2

What, Where, When?

This chapter covers temporal and spatial issues that will hopefully provide clues as to what lighting setup to start with. By the time you have finished this chapter, you should be able to observe a lighting environment and define the time of day (if relevant), time of year (if relevant), atmospheric conditions (if relevant), and whether the environment is interior or exterior. You should be able to analyze a photograph's lighting (or the lighting outside your window, under your desk, or anywhere). You should also be able to start planning your own basic lighting setup based on the scenic information you observe about place, time, and atmospheric conditions.

It is always good to have a defined starting point for your lighting. Where do you begin? I begin lighting a scene by considering a number of questions that help me decide what lights to use, where to place them, how to color them, and what sort of intensity mixtures (or ratios) I will use. We begin with the largest, most obvious questions and move on to finer points. As in any analysis, "Start big, go small."

Interior or Exterior

Perhaps one of the first decisions you will have to make about your lighting is whether it is an interior or exterior shot. This is a basic and general question that will provide you with a great deal of information about your lighting setup. The shot might contain both interior and exterior elements, such as a room interior with a window through which the street outside is visible. Or it might be an exterior shot that includes someone leaning out a window and waving. There is interior lighting behind that person. It may be subtle, but illuminating that interior properly might make the difference between a shot that is believable to the audience and one that is not. The question is whether the camera is inside a building or out on the street. Interior and exterior light sources may both play a part in the shot, but the location of the camera dramatically changes how the sources will be handled and what the relative light intensities will be between interior and exterior.

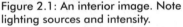

Figure 2.1: An interior image. Note lighting sources and intensity.

Figure 2.2: An exterior image. Also note light sources, intensity, and diffuseness.

Interior and exterior light react and complement each other all the time, everywhere. Knowing how to create these complex interactions is as simple as identifying and simulating each individual source.

Interior light sources, for example, are usually incandescent or fluorescent. Exterior light sources are usually the sun, the sky, clouds, the moon, reflected sources, and reflected diffuse sources (technically, all these sources are the sun, but let's not wear our picky hats today). The sun's light, diffused through the air molecules in the sky, creates a global, diffused source. Or the sun may be occluded by clouds that block the direct rays from the sun, in which case the light is diffused among the water droplets in the clouds, creating yet another diffuse source. Direct sunlight may strike a wall or the ground, picking up the color of that wall or ground and reflecting it onto another surface. (Don't get all nitpicky about the actual physics of light reflection and radiosity yet. We'll discuss all that later.) Sunlight may reflect off the surface of a swimming pool, creating a hard reflection against the pool house. In each circumstance, the sun is the light source. All the other lighting events, with the exception of artificial light, are diffusions or reflections of that primary source.

While it is theoretically possible to create a global lighting environment with only one source and to provide diffusion and reflection events consistent with the real world, render times would probably be measured in weeks or months per frame. Instead of that, we have decided to make each diffusion and reflection event into a separate light source. NewTek, maker of LightWave, has provided us with the tools to create these sources, and years of experimentation and research among the LightWave community, and indeed the whole CG community, have provided us with innumerable methods for accurately capturing the correct look with the available tools. The lighting tools are not physically accurate but are close approximations. Some of the lighting tools reflect only a portion of the real properties of a light source. This makes render times manageable. In general, the closer a lighting tool is to physical accuracy, the exponentially longer it takes to render.

Note: Bear in mind that it is the look, not the physical accuracy of the lighting model, that matters to producers, directors, and supervisors. The production reality is that any method you can use to create great lighting is valuable. If it is quicker to render and still looks as good, it is more valuable. There are many "tricks" to creating great lighting without the monstrous rendering times. Many of them are covered later in this book. But the main purpose here is to provide you with enough knowledge to create your own tricks that are most relevant to the job you are working on right now. Remember that not all techniques or methods are relevant to all lighting challenges.

Imagine a living room with a fireplace crackling brightly at one end. There is a soft, indirect incandescent source illuminating the pale yellow ceiling and casting a reflected diffuse light throughout the room. Halogen track lighting in the kitchen is spilling a crisp, sharp light from the pass-through into the dining area where it reflects off and refracts through the glass tabletop. The large glass windows reveal a wide cityscape many floors below and a moonlit sky twinkles above. In the distance, moonlight reflects off the Pacific Ocean.

Sound complex? This scene could be lit with as few as three lights. Why? That is how many light sources that have been described are acting on the foreground of the shot. Adding a few more lights to mimic some of the diffusion and reflection events, rather than calculating real reflections and diffusions, can dramatically improve render times. LightWave is equipped with a robust and full-featured lighting toolkit to help you mimic all the lighting events in the scene without having to create a physically accurate lighting model which, while it may look marginally superior, will likely send render times through the roof.

One last note about interior and exterior lighting: When we talk about exterior sources, we are usually referring to "natural" sources such as the sun. When discussing interior sources, we are usually referring to "artificial" sources such as lightbulbs. Of course, sunlight can pass through a window into a room, and tiki lamps or neon signs are usually found outdoors, but don't be confused. By the time you are finished with this book, you'll know how to create a neon source whether indoors or outdoors and how to create a sunny day whether on the beach or viewed through a tiny basement window. Just remember to think about whether your camera is interior or exterior, and the sources will fall into place.

Time of Day

What time of day is it? Is it midday or sunset? Is it midnight or early morning? Each of these situations requires a completely different lighting solution. Midday might require a bright, hard-shadowed light source at a high angle to represent direct sunlight, while sunset might also require a hard-shadowed light source, but with less intensity, more color saturation, and a much more obtuse angle or direction. Early morning could mean the sun has not yet risen, so all the light in the scene is indirect, diffused, and colored according to atmospheric conditions. Midnight, on the other hand, might be lit by the moon, which acts as a direct lighting source although it is in fact a diffuse, reflected source, and displays the properties of both. Finally, starlight may be the only source of illumination, or it could be light from a nearby window, a distant street lamp, or a neon sign. How do we deal with these? How do we balance the dim starlight with the bright neon sign and still tell our audience that it is nighttime?

So much depends on the time of day. Go out and look at lighting conditions around you at different times of the day. You will find infinite combinations of light sources and situations.

Figure 2.3: A daytime image. Note lighting sources and intensity.

Figure 2.4: A nighttime image.

Time of Year

Time of year, while more subtle, is also valuable in establishing lighting conditions, mood, and setting in your scene, especially if the scene is outdoors. Imagine, for example, the kind of light you might see at 3 p.m. on a clear day in the summer. Contrast that with what the lighting might be like at 3 p.m. in the autumn or in the winter. The difference is the direction, intensity, and color of our light source (the sun). In the summer, the source is high, very bright, and very white, reaching a color temperature of about 5800 Kelvin degrees, while autumn light is warmer and less intense, with a color temperature perhaps closer to 4500 Kelvin degrees.

> **Note:** See the discussion on color temperature in Chapter 8.

This change in color from summer to autumn occurs because of the ever-changing angle of the earth relative to the sun and what happens to the light rays as they diffuse through the atmosphere at a more obtuse angle. In the winter, the sunlight must actually pass through more atmosphere to reach the ground than it does in the summer. This is because the hemisphere (Northern in June and Southern in December) is tilted toward the sun in summer, making the light rays reach the earth at an acute angle, making the sun appear higher in the sky, and letting the sunlight take the most direct route through the atmosphere. In winter, the hemisphere is tilted away from the sun, making the sun appear lower in the sky and causing the light rays to reach the hemisphere at a lower, more obtuse angle. In this case, sunlight takes a longer path through the atmosphere.

Regardless of the calendar month or hemisphere, winter sunlight is always closer to the horizon than summer sunlight, resulting in a lower average angle in winter and a higher average angle in summer. Spring and autumn light are phases between summer and winter, so the light source will be somewhere in between the extremes of summer sunlight and winter sunlight. If you plan on lighting a scene within one of the polar regions, perhaps it's best to go to the library and start studying geography!

> **Note:** Lest we confuse any readers, be it known that summer starts in June in the Northern Hemisphere and in December in the Southern Hemisphere.

Time of year may be a subtle consideration. It may not matter at all in many cases, but in some cases, illustrating the season can make the difference, giving the shot a temporal anchor.

Atmospheric Conditions

Not every day is sunny and clear. Changes in the weather make a dramatic difference in the way your scene is lit.

Figure 2.5: A sunny day. Note the hard shadows and high contrast.

Figure 2.6: A cloudy day. Note the soft shadows and low contrast.

Take, for example, a clear sunny day and contrast that with a cloudy or rainy day. Sunny days have a hard, bright, warm main or *key* source (the sun), complemented by a diffuse, cool secondary or *fill* source (the sky). On rainy days, however, the key source is usually the clouds — most likely a grayscale diffuse source.

> **Note:** For more discussion on what constitutes key and fill sources, please see Chapter 6, "Principles of Lighting."

The eye can tell instantly, without seeing either the light source or the sky, what the atmospheric conditions are by seeing the color and diffuse qualities of the light. When you wake up in the morning and look out the window, you don't need to look into the sky to see if the sun is out or if it is raining. The signals are in the buildings and environment around you and in the shadows and the quality of the light.

Knowing how to identify and replicate atmospheric conditions is a powerful tool in visual effects situations where the artist is required to match lighting to a background plate. In design, it is crucial to delivering not only the environmental message you wish but also the emotional message.

How does a rainy, cloudy day make you feel? What about a bright, sunny day with a few puffy clouds? How about a dry, hot afternoon with dark, foreboding clouds hanging overhead? What about a foggy day, or a deep red sunset where the red is not from clouds but from the massive forest fire approaching your town? Think through all these examples and listen to your own emotional reactions to each one.

Atmospheric conditions can send a scene down a desired emotional path, easily and unconsciously drawing the audience into a desired mindset.

You should now be able to view a scene or photograph and understand that atmospheric conditions play an important part in many cases, primarily outdoors. But don't forget the smoky room or the steamy shower. These are also atmospheric conditions that play a part in how you will light your scene. Lights interact with these elements to create an effect known as volumetric lighting in which the light beams become visible due to their interaction with the atmospheric particles of smoke or steam. There is more discussion of volumetrics later.

• • •

Let's sum up the questions we ask when examining a scene for lighting.

- Is the scene an interior or exterior (or both)?
- What time of day is depicted in the scene?
- What time of year is depicted in the scene?
- What are the atmospheric conditions present in the scene?

Remembering these four areas of consideration should provide you with great assistance in identifying just what the lighting conditions are in your scene.

Hopefully by now you are able to define the temporal and spatial issues that are present in various lighting environments. You should now be able to observe a lighting environment and define the time of day (if relevant), time of year (if relevant), atmospheric conditions (if relevant), and whether the environment is interior or exterior.

Chapter 3

Light Sources

This chapter will help you understand some specific types of light sources. There are many different sources of light in the world. Each has similarities and differences and must be handled appropriately in Light-Wave. Once you understand these specific light sources, you should be able to look at any light source and understand its properties.

In the real world, a light source is defined as the direct source of illumination. The sun is a light source. So are a fluorescent tube, a lightbulb, a candle, and a tiki lamp. Described another way, physicists consider light sources to be events in which energy is spent, resulting in the emission of photons. Since this is not a physics manual, we will ignore that particular law. Apologies to physicists everywhere.

For the purposes of this book and CG lighting in general, a light source is also defined as an indirect source of illumination such as diffuse or reflected light. The sky, for example, is considered a diffuse light source, although all of its light comes indirectly from the sun. Reflected light such as light from a mirror and diffuse reflected light, also known as *radiosity*, is considered a light source in the CG world.

There is a good reason for this. Rather than create a physically accurate lighting environment in which diffuse light sources are actually diffused from the direct source, and in which reflected light is actually reflected 20, 30, or 100 (or infinite!) times, bouncing around the environment, we use cheats and tricks to create these effects. Why? There isn't enough rendering time. Computers are not fast enough. Deadlines must be met. Rendering diffuse and reflecting light sources accurately is very CPU intensive and takes a great deal of time. So instead of actually diffusing the light from the sun by creating a physically accurate diffusion event the size of the earth's atmosphere, we add a local diffuse light source that only affects the area within view of the camera. Instead of actually reflecting the light from the sun, we use no reflection but instead add a light source at the reflection point to simulate the effect. Usually the results are acceptable and save us hours per frame of rendering time.

What's the big deal about rendering time if the final render looks great? You're right. If you're working on a personal project at home and you want to leave your dual proc machine rendering for six weeks to get a great four-second shot, go for it. But if you are working in a production environment, you are probably not the only artist trying to get frames rendered. If you hog the render farm with frames that take an unreasonable amount of time to render, you risk missing your deadline (and incurring the wrath of the other artists). Trust me on this — CG artists can be very creative with their punishment. Many tricks and tips are covered in this manual to help you create the best "bang for your buck." These tricks do not work for every situation, but you will find that most cases do not require the long render times, and you won't have to find out what punishments are inflicted on "render hogs."

Sunlight

Intensity	High to medium
Color	Warm spectrum
Direction	Side to top
Diffuseness	Low
Shadow	Usually very hard to soft
Shape	Usually omni
Contrast	High
Movement	Usually imperceptible
Size	Medium or small

The first and most common light source in the world is the sun. It is the source of almost all light on our planet, actually. All the photochemical or electromagnetic energy in the world originates with radiations from the sun. As a lighting artist you are most certainly going to run into situations where you will have to create sunlight for your scene.

This section deals only with direct sunlight — the stuff you see when the sun is visible in the sky, the stuff that gives you a sunburn, the bright light that blows out your photos and makes you squint, the stuff your mother told you not to look at during a solar eclipse.

A very simplistic description of sunlight may refer to it as a distant light source in which all the light rays are parallel and all the shadows are hard. The parallel light rays mean that objects in the path of the sunlight will cast shadows that are exactly the same size as the object itself. Some describe the sun as a point source that emits light omnidirectionally and is so distant that the light rays reaching the earth merely appear to be parallel because the angle is so negligible as to be imperceptible. Some see the sun as an area source. In other words, they see the sun as a flat disc in space, the whole surface of which is emitting light omnidirectionally. Area sources behave as diffused sources and therefore result in soft shadows. In truth, all these descriptions are elements of how sunlight behaves.

Figure 3.1: A distant light with parallel rays and hard shadows.

Figure 3.2: A point source with omnidirectional rays and hard shadows.

Figure 3.3: An area source with omnidirectional rays and soft shadows.

Before we deal with lighting types used in CG, let's discuss reality. In reality, all light sources are omnidirectional area sources. In reality, there are no point lights or distant lights like the tools we use in LightWave. This is because 1) all light sources have dimension and volume and cannot, therefore, be nondimensional point sources, 2) all light sources have limited dimension and cannot, therefore, emit the same parallel beams in the same direction regardless of your position in space, and 3) no light sources emit only parallel light rays.

"But wait," you say, "a candle is a point source and so is an LED."

Actually no. Candles and LEDs are small area sources, to be sure, but a point source by definition emits all light omnidirectionally from a single nondimensional point in space. There are no such light sources in existence. Candle flames have dimension; so do lightbulb filaments. This means that every nondimensional spatial point within the shape of the flame and on the filament is emitting light in every direction, producing not only an area source but a diffused result.

"Who cares?" you say. "If you can't tell, what's the difference?"

The difference is in the details. But it is true that sometimes you can get away with using a distant light or a point light to simulate the sun.

> **Note:** In Part III, we deal extensively with different ways of creating sunlight and skylight using different light types for different quality results and different render times.

31

The sun is larger than the earth. This means that there are light rays running exactly parallel to each other that cover the entire sunward face of our planet.

If the sun's rays were all parallel, the shadow behind earth would look like this

Figure 3.4: If the sun's rays were all parallel, all shadows would behave the way those in this image are behaving, all parallel and hard-edged, and the shadow would remain exactly the same size as the object that cast it.

In addition to these parallel rays, there are nonparallel light rays coming from the entire earthward face of the sun in every direction, some of which reach the earth.

Of those light rays that reach the earth, some come from near the edge of the sun's disc, some come from the middle, some come from everywhere on the sun. Since the sun is larger than the earth, some rays will angle behind the earth while rays originating near the center of the disc will either hit the earth or angle away from the earth after they pass it. A lunar eclipse is a good example of this effect.

Sunlight acts this way on every object on the earth but on a smaller local scale. The *penumbra* is the area behind the earth — or building or chair or anything on earth — where there is partial shadow. It is partial shadow because while some sunlight is blocked out, the sun is so large that some of the light still reaches that area behind the object. The *umbra* is the area behind the earth — or building or chair — where there is no sunlight at all and the shadow is complete. This is why you can look at a chair leg with sunlight shining on it and see near the leg that the shadows are dark and hard-edged. But the farther away you move from the leg, the softer and lighter the shadows become. It is because the sun is so much larger than the chair leg that some of the light manages to reach those areas behind the leg.

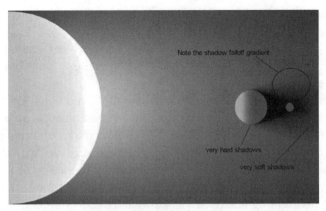

Figure 3.5: This image demonstrates how the sun's light acts on the earth and especially how sunlight gets behind the earth. Note that as less of the sun's surface is visible behind the earth, the light intensity falls off. The area of falloff is very narrow nearest the earth and grows larger the farther from the earth you look. Effectively, since the earth is the shadow-casting object, it is the focal point of the shadow, which grows softer as you get farther away. *Remember this. It is crucial!*

Figure 3.6: This image uses an area light far enough away to create natural hard shadows near the chair and natural soft shadows farther away. This simulates the way sunlight acts on an object here on earth.

So hopefully you now grasp how the sun emits parallel rays similar to a distant light in LightWave, emits omnidirectional light similar to a point light in LightWave, and emits light over an area similar to an area light in LightWave. LightWave's area lights are closest, but they, too, fall short since they are planar and the sun is a volume; however, this physical inaccuracy will almost never be an issue.

"OK," you say, "if sunlight doesn't work exactly like distant, point, or area lights in LightWave, then why do we have these types of lights in LightWave?"

The answer is that these lights calculate much more quickly than a physically perfect model, and that often, the precise physical accuracy may be unimportant or unnoticeable. The camera may be framed on an area very close to the object so that only the hard shadows are visible and the more distant softening shadows are out of frame. In this instance, you could use a distant light or even a point light or a spotlight to create the bright light and hard shadows needed to simulate sunlight. Or there could be enough motion in the shot that physically precise shadows would never be noticed.

Now that you understand how sunlight really acts on objects, you will have to look at the requirements of your shot and decide how far to take it and how far to fake it. The trade-off is that the most physically accurate solutions generally take longer to render. If the final render is no different whether you use a distant light or an area light, then there is no point in using the area light. Do the quick renders. Make the boss smile.

Skylight

Intensity	Medium to low
Color	Cool spectrum
Direction	Omni
Diffuseness	High
Shadow	Soft
Shape	Usually none
Contrast	Low
Movement	Usually none
Size	Very large

Skylight is the ultimate filler when it comes to lighting. Whether it is bright, blue sky or dark, gray clouds, skylight is a diffuse source that epitomizes the expression "global illumination." This is because skylight is global. It is a big ball around the earth that emits light omnidirectionally during the day. It is a gigantic, spherical area light. It is a luminous ball turned inward. Surprise! I have just described three different ways in which skylight can be simulated by LightWave.

Skylight produces only soft shadows, yet it is remarkably similar to sunlight. Skylight is sunlight that has been diffused and spread around randomly in many directions. There are two primary differences between skylight and sunlight. First, sunlight appears mainly unidirectional, or traveling all in parallel rays, creating hard shadows. (I know we just spent a whole section describing how sunlight is omnidirectional, but compared to how random skylight is, sunlight appears relatively uniform.) The sky's light is omnidirectional relative to any place on the earth's surface, except where it is occluded by the earth, so it causes only soft shadows. Look at the underside of your chair outside on a cloudy day. See the shadows? Remember that objects cast shadows? What object is casting that shadow? Is it the chair? Partly. Mostly, however, it is the planet beneath your feet. Think of it this way: The sky is a big, luminous globe. You can't see most of it because the planet is in the way. If the whole ball of sky were not occluded by the planet (in other words, if you were just floating in a giant ball of luminous atmosphere with no planet), then everything would be lit from all angles. The reason most objects on the earth are dark on the bottom is because the earth is getting in the way and creating a shadow. Think also of nighttime. Night occurs because the earth is casting a big shadow and half the planet is sitting in it. This is an important consideration when building a diffuse global lighting solution. The earth is a big, fat shadow-caster. Don't forget it. Let's look at our chair again and see what a global light source like the sky will do to the shadows.

Figure 3.7: You can see in this image that there are no dark "umbra" type shadows. The area under the chair does have a soft shadow because some of the light is occluded by the chair, but some amount of light reaches everywhere. This is because light is coming in from all directions. So a soft shadow is not about whether or not light is reaching the spot but *how much* of the total light is reaching the spot.

Whereas the sun's light comes from one general direction and causes shadows on the opposite side of the object, skylight comes from all directions. There is no complete shadow from any direction as long as a line can be drawn between that point and any portion of the sky. This means that under skylight, most of the shadows are of the penumbra type. This is also known as "accessibility" lighting. If any part of the light source has "access" to any part of a surface, then there is some light. If a great deal of the light source has access to the surface, there is a great deal of light. If very little of the light source has access to the surface, there is very little light.

Incandescent

Intensity	Variable
Color	Warm spectrum (can be altered)
Direction	Any
Diffuseness	Usually low
Shadow	Very hard to soft
Shape	Any
Contrast	High to medium
Movement	Any
Size	Any

Incandescent sources can be as simple as a household frosted lightbulb or a tiny halogen lamp. They can also be a burning fireplace, a candle, a stove element, an electric heater, or even a tiny LED. Incandescence involves the expenditure of energy at high temperature, resulting in light. So anything that is so hot it emits light can be said to be incandescent. Lava flows, for example, or fire embers, or a lit cigarette are all incandescent. Fireflies are not.

> **Note:** Some organisms emit light through photoluminescence. This happens because the organisms absorb infrared or ultraviolet radiation from sunlight during the day and then emit it when they move. We're not going to deal with the science of photo or chemical luminescence. Suffice it to say that by the time you finish this book, you will be able to look at any light source, identify its properties, and simulate it in LightWave.

Because incandescence is caused by high heat, most incandescent light is on the warm or red side of the spectrum. Of course, clever stage and film lighting designers alter the color of incandescent light by placing a colored filter in front, which means you can get blue light out of an incandescent light source. Bear in mind that larger incandescent sources are likely to cause softer shadows, while smaller incandescent sources usually cause harder shadows.

Fluorescent

Intensity	Medium to low
Color	Cool spectrum (can be altered)
Direction	Any
Diffuseness	High to medium
Shadow	Usually soft
Shape	Usually none
Contrast	Usually medium to low
Movement	Usually none
Size	Usually medium to small

Fluorescent sources include, coincidentally, fluorescent lamps, neon lamps, computer monitors, televisions, and any other sources created by making a phosphor glow due to particle bombardment or electrical excitation. Technically, only lights containing fluorine are fluorescent. While neon lights, monitors, and fluorescents are technically different from each other, for the purpose of CG lighting their properties are similar enough that they will be dealt with pretty much identically, except for color and shape. For brevity we will refer to all such sources as "fluorescent" sources.

The primary difference between incandescent and fluorescent light, as far as we are concerned, is that incandescent sources are considered direct light sources and usually result in hard shadows, while fluorescent sources are considered diffused light and usually result in soft shadows.

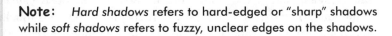

Note: *Hard shadows* refers to hard-edged or "sharp" shadows while *soft shadows* refers to fuzzy, unclear edges on the shadows.

Reflected

Intensity	Any (depends on physical source)
Color	Any
Direction	Any
Diffuseness	Usually low
Shadow	Usually hard

Shape	Any
Contrast	Usually high
Movement	Any
Size	Any

Reflected light sources have distinct differences from other sources. Light reflected from a mirror, a water surface, a window, or other highly reflective surface displays many of the properties of the original light source. For example, sunlight reflecting off a pool onto a wall will retain most of the hard-edged properties as well as a good portion of the intensity, color, shape, and contrast. Skylight reflecting off the pool will retain all its diffuse properties as well. But adding light-reflective properties (called *caustics*) to a surface means a huge increase in rendering time. It is often simpler and quicker to place a new light at the place where the reflection would occur, replicate the properties of the original source (except for direction), and aim it in the direction that the reflected light would go.

Diffuse Reflected

Intensity	Any (depends on physical source)
Color	Any
Direction	Any
Diffuseness	High
Shadow	Soft
Shape	Usually none
Contrast	Usually low
Movement	Any
Size	Usually large

Diffuse reflected light is referred to in CG terminology as *radiosity*. What this means is that light coming from any source will touch a surface of some kind, then part of that light will reflect away, perhaps touching another surface and reflecting again. Radiosity reflections can continue infinitely until all photonic energy has been spent.

As with all reflections, the angle of incidence (the angle at which the light reaches the surface) must be equal to the angle of reflection. In the case of diffuse reflection, the surface is usually uneven or rough, causing the light rays to reflect away in numerous directions and effectively diffusing the reflected light.

A good example is that of sunlight illuminating the pavement in front of a wall. There is no direct lighting on the wall, and it is shaded by an overhanging roof. Blue skylight is filling in and lighting the wall, but there is a brighter, more yellow light on the wall coming from below. This is the light reflecting off the pavement and up onto the wall. The pavement is very uneven and so the light reflection is very diffuse. This is the most common form of lighting in nature. More than sunlight or skylight, the world is illuminated by this type of lighting. The light rays in nature can reflect from surface to surface an infinite number of times, radiating from pavement to wall, back to pavement, to nearby fences, trees, or whatever. Each time the sunlight strikes a surface, it diffuses into many new directions, so the more reflections that occur, the lower the overall intensity of the reflection becomes. As a lighting artist, you will learn to have a love-hate relationship with radiosity. On one hand, it adds a realism to LightWave's renders that no other tool can match. On the other hand, the render times can become galactic very quickly, sometimes making radiosity impractical. We will spend some time later on discussing how best to fake radiosity and when it is best to use the real deal.

A Note about Proportion and Scale

These light sources have all been described according to their normal world scale, that is, as though you were the viewer standing there, looking at them. But the camera often sees things differently. What if, for example, there was a close-up of a candle? Well then, that incandescent source would not be tiny. It would be a major consideration in your lighting setup. What about the skylight? It is global and very large, unless you can only see a small square of it through a skylight. So in many ways the properties we have assigned to these light types are highly variable and will depend on the situation. Don't get stuck into one way of thinking about a light type or its properties. Infinite possibilities exist. Be prepared to create a technique never before tried for a situation never before seen. There are no rules. Look at the situation, analyze the light sources and their properties, and then proceed.

• • •

By now, it is probably becoming obvious to you that many different light sources can behave in many different ways and can display a number of variable properties. Just like the analogy of the auto mechanic who knows everything about the car, but only thinks about fixing one system at a time, if you take each light source one at a time and analyze its particular properties and behaviors in a photograph, you should have enough information to understand what properties are present and you'll be able to add each light source, one at a time, into your scene. Later in this book, we discuss the tools we can use to simulate each of the many properties that we've discussed.

In this chapter, we have covered the properties of a number of specific real-world light sources. Hopefully by now you can analyze each light source type and recognize them in a photograph.

Chapter 4

Surface Considerations

Your job as a lighting artist is to light objects. These objects have surfaces. In order to enable your lights to interact properly with your surfaces, you will need to understand some surface properties that pertain to lighting. This is, by no means, a definitive guide to texturing. For that, I recommend you consult *LightWave 3D 8 Texturing* by Leigh van der Byl. This chapter covers some of the basic surface properties you need to consider when building your lighting environment, since the look of light and your texture properties are so closely interrelated. By the time you finish this chapter you should have a basic understanding of how color, specularity and glossiness, reflectivity, diffuseness, and luminosity affect your textures and your lighting.

Color in the Real World

The first and most significant property we discuss is color. We get into the dark art of color mixing in Chapter 19, but for now, suffice it to say that in the real world, the solid colors found on surfaces interact differently with colored light than they do by mixing other color into the surface. For example, if you mix paint colors of primary red, primary blue, and primary yellow, you will, theoretically, get black paint. If you mix light colors of primary red, primary green, and primary blue, you will, theoretically, get white light.

Note: The reality of paint and light in the real world is that it is practically impossible to create true primary colors. A primary color is one that contains only a single wavelength. While it is possible to create this digitally, it is very difficult in the world of chemicals and pigments. So in reality, if you were to take paints labeled primary red, yellow, and blue, you will probably get a brownish gray. Keep this in mind when painting textures digitally, especially if you are trying to make it look photo-real.

The most obvious difference between solid pigment colors and lighting colors is that the primaries are different. For solids, it is red, yellow, and blue. For light, it is red, green, and blue. We deal with the reasons for this in Chapter 19, which covers color in depth.

Color is measured in wavelength. If we look at a spectrum of visible light, we see red colors at one end and blue colors at the other end. Blue and violet have the shortest wavelengths, while the red end has the longest wavelengths. Our eyes perceive these wavelengths and translate them into different colors. Various surfaces and materials in the real world will either absorb or reflect certain wavelengths based on the surfaces' own physical properties. A surface that absorbs only red and green wavelengths of light, for example, will appear mostly blue because it is reflecting the blue part of the spectrum. Furthermore, the reflected blue wavelengths will then reflect on another nearby surface. This is why if you put two objects of different colors near each other in bright light, they appear to gain some of the reflected color of each other. In the world of CG, this effect is called radiosity, or diffuse reflection.

Note: It's the old trick of putting a buttercup under the chin to see if the yellow light reflects on the underside of the chin. OK, maybe you didn't do that as a child, but I did. The trick was that if you saw yellow light reflected under the chin, it meant you liked butter. Hey, it makes sense when you're six.

Be aware that if you shine a yellow light onto a blue surface, there will be little reflected light because the incoming wavelengths are opposite the surface wavelengths on a color wheel. This means that the yellow light is in the range most likely to be absorbed by the blue surface. Yellow light is yellow because it is missing most of the blue wavelengths, so there is little light left for the blue surface to reflect. More detail on color wheels, mixing, and the behavior of colors is in Chapter 19. Understanding the difference and interactions between solid colors and lighting colors can be confusing at first. This is all covered in Chapter 19 as well.

Specularity and Glossiness

If you were a physicist, you might comment that the reflectivity of a surface is based on its specularity. In the real world, *specularity* refers to the surface properties of an object that cause light to reflect in a directed manner, as from a smooth, polished surface, so that parallel light rays reaching the surface will still all be parallel light rays when reflected. In the real world, high specularity usually refers to mirror-like and other highly reflective surfaces.

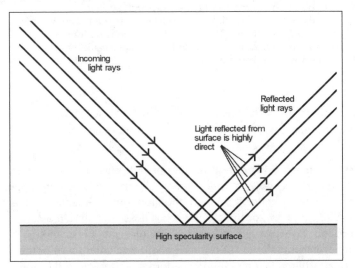

Figure 4.1: This image demonstrates how a very smooth surface reflects light information. The light information retains its original form and is therefore still easy to identify as an image. This is what occurs in a mirror. In the real world, shininess (or glossiness), reflectivity, and specularity are the same thing.

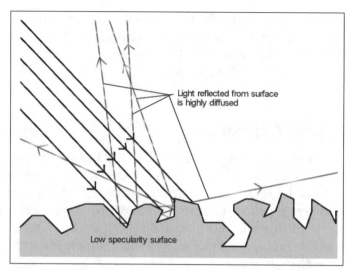

Figure 4.2: This image demonstrates how a rough surface reflects light information. The light information does not retain its original form and is scattered. The light information is no longer identifiable as the original light information. This occurs on any rough surface such as a sheet of paper or a wall painted with a matte paint.

In LightWave, however, specularity and reflectivity are two entirely different animals.

> **Note:** Specularity and glossiness in LightWave are misnomers. The control we know as Specularity really should be called "Specular Intensity" because it refers to the illumination intensity of the specular highlight, or how bright it is. Glossiness should actually be called "Specularity," because a high glossiness is a smaller, sharper, more defined specular highlight, indicating a smoother surface, while a low glossiness is a larger, softer, more diffused specular highlight, which indicates a rougher surface texture. The Specularity control in LightWave actually is like a light intensity control that only affects the intensity of the specular highlight but not the illumination value.

Specularity in LightWave refers to the "shininess" of a surface. It's like that bright, white highlight you see on a polished apple. It refers to how much "brightness" or "lighting" information is reflected. But specularity in LightWave does not include reflective information. *Reflectivity,* on the other hand, refers to how much clear image information is reflected. In the real world, these two are inextricably tied together because image information *is* light information. The light seen in the mirror has reflected off the surface. One great reason why specularity and reflectivity are separate in LightWave is that you can dramatically decrease rendering times by using only one or the other. A marble, for example, is usually highly specular. This means that there's a nice bright highlight on the surface, and it is reflecting all the image information around it. But if you are standing in a room and there are a few marbles on the floor ten feet away from you, it is unlikely that you will clearly see any of the image information unless you look very closely. Why, then, spend time calculating it, when a nice specular light hit will complete the illusion quite adequately? For many surfaces, you will use specularity only and never turn on reflectivity, especially for surfaces with low specularity such as rough plastic or perhaps even skin. They both have some shininess, but the reflective value is so low and the reflected image so diffused by the rough surface that you will never really see an image reflected. You can save a good deal of render time by simply not calculating the reflectivity.

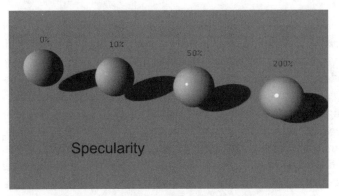

Figure 4.3: This image displays various levels of specularity. The Specularity setting in the Surface Editor determines the brightness or intensity of the specular highlight and really should, therefore, be named "Specular Intensity."

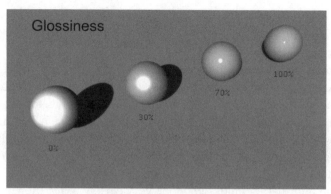

Figure 4.4: This image displays various levels of glossiness. The Glossiness setting in the Surface Editor determines smoothness (or specularity) of the surface and really should, therefore, be named "Specularity." Note that the lower the Glossiness setting, the more spread out the specular highlight becomes. Wider specular highlights indicate a surface that is rough and is diffusing the light information more.

Reflectivity

Reflectivity in the real world refers to how much light is not absorbed by a material. For example, coal is not very reflective, but snow is highly reflective. A mirror is highly reflective, but a cast-iron frying pan is not.

Colloquially, however, we think of reflectivity as meaning how well you can see the reflection of an image in a surface. We think that a mirror is highly reflective, but a white wall is not. In truth, both the mirror and the white wall are highly reflective. The difference is that one material diffuses the light that it reflects, and the other does not. If you go back and look at the images in the previous section of this chapter, you will understand that the white wall has a very rough surface at the microscopic level, and so the image information is scattered so widely that we can no longer discern any image information in the reflection. However, a mirror's surface is so smooth that the image information is not scattered at all and the reflected light is in almost the same form as it was before striking the mirror's surface; therefore, we can see the image information clearly.

In LightWave, however, reflectivity refers only to image reflection and has nothing to do with diffuseness, specularity, or glossiness, all of which are separate controls in the LightWave Surface Editor panel.

So this means that you use the Reflectivity setting if you specifically want to reflect the surrounding environment in your object's surface, such as a mirror, a glass, or a shiny marble floor, but you can leave it off for diffuse surfaces that don't reflect images.

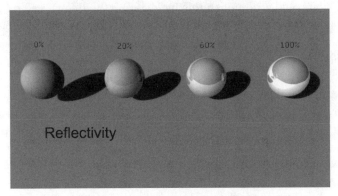

Figure 4.5: This image demonstrates the Reflectivity value at different levels. The higher the value, the more image information is reflected in the texture. Very simple.

Note: In order to have reflection work, you must enable Ray Trace Reflection in your Render Options panel.

Diffuseness

In LightWave, *diffuseness* is a surface property that refers to the amount of light that acts on a surface. For example, a beach ball has a high diffuseness. When light hits it, you can see that it is brightly lit and easily visible. Technically, we are saying that because light hits the object and is widely diffused, or dispersed, the object is easy to see from any direction because a great deal of light is reflecting from its surface in all directions. As another example, a mirror has very low diffuse value. While it does reflect all the light away, it is not diffused. The reflections are direct. All you see is a reflection of whatever image is before the mirror. It is technically possible in the real world for a material to have no reflectivity and no diffuseness. A material such as this would be invisible because no light is reflected or diffused from its surfaces. The only item known to have these properties is a black hole, which does not reflect or diffuse light from its surface. But this is mainly due to gravity rather than surface properties. If black holes did not have the immense gravity necessary to suck in light, then they would be visible because all surfaces have some measure of diffuse value. Even the surface of the sun has a diffuse value, but it is completely overwhelmed by the luminosity of the sun.

In LightWave, if you wished to remove shadows from an object's surface, you could accomplish this by lowering the diffuse value of the surface and by increasing the luminosity value. Or if you want to look at it another way, in the real world, a white surface like a piece of paper has a high diffuse value because it diffuses a great deal of light and is, therefore, highly visible. A black surface, on the other hand, has a low diffuse value because it diffuses very little light. The easiest way to envision this is by imagining driving down a dark road at night. If a person is wearing all white clothes, your car headlights will pick him up sooner and he will be visible much farther away because his clothes have a high diffuse value. Someone dressed entirely in black might not be seen until you are very close, because very little light is being diffused back toward you, and therefore there is very little light information entering your eyes. The person is very difficult to see.

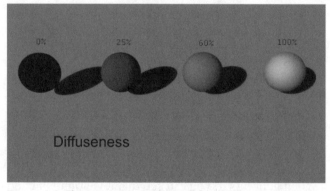

Figure 4.6: The texture settings on all four balls are exactly the same except for the diffuseness values. Diffuseness indicates how much of the light received by the surface is reflected back. A low diffuseness value means very little light is reflected, while a high diffuseness value means a great deal of light is reflected. The more visible light that is reflected by the surface, the more visible it is to the human eye.

Luminosity

Some objects in your shot will have surfaces that emit light. These surfaces are said to be *luminous*. In other words, they display the property of *luminosity*. The surface of a lightbulb, for example, has a pretty high luminosity value. So does a computer monitor. Any surface that emits light can be said to be luminous. NewTek, the makers of LightWave, has provided us with some great tools to simulate the luminosity of a surface. One is the luminosity value found on the Surface Editor panel. This luminosity value brightens the surface, eliminating shadows as though the brightness were overpowering any shadows. This value, however, does not actually emit light. It does not actually transmit illumination to nearby surfaces unless you turn on LightWave's radiosity. In this case, the luminous surface does emit light to nearby surfaces.

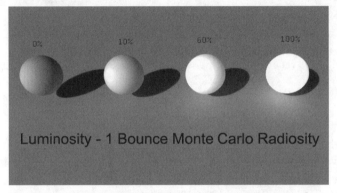

Luminosity - 1 Bounce Monte Carlo Radiosity

Figure 4.7: In this image, the texture values are the same for all four balls, except for luminosity. The higher the luminosity value, the more light a surface is apparently emitting. A lightbulb, for example, has a low luminosity value when it is turned off but a high luminosity value when it is turned on. Note how, as the luminosity increases, the shadows are filled in. Just for the fun of it, I turned on single-bounce Monte Carlo radiosity for this render so that the balls emit light onto nearby surfaces.

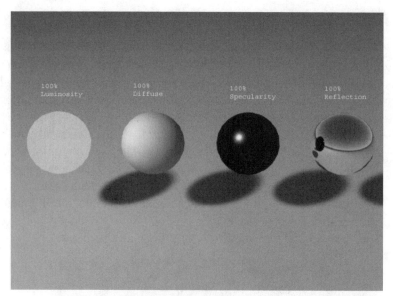

Figure 4.8: This image demonstrates the use of luminosity, diffuseness, specularity, and reflectivity. All other settings are at 0%.

•　•　•

I hope this chapter has helped you understand some of the surface properties we deal with when lighting our scenes. Lighting is only half about the lights we use and how we use them. The other half of lighting is about the surfaces that we light. The surface properties have a direct effect on how the light looks when it reaches them.

Chapter 5

Studying Light

This chapter deals with the observation of light in the real world. By the time you have finished this chapter, you should be able to observe and identify the light properties specific to various types of natural and artificial light sources and to shadows.

Being a great lighting artist is all about understanding how real light works so that you can recreate it in your virtual environment. The only way to really understand the nature of light and shadows is to study it.

Studying light is really as simple as it sounds. As an artist, you wish to recreate something in the medium of your choice. If you are a painter, you might wish to paint a portrait. This requires you to understand human skeletal and muscular structures, the behavior of fabrics, the visible properties of skin, iris, lens, and hair. Perhaps there is a chair in the portrait. You must understand the grain of the wood and the properties of the velvet or leather upholstery. You must understand how the light will play off each surface, how the specular highlights and reflections should look, how shadows are formed and where, what the diffuse reflected light will do to the underside of the chin and the nose, how back-lit cotton will react translucently, and so on.

Studying to be an artist means studying the art of the masters. It also means studying the natural elements that come together to create an image. In this case, the element we are talking about is light. Light deserves as much study as any other element of your composition — perhaps even more. In the world of CG, your lighting is mission critical to making your shot look real. So start by spending some time just looking around. You don't have to go to a gallery. Light is everywhere, in every form. A trick used by many lighting designers is to hold up one hand or a piece of paper and stare at it, turning it over and around to see how the light plays across it. Look at the shadows and where they are, what color they are, and what sort of light is filling the shadows. Check out the contrast, the shape and softness of the shadows, and the direction of the light source. Can you identify all the light sources around just by looking at your hand? You should be able to, but if you can't, don't worry — you will be by the time you've finished this book!

Some artists like to put a white or gray ball in an environment to study the lighting. This works, but I find it sterile. A hand is a much more interesting shape and will provide much more information. That's not to disparage the white or gray ball. If you can get the VFX supervisor to stick a ball (especially a reflective ball!) on the set and take a photo or provide some extra footage from the plate, it will provide valuable information for matching the shot's lighting.

> **Note:**   18% gray balls and reflective balls are commonly used as lighting references on the set. A good VFX supervisor will be sure to provide these references to the visual effects department where the CG lighting will take place. The gray ball shows general light effects on a diffuse, round shape, while the reflective ball works like a 180 degree mirror, showing you the precise position and color of the light sources and giving you a rough approximation of the intensity ratio between light sources.

Here are some of the light types you may encounter, along with some suggestions on how to start looking at them.

Natural Light

Natural light refers to the light we find in nature — light that is not made by people. I am going to tell you many times in this section that the best way to really understand these light types is to go out and study them. No book, no video, and no plug into your brain will take the place of observing, experiencing, and understanding for yourself the way real-world light interacts with things in your environment.

Sunlight

The most obvious natural light source is the sun. Understanding how sunlight reaches the earth and how it lights objects in your environment is important to creating realistic sunlight in your CG scene. A common misconception is that the sun is equivalent to a point source with light rays radiating outward omnidirectionally. Another misconception is that the sun is a distant light that is so far away that all its rays are parallel by the time they reach the earth. The fact is that these are both true in part, but there are more qualities not yet discussed.

The sun is about 149,597,890 kilometers away from the earth and its diameter is about 100 times that of the earth. The entire surface of the sun is radiating light in every direction at once. This means that over the width of the sun's disc as viewed from the earth, parallel rays of light are approaching the earth. There are also rays of light spreading out in all directions from every point on the surface of the sun and rays of light converging on the earth and all things on it from many directions. The result of the size differential between the sun and the earth can be observed during a lunar eclipse when the earth passes directly between the sun and the moon. The moon first passes into the penumbra, that area behind the earth where the sun's light is partially obscured. The sun is so much larger than the earth that some of the sun's light manages to reach behind the earth, creating a partial shadow. The moon then passes into the umbra, that area where there is no direct sunlight at all.

Let's look at an illustration of a lunar eclipse to describe this phenomenon.

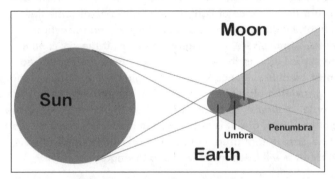

Figure 5.1: This effect occurs for every object lit by direct sunlight, but the angles are usually so slight as to be imperceptible. The light rays often appear to be parallel. In many cases, this effect will not need to be addressed in CG lighting. Sometimes, however, understanding this effect is critical to your lighting.

If you place a chair in the sunlight, you will notice that the shadow cast by the chair is sharpest near where the chair is touching the ground and becomes fuzzier with distance. This is the same effect that is found in the lunar eclipse. In the case of our chair, the sun is much larger than the chair, so the converging light rays are able to reach around behind it, "softening" the shadow. See Figure 3.6.

Skylight

When we say "skylight" we are usually referring to a clear, blue sky. When the sky is blue, you will notice that shadows have a bluish tint to them. It does not seem obvious at first, but look closely. If you look outside on a snowy day, it is very obvious. Skylight is a global light source that has several immediately obvious effects.

> **Note:** Since the release of *LightWave 3D 7.5 Lighting*, more than any other topic, this has become one of debate. Some artists outright refuse to believe that the blue sky illuminates and fills in the shadows cast by objects on a clear, sunny day. Some insist that shadows are the absence of light and, therefore, contain no illumination at all. Others, recognizing that there is some light in the shadowed area, insist that the shadows must be gray because, well, isn't it just lit at a lower intensity? To address these directly, lest you become befuddled by these non-thinkers, a shadow on earth is not the absence of light. It is the absence of *some* light but not all light, because light is always reflecting and refracting around the atmosphere. As for gray shadows, if the sky is blue, and the sky is filling in the shadowed area, then the shadowed area must be blue…just as blue as it would be if you were shining a flashlight with a blue filter in front of it. The problem seems to be that people let their eyes be fooled by their preconceptions. If the tablecloth is white, and it is less lit in one area then another, then it must be gray in that area, not blue. Read on, though. If this is not yet clear, it will become so in the following pages.

Skylight fills the shadows with a blue, low-intensity light. It illuminates almost every surface except the most obscurely hidden. Skylight is most visible in areas where direct sunlight does not reach. That's one of the main reasons you can see down a narrow back alley between two tall buildings even if it is not directly lit by sunlight.

Skylight, which seems relatively dim in broad daylight, can seem blinding if you are indoors. (Ever leave a movie theater on a bright but cloudy day?) Skylight can also be orange, red, or yellow if it is sunset or sunrise. It can even have a greenish tint under some strange atmospheric conditions. Keep in mind that a surface lit by direct sunlight is also additively lit by the sky. In other words, on a clear, sunny day, both skylight and sunlight are illuminating most surfaces outside. There are two light sources, two colors, two completely different sets of properties at work on that surface. The reason that light on a surface looks whiter than the sun is that the relatively yellow light of the sun is being mixed with the blue skylight. This phenomenon pushes the final, mixed color much closer to white than either skylight or sunlight emissions. Go out and observe. Record your findings. Get to know the sky.

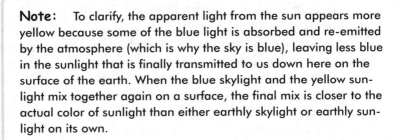

Note: To clarify, the apparent light from the sun appears more yellow because some of the blue light is absorbed and re-emitted by the atmosphere (which is why the sky is blue), leaving less blue in the sunlight that is finally transmitted to us down here on the surface of the earth. When the blue skylight and the yellow sunlight mix together again on a surface, the final mix is closer to the actual color of sunlight than either earthly skylight or earthly sunlight on its own.

Cloudy Day

A cloudy sky can throw some pretty wild changes into an otherwise simple lighting situation. While a cloudy day still provides a global illumination (or "sky dome") scenario, there can be several key differences. First, there is usually little or no direct sunlight, meaning the skylight becomes the key source of light. Second, clouds can range from white to dark gray, pink, red, orange, or even greenish. This means variations in color and intensity. Third, there are unlikely to be any hard shadows. Fourth, these factors will often change more rapidly than on a clear, sunny day (depending on your weatherman). Check out your next cloudy day. Imagine what tools in LightWave you might use to simulate the soft lighting environment you see outside on a cloudy day.

Moonlight

Moonlight is very interesting. Because it is 100% reflected light, it comes to earth roughly the color of the moon, which appears far more white than sunlight. Sometimes moonlight is perceived as blue light and is often simulated this way on set. Since the human eye is accustomed to a more yellowish light from the sun, the relative whiteness of the moonlight is closer to the blue end of the visible spectrum. This relative color shift is often misinterpreted as blue light. Also, the blueness of moonlight is simply near-white reflected moonlight that has been diffused through the atmosphere. Just as daytime skylight is blue, nighttime skylight is also blue but at a much lower intensity. The mix of white moonlight and blue nighttime skylight gives the real impression of blue-tinted light. The moonlight is reflecting from a highly diffuse surface, but the light comes so far that most of it is lost in directions away from the earth. We actually receive only a tiny fraction of the light that hits the moon, just as we receive only a tiny fraction of the light that leaves the sun.

A night lit by a full moon can seem quite bright when it is, in fact, only slightly lighter than pitch black. The key to understanding moonlight and how to simulate it is in knowing how the human eye reacts to low-light situations. The eye is far more sensitive than a computer monitor, a painter's canvas, or a photograph. The iris will dilate to let in more light when it is dark and will contract to let in less light when it is very bright. This keeps the illuminated world within a range that is comfortable and understandable to the light receptors in the eye. So while a moonlit night is much darker than a sky-lit shadow on a bright sunny day, the eye may be able to see clear details in the moonlight but almost no details in the shadows on a sunny day, perceiving those shadows to be nearly black. This is because the eye has adjusted. It all comes down to these three words: "It's all relative."

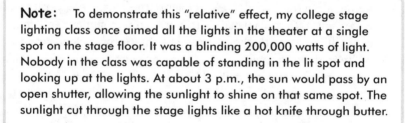

Note: To demonstrate this "relative" effect, my college stage lighting class once aimed all the lights in the theater at a single spot on the stage floor. It was a blinding 200,000 watts of light. Nobody in the class was capable of standing in the lit spot and looking up at the lights. At about 3 p.m., the sun would pass by an open shutter, allowing the sunlight to shine on that same spot. The sunlight cut through the stage lights like a hot knife through butter.

Starlight

Starlight is very similar to moonlight except that it is usually lower intensity, it is usually either white or a steel blue in color, and it does not cast hard shadows being, by nature, a rather omnidirectional source. The best way to understand starlight (or any light) is to go out into it and look around. You'll see soft shadows and gentle, very low illumination.

Starlight behaves exactly the same as skylight, but at a much lower intensity level and a much more saturated color.

Artificial Light

Artificial light refers to light emitted by manufactured devices. This usually means electric light, but one can also argue torches, lighters, fireplaces, rocket engines, lasers, gasoline fires, and H-bomb explosions. Let's not be nitpicky.

Incandescent Sources

Incandescent sources usually mean light sources that emit light by the conversion of electricity to heat such as common household lightbulbs. We can also include flame sources such as candles, fireplaces, or torches that do not use electricity but emit light through the production of high heat through a chemical conversion (burning or rapid oxidation). We generally consider flame sources incandescent because the color temperature of these processes falls into the same range as those of electric incandescent light sources.

Diffuse Sources

Diffuse incandescent sources are very common. A frosted lightbulb, for example, is a diffuse incandescent source. Notice how much like the sun these lights behave. Shadows are sharpest near the object and become softer farther away. This is because the area of light emission is relatively large, causing the shadow falloff or "penumbra" gradient-like effect. They are just a much smaller-scale version of the same type of light.

Point Sources

Incandescent point sources include light-emitting diodes, small candle flames, and tiny lightbulbs. In truth, none of these are technically point sources because a point source should, by strict physical definition, have no dimension or no measurable size in any direction (because that is how point lights behave inside LightWave). But these examples are usually small enough to qualify for "point source" status in the CG world. In some cases, the sun can be considered a point source for CG purposes because it is so far away that it may seem small. You can get away with it under the right conditions. Point light sources, whether in the real world or in CG, result in harder, diverging shadows. Point sources are always smaller than the objects they strike; therefore, the shadows from point sources are always diverging (getting larger with distance). Since these sources are usually physically small, they are also usually appropriately less intense. But that doesn't mean you can't think up some completely strange and unique use for a point source that follows none of the normal properties.

Fluorescent Sources

Fluorescent sources refer to lights such as neon or fluorescent fixtures where illumination is achieved by bombarding "phosphors" with electrons. These light sources are always diffuse, since the illumination occurs over a relatively large area. Take a neon sign or a fluorescent tube, for example. Look at the type of light cast by these fixtures. Examine the shadows. They are soft because of the wide area of light emission. Note that neon lights also come in a wide range of colors, shapes, and sizes, far more variable than any natural source. For the purposes of this text, we can include in this category other wide and soft light sources such as computer monitors, televisions, and plasma screens. These aren't technically fluorescent, but the light and shadow properties work the same.

Shadow

Perhaps the most common misconception about shadows is that they are an effect created by a light source. Some say lights cast shadows. If you take a moment to think about this, it is obvious that lights do not cast shadows. Shadows are cast by objects that are being illuminated by the light. Shadows are the absence of light from a particular source. Shadows are the space behind an object where the light cannot reach. This is not to say that all shadows are completely void of light. In fact, almost all shadows have some visible light spilling into them from other sources. Shadows occur where some or all of the light sources are completely or partially occluded. Normally, the most obvious shadow cast by an object is the area where the key, or main, light does not reach.

Shadows are critical in our everyday life. They allow our visual systems to understand where a stair ends or where the curb edge is on the sidewalk. Without shadows we would constantly be tripping over and bumping into things. When you walk through a doorway into a room beyond, one of the main identifiers of that doorway is the difference in lighting between one room and the next or of the shadows defining the shape of the door or the molding around the doorway. If all surfaces were evenly lit and without shadow, the only differentiation between the surfaces would be color. What if you are trying to find a white door in a white wall? It would be impossible without some lighting differentiation, that is, shadows of some sort. Look around you and find a door. If it is the same color as the wall, then the only reason you can see it is because of the shadows that give it form.

Figure 5.2: In this image, the shadow is cast by the railing. Its position is exactly opposite the sun relative to the railing. Some detail is still visible inside the shadow though. This is because while skylight is present everywhere in this image, the sunlight is partly occluded by the rail.

The qualities of shadows can provide a great deal of information about the lighting environment. Are the shadows hard or soft? Are they deep or subtle? Are they long or short? What colors fill the shadow, if any? What shapes do we see within the shadow or outlining the shadow? Is it only the shape of the object casting the shadow? Or are there other shapes? What causes the other shapes? Shadow shows the direction of the light source. Do the shadows demonstrate a natural light source or a strange, unusual one? Are the shadows uniform, or does light and darkness vary over the surface of the shadow? What causes the variations?

Shadows come in infinite shape, size, and quality. Pay special attention to what the shadow qualities are for your particular light source. Hard shadows, for example, are actually pretty uncommon in the real world. They are created by point sources or any source that does not have an area of illumination. In the real world, there is no such source, but in the CG world, point lights and distant lights create hard (and only hard) shadows. We will get into the reasons for this later on. For now, suffice it to say that even though the shadows are physically incorrect, these lights are not useless. They are very useful indeed, but must be used judiciously (and cleverly) to accomplish a realistic simulation of real-world lighting.

In the real world, both diffuse reflection and area source lights create soft shadows. Fortunately, we can fake soft shadows in CG with a great little tool called Shadow Fuzziness, which is available for LightWave's spotlights when using shadow maps instead of ray-traced shadows. For more on spotlights, see Chapter 7.

Most real-world shadows will be filled with a secondary light source. This secondary light source is likely to be a global source such as sky or cloud or a diffuse reflected source such as the light bounced off a road or wall. Most likely, the secondary or "fill" source is colored, either because the sky is blue or because the wall is yellow or whatnot. Either way, the fill source is probably colored, which means the shadow is colored. We take note of these real-world lighting properties and recreate them in LightWave. For more on key and fill lighting, see Chapter 6.

Light Color

We should begin here with a short discussion of "color" versus "color temperature." Colors in the red side of the spectrum (including orange and yellow) are considered to be "warm" colors because they remind us of fire and heat, while colors in the blue side of the spectrum are considered to be "cool" because they remind us of ice and snow.

The reality is that when a chunk of metal is heated up, it begins with a red glow, and as it gets hotter goes to orange, yellow white, and even blue provided it hasn't melted already. This is where the term "color temperature" comes from. The higher color temperatures are closer to the so-called "cool" end of the color spectrum, while the lower color temperatures are closer to the so-called "warm" end of the color spectrum. In astronomy, red giant stars are considered relatively cool (temperature-wise) while blue dwarfs are considered to be extremely hot stars. Confusing enough? We use both terms in this book, but for convention's sake, a color that is described as "cool" will be in the blue end and a color described as "warm" will be in the red end. If I want to talk about color temperature, I will specify it as "color temperature." Don't worry if you don't have a handle on this yet; we cover color and color temperature in the "Kelvin" section of Chapter 8.

· · ·

Hopefully this chapter has provided you with a place to start observing light in your world. Observation and understanding are absolutely essential to creating believable lighting in your CG work. There will be examples later in the book to help you understand exactly how to replicate the light you see around you once you understand it.

By now, you should be able to observe and identify the light properties specific to various types of natural and artificial light sources and to shadows. Whether it is sunlight, neon lights, or a ball of flame, you should have a good idea about what differentiates one set of light properties from another.

Chapter 6

Principles of Lighting

This chapter covers basic lighting principles including concepts such as the key light, the fill light, the highlight (or rim light), three- and four-point lighting, basic coloring, intensity ratios, and a little history discussing how lighting became what it is. By the end of this chapter, you should have a grasp of these basic concepts and how they relate to not only photographic lighting but also light in the real world.

Lighting has four primary purposes. First, we light a scene to illuminate the subject, to make it visible. Second, we try to focus the viewer's attention on specific areas of the shot and to subtly make other areas less prominent. Third, we give form or shape to the subjects, the set, and other elements in frame so they don't seem flat and unreal. And fourth, we wish to build an emotional framework for the scene so that our viewers will follow along with the story just as we wish.

As with any other visual element, there are certain principles that apply to most lighting situations. I hesitate to call any of these rules, since this is art and artists tend to make hamburger out of anything they are told is a rule. So consider these principles a starting point. Once you have fully grasped the principles, do with them as you will. Please don't misinterpret that statement as meaning that the principles in this chapter are not important. They are crucial in being able to move on to more advanced lighting concepts, just as when learning to play a piano, the artist must first learn which key is middle C, what a scale is, and what keys are. The pianist later forgets about these things. They simply become second nature to the pianist, but they remain there in the subconscious, the absolute core of knowledge that allows the pianist to play the piano. In the same way, these principles will become your keys, scales, and "middle C." You must know them so well that you can forget about them and carry on playing and composing.

The Key Light

The *key light* in a scene is the primary source of light. It can be any light source from any angle. It is the light that provides primary illumination. Sunlight is an easy example. On a sunny day, sunlight is the key source. There are no brighter lights on earth that you are likely to see in your shot. Make it a cloudy day and the sky becomes the key light because it is now the primary source of illumination. (Yes, the clouds are luminous because they absorb and diffuse the sunlight, re-emitting it toward us.) This is an entirely different type of source, but in this situation, the clouds become the key light. In your living room, a floor lamp may be the key, or the fireplace could be the key if the electric lights are all off. It's a simple concept.

Figure 6.1: This image demonstrates a single key light alone on a chair.

The Fill Light

Look in any shadow in front of you. There it is — the *fill light*. Fill light does two main things. Most obviously, it illuminates areas that are shadowed from the key light. It also usually illuminates all the areas that are lit by the key light, or at least some of them where the key light and fill light overlap on a surface. In other words, in a situation with a key light and fill light, the shadows are illuminated by the fill light and the unshadowed areas are illuminated by the key light and the fill light wherever they overlap.

If there were no fill light, shadows would be pitch black and you would see no details inside them. This is not likely to happen on or near our planet, although there is a good deal less fill light available in space, since there is little or no atmospheric diffusion going on.

Fill light can be created by any secondary source. Usually, however, it is either a global source like skylight and cloud light or it is a diffuse reflection (radiosity). But since fill light is simply a lower intensity light filling up the shadows, you can use any tool in your CG arsenal to create this illumination. For a skylight fill, for example, I would probably choose an area light as my first choice for accuracy and speed. My second choice might be backdrop-only global illumination. My third choice would probably be a spotlight with high shadow fuzziness. These are all covered in detail later. Suffice it to say that the fill light mainly "fills" the shadowy spaces left over by the key light.

Figure 6.2: This image includes both a key light and a fill light. Note the soft shadows created by the area light used for the fill.

The Highlight

The *highlight* is also known as the top light, the back light, the tip light, and the rim light, depending on where you learned your lighting. Its primary purpose is to make an object stand out from its background, to help define the shape, and to provide a nice, defined edge for those nasty green-screen or blue-screen shots.

Figure 6.3: This image illustrates a highlight, or "rim" light. The top edges are clearly outlined by a specular hit and heightened illumination. This makes the object stand out sharply from the background.

Figure 6.4: Here is a good example of a highlight in nature. In this example, one could argue that the key light is the highlight, or rim light. Others may say there is no key, just a fill and a rim. (See color image.)

Some artists go pretty wild with highlighting, adding a rim light for every shot. But like all other light sources in your shot, there had better be some motivation for the light.

> **Note:** The rim light is the most overused light in the CG world. It has become almost a joke to see an animated CG film in which every character has a strong rim light in every shot from every angle, regardless of the lighting environment around them. It's getting downright cheesy. Please, I beg you, as up-and-coming lighting artists, for the love of all that's good, break the "cheese" barrier and start using rim lights judiciously and subtly!

> **Note:** Sometimes what appears to be a rim light on a texture is really a texture shader such as LightWave's Fast Fresnel shader that makes the surface change luminosity based on its angle to the camera. So lights are not always to blame, but the result, effect, and "cheese factor" are still the same. For more detail on LightWave's Fast Fresnel shader, check out the LightWave manual or take a look at the "Fast Fresnel" section of Chapter 16.

If, for example, a person is sitting in a small room and the only light is from a window to the subject's left, there had better not be a rim light making a nice halo over the subject's hair. There is no light source to justify it. It will definitely look very wrong. If you really want or need this nice rim, find a way to create a justification or find another solution. Don't add lights that have no source in the "real" world.

McCandless Lighting

Once upon a time, a lighting designer named Stanley McCandless observed the natural interaction between key and fill lighting and desired to recreate this effect for the stage. McCandless observed that a very bright, very large light source (the sun) approached the subject from one angle. He thought to recreate this using a large array of "key" lights all pointing in the same direction. He also observed a secondary, very uniform source (the sky) filling in all the shadows. He sought to recreate this using a large array of "fill" lights also all pointing in the same direction but opposite the key array. Thus, the McCandless lighting system was born. Each area on the stage (of which there were usually six or nine) was lit with two spotlights, one 45 degrees to the left and one 45 degrees to the right. Both lights came from 45 degrees above. One set of lights was the key light and the other was the fill light. Usually the key was colored warm and the fill was cool.

Note: Of course for a nighttime scene, one might have both the key and fill on the cool side of the spectrum. For a very hot summer day in a desert, one might make both key and fill on the warm side. Much depends on individual taste, style, and desired emotional impact.

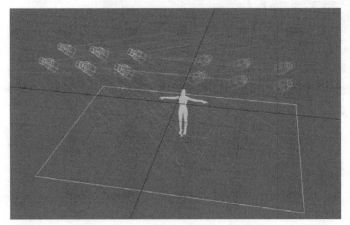

Figure 6.5: This illustration shows a basic McCandless lighting setup.

Try a render using two plain spotlights in the McCandless setup, 45 degrees to either side of the subject and 45 degrees above. Make one slightly amber and the other steel (faint) blue. Light any subject you wish; it doesn't matter. You should get an image something like this:

Figure 6.6: McCandless lighting. (See color image.)

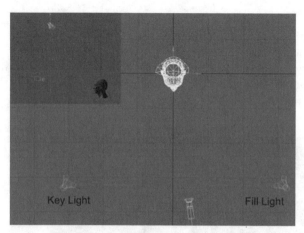

Figure 6.7: You've just created a key/fill lighting setup. Hold onto it. We'll be adding more light.

Key/Fill Lighting

Key/fill lighting is McCandless lighting boiled down to its most basic principles. It doesn't require the formal rules or rigidity of the original theatrical system that defined specific lighting angles relative to the audience or viewer. In a theater, the audience sits in a specific spot relative to the action and to the lighting. In film, the camera has the advantage of taking any point of view (POV), even if it is from within a mouse hole or atop a giant chandelier. This means the lighting designer must be much more flexible in planning than Stanley McCandless had to be. In the world of CG, the camera can even be placed within or behind light sources — something that is not possible in the real world.

Observe key/fill lighting in the world around you. You can see that the lighting angles, colors, shapes, sizes, and source types combine into infinite variety. In some cases, the key light may also act as a highlight. In some cases the key and fill light are the same source. Sometimes the key is cool and the fill is warm. Sometimes both are cool or both are warm. Sometimes the fill light is also the rim light, or the rim light could be the key. The primary source does not necessarily have to be the light that presents the most illumination toward the camera.

It comes down to this: You have a key light shining on an object. Whatever light is illuminating the shadows is the fill light. Any angle, any light source, any property is allowed. The key light illuminates; the fill light shapes.

Three-Point Lighting

Yet another step beyond key/fill lighting, three-point lighting is a key light, a fill light, and a highlight (or rim light). It is a simple combination that provides illumination, form, and dimension. Three-point lighting is, perhaps, one of the best known, most used, and most misused lighting setups known. Although it is a very functional setup, it is often used in completely inappropriate environments. Remember: Every light must be justified.

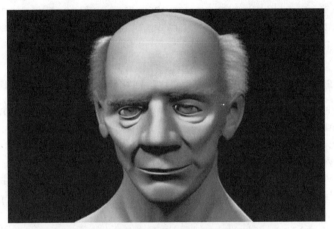

Figure 6.8: Three-point lighting. (See color image.)

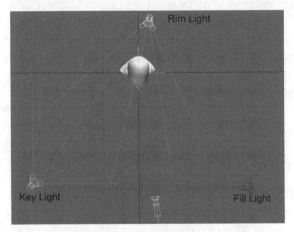

Figure 6.9: This render demonstrates a typical three-point light setup. Here we have a key light as the primary illumination, a fill light providing secondary illumination within the shadows, and a highlight giving a sharp outline to the subject.

Simple, right? Now you are a studio lighting god.

What is Great about Three-Point Lighting

Three-point lighting is a simple, versatile, and powerful method of providing an immediate "beauty" lighting scenario in which most elements are likely to be visible and attractively lit. The key light provides primary illumination, the fill light provides form and shadow fill, while the highlight provides dimension.

Three-point lighting using spotlights is also extremely fast to render with shadow maps.

No scene or lighting analysis is necessary and the artist can import a generic three-point lighting rig from a prepared scene any time, scale the rig, and start a render.

What Is Not So Great about Three-Point Lighting

Three-point lighting is probably the most grossly overused and most inappropriately used lighting setup in the world of CG. Mostly this is because artists know it is a rig that will make their 3D objects look attractive without having to learn anything about lighting. Consequently, CG artwork from animated TV series to feature visual effects is lit using this technique with little consideration for whether or not it is appropriate to the shot. It's a travesty that so many scenes that call for great, creative lighting are shortchanged by artists who don't wish to take the time to learn how to provide really good lighting or by those who think they know how to light, simply because they have been pointing lights at a computer terminal for years. Make no mistake about this: You cannot learn lighting by sitting at a computer monitor with 3D software in front of you, no matter how many hours a day, no matter how many years you have been doing it. An experienced lighting artist will see a shot with three-point lighting at the movie theater and will shrug and wonder sadly why there weren't any real lighting artists available at the time.

Four-Point Lighting

Just to add another monkey wrench to the works, I'm going to include one of my favorite "beauty" techniques. It's a variation on the age-old three-point technique. One of the limitations of three-point lighting is that it doesn't account for any "bounce" source reflected from the ground in front of objects. Key, fill, and rim light all come from above, leaving any underside surfaces in the dark. Bounce light is often forgotten simply because it is a subtle and usually low-intensity light source in the scene, but adding this one light to create a four-point rig can really make a big difference.

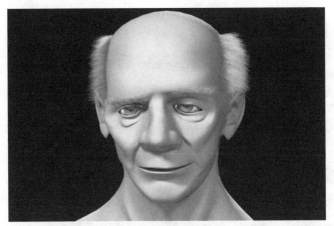

Figure 6.10: In this image, the "bounce" light behaves like radiosity reflected from the floor or road in front of the man, also filling in where lesser experienced lighting artists might be tempted to use ambient intensity — a big no-no in most cases. (See color image.)

> **Note:** There are some, but few, instances in which ambient intensity is appropriate for use in your CG artwork. The main reason it is so infrequently used is that ambient intensity simply adds an even illumination to every surface regardless of light direction or intensity. This has the effect of "flattening out" your beautiful 3D work. That doesn't mean we *never* use it, just rarely (unless employing Monte Carlo or Interpolated Radiosity).

Other Lighting Angles

Lighting designers in film, TV, and especially in theater are constrained to the physical and technical requirements of their lighting instruments. A light must be placed where it has access to electricity, where an operator can reach it if necessary, and where it is not in the way of the camera or the audience. In the beautiful, versatile world of CG, we have no such constraints. We can place any light anywhere at any angle, even directly in front of the camera. Let your imagination go wild. Play with lighting angles and see what they do.

In addition to key, fill, and highlight angles, two of the most common additional angles used are sidelight and footlight. Sidelight is a valuable tool for its ability to punctuate an object's form using a slightly dramatic angle. This usually results in a strong emotional response from the viewer.

Figure 6.11: Sidelight. (See color image.)

The term "footlight" derives from the early days of the stage when lighting was either candles, gas light, or early electric light and was placed at the front of the stage on the floor (where actors often kicked them). These days, this lighting angle is more often referred to as "dramatic" lighting, due to the dramatic effect achieved by this angle.

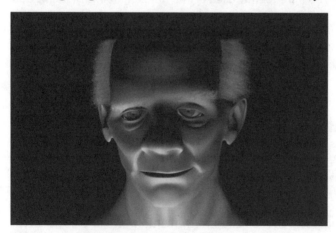

Figure 6.12: Footlight. (See color image.)

We know from our childhood that a flashlight under the chin is a great effect when telling spooky stories. But why? Simply put, the lighting angle is very strange and unnatural. Natural light almost always comes from above. Millions of years of living in nature has taught animals (including us) what feels right and what feels wrong as far as lighting angles are concerned. Here's an important tip: If you want your scene to feel strange, try unusual lighting angles.

Coloring Your Light

We have dealt with a few coloring issues. Key light, for example, will be warm if it is the sun, a candle, flashlight, household bulb, or red neon lamp. Fill light will be cool if it is the sky. Natural lighting generally falls within the Kelvin scale of color temperature, although natural lighting on Mars or beneath the ocean's surface may be radically different from natural lighting in downtown Vancouver. For more on the Kelvin scale, see Chapter 8. Artificial lighting has a color range as wide as the visible spectrum.

Regardless of what colors you choose for your lighting palette, chances are you will have at least one key source and at least one fill source. We differentiate between key and fill not only by angle and intensity but also by color. The fill color is almost always different from the key color, even if it is in the same side of the color spectrum.

Complementary Tint

A key/fill lighting setup in which the key and fill colors come from opposite sides of the color spectrum or color wheel are said to be complementary. In other words, a red key with a blue fill is complementary. So is a blue key with an amber fill, or a purple key with a yellow fill.

Daylight is a typical example of basic complementary key/fill coloring. The sun is a warm key and the skylight provides a cool fill.

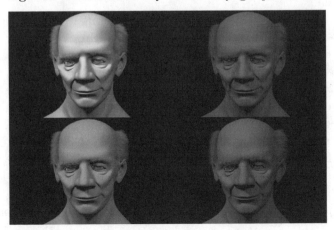

Figure 6.13: Complementary tint. (See color image.)

Related Tint

Related tint also employs a basic key/fill setup; however, this method uses colors that come from the same side of the color spectrum. An amber key with a yellow fill would fall into this category, as would a light blue key with a dark blue fill.

You may find a related tint key/fill scenario where the primary source is warm, such as a lightbulb, and the fill light is diffuse reflected light from a warm-colored wall.

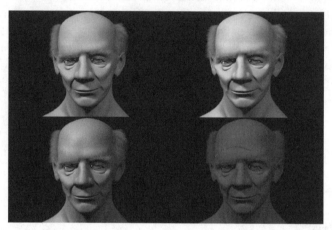

Figure 6.14: Related tint. (See color image.)

Intensity Ratios

Just as important as the key/fill color selection is the key/fill intensity ratio, and the ratio between these two lights and any other light sources in the scene.

As a rule of thumb, you can start by considering that the fill light should be about 60% of the intensity of the key light. Why is this? If both the key and the fill light were the same intensities, there would be no distinction between the two. Also, the fill light is distinguished by its lower intensity and tendency to "fill" shadowed areas left over by the key. If the fill were the same intensity as the key, there would be few shadowed areas left and the lighting would become flat.

The rim will generally be about the same value as the key intensity plus the fill intensity. For example, if you have a key light at 150% and a fill light at 90%, then you'd want to start your rim light at about 240%. Why so high? Well, the rim light isn't there to illuminate anything; it's there to provide a bright "halo" around the exterior shape of the object.

If the rim light isn't brighter than the key and the fill, you won't see it at all.

The bounce light, being a diffuse, reflected light source, will usually be the most subtle of all light sources and is likely to be lower in intensity than the fill light. I'd be inclined to start around the 40% range.

Of course, these values are thumbnails only and might not be appropriate for your scene. As a matter of fact, you might find that your scene calls for completely different intensity ratios. Just bear in mind that certain light types have certain intensities relative to the other lights, and that these intensities are determined by the light type, properties, and environment. There's a very good reason for them. Analyze your scene, find out what they are, and proceed with your lighting levels appropriately.

Intensity ratios are used throughout the book. Watch for differences in intensity between key, fill, and other lights and see if you can detect a pattern.

Options in Lighting a Scene

If you start thinking about all the options and using these few simple principles, the possibilities are mind-boggling. Infinite angles and colors alone should keep you experimenting for quite some time.

• • •

Now that we have covered some of the basic principles used for lighting a scene, you should start seeing how you can alter, mangle, and even completely ignore much of what has been discussed here. Now that you are grasping why key and fill light are used and why the three-point technique was invented, you should start seeing how you can develop your own techniques to illuminate and to focus the viewer's attention while helping to shape the subjects and convey an emotional framework for the scene.

You should now have a grasp of these basic lighting principles and concepts. The key light, the fill light, the highlight (or rim light), three- and four-point lighting, basic coloring, and intensity ratios are used in lighting every day, so it is important that you clearly understand them. If you don't, go back over the chapter, as these concepts will form the underpinning of any lighting work you do.

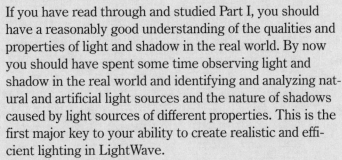

Part II

LightWave's Lighting Tools

If you have read through and studied Part I, you should have a reasonably good understanding of the qualities and properties of light and shadow in the real world. By now you should have spent some time observing light and shadow in the real world and identifying and analyzing natural and artificial light sources and the nature of shadows caused by light sources of different properties. This is the first major key to your ability to create realistic and efficient lighting in LightWave.

The second major key is the understanding of all the available tools. In this case, the tools include not only those that arrive with LightWave fresh out of the box but also many available third-party LScripts and plug-ins that are available for purchase or for free. Start out by learning LightWave's basic toolkit. Take note of the plug-ins mentioned herein but remember that there are many, many more available and many more becoming available all the time. Prices range from free to very expensive indeed. High-priced plug-ins are usually intended for the professional production market. Some of these have demos available and some do not. If you are considering purchasing a plug-in but can't decide whether or not to make the cash outlay, here is my advice: If you have a project where you need the plug-in, factor it into your budget. If the project can pay for it, then by all means get it. If, on the other hand, your own work won't support either the need or the expense, then find another way. There's always another way.

Hopefully, by the end of this part, you will have a reasonably complete understanding of LightWave's toolkit and of other tools that are available for LightWave. This part presents the tools but does not teach their use much. See Part III for tutorials. Better yet, buckle down and start using the tools, go through the LightWave manual, and spend some time searching online for tutorials about their use. www.Flay.com is a great place to start looking. You should also check out www.newtek.com. There are loads of tutorials there. You will become familiar with all the tools soon enough.

Chapter 7

Light Types, Their Properties, and Typical Uses

Part II deals specifically with the LightWave 3D toolset. Rather than just regurgitating what can be found in the manuals, this part attempts to demonstrate some typical real-world uses and examples for the tools. There is certain to be information here that is also found in the manual, but in writing this chapter I decided it would be easier for the reader to have the information right at hand rather than having to flip back and forth between this book and the manual. There is practical, production-based information found in this book — and in this chapter in particular — that is not available in the manual. Furthermore, there is a great deal of information in the manual on a wide variety of subjects that is not covered in this book. I strongly urge you to have a serious look through the manual, not just when you need some specific information. I have discovered many gems of information by casually flipping through the manual. This chapter is designed to expand on the manual by providing a production-based context for each of the tools. Certainly, many of the tools in LightWave have been used for purposes other than those for which they were originally intended by the creators.

By the time you have finished this chapter, you should have a good understanding of the different light types available, what each does, and some ideas on how best to use each of the various light types in different lighting situations.

Light Properties

One thing common to all lighting instruments within LightWave is the properties panel. Each light type has a finite number of properties that can be adjusted. Not all properties are available for all light types, but they can all be found on the properties panel or on one of the sub-tabs. There are a few different ways to open this panel. You can click the Lights mode button at the bottom left of Layout and then click the Properties button. Or, if you have the Lights mode button selected, just hit the "p" key on your keyboard. Incidentally, the p key is, by default, the key you press to bring up the properties panel for any selected item, whether it's a camera, bone, object, or light.

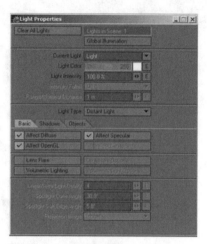

Figure 7.1: The Light Properties panel. You will notice that the Light Properties panel is wider now than it was in previous versions. Now all properties panels are the same width.

> **Tip:** There are four buttons at the bottom left of the Layout interface: Objects, Bones, Lights, and Cameras. These buttons determine which edit mode you are in. When you are in one of the edit modes, the properties panel will display properties of whichever item is currently selected for that mode. Thus, if you have a bone selected and the properties panel is up, and you then select a light with the middle mouse button (or left mouse button if that option is chosen in the Options panel), the edit mode and the properties panel will automatically change to Light Properties.

The first thing you will see at the top of the Light Properties panel is the Clear All Lights button. This will not clear all your lights. It will always leave one. If you wish to light your scene without lights, you'll have to set the intensity on this last light to 0%. Next to this button is a small box showing you how many lights are currently in the scene. Beneath this is the Global Illumination button. This is a can of worms that we will deal with later. Below is a drop-down box that allows us to quickly select any light from a list of all the lights in the scene. Below this we find the five most basic settings for each individual lighting instrument.

The first is Light Color. There are several ways to select a color for your light. A quick-and-dirty method is simply to click on each one of the RGB values one at a time and slide the mouse left and right. This is good for quick eyeballing. Right-click in this window and the values switch from RGB to HSV, which you can alter in the same fashion. A second method for changing color is to click on the colored square to the right of the RGB/HSV values. This will bring up a color picker.

> **Tip:** If you have not done so already, open up your Layout General Options panel by pressing the "o" key. About a third of the way down you will see the Color Picker entry. If it is on Default, switch it to LW_ColrPikr. The LightWave Color Picker is vastly superior to and more versatile than the Windows default color picker.

Once you are in the LightWave Color Picker, you will find many different ways to select the color you wish. We deal extensively with the LightWave Color Picker in Chapter 8.

A third method for picking your color is to click the "E" envelope button to the right of the color square. This opens a graph editor in which you can numerically set each of the RGB values and change them over time. One particularly great feature of this graph editor is that it includes a color gradient that shows you the exact color mix and change over time.

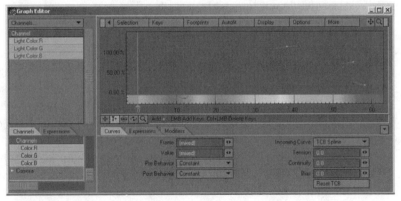

Figure 7.2: The LightWave RGB Color Graph Editor. (See color image.)

Below the color selectors are the intensity controls. They control how bright your light will be. You can change the intensity numerically simply by typing in the numeric field, or you can use your mouse by clicking on the arrows to the right of the numeric input and sliding your mouse back and forth. Once again, you can also hit the envelope button to the right of the arrows and open a graph editor in which you can change the intensity over time.

Below the intensity option are Intensity Falloff and Range/Nominal Distance. You must set a distance and choose between four falloff types. If you choose Off, the light intensity will remain the same whether the light is one centimeter or one million kilometers away. If you choose any of the other options, you will need to set the Range/Nominal Distance parameter. This setting determines the maximum distance the light reaches. For example, if I set a Linear falloff and a Range/Nominal Distance of 10 meters, there would be no light transmitted from that light 10 meters away from it. If I set Intensity Falloff to Linear, the light intensity would be 100% at the center of the source, 50% five meters from the source, and 0% 10 meters from the source. It is very linear and refers to the distance at which light falloff ends. If the falloff parameter is set to Inverse Distance or Inverse Distance ^ 2, the Range/Nominal Distance refers to the distance at which light falloff begins.

> **Note:** A linear falloff is not physically accurate, but it calculates much more quickly than real light falloff, which is the inverse square of the distance traveled by the light. It's like this: A light emits a specific quantity of light. When the light is near the light-bulb, it is very dense and compressed together into a small area. As the light travels away from the light, it spreads out and dissipates. The light is less dense and, therefore, provides less illumination on a surface.

You can also select a curved falloff shape instead of linear. You can choose between inverse to the distance traveled or the inverse square of the distance traveled. Inverse square is what occurs in nature, although I have found that a linear falloff usually looks fine and seems to calculate faster.

You will discover that you can apply intensity falloff to all light types except distant lights. Falloff is not allowed for distant lights because a distant light is supposed to simulate the sun. While the sun does indeed have an intensity falloff, it is so astronomically huge (measured in millions of light-years) that any amount of falloff occurring on our puny little planet is probably immeasurable and certainly not visible. Smaller light sources such as lightbulbs and candles have an easily visible intensity falloff. If you light a candle in a dark room, you will see that there is a relatively intense area of light quite close to the candle that falls off quickly to dimness. If you stand outside this "circle of light" however, you will see that the illumination still continues to the very walls of the room, no matter how far away they are. It may be extremely dim light and may be extremely difficult to see, but it is there. In reality, the light beams do not stop at any range as they do in LightWave. They keep going and spreading out until they can no longer be sensed by human visual systems. The Range setting allows us to set a cap on how far away LightWave calculates lighting. If we didn't do this, renders might take a very long time indeed.

Below the Range/Nominal Distance setting is Light Type. You have five choices here: Distant, Point, Spot, Linear, and Area. All five of these light types are covered in more detail later in this chapter.

Basic Sub-Tab

The first segment under the Light Properties Basic sub-tab contains four toggles (on/off switches) that let you decide what aspects of the scene your light will affect. The Affect Diffuse button determines whether or not the light will provide any illumination to the objects in your scene, while the Affect Specular button determines

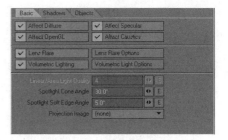

Figure 7.3: The Basic sub-tab.

whether or not the light will provide a specular light source for the surfaces in the scene that have some amount of specularity turned on. In the real world, Affect Diffuse and Affect Specular would be one and the same (and so would reflectivity and glossiness, for that matter). In the world of CG, however, we can use these qualities separately. Why? Say you have a surface illuminated just exactly as you like it, but you wish there was a higher specular highlight along one edge. In the real world, you would not be able to increase the specular lighting without increasing the diffuse lighting, since it would be a simple matter of increasing the overall intensity of the light. In LightWave, however, you could clone your light source and turn off all affect attributes except Affect Specular. That new light would now add additional specular intensity without brightening up the surface of the object. The Affect OpenGL button determines whether or not the illumination from the light will be visible in Layout's OpenGL viewports.

> **Note:** Currently the maximum number of lights available in OpenGL is eight. New to LightWave 8, the eight *brightest* lights will be selected as the eight OpenGL lights, instead of the first eight lights loaded. Or you can specify which eight lights you want to affect OpenGL by using Affect OpenGL. Any illumination from other lights will still be rendered but will not be visible in OpenGL.

The Affect Caustics button determines whether or not light emitted from the light will be considered in any caustics calculations that may be occurring in the scene, provided caustics has been turned on in the Global Illumination panel.

Lens Flare/Lens Flare Options

The Lens Flare check box enables lens flares for the selected light and also enables the Lens Flare Options button next to it. Clicking this button opens a new panel where you can adjust all the properties of the lens flare. Lens flares are covered in more detail in Chapter 15.

Volumetric Lighting/Volumetric Light Options

The Volumetric Lighting check box enables lens flares for the selected light and also enables the Volumetric Light Options button next to it. Clicking this button opens a new panel where you can adjust all the light's volumetric properties. Volumetrics are covered in more detail in Chapter 14.

Linear/Area Light Quality

> **Note:** New to LightWave 8, Linear/Area Light Quality is now envelopable. The most immediate advantage to this is that the light quality can be tied to expressions. This means that you could lower the light quality when the camera is very far away and increase the quality as the camera draws near, thereby saving precious render time when the camera is too far away to see the better quality.

Linear and area lights are render intensive by nature. Because they calculate like linear or two-dimensional arrays of point lights, they take much longer to render than LightWave's simple lights (distant, point, and spot). You can speed up your render times by lowering the quality of the area or linear lights in your scene. This is especially good for rendering previews where final light quality is not so important. Also, with Shading Noise Reduction enabled in the Global Illumination panel, you may actually get away with lower quality settings for the final render. The default quality setting is 4. The quality range for linear and area lights is 1 to 5.

Spotlight Cone Angle

The Spotlight Cone Angle setting defines the angle from perpendicular at which we find the edge of the light beam. If, for example, you set a spotlight cone angle to 45 degrees, the total beam angle from one side to the other would be 90 degrees. Make this angle smaller for a tighter spotlight and larger for a wider spotlight. If you decided to make your spotlight cone angle 180 degrees, your spotlight would behave somewhat like a point light, emitting light in all directions.

If you use Light View in Layout, you will see that the spotlight cone angle is defined by a shaded area around the outside of the spotlight cone angle.

Spotlight Soft Edge Angle

The Spotlight Soft Edge Angle option determines how far inside the cone angle the soft falloff begins. If you had a spotlight soft edge angle of 0 degrees, the spotlight edge would be hard. The higher the angle, the softer the spotlight edge becomes. You can see the spotlight soft edge angle as a dotted line inside the shaded area when using Layout's Light View.

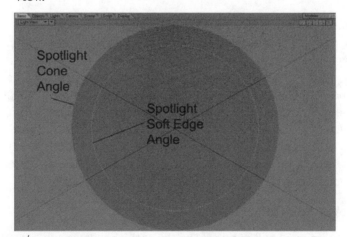

Figure 7.4: Looking through the Light View, you can see both the spotlight cone angle and the spotlight soft edge angle. This is a great way to set these angles if you are the type who prefers to work visually rather than by the numbers.

The spotlight soft edge plays a major role in defining the scale of the spotlight. Much larger or more distant light sources have a smaller soft edge angle, while spotlight sources that are closer, diffused, or defocused usually have a larger soft edge angle.

Projection Image

> **Note:**   New to LightWave 8, projection images are now visible through the Light View. This makes it much easier to line up your projection images just the way you'd like.

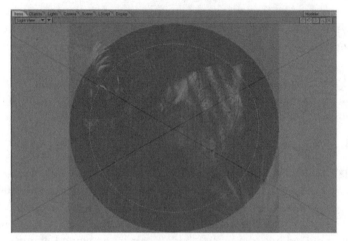

Figure 7.5: Projection image as viewed through the Light View.

LightWave provides the ability to project an image through a spotlight just like a slide projector or a film projector, depending on whether the image is a still or an image sequence. This has many useful applications such as projecting a background sequence onto some geometry at the angle and position of your choice. You could always apply the image or image sequence to the geometry, but projecting it through a spotlight allows you to easily and quickly position the projected image anywhere you like without having to rename surfaces to accommodate the image.

For more details and a tutorial on using projection images, please see Chapter 10.

Shadows Sub-Tab

The first thing you will notice at the top of the Shadows sub-tab is the Shadow Type menu. Clicking on this menu opens a drop-down that provides three options: Off, Ray Trace, and Shadow Map. The options Off and Ray Trace are available for all lights. For spotlights, however, there is a third option called Shadow Map. You will soon discover that shadow maps (and therefore spotlights) are one of your best friends.

Figure 7.6: The Light Properties Shadows sub-tab.

If you choose to leave shadows off for a particular light, this means that no shadows will be cast behind objects on which that light is shining. The object will still cast shadows on itself (provided you have not disabled that option for the object in its properties panel), resulting in less illumination on surfaces that are facing away from the light, but it will not cast shadows on other objects or surfaces.

Figure 7.7: This image demonstrates the three shadow states. The far left image is rendered using a spotlight with shadows off, the middle image uses ray tracing, and the right image uses a shadow map.

Ray tracing is calculated by tracing a line from the light source to the edge of the object that casts the shadow. Many lines are traced from the light source to the object until its entire shape has been traced with these light "rays." The result is an extremely hard-edged shadow that is accurate in shape, if not in softness.

Shadow mapping is done by looking toward the object from the light, taking the shape of the object in view (in this case a chair), and then using that "shape" of light to illuminate surfaces and objects behind the chair. It is not very physically accurate but has several significant advantages over ray tracing.

Beneath the Shadow Type selector is the Shadow Color box, used to choose the color of your shadows. This can be a very cheap and easy way of simulating a fill light without actually including one in the scene. As we discovered earlier in this book, colored shadows are the result of a secondary, or "fill," light source providing additional illumination within the shadow of the primary, or "key," light source.

> **Note:** Unfortunately, the shadow color only affects shadows cast by one object onto another object and does not include self-shadowing. This severely limits the use of shadow color in real applications.

Everything beneath Shadow Color in the Shadows sub-tab relates only to spotlights with shadow maps enabled. Shadow maps are one of the most useful lighting tools in the LightWave lighting toolset for a number of reasons: First, it is much, much faster to render with shadow-mapped spotlights than to do all that ray tracing. Second, you have the option of changing the resolution size of the shadow map. Keeping it as small as possible provides the quickest render times; however, if the light is illuminating a very large area, you may begin to see pixelation, or "jaggies," in the shadows. This is corrected by making the shadow map resolution larger. You will see the Shadow Map Size option a little farther down the Shadows sub-tab. You can also add "fuzziness" to shadow maps using the Shadow Fuzziness setting. This is a simple blurring algorithm that is applied to the shadow map. It's cheap and dirty but frequently passes for natural soft shadows as photo-realistically as radiosity.

The Cache Shadow Map button tells LightWave to calculate the shadow map only once, at the first frame of the render, then use that calculation for all subsequent frames. If you have large shadow maps, or many of them, and if your objects and lights do not move during the animation, then this option could save you significant render time. It is like casting a "freeze frame" shadow. If you use this option and your objects or lights move, the shadow will not move with them but will stay in the original place.

The Fit Spotlight Cone button, very simply, tells LightWave to make the shadow map fit the spotlight cone angle, whatever angle that may be. If you wish to choose your own size for the shadow map or zoom the shadow map larger or smaller than the spotlight's cone of illumination, simply uncheck the box and enter the desired shadow map angle in the box below. You can, for example, have a spotlight with a cone angle of 30 degrees and a shadow map with an angle of 5 degrees, or 90 degrees, or whatever you wish.

Note: If you use a smaller shadow map angle than the spotlight cone angle, you can see a representation of it in the Light View of the spotlight. The secret is to use as small an angle as possible for the shadow map while using as high a resolution as needed.

More detail on all these tools is available in the LightWave manuals.

Objects Sub-Tab

Next to the Shadows sub-tab you will find the Objects sub-tab. This is pretty simple.

If you wish to exclude the currently selected light from shining on any particular object or objects, simply click the object in the Object list.

Figure 7.8: The Objects sub-tab.

Note: In LightWave 8, you can now click in the gray bar (where it says Exclude and Object) and you will get the option to select all, clear all, or invert your selection. This comes in handy when you want to select all but one object. It saves you from having to go down the list selecting or deselecting everything. This same feature is available in the Object Properties panel where you can exclude lights from individual objects.

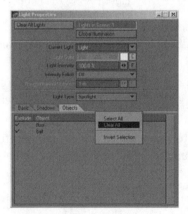

Figure 7.9: Object exclusion options in the Light Properties panel

Figure 7.10: Light exclusion options in the Object Properties panel. Note you can also exclude radiosity and caustics calculations from individual objects.

Why would you wish to exclude a particular light from a particular object? This is one of the true beauties of CG lighting. In the world of real lights and electricity, one of the biggest problems is "spill" light — undesired light falling on the subject. For example, you may be illuminating a wall with one light and your foreground subject with another light. You may not want the color or intensity of the wall light on your foreground subject. But if the foreground subject and the wall are very close, spill is almost a foregone conclusion. Many devices have been invented to deal with this problem including shutters, barn doors, and flags of various shapes and sizes. In LightWave, however, all we have to do is click the Exclude object list. Very nice, indeed!

The Global Illumination Button

Near the top of the Light Properties panel is the Global Illumination button. Clicking this button opens a new panel filled with all sorts of good things.

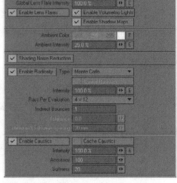

Figure 7.11: The Global Illumination panel.

Tread carefully here. While these tools offer unparalleled photo-realism to your lighting, they come at a cost of drastically increased render times. Know these four things:

- You will be able to use these tools occasionally when time permits.

- Processors are always getting faster. (When area lights were first introduced, they were discarded as useless due to the phenomenal rendering time required to calculate their lighting solution.)

- You don't have to use these tools at the highest quality. Sometimes you can get away with lower quality settings that render much faster.

- Sometimes you have to say "to hell with it" and crank everything up just to enjoy yourself, then come back in the morning to view the frame.

At the top of the panel are the Global Light Intensity and the Global Lens Flare Intensity settings. These do exactly what they say. The Global Light Intensity setting will allow you to control the intensity of all lights at once. Beware, however, that if Light(1) is set to 100% and Light(2) is set to 50% and you then make your Global Light Intensity

50%, Light(1) will be emitting 50% and Light(2) will now be emitting 25%. In other words, the global setting does not override the light's intensity but reduces (or increases) it by the displayed percentage. It is simply a multiplier that is applied to each light's intensity value.

Global Lens Flare Intensity works exactly the same way but on lens flares instead, if you have any activated in your scene.

The next three buttons allow you to toggle lens flares, volumetric lights, and shadow maps. The practical use of these buttons is for making quick renders. Rather than going through each light individually and disabling these features, you can turn all of them off at once with these buttons, do your quick render, then easily enable them again later.

Ambient Light

There seems to have always been a raging controversy over the use of ambient light for photo-real work. Why? Well, it seems to wash out the image, reducing form and direction and flattening everything. This is because ambient light adds a diffuse lighting value evenly to everything in the scene. Why use it then? I mainly use ambient light to see what I'm doing in OpenGL. Ambient light can also be an extremely quick rendering solution for a global fill light if used properly. Most really good artists will tell you to automatically turn off ambient lighting and use "real" lights. While this has been largely true in the past, it is not so now. Ambient light has been reborn as a tool to help with radiosity scenarios. We will get into more detail on this when we deal with radiosity lighting solutions. Suffice it to say that it's time to re-evaluate the old ambient setting.

Here's what Arnie Cachelin, senior programmer at NewTek, had to say about it:

> "Ambient intensity adds an even amount of diffuse lighting, so it will be something like ambient*diffuse*color on a surface EXCEPT IN THE CASE OF RADIOSITY RENDERING.
>
> "With radiosity rendering, the ambient amount/color is used as a background illumination amount, so the accessibility still applies, but the ambient light makes up for the diffuse bounces skipped in the indirect lighting calculation. This is why ambient is very useful in radiosity rendering, and is actually a relatively accurate approximation of scattered diffuse light."

The more time I spend cranking out visual effects, the more uses I have found for ambient intensity. While it is certainly to be used judiciously and mainly where other, more elegant solutions are not possible for one reason or another, don't count it out entirely. It's likely to save your bacon at some time. My latest experience was building talking animal heads for a couple of feature films. We used Worley's Sasquatch to fur all our animals. Sasquatch is an extremely powerful tool, but simply due to the nature of millions of fur fibers, we couldn't render with ray tracing on due to the immense rendering times. That's fine, because Sasquatch uses shadow maps. But the deepest shadows remained too deep, and we couldn't fill them ambiently using our usual methods: Backdrop Only radiosity and area lights. The only real solution left was ambient intensity. The pleasant surprise was that since fur is so random and fine, you couldn't tell that the ambient intensity was flattening things out. It simply decreased the shadow density perfectly and we went on our merry way. I was so stuck on not using ambient intensity that it took me a long time to get around to trying it. The lesson here is, don't take anything for granted. Don't think you know everything, and be willing to try things out, even if you think they probably won't work. You might be as pleasantly surprised as I was!

Shading Noise Reduction

Shading Noise Reduction is a great tool. As I am in the habit of using area lights, it's especially useful, as it allows me to set the light quality lower and still achieve good results with faster rendering times. This option reduces the graininess produced by linear and area lights. It also reduces the graininess from radiosity with lower quality settings.

Radiosity and Caustics

The next two sections on the Global Illumination panel deal with radiosity and caustics settings. If you want to jump right into it, they are dealt with in depth in Chapters 12 and 13, respectively.

LightWave's Light Types

Following is a description of the lights available in LightWave's Layout. Rather than simply quoting the manual, I try to put each light type into a production context, describing the strengths and weaknesses of each, providing real-world examples for each, and demonstrating some typical uses for each light type.

Distant Lights

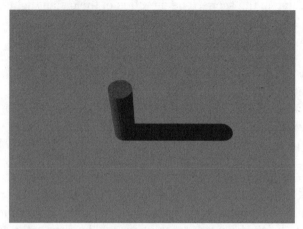

7.12: Shadows cast by a distant light are the same shape as the object casting them. The shadow edges are always hard.

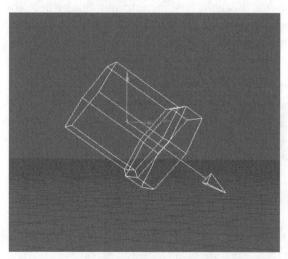

7.13: Distant lights have a new look in LightWave 8. This was done mainly to help differentiate spotlights and distant lights.

Distant lights in LightWave are intended to simulate sunlight. The light "rays" from a distant light are all parallel to each other, have no falloff, and extend infinitely in whatever direction the light is pointed, so your subject cannot travel out of the light as though it were lit by a spotlight. While none of these properties exactly describe sunlight, they are similar enough that a distant light can often pass for sunlight. It does not matter where you position your distant light. It could be inside, below, or above anything in the scene. The direction of the distant light is all that matters. The direction of the distant light defines only the direction of the light rays, not their origin.

What's good about distant lights? They render relatively quickly, even with ray-tracing on and they provide an adequate simulation for direct sunlight.

What's not so good? Because of the "ray-tracing only" shadows option and the parallel rays, all shadows from this light are very hard-edged. As we previously discussed, sunlight produces fairly hard shadows close to an object, but the shadows become increasingly fuzzy the farther away from the object the shadow is cast. This means a distant light is not the best choice for a scene in which long shadows are visible and need to be accurate. Because the light rays of a distant light are all parallel, the shadows cast by an object will be exactly the same size and shape as the object no matter how far away the shadow falls. This is not very accurate but also may not be noticeable in many shots.

Practical uses for this light type include situations where the subject is in the foreground and background shadows are not visible in frame such as in a close-up.

Spotlights

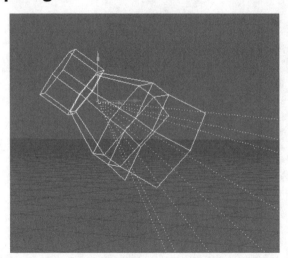

Figure 7.14: Spotlights also have a new look in LightWave 8.

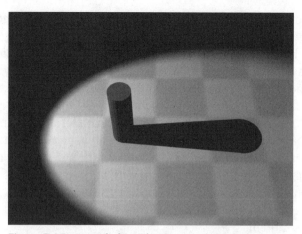

Figure 7.15: A spotlight with ray-traced shadows.

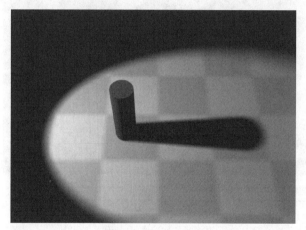

Figure 7.16: A spotlight with shadow-mapped shadows
and a high shadow fuzziness.

Spotlights are extremely versatile and useful lights. They are perhaps
the most useful lighting tool in the set. What makes them so special?
Well, spotlights can certainly be used just like a typical stage or studio
spotlight with a cone angle, shadow softness, gobos, shutters, and whatnot. But they can also be transformed into fake point lights, area lights,
and distant lights, with the distinct advantage of utilizing shadow maps
and shadow fuzziness, meaning that they render much faster. But wait,
there's more — unlike the real world, spotlights are not limited to spotlight cone angles within their lenses' focal range. You can set a spotlight
to a cone angle of 180 degrees if you like, effectively creating a point
light or omnidirectional light source that can be shadow mapped. No ray

tracing required. A warning, however: The higher you set the cone angle, the larger your shadow map will need to be to avoid pixelation (aka aliasing). Experiment with this and you will find the right balance.

Spotlights can also be used as fake distant or area lights. How? Simply set the cone angle to an extremely small angle like 1 or 2 degrees, back the light off until it is far away enough to cover your subject area, and render away. The light rays are not quite as parallel as a distant light, but they're close. Once again, using a shadow map instead of ray tracing will speed things up. As an added bonus, you can turn up the shadow fuzziness to simulate a global or area light with very soft shadows. These solutions will not always work for every situation, but I hope you can see how versatile these lights can be and how easy it is to think up different uses for them.

Copyright 2002 Nicholas Boughen

Figure 7.17: Note the apparent "radiosity" lighting on the columns and ceiling. It appears that the light has come in through a window and bounced off the floor, thus illuminating the ceiling and interior columns. This radiosity effect was achieved using a single spotlight with a very wide cone angle (85 degrees) and a high shadow fuzziness.

What's wrong with spotlights? Well, there's always a bad side. With ray tracing on, the spotlight behaves exactly like a distant light except that the light rays are diverging from a single point instead of being all parallel. Shadows are very hard. Shadow maps and fuzziness can solve much of this, but they are not physically accurate and don't always look right. Furthermore, as I stated earlier, shadows tend to be sharper close to the subject and softer farther away. Shadow maps are soft everywhere. It can be a dead giveaway. Look again at Figure 7.7. The image on the right shows a shadow-mapped shadow with a relatively high fuzziness level. Note how the shadows do not touch the chair legs. They have been "fuzzed out." It's a quick-and-dirty solution, but it can work if key areas of the shadow are not visible in frame, hiding the inaccuracy.

Point Lights

Figure 7.18: Surprise! Point lights have been redesigned too. Not just a poor, back-alley asterisk anymore. And besides, it's a lot easier to tell the difference between a point light and a null object now. Good going, NewTek!

Figure 7.19: A point light.

A point light is an omnidirectional source emitting from a nondimensional point in space. Some equate this to the sun or to a bare lightbulb. Both of these are pretty much omnidirectional, but what makes them different is that they both also have area or size, which a point light does not. The difference is in the shadows. Point lights ray trace shadows, which means that all shadows are very hard. There is no "penumbra" effect and therefore no softening shadows. In fact, there are no light sources in the real world that are nondimensional. Even the smallest filaments or arcs on the smallest light sources have some measure of size. Now when we get into extremely small sources like LEDs, this point becomes moot because you usually can't see the difference, but if you try to light a room with a bare lightbulb, the physical inaccuracies are certain to be visible and obvious. The hard shadows of ray-traced lights are one of the dead giveaways that elements are CG.

So what are point lights good for? I like to use them for point sources where scale is very large and, therefore, the shadow details are invisible. They're excellent for this because, as ray-traced lights, they render relatively quickly. And remember, you don't have to have shadows turned on. You can use point lights as ambient or "fill" lights with their shadows turned off if all you need is a little generic illumination.

Area Lights

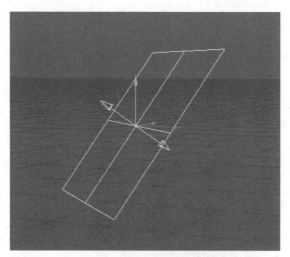

Figure 7.20: Guess what? Area lights have a new look! That should help you tell the difference between your white card and your area light. The area lights now sport an arrow pointing from both sides. This helps new users realize that area lights light identically out of both sides.

Figure 7.21: An area light.

Area lights are by far my favorite lighting tool. For one thing, they are far more physically accurate than most any other light type in LightWave. Second, they can be just about any light source you need simply by varying their size and shape. Third, they render more quickly than radiosity, although they are significantly slower than ray-traced or shadow-mapped lights. But the render hit is easily paid for by the beautiful quality of the shadows. If render time were not an issue, I would probably light everything with area lights and forget the rest of them.

What is an area light? It works somewhat like a rectangular space that is filled with ray-traced point lights. The rays are tracing from over the entire area of the rectangle, so light "wraps around" objects, creating the "penumbra" effect, or soft, beautiful shadows. Because area lights are based on an "area" of luminance, they are much more physically accurate than any of the other light types in LightWave, which is why the shadow quality is so realistic. If, for example, I used a large, distant area light for the sun, the shadows would behave realistically, being hard near the object and softening out farther away as opposed to a ray-traced distant light, which would cause hard edged shadows everywhere. But a large, distant area light will probably take a very long time to render, so we make compromises, we cheat, we fake, we try to make it look as close to "real" as possible, hopefully close enough that the audience won't see the difference. That said, area lights are still my favorite and my most used lighting instrument of choice.

Area lights have a quality setting on the Basic sub-tab of the Light Properties panel. Sometimes you can get away with a setting that is lower than the default of 4. This will speed up your renders and is especially great when doing test renders where final quality is not required.

Also, if you turn on Shading Noise Reduction on the Global Illumination panel, it may allow you to keep your quality setting lower, thereby reducing render times. Note that there is also a setting of 5 that is of higher quality than the default of 4 for when you need it.

A great new tool in LW8 that applies to both area lights and linear lights is that light quality is now envelopable. In other words, you can make the area light quality low when the camera is very far away and have it increase as the camera draws near. When the camera is far away, you can't tell the difference anyway, so why take all that extra render time to calculate high quality when you can save it up for when the camera draws really near??!!

> **Note:** If, like me, you use area lights all the time, then you should know that G2 is just about the best investment you could make. This is because G2 uses its own rendering engine to calculate area light shadows and includes, within its interface, an area light shadow quality control. The resulting area light shadows on G2 surfaces are far smoother and more beautiful than those from LightWave alone. It is an expensive plug-in, but if quality is your top concern, you really owe it to your clients. This one feature, in my opinion, makes G2 worth the asking price. No, I am not getting sales commissions! For more on G2, see Chapter 16.

Linear Lights

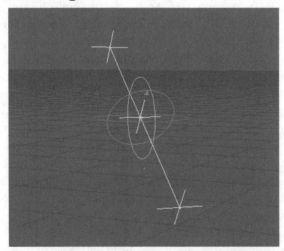

Figure 7.22: Note that linear lights also have a new graphical look. The new crosshairs at either end and at the middle of the light make it easier to align the light in your scene.

Figure 7.23: A linear light.

Linear lights are similar to area lights except that instead of being a two-dimensional rectangular array of point lights, they behave like a one-dimensional line of point lights. The net effect of this setup is that a linear light has an axis and that shadows cast will only be soft along that one axis. It's a rather strange shadow and not very useful in photo-real work. Still, the linear light can be very useful with shadows turned off when you need to simulate a light source such as a fluorescent tube. If I had the time, however, I would choose a long, narrow area light to serve as a fluorescent tube, as the shadows are much nicer.

Because linear lights only have to deal with one dimension of calculation, they calculate more quickly than area lights. As a matter of fact, if one wished, one could create a quicker rendering area light by building an array of linear lights side by side. Not as perfectly accurate as an area light, but a good approximation in many cases, no doubt.

As mentioned previously, LW8 includes a new tool that allows you to make both area lights and linear lights envelopable. Its use can save render time.

Objects as Lights

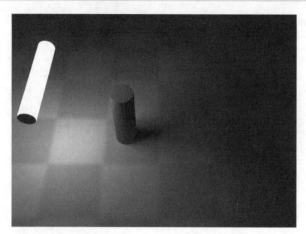

Figure 7.24

With the addition of radiosity to LightWave's lighting toolset in version 6.0, CG artists were blessed with the ability to create custom lights in any shape they wished. Radiosity is actually based on surfaces, not objects, but that provides you with greater flexibility. Any surface with a luminosity value will emit illumination into the scene if you have radiosity turned on. The trade-off is that radiosity can be a painfully long render. But used judiciously, this can still be an invaluable tool in your search for photo-real perfection.

When you think about it, this feature makes sense. There are numerous ways you can use radiosity. A lampshade, for example, might appear luminous if it's translucent. A neon sign or a frosted lightbulb also fall into this category. Any item that is either luminous or translucent might be handled in this manner. Remember that small items in your scene that use this technique will not necessarily automatically make render times huge. There are a number of choices and settings in the radiosity panel that will improve render times as well. So don't write off radiosity as too expensive. It's a great tool and can make the difference if you are trying to achieve photo-realism.

Perhaps the single greatest thing about this technique is that for the first time, we can create physically accurate light sources in LightWave. The simple lights — point, spot, and distant — are not physically accurate at all, and the complex lights — area and linear — only display some physically accurate light properties. The main problem is that all light sources are contained within a volume, such as a volume of flame or a filament that makes up a physical volume in space. Volume, by definition, requires three dimensions. The most dimension any LightWave light covers is two and that's with the area light. Since we can emit light from object shapes, we can create three-dimensional volumes, make them luminous, and have them behave very much like real light sources in the real world.

It's not that you will have use for this very often, but it's fun and cool, and you can do some kick-ass lighting this way.

Examples

Following are a few examples illustrating the different looks from different light and shadow types. Area lights and radiosity are the most attractive and accurate options but not the only ones. There are often ways to create subtle, realistic solutions without them.

Figure 7.25: In this image, a spotlight with high fuzziness has been used as the key source. The shadows are fairly realistic along most of the surface but not at the base.

Figure 7.26: An area light has been substitued as the key in this image. Note the highly accurate shadows across the face and on the wooden base.

Figure 7.27: The key light is a point light here. This still looks fairly real, but all the shadows are hard due to the ray tracing and the nondimensional point source of illumination.

All three of these examples are reasonably well lit. The question becomes one of detail. What is the audience looking at? How long is the shot? Long enough to notice the details? Does the camera zoom in on any particular area?

If the audience has enough time to really notice the shadows, you'll likely want to go for a shadow-mapped or even an area light solution. If it's a short shot or if the camera simply pans past the object, you will probably be able to get away with cheaper solutions. Remember, motion blur hides many tricks.

• • •

This chapter has dealt with the different light types in the LightWave toolset. Hopefully you now have a richer understanding of the qualities and uses of these lights. I hope I have been able to provide a more insightful and less technical view on them. Later chapters will go into detail describing practical uses for each light type. In the meantime, don't be afraid to load up some of the sample scenes from the companion CD and play with them. The absolute best way to know which light type to use is to know the exact capabilities of each light type. I can write at length what I think each light type is capable of, but it will never take the place of your experience. This book is only half of the lesson; the rest is up to you.

Chapter 8

The LightWave Color Picker

This chapter covers the different color picking tools available in LightWave's custom color picker. By the time you have finished this chapter, you should have a good grasp of LightWave's QuickColor, HSV<-->RGB, Tint & Shade, Wavelength, and Kelvin color pickers and their specific uses.

LightWave comes equipped with two choices for color pickers. You can use the standard Windows or Mac color picker, which is fairly basic, or you can have a look at the arsenal of color picking tools in the LightWave color picker. You can select the LightWave color picker in Modeler by going to the Display Options Interface tab and selecting it in the Color Picker drop-down. In Layout, open the General Options panel and select from the Color Picker drop-down.

Before we look at the LightWave color picker, however, here are a few words about color.

In your virtual world, there are two primary reasons why a light source is emitting a particular color of light.

In the first place, lights emit heat.

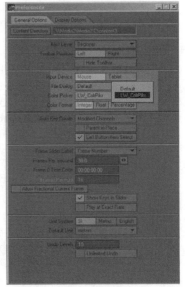

Figure 8.1: Selecting the LightWave color picker in Layout's General Options panel.

The higher the temperature, the brighter and whiter the light becomes. The brightness is known as intensity and the color is known as color temperature. Imagine a piece of metal heating up in a forge. It first begins to glow very dim red, then heats up to orange, then to white. If you could keep heating it, it would start to go into the blue end of the spectrum until it was too bright to look at. So low color temperatures are in the red end of the spectrum while high color temperatures are in the blue end of the spectrum with white in the middle. Ironically, humans tend to equate blue with icy, cold things and red with fire and brimstone, so we refer to colors in the red end as "warm" and colors in the blue end as "cool," which is completely backward. Just read it over a couple of times — you'll get it!

The second reason for a light's color is that it may be filtered by something. In other words, the light is passing through or reflecting off some substance that is absorbing some of the color wavelengths and allowing other wavelengths to pass through or reflect away. Take a piece of green glass, for example. If you shine a white light through a piece of green glass, the glass will absorb most of the red and blue wavelengths from the light but will allow most of the green light to pass through.

> **Note:** Why do I say "most" of the red and blue light is absorbed and "most" of the green light passes through? In the theoretical world, there are primary colors. Primary colors consist of only a single pure wavelength. So if we had a pure white light that consisted of all three primary colors (red, green, and blue), and if we also had a green glass filter that only filtered out the primary red and blue but allowed primary green to pass through, then we could say all the red and blue was absorbed and all the green was allowed to pass through. Trouble is, in the real world, primary colors don't usually exist anywhere except laboratories. So while most of the red and blue light is absorbed by the green filter, a little bit will still seep through because the filter is not perfect. And while most of the green light is allowed to pass through, some is absorbed, again because the filter is not perfect. This may seem like nit-picking, but understanding how imperfect light coloring and filtering is in the real world can help you add realism to your work. You can use numeric values to choose your technically perfect colors, but you should trust your eyes to tell you whether or not it looks right.

Almost all light is filtered by something. The sunlight is filtered by the sky, the light in a neon sign is filtered by the colored glass tube, the floor lamp light is filtered by its amber shade. You get the idea. Hopefully this will help you make your color choices.

QuickColor

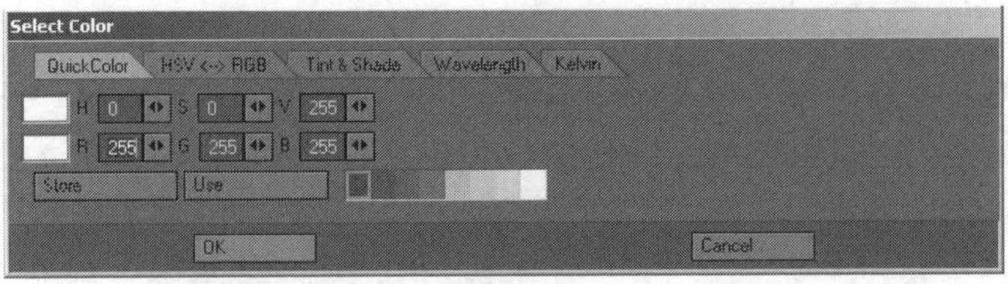

Figure 8.2: The QuickColor panel.

QuickColor is a good, speedy tool if you know exactly what you want and understand HSV or RGB colors. Both HSV and RGB values can be entered numerically in the boxes, or you can drag the values up and down by clicking on the arrow buttons and moving the mouse left or right. All these values can range from 0 to 255.

HSV refers to choosing color by selecting the hue, saturation, and value of the color. *Hue* tells you what the pure color is, such as red, green, pink, purple, etc. *Saturation* refers to how much of that color you want. For example, pale blue has a low saturation of blue, while midnight blue has a high saturation. A saturation of 0 means the color is white. Finally, *value* refers to how bright or dark the color will be. Crimson, for example, is a dark red with a low value, while hot pink has a very high value. A value of 0 means the color is black. Play with these sliders to get a feel for how they work.

RGB refers to choosing your color by mixing specific amounts of red, green, and blue. Each color has a range of 0 to 255. You change these numbers exactly as you change HSV numbers, either by entering numbers in the boxes or by clicking the slider arrows and dragging the mouse left or right. An RGB value of 255, 255, 255 means that all colors are included to their maximum amount, resulting in white. An RGB value of 0, 0, 0, is black because no color is included at all. An RGB value of 255, 0, 0 is red. If you still don't quite get it, play with the sliders. It will soon all make sense.

QuickColor also has eight slots in which you can store custom colors. Once you have picked a color you like, select one of the eight boxes next to the Use button, then click the Store button. You will see your color fill the selected box. To save a second color, first choose the color, then select the second box, click the Store button, and so on. To use the color, simply open the panel, select the color box you want, then click the Use button. That color will be assigned to your item.

HSV <--> RGB

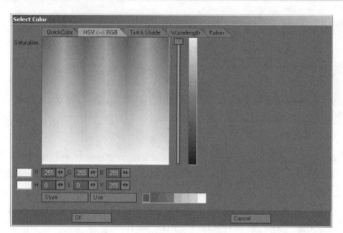

Figure 8.3: The HSV <--> RGB panel. (See color image.)

HSV<-->RGB is exactly the same as QuickColor but with a couple of added features that make it visually easier to understand how HSV works.

If you look at the color palette, you will see that the hue is left to right and the saturation is top to bottom. The purest, brightest colors with the highest saturation are at the top, while the most faded colors with the lowest saturation are near the bottom. At the very bottom, where saturation is 0, all colors become white. An up and down slider to the right of the color palette lets you choose the value or brightness of the color. Colors with the lowest values are darker and near the bottom, while the brightest colors with the highest value or brightness are at the top. Colors with a value of 0 are black.

All the tools from the QuickColor panel can be found below the palette, including numeric and slider inputs for both HSV and RGB values as well as eight slots to save custom colors.

Tint & Shade

According to NewTek, the Tint & Shade panel is intended to more or less match the way painters think about tones and shades. It apparently avoids some of the flaws found in both the RGB and HSV models. This model is called the HWB, or hue, whiteness, blackness model.

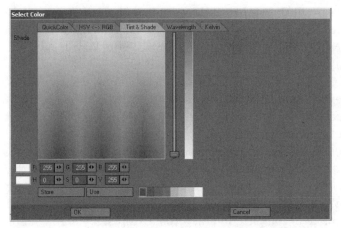

Figure 8.4: The Tint & Shade panel. (See color image.)

The most practical use I have found for this palette is that it's a snappy way of finding a complementary color. Simply click on a hue in the bottom half of the screen. The slider at the right will then show you your selected color and a range of related and complementary tints along the slider. It's a very easy way to find good complementary and related tints.

Wavelength

Figure 8.5: The Wavelength panel. (See color image.)

Visible light is near the middle of the color spectrum and is found between the infrared on the low end and the ultraviolet on the high end. Light "waves" are measured like a sine wave from one peak to the next, and this distance is called the wave "length." Cooler colors in the blue end of the visible spectrum have shorter wavelengths than colors in the red end of the visible spectrum. For example, blue or violet light has a shorter wavelength than red light, therefore, violet light has more waves per meter than red light. Since both red and violet light moves at the same speed, the shorter violet waves will pass by more frequently. In other words, a shorter wavelength means a higher "frequency."

You can select your color wavelength within the visible spectrum either by clicking on the palette or by selecting the exact wavelength numerically in the box to the right of the palette. Wavelength is measured in nanometers.

The other tools at the bottom of this panel are similar to previous panels except that HSV values are missing. This is because the Wavelength panel deals only with pure color wavelengths and does not account for saturation or value.

Once again, you have the tools to save and use up to eight custom colors. If you ever need more than eight, you can always save the color in the surface settings in the Surface Presets shelf. This can be opened via the Window drop-down in Layout. Textures can be stored there, from simple colors to complex, multilayered textures. If you run out of color slots on the LightWave color picker, you can store them in this shelf.

Kelvin

Figure 8.6: The Kelvin panel. (See color image.)

The Kelvin panel is my favorite color picker feature. It works exactly the same as the Wavelength panel except instead of measuring wavelength, it measures the color temperature in Kelvin degrees. What's so great about this? Well, if you have any experience on set, you'll know that the most often used lighting gels all have a color temperature that corresponds to their color filtering properties. So if you know the color temperature of the gels, you would know exactly what color to make your lights if you have to match a plate. Furthermore, most natural lighting colors are within this range. Here is a short list of some of the most common natural light sources and their color temperatures:

Color Temperatures of Various Sources

Lighting Source	Kelvin Degrees
Candle	1900
Lightbulb	2000-2500
Tungsten/halogen bulb	3200

Lighting Source	Kelvin Degrees
Afternoon sunlight	4500
Summer sunlight	5500-5700
Sunlight with blue/white sky	6500
Summer shade	7000
Overcast sky	7000
Skylight	10,000-20,000

From *Set Lighting Technician's Handbook: Film Lighting Equipment, Practice, and Electrical Distribution* by Harry C. Box (Focal Press, 1993).

The only complaint I have about this color panel is that its maximum value is 11,000. There are some circumstances where a higher color temperature is required. But one can always find those colors in another panel or by increasing the RGB values. Try out some of these settings. You will quickly see what a useful tool this is when you are lighting a shot.

As with all the other panels, tools are available to store and use up to eight custom colors.

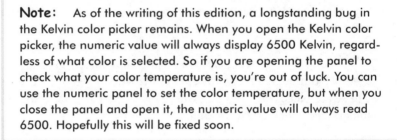

Note: As of the writing of this edition, a longstanding bug in the Kelvin color picker remains. When you open the Kelvin color picker, the numeric value will always display 6500 Kelvin, regardless of what color is selected. So if you are opening the panel to check what your color temperature is, you're out of luck. You can use the numeric panel to set the color temperature, but when you close the panel and open it, the numeric value will always read 6500. Hopefully this will be fixed soon.

• • •

This ends our overview of the LightWave color picker. As you can see, there are numerous ways to choose your colors not only for your lights, but for your surfaces as well.

By now, you should have a good grasp of LightWave's QuickColor, HSV<-->RGB, Tint & Shade, Wavelength, and Kelvin color pickers and their specific uses. It's easy to see that each have specific uses and can be used for different purposes. You may eventually settle on only one or two of the pickers, but I use them all!

Chapter 9

Shadow Types and Their Typical Uses

This chapter deals with LightWave's various shadow types and properties. By the time you have finished this chapter, you should understand ray-traced shadows, shadow maps, and the effects of shadow sizes and softness and how they relate to the type of light source that creates them.

Among the following paragraphs are some of my greatest pet peeves — those things that make my skin crawl when I see or hear about them. These are basic concepts that will really mess you up if you don't fully understand them, so *pay attention*!

First, let's get a few things straight:

- There is no such thing as a light source that causes only hard-edged shadows.

  The shape of a shadow depends upon the shape of the object that is casting it, but the size and softness of the shadow is dependent completely upon the light source. A light capable of causing a completely hard-edged shadow must have zero dimension and be a point in space with no size or shape. While this light type may very well exist in a virtual environment such as LightWave, it certainly does not exist in the real world. All light sources have some size, even the tiniest light-emitting diode or electrical arc. All light sources, therefore, cause some amount of softness to occur in the shadow. This means that all lights are volume lights (which is like an area light shaped like a cube instead of a plane).

- Lights do not cast shadows. Lights never cast shadows. No light has ever cast a shadow. Well, that's not entirely true. If you put an ellipsoidal reflector spotlight in front of a lit 5K Fresnel, it will cast a shadow. My point? Only objects cast shadows.

- One light results in one shadow. I have seen numerous shots where a single light source existed in the plate, yet there were multiple shadows on the floor cast by multiple CG light sources. That's another dead giveaway that something isn't right. CG artists are not the only ones to make this mistake; gaffers make the same mistake on set.

These are real-world scenarios. As CG artists, we often find ourselves trying to simulate real-world lighting. You will never succeed unless you know that a completely hard-edged shadow is wrong, lights do not cast shadows, and one light source results in one shadow for each object. I know there are nitpicky people out there who will argue that a reflection can cause a second shadow from the single light source and that is true, but it could be argued that the "mirror" is a second light source. Let's not get into an arm-wrestling match about it. Physicists, be gone!

Shadow Size and Softness

In general, we can state that a very small light source will result in a very large shadow and conversely that a very large light source will result in a very small shadow. Let's look at some examples.

Figure 9.1: Small light source.

Notice in this image that the shadows are hard-edged and grow wider farther away from the pillar object. Since the light source is much smaller than the pillar, the light rays that get past the pillar are diverging as in Figure 9.2.

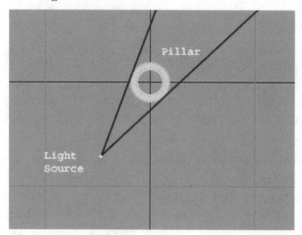

Figure 9.2: Small light source setup.

In Figure 9.3, a light source was used that is much larger than the pillar. The result is that the light rays are able to converge behind the pillar object, thereby lighting that area. The result is that the shadows (or occluded areas) are much smaller and softer edged.

Figure 9.3: Large light source.

This phenomenon is described in Figure 9.4. You can see that the area light is large enough that some of the light rays will reach areas behind the pillar.

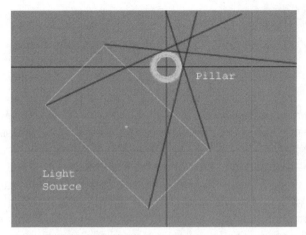

Figure 9.4: Large light source setup.

Will it surprise you to learn that both of the rendered images were created using an area light? The first image simply used a very small area light. If you look carefully, you will see that the shadows become slightly soft farther away from the pillar, just as in the real world.

Take a look at Figure 9.5. Note that the shadows cast by the car in the foreground are very hard-edged while the shadows of the trees are very soft. The sun is the light source for both car and tree, so why is this? Well, we know that the trees are much farther away from the foreground of the image than the car is. It is further evidence that shadows are hard near the object that is casting the shadow and get softer farther away due to the penumbra effect.

Figure 9.5

115

LightWave's Shadow Types

Following is a description of the shadow types available in LightWave.

Ray Trace

Take a red thumbtack and stick it into your ceiling. Then take a spool of thread and tie one end of the thread to the thumbtack. Walk away from the thumbtack, letting the spool play out the thread until you reach a wall. Cut the thread and tape the end to the wall. Make sure the thread is taut and straight. You now have a line drawn from a source point to a target point. Add a million more threads all originating at the red thumb tack (your light source) and hitting walls, floor, chairs, tables, and everything else in the room. That's how ray-traced shadows work.

Whenever an object gets in the way of your thread, the ray stops. There is no ray behind it. That's a shadow. And it's sort of how light works too. A photon is flung from the surface of the sun and flies through space in a reasonably straight line, analogous to the threads (not counting gravity, you bad physicists), until it impacts some opaque material that stops its travel.

So what's the difference between real sunlight and ray-traced light? The thumbtack-and-thread example we just looked at has all the threads starting at a single point in space. But the sun is not a single point. It's a big, luminous ball. If we wish to create a more realistic model, we will need to take a very large box of thumbtacks, stick them into the ceiling in a big circle as close to each other as possible and then run a million threads from each pin to points all over the walls, floor, ceiling, and anything else in the room. You can see how this requires a great deal more work. You can also see why a point source ray-traced light calculates much more quickly than an area light, which is, in essence, just like the big circle of thumbtacks on the ceiling.

Distant lights also ray trace shadows, but they work a little differently. Instead of all the light originating from a single point and radiating outward, the light rays all run parallel to each other from the beginning to eternity. They have no origin and no position in space, only direction. For more on how distant lights work, see Chapter 7.

All the light types in LightWave's toolset are equipped for ray tracing. The only real disadvantage to shadows produced by a ray-tracing light source is that they are very hard-edged. In reality, since all lights have some amount of size, all shadows must therefore have some amount of softness since the light rays will "wrap around" objects, even if it is just a small amount. Smaller lights will tend to have harder shadows than larger lights because the light wraps around less, but none of them cause completely hard-edged shadows.

Ray-traced shadows are typically used where sunlight is your main light source or where you see shadows that are very near the object that is casting them. Most people seem to perceive sunlit shadows as hard-edged, and most shadows are harder edged close to their object. But beware of this. People *think* sunlight causes hard-edged shadows, but when they see the hard shadows in your CG work, they subconsciously *know* that it looks wrong.

Shadow Map

This is where one of my favorite features comes in — shadow maps. The real beauty of shadow maps is how good they can look compared to what a cheap trick they actually are.

First of all, shadow maps can only be used with spotlights. Unfortunate, but true.

Shadow mapping uses a technique similar to how the camera determines whether or not areas are hidden from the camera's view, but instead of the camera, they determine what areas are hidden from the light's view. Areas that are hidden from the light's view are in shadow.

Now the true beauty of shadow mapping is not how it calculates its shadows but rather the fact that you can add fuzziness to the shadows. As with ray tracing, shadow maps and shadow fuzziness have their advantages and disadvantages. The great advantage to shadow fuzziness is that it is calculated very quickly and lets you avoid the very CG hard-shadow look. LightWave simply blurs the shadow outline to make the shadow soft. Let's take another look at the shadow map options.

Figure 9.6: The Shadows sub-tab.

Shadow Map Size refers to the pixel dimension of the map. The default is 512, meaning the shadow map is 512 x 512 pixels. I often find this to be too small, resulting in obvious pixelation, or "jaggy" edges. You can either change the setting to create a higher resolution shadow map or increase the fuzziness to blur out the pixels, or both. I often use a fuzziness in the 10 to 20 range. Using a fuzziness of 0 will not blur the shadow map at all. You will see the sharp edge of the pixels unless you use a very high-resolution shadow map. Beware: Shadow Fuzziness values that are too high can result in crawling shadow artifacts over an image sequence.

The only real disadvantage to shadow maps is that they are soft-edged all the way around. Once again, real shadows tend to be harder near the object and softer farther away. If the area near an object is not obvious or not visible in the shot, you can safely use shadow mapping to add the softness to your shadows instead of the render-intensive area light method.

Shadow maps are typically used in situations where render speed is a big issue and the sharpness of shadows is not obvious or visible in frame, or where you only require soft shadows for the shot. Spotlights with shadow maps can be used as skylight fill lights, for example. You might move a spotlight way up the Y-axis and spot the light down to a very small cone angle so that the light rays are somewhat parallel.

> **Note:** To "spot" a light means to narrow its beam angle, while to "flood" a light means to widen its beam angle.

If you then turn on a high fuzziness and use a nice large shadow map size, the spotlight can provide a reasonable and very quick-rendering replacement of an area light or even a global illumination solution.

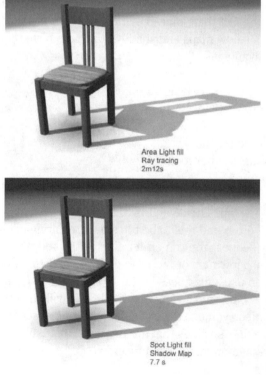

Area Light fill
Ray tracing
2m12s

Spot Light fill
Shadow Map
7.7 s

Figure 9.7: The top image used an area light for fill with ray tracing turned on. The bottom image, which is nearly identical, rendered in 0.06 the time — a significant speed increase for such an easy and effective trick. The second image simply used the above-mentioned technique of using a spotted down spotlight with a high fuzziness. I set up the light, rendered once, adjusted the intensity once, rendered again, and very closely matched the original area-lit image.

No Shadows

There are many situations in which it is perfectly acceptable to simply turn shadows off for a light. For example, if you are using a distant light as your key and you need a blue skylight fill but there are no areas in frame where a shadow would be cast, you can place a large area light for the fill and turn off shadows. The render will be much quicker and will still look fine. Also, if you wish to decrease your shadow density, using a light with no shadows provides you much, much more control than using ambient intensity to fill in the shadows. Of course, if you have all the render time in the world, just skip straight to Chapter 12 and start rendering with Monte Carlo radiosity set to 5 bounces.

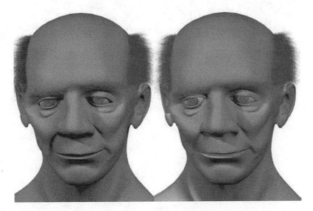

Figure 9.8: The head on the left uses an area light with ray tracing on for the fill source. It took 2 minutes and 6 seconds to render. For the head on the right, I turned off shadows for the area light. It took 18 seconds to render. The images are fairly similar except that the right one has a little more illumination in areas that are shaded from the key light. It's a massive speed increase, but you will have to decide if the results are acceptable for your particular shot.

You also have the option under Light Properties to turn off shadows only for particular objects and under Object Properties to turn off shadows only for particular lights. As you can see, there are many options and combinations when it comes to shadows.

• • •

I hope this chapter has successfully demonstrated the importance of accurate shadows as well as the flexibility of the tools available within LightWave. Later chapters deal with specific techniques and technique-building methods.

You should now have a good understanding of ray-traced shadows, shadow maps, and the effects of shadow size and softness and how they relate to the type of light source that creates them. As you will see in Part III, there are numerous ways to use lights with both ray-traced and shadow-mapped shadows.

Chapter 10

Projection Images

This chapter covers some ideas for the use of projection images in lighting. By the time you have finished this chapter, you should have a few good ideas about how you can enhance your effect lighting using projection images.

Images can be projected out of spotlights (and only spotlights). You may use either ray-traced or shadow-mapped shadows in the spotlight; however, no shadows are required to project the image. This is just like slipping a slide into a slide projector. You can take any image you like, such as a stained glass window, and project it out of a spotlight. If your image is black and white, it will appear that shadows are being cast, but it is only the image with no actual shadow casting.

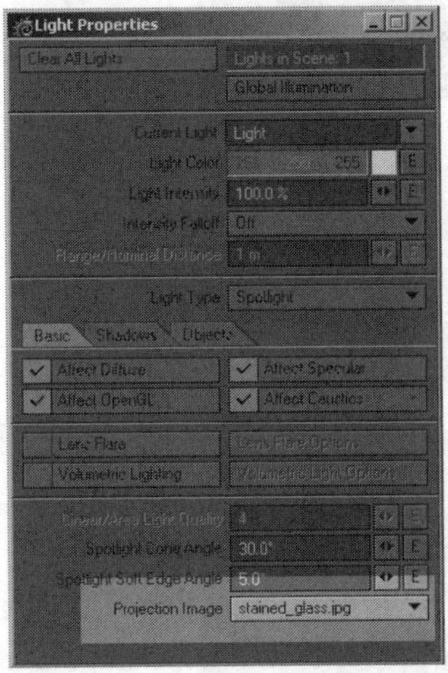

Figure 10.1:
The Light Properties
panel with an image
loaded in the Projection
Image drop-down.

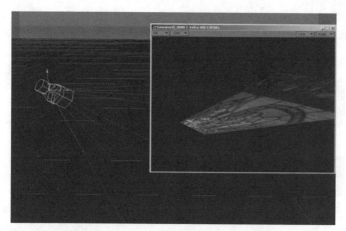

Figure 10.2: The spotlight position is shown on the left. The projection image is projected on the ground plane.

Figure 10.3: Even with a projection image, there will be no shadows unless a shadow option is selected. Here, there are no shadows.

Figure 10.4: This render has shadow maps enabled for the spotlight.

A cool new feature in LightWave 8 is the ability to see the projection images through the Light View in Layout.

Figure 10.5

This new feature allows much quicker and more precise alignment of the projection image in the scene, since you can see exactly where the image will lie.

You can also use the projection image feature to create shaped shadows.

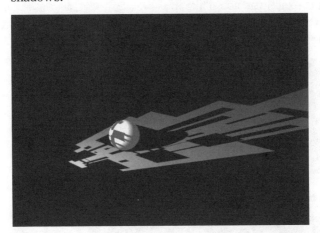

Figure 10.6

Simply by using a grayscale image, and making the image black where you don't wish the light to be projected, you can create shaped lighting.

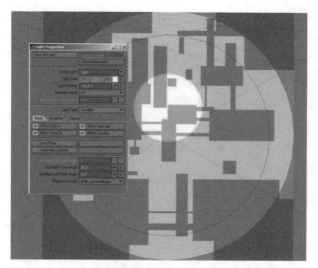

Figure 10.7

In the real world, gaffers use a variety of tools such as flags, shutters, barn doors, flats, and foliage (and anything else that will work without burning to a crisp) to shape light beams, allowing the gaffer to place light only where he wants it. You can do this much more easily by simply painting a black and white map, loading it into your light as a projection image, and then aligning it either by moving the light or by adjusting the map until it is exactly as you'd like it.

You can also use projection images to create custom textures for your volumetrics.

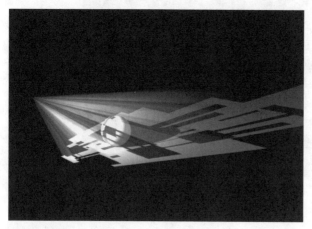

Figure 10.8

There are a variety of procedural textures you can use from LightWave's Texture Editor, but often those are too generic and don't do the job. There are also a couple of tricks that can be used to get procedural textures into your projection image. What if you have light streaming through a broken casement window into a dusty barn? You'll need the shapes of the window frame and broken glass in the shadow. You can always do this by tracing shadows and transparency, but it will render much, much more quickly if you simply use a clever projection image. Make the image black where the window frame stops light completely, and make it gray where the dirty, broken glass stops some but not all of the light.

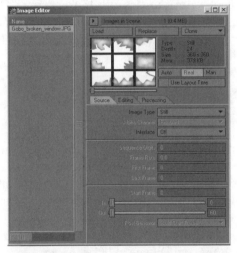

Figure 10.9

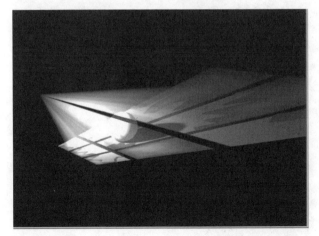

Figure 10.10

Here's another really cool use for this tool. What if you want to have waving palm trees? You could always build palm tree models, animate them, and place them in front of your light. Or you could get some footage of a waving palm, or build an image sequence in 2D, grayscale it, then apply that to the light. It's a great deal less work, and much less rendering time, to simply project the moving shadows, rather than building, animating, and tracing shadows.

You might also use this technique to project the light from a blazing building across the street. Get some footage of a fire (you might want to blur it considerably, since it is a diffused light and will not retain its image information) and project it into your shot. Or what about that ever-elusive swimming pool water caustics effect? You know — the one you see on a nearby wall from the light reflecting through the water and back up? LightWave actually has an "underwater" procedural that you can project through the light to get this effect.

Using a LightWave Procedural Texture as a Projection Image

LightWave procedural textures are not available to the projection image slot. Only images can be used here. This means that if you wish to use a procedural texture in the projection image, you must first generate an image sequence using the procedural texture. Following is a short tutorial detailing how this is done.

Load a single polygon and point the camera straight at it. Set Luminosity for the polygon at 100% and Diffuse at 0%.

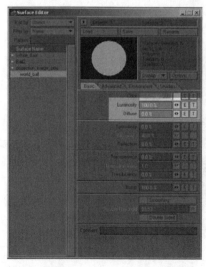

Figure 10.11

Open the Surface Editor and select the polygon's surface. Click the
Color Texture button.

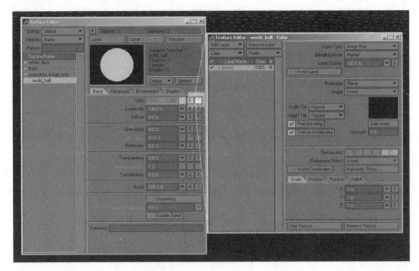

Figure 10.12

Change Layer Type to Procedural Texture and select the procedural texture you'd like to use from the Procedural Type drop-down. We're going
to use Underwater.

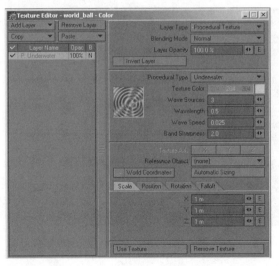

Figure 10.13

You'll have to render out an image sequence to see if you have your settings right. Settings such as Scale, Wavelength, Wave Speed, and Wave Sources can have a significant impact on the look and feel of your waves.

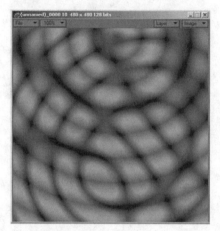

Figure 10.14

Once you have the procedural behaving the way you'd like, render out an image sequence as long as you need for your shot. I have included on the companion CD a 60-frame underwater image sequence that I made for this chapter.

Figure 10.15

Apply the image sequence to your spotlight as a projection image. Be sure that Image Type is set to Sequence.

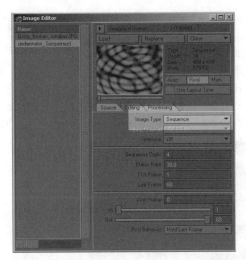

Figure 10.16

Since we are recreating the light reflected off a swimming pool, the projection light should be pointing upward toward a wall. Load another polygon object to act as a wall and set your projection light below the polygon and pointing upward toward it.

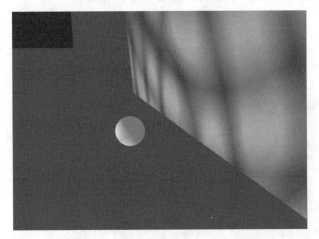

Figure 10.17

When you render the sequence, you should get a swimming pool light reflection sort of effect without having to use radiosity, caustics, or reflection, all of which occur in reality for a lighting situation like this one. Your renders should be blistering fast too!

Using a LightWave Procedural Texture as a Clip Map

This isn't exactly using projection images, but it functions sort of the same way and it's a cool little technique so we'll discuss it here.

Simply take a single rectangular polygon and parent it to your spotlight. Scale and position it so that the polygon just covers the Light View.

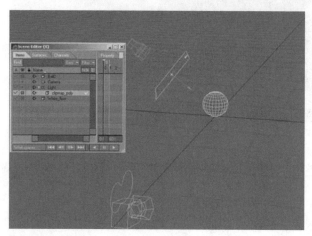

Figure 10.18

Under the polygon's Object Properties panel Render tab, click the Clip Map Texture button.

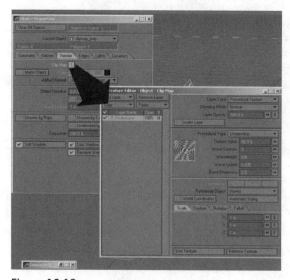

Figure 10.19

Here you can add any procedural texture you like, including animated textures such as Underwater or textures with world coordinates so the texture changes only as the light (and its projection polygon) move through world space.

Figure 10.20

The only disadvantage to this technique is that clip maps are absolute, that is, black or white. My tests show that any value below 50% is clipped, so light will pass through, while any value above 50% is not clipped and remains opaque to the light.

Using a LightWave Procedural Texture as a Transparency Map

If you really need the subtle variations in grayscale, as you would if you were using this technique for underwater caustics, then instead of using a clip map, open up the polygon's Surface Editor, open the Texture Editor in the transparency channel, and add the Underwater procedural texture.

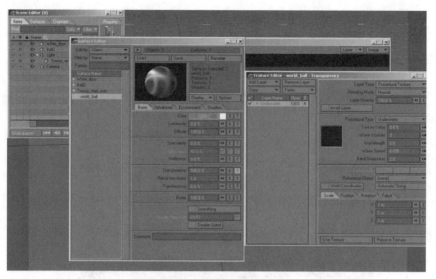

Figure 10.21

Be sure ray trace shadows is on, so shadows will be ray-traced through the transparency. This is an even better look and technique. It acts like a projection image but allows you to access LightWave's procedural textures.

Figure 10.22

> **Note:** If your polygon is not casting shadows, be sure Double Sided is on in the Texture Editor.

• • •

By now you should have a good idea of some of the creative uses to which you can put projection images. The clever artist will now try a few experiments with projection images to see how realistic a simulation can be created using these techniques.

Chapter 11

General Light Properties

This chapter discusses practical uses for the light properties and settings available within the LightWave Light Properties panel. Each of these settings is crucial to how your final render will work. Take the time to understand each tool. Try them out and experiment. I'm constantly learning new ways of doing things by fiddling with the controls.

We'll start our look at the tools with the Affect toggles. These turn on or off the ability of a light to affect the surface diffuse, specular, OpenGL, and caustics properties of objects in your scene.

Affect Diffuse

The Affect Diffuse button determines whether or not the selected light will add any "light" to the objects in your scene. In reality, diffuseness refers to how much light is reflected by a surface, thereby making the surface visible (or not if there is no diffuseness). Diffuseness values can be set and varied for individual surfaces in the Surfaces panel, but the Affect Diffuse button will determine whether the selected light will affect any of the diffuse values of objects in the scene.

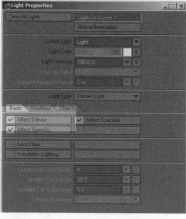

Figure 11.1: The Affect Diffuse button.

What is the practical application of this tool? If you want to add a specific specular hit to an object without affecting the rest of the lighting in the scene, you could add the light and turn off Affect Diffuse. Objects illuminated by that light will not appear brighter because of the added light but will receive an additional specular hit.

Affect Specular

Affect Specular works the same as Affect Diffuse but on the specular component of a surface instead. If you wish a particular light not to have an effect on the specularity of a particular surface, simply disable this button. What is specularity? Specularity is a simple reflection. For example, if you were outside on a sunny day and you had a big, chrome ball in front of you, you would see a reflection of the sun somewhere on the ball. On the other hand, if you had a big white balloon, you would not see a reflection of the sun because the balloon material dif-

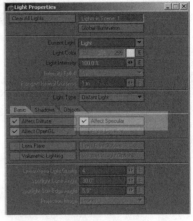

Figure 11.2: The Affect Specular button.

fuses the light image. So instead of seeing the light of the sun reflected as an image, you see the reflection diffused in all directions. The image is so diffused that it is no longer distinguishable as anything but a bright highlight on the balloon. In the real world, specularity and reflectivity are the same thing, but in LightWave, reflection and specularity have been separated into two different properties. This is so that LightWave can quickly render a specular highlight without having to calculate real reflections. It's much simpler to calculate, and therefore much quicker to render. Simply put, a specular highlight on a surface is just a brighter area than the rest of the surface; in essence, it is a "shiny" spot.

> **Note:** Bear in mind that Specularity and Glossiness in LightWave's Surface Editor are misnomers. Specularity should really be called "Specular Intensity" because it determines how bright the specular highlight is. In effect, it is like changing the intensity of the light from which the specular highlight originates without changing the illumination value in any other part of the scene. Glossiness refers to how diffuse the surface texture is and should really be called "Specularity," which is its real-world equivalent.

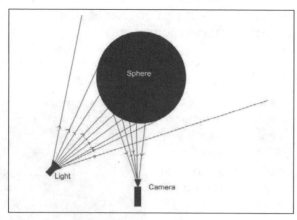

Figure 11.3: Specularity.

Note how the light beams reflect toward the camera due to the spherical shape of the object. This reflection of the light source on the surface of an object is what we know in LightWave as specularity. The position of the specular highlight is determined by the angle of incidence (from the light) and the angle of reflection (to the camera) as oriented to the surface normals.

Figure 11.4: Example of specularity.

Affect OpenGL

For the uninitiated, OpenGL is the technology used to display the geometry, basic textures, lighting, specularity, and anything else it can in your Layout window.

In LightWave 8, instead of only the first eight lights being available for OpenGL, now the eight brightest lights will automatically be used in

OpenGL. You can change exactly which lights you want Affect OpenGL applied to simply by deselecting this control on those lights.

This button determines whether or not the selected light will illuminate objects in your OpenGL Layout. Be aware that OpenGL currently supports a maximum of eight lights. You may have Affect OpenGL activated for 20 lights, but only the eight brightest in the list will affect objects within Layout's OpenGL View, unless you specify the eight lights you want OpenGL to use by disabling the Affect

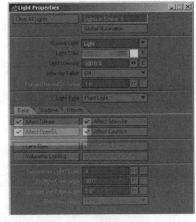

Figure 11.5: Affect OpenGL button.

OpenGL switch in all the other lights. Note that this does not affect rendered images in any way but only whether the effects of the selected light are visible in Layout's OpenGL View.

Affect Caustics

The Affect Caustics button can actually save you significant render time if you have enabled caustics in your scene because you can eliminate all the lights from caustics calculations except the specific ones involved in the caustic effect. What are caustics? In the real world, caustics are very similar to specularity, except that instead of the light intensifying toward the camera, it reflects off the surface and intensifies on another surface. Caustics is similar to radiosity in that it is light that is reflected off one surface onto another or focused by refraction onto another surface. The difference is that caustic light is

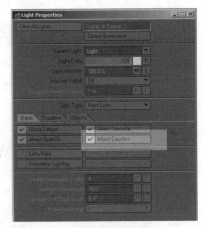

Figure 11.6: The Affect Caustics button.

focused and highly intensified to create a bright area of reflection or refraction.

By having the Affect Caustics button enabled only for a specific light or a couple of lights, all other lights will not calculate caustics. This means more predictable results and less render time than if you had caustics enabled for all lights.

> **Note:** Caustics must be enabled in the Global Illumination panel.

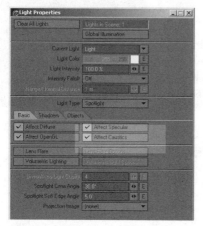

Figure 11.7

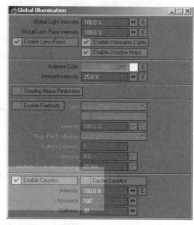

Figure 11.8

Enable caustics both on the individual light (in the Light Properties Basic sub-tab) and in the Global Illumination panel.

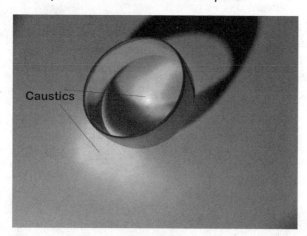

Figure 11.9: Example of caustics.

Caustics are pretty render-intensive and finicky so you may find that this is a tool you don't often use. Of course, render power and speed is always increasing. Not long ago we all thought area lights were too render-intensive to use.

Intensity

Light "intensity" refers to the brightness of your lighting instrument or how much brightness it is adding to the objects in your scene; that is, how much light it is putting out. We would consider that a 1000-watt lightbulb has an intensity ten times greater than a 100-watt lightbulb. In the world of real lighting, 0% is where the light is off and 100% is where maximum voltage has been applied, usually 110 volts or 220 volts (or other voltages depending on where you live). Fortunately for us, we CG artists are not limited by available electricity. The

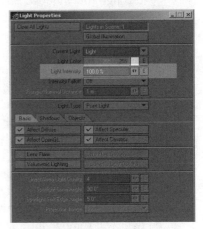

Figure 11.10: The Light Intensity setting.

percentage range of 0% to 100% is by no means an upper or lower limit. Light intensity is a multiplier that is used to calculate the final color of a surface. For instance, if you have a light with an intensity value of 100% aimed exactly perpendicular to a flat colored surface that has an RGB value of 200, 200, 200 and a diffuse value of 100%, the color that will be rendered out is 200, 200, 200. If the light has a value of 50%, you will receive a color of 100, 100, 100. In practical application however, choosing the proper intensity value is not always that straightforward, as there are many more calculations involved with varying surface parameters, light angles, etc., that often require you to use values outside the range of 0 to 100. There is no (practical) upper or lower limit to your light's intensity value. Your light can be 1,000,000% if you like or –38,465%. There is actually a numerical limit to how high or low LightWave will allow you to adjust the intensity, but the values are so extreme that it is generally not practical to use them.

> **Note:** Intensity values above 100% and below 0% must be entered numerically. The slider arrows only work from 0% to 100%.

What's the use of a light intensity over 100%? You'll find that you often use lighting values over 100%. Remember earlier on in the book when I mentioned that lighting levels are completely relative? This is where that principle comes into play. Say, for example, you have a nice interior shot beautifully lit with lamps and diffuse reflections from light sources within the room. Then the client says she wants sunlight streaming in through the window. So you place a light outside the window, crank it up to 100% and render. But you can barely see the light because all the other lights inside are between 50% and 100%. The sunlight should be predominant, but it's just washed out by all the other lights. Relative to the interior lights, the sun should be many times brighter. So make it many times brighter. Start by cranking it up to 500%. This may be too bright, but it's a place to start. You get the idea.

Intensities are highly subjective. They're easy to set, and one intensity takes pretty much the same amount of time to render as another. Feel free to experiment with wildly strange intensities. Push the limits of your scene to see what your lights are capable of.

What about lights of negative intensities? This is a truly great tool that every gaffer in the world wishes he had available on set. A negative light will remove intensity from the scene, resulting in lower diffuse and/or specular values of surfaces illuminated by that light. It can be used like a carving tool, removing only specific light from specific areas of the scene. You can even use a light with a negative value to remove volumetrics from a volumetric light of positive intensity. For example, if I have a surface lit with a distant light at 100% and I aim a spotlight with an intensity of –50% at the middle of the surface, there will be an area in the middle of the surface that is illuminated at only 50%.

Figure 11.11: Layout View of intensity example.

Figure 11.12: Render of intensity example.

There are a number of practical applications for using negative lights. For one, you can carefully sculpt exactly where you wish your light and dark areas to be in the shot. You can also use a negative light to remove color from another light. For example, white light is composed of the three primaries: red, green, and blue. If you shine a negative green light on a white light, some of the green will be removed, leaving mostly red and blue, or magenta.

Figure 11.13: The main light is a distant light with a color of 255, 255, 255, or pure white. The spotlight has been set to –50% intensity and has a color of 0, 255, 0, or pure green. This means that 50% of the green has been removed from the area where the spotlight is shining. (See color image.)

Understanding the color wheel and how to mix colors is key to using this trick effectively. The color wheel and color mixing are covered in detail in Chapter 19. This technique is a great way of coloring your lights without having to compete with the intensity already in the scene. In other words, if all the lights in the room are relatively bright, you don't have to crank a particular red light up to 1000% just to see some of the red color in that spotlight (or whatever light type you choose). Instead, add a negative intensity and remove the colors you don't want to see.

As another example, let's say you have a scene perfectly lit, but the color values of the lights aren't quite right. Perhaps they are too warm for the intended environment. Instead of adjusting the color values of all the lights in your scene, you could add a negative light or two with the proper color values selected to "pull" some of the unwanted color values out of the scene. To be really sneaky, you could also apply a negative Ambient Intensity value with an appropriate color choice to accomplish a global reduction of color values of surfaces in your scene

Now just to throw a monkey wrench into the works, if you place an object in front of the negative light, the object will cast a shadow but not one you might expect. In this shadow, the negative light will not have any effect at all on the original surface value. In other words, light will not be subtracted from the area in shadow. Think of it this way: With a "normal" light of positive intensity, there is no light added into an area of shadow. With a light of negative intensity, just the opposite happens — no light is subtracted from the area of shadow.

Figure 11.14: If the spotlight had a positive intensity value, the shadow area behind the ball would not receive illumination from the spotlight. Since the spotlight has a negative intensity value, the shadowed area behind the ball is not having light removed and you get a sort of "photo-negative" effect. (See color image.)

Now to add a second monkey wrench: In LightWave 7.5, we were given the option of coloring the shadows in our scene. This is done in the Light Properties panel Shadows sub-tab.

If the light is negative, however, the shadowed area will have the selected shadow color removed. Using our example scene with a negative spotlight colored 0, 255, 0 (pure green), this produces an area in which some of the green has been removed. If we then make the shadow color 255, 0, 0 (pure red), then the shadowed area from the negative spotlight will have some of the red removed, resulting in a shadowed area containing mainly blue and green.

Figure 11.15: This checkerboard polygon is lit with a white distant light. We have added a green negative spotlight that removes the green, resulting in a magenta area (magenta is composed of red and blue). We have also made the shadow of the negative spotlight red; therefore, red is removed from the shadowed area, resulting in a cyan colored shadow (cyan is composed of blue and green). (See color image.)

> **Note:**   Bear in mind that the shadow color setting only changes the color of the shadow cast by one object onto another object. The color of the self shadows on the object are not affected, so you might end up with two different colored shadows beside each other. This severely limits the practical use of shadow color.

So you can see how versatile light intensity can be. It's much more than simple illumination. Intensity can define a light source. The sun, for example, is usually blinding. Put an extremely bright light source in your scene and most people will assume it is the sun. Conversely, if you put a very small, dim source in your scene, people will have no trouble accepting that as a candle flame. Experiment with intensity. Try out different relationships. For example, fill light is usually at a lower intensity than the key light. That doesn't mean it must always be so. Try out different combinations.

Falloff

Light falloff is probably one of the most important yet subtle properties of your CG light. Let's begin with a discussion of how falloff works.

You know that if you turn your radio on you will hear sound. You know that if you walk away from the radio, the sound will get quieter and that at a certain point, you will be so far away that your ears can no longer perceive any sound from the radio even though it is on, even though the speakers are vibrating, compressing, and rarifying the air molecules in the room. The density of the molecular

Figure 11.16: The Intensity Falloff setting.

motion decreases the farther away you get from the speaker and the more the sound spreads out over three-dimensional space. That is sound falloff. It is very similar to how light falloff works.

When light is emitted from a light source, a quantifiable number of photons are released. These photons spread out in all directions, becoming less dense as they spread out. The farther away from the light source, the lower the density of photons. This means that a 1 cm square piece of paper held very near the light source will be struck by many more photons than the same 1 cm square piece of paper held very far from the light source. Very far away from the light source, only a tiny fraction of the photons reach the 1 cm square piece of paper. This is the reason why stars seem so dim. Many of the stars are much, much brighter than our own sun, yet because of their distance from us, they appear so dim as to be invisible during the day and cast almost no visible light on the earth during the night.

Natural falloff is exponential or curved because it follows the inverse square law; in other words, the light is spreading out both horizontally and vertically as it moves away from the light source. To understand this, you must first know that the area illuminated by a light source corresponds to the square of its distance from the light source. For instance, let's say that you have a spotlight that has been "barn-doored" to project light in the shape of a square. Furthermore, it is aimed at a surface that is 1 meter away and happens to illuminate an area that is 50 centimeters wide and tall (50 square centimeters). If you were to move the light or the surface so that they are now 2 meters apart, you would get an area of light on the surface that is 100 centimeters square, or four times the previous area (2 squared = 4). Increasing the distance to 3 meters would give you an area of light that is nine times greater than it is at 1 meter apart (3 squared = 9). We know that the farther away a surface is from a light source, the more the same number of photons are spread out, so each time we increase our distance, we have a larger area of light, but it is less bright—sort of like having enough paint to cover a 1 meter square area. If we have to cover 10 square meters with the same quantity of paint, the paint is going to be a lot thinner. Since the area of illumination corresponds to the square of the distance, the intensity of the light must fall off by the inverse square of the distance. With our example above, let's say that the area illuminated at 1 meter away receives 100% of the light. This means that at 2 meters away, the area being illuminated would only receive 25% of the light (the square of the distance is 4 and the inverse of that is $\frac{1}{4}$, or 25%). As we increase our distance to 3 meters, the area being illuminated would only receive 11.11% of the light value (3 squared = 9, and 1/9th of 100% = 11.11%). You can see that in nature, we can never actually get to 0% falloff. To actually calculate this in LightWave would take forever and so we are able to adjust the range of lights so they do not illuminate anything after the defined range. Of course, it would take a very long time to model the entire universe to test this, so the point is moot anyway.

In LightWave you have the option of choosing other falloff calculations. A linear falloff, for example, means that if you set the range of the light to 1 meter, the intensity will be 100% (or whatever intensity you set) at the light source and 0% at 1 meter away from the light. There will be no illumination outside the 1 meter circle around the light source. At 0.5 meters, the intensity will be 50%, and so on. This is not a physically accurate model of light falloff; however, I have found that few people can look at a falloff gradient and tell whether it's linear, inverse distance, or inverse square.

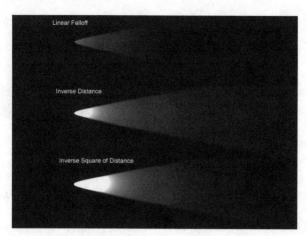

Figure 11.17: Falloff types

Figure 11.17 clearly demonstrates the differences in falloff type. The bottom segment shows a natural falloff using the inverse square. This is how real light falls off. But you may not always wish to have that much intensity so close to the light source. You can lower the near intensity by selecting either Inverse Distance or Linear. Or you can decrease the nominal distance. The nominal distance used with inverse or inverse square falloff determines where the light falloff begins, so light within the nominal distance circle will be at the full intensity set in the Light Properties panel. This is an instance in which real-world calculations often don't seem to be very important. I usually use linear falloff and only occasionally switch to one of the other types.

Distant lights are not equipped with falloff. This is because distant lights are meant to simulate sunlight. The sun has falloff just like any other light source, but the amount of falloff occurring within the human perceptual range is so slight as to be virtually unnoticeable. Why calculate something that can never be perceived?

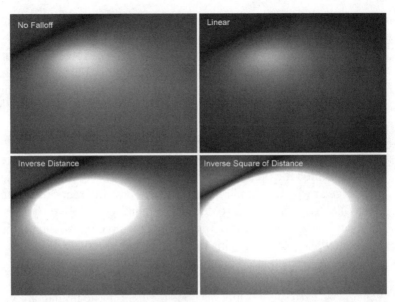

Figure 11.18: Area light falloff types.

Falloff is available for any lights other than distant lights. In Figure 11.18, an area light is used to demonstrate how falloff works. Note that an area light with no falloff still appears similar to an area light with linear falloff. This is because the ray-traced light rays are diverging and becoming less dense farther away from the area light, much like real-world light behavior.

Range/Nominal Distance

The Range/Nominal Distance setting pertains to falloff. There are two modes: Range and Nominal Distance. If you are in linear falloff mode and look through one of the orthogonal views, you will see a yellow circle around the light depicting the range. The light intensity falls off to 0% at this range. For example, if you set the Range/Nominal Distance to 1 meter, when using linear falloff the light intensity will be 100% at the light's origin, 50% at a range of 0.5 meters, and 0% at a range of 1 meter. This

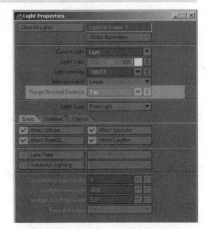

Figure 11.19: The Range/Nominal Distance setting.

effect does not exist in the real world. Light can continue traveling billions of light-years or until it impacts an opaque material. There is no known upper limit to the distance light can travel. However, we often wish to limit exactly what our light will illuminate. This is a tool that every gaffer wishes he had in his toolkit. Besides, it is much easier and quicker to calculate a 1 meter spheroid area of illumination than it is to calculate 1 billion light-years in every direction.

If, on the other hand, you select one of the inverse modes of falloff such as Inverse Distance or Inverse Distance Squared, then the yellow circle becomes the nominal distance. In other words, this is no longer the range at which light falls off to 0%; it is now the range at which the light falloff *begins*. Therefore, the light intensity is 100% (or whatever intensity you have selected) from the light source out to the nominal distance, at which place it begins to fall off either inversely or inverse squared. Inverse squared most closely resembles real-world lighting in behavior. Bear in mind that the light within the nominal distance circle will appear extremely bright, as does the light in the immediate vicinity of a lightbulb. It may take you a while to get used to using this setting, but it is by far the most realistic.

Exclude Objects

You will not always want every object lit by every light. On set, we use "flags" of various shapes and sizes to prevent certain lights from illuminating certain areas on the set. We use barn doors and shutters as well to control exactly where the light reaches.

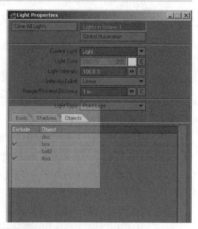

Figure 11.20: Excluding objects in the Objects sub-tab.

Fortunately for CG artists, preventing a light from spilling into undesired areas is as simple as opening up the Light Properties Objects sub-tab, and clicking in the Exclude column beside the object you wish not to be lit by the selected lighting instrument. If you exclude your selected light from a certain object, no illumination from that light will reach the object, even if you point the light directly at it.

In LightWave 3D 8, we can now click on the dark gray bar in the Exclude window to access Select All, Clear All, or Invert Selection options. This is very handy when you have many items in the scene to select or deselect.

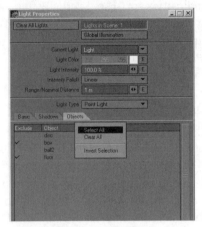

Figure 11.21: Exclude options.

Ambient Intensity

Found in Light Properties on the Global Illumination panel, ambient intensity is the oft-maligned bastard child of CG lighting. Most experienced CG artists will automatically set Ambient Intensity to 0. Simply put, ambient intensity adds a perfectly even amount of diffuse illumination to all surfaces in the scene. The problem with this is that it is extremely unnatural because it is much too perfect and therefore is a dead giveaway that your work is computer generated.

Take heart, though. Ambient intensity is still a good tool and has recently been given an entirely new and very crucial importance in LightWave's world thanks to the addition of radiosity.

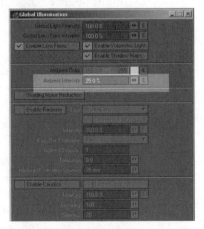

Figure 11.22: The Ambient Intensity setting.

The biggest advantage to ambient intensity is that it is dirt-cheap to render. Also, it is somewhat reminiscent of fill light. Sometimes you can get away with using only ambient intensity as your fill source which is very good, considering that ambient intensity is the proverbial hare compared to an area light's or radiosity's tortoise. I actually find ambient intensity most useful for seeing what I am doing in Layout. Often times, even if I am not using ambient intensity in the shot, I will have it turned up to illuminate the OpenGL interface, and then I'll turn it off for the render. But there are a few instances where ambient intensity can save the day.

The following are remarks by Arnie Cachelin about using ambient intensity with LightWave's radiosity. The full text can be found in Kenneth Woodruff's document "LightWave's 'Full Precision' Renderer and You," which is printed in the appendix:

"When radiosity is enabled, the ambient light value is added only to the indirect diffuse lighting of surfaces, not to the direct lighting. This means that the ambient level functions as the sum of all the higher order diffuse light 'bounces.' This little-known solution provides adjustable levels of higher-order lighting, which is generally a very subtle effect, while avoiding the exponential increase in the number of expensive ray-trace operations otherwise required by multi-bounce global illumination solutions. Contrary to your well-honed instinct for LW photorealism, ambient intensity should NOT automatically be set to negligible levels for radiosity. In general, the ambient level will need to account for second and higher-order bounces from many directions. These bounces will tend to contribute more if there are very bright lights in the scene, or bright luminous objects or bright spots in HDR ImageWorld environments. In these cases, bumping up the ambient intensity will increase accuracy. It will also help smooth noisy artifacts of undersampling, and light nooks and crannies which may otherwise not sample enough of the environment. This is better than just a hack, because every level of bounce makes the lighting less directional, of far lower intensity, and more susceptible to undersampling. Subsuming these bounces into a uniform level takes advantage of these characteristics, and eliminates the extra sampling requirements."

What this comes down to is that using ambient intensity with radiosity is not merely a good thing, it is highly desirable, especially as one of the main problems with radiosity is the graininess produced by under-sampling. Try it out. I think it will give you a new respect for ambient intensity.

· · ·

This chapter has covered numerous capabilities of the lighting tools available in LightWave. By now you should have a good grasp of most of the tools discussed herein. No doubt there are dozens more that I haven't thought of, and probably thousands more invented by other artists in times of need. Use your creativity to find new, effective, and cheap ways to use these great tools.

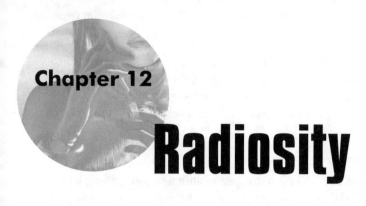

Chapter 12

Radiosity

This chapter deals with the wacky world of radiosity. By the time you have finished this chapter, you should have a good understanding of what radiosity is and how to decide when to use it and when not to use it, along with a few good ideas about how to improve render times while still using radiosity.

I know many artists have written off radiosity as too expensive, requiring too much render time to make it practical. And, in fact, there are many clever ways to fake radiosity and achieve very good results without the hideous render times, but nonetheless I'm here to change your mind. There are many ways to use radiosity that do not make render times unacceptable. The simple fact is that no other lighting tool in the LightWave arsenal will provide you with the photo-realism that radiosity will. This is because radiosity behaves more like real light than any of LightWave's other tools. Read on and be converted.

Radiosity Defined

Simply put, radiosity is the reflection of light. Light comes out of the sun, hits the white concrete in front of your house, bounces up, and hits your yellow house. The fir tree beside your house tree is green but now has a yellow sheen from the light that diffused and bounced off your house.

This light bouncing goes on and on. Light reflects or bounces hundreds or thousands of times until it is completely absorbed; however, humans are usually unable to perceive more than just a few bounces before the light become too subtle to see. The sky is also a radiosity light source. Light is diffused through the atmosphere and bounced around in all directions through impacts with air molecules.

One of the key properties of radiosity besides its random diffusion is that it appears to "pick up" the color of the surface from which it bounces, such as the yellow light bouncing off the yellow house. What is really happening is that the yellow house absorbs most of the blue wavelengths and reflects the remaining red and green light onto the fir tree beside your house. Red and green light mix to make yellow or amber light. In reality the light bouncing off the house simply contains fewer visible wavelengths than the light that reached it. Understanding this principle will help you know what color to make your reflecting source when you are faking radiosity as discussed later in this chapter.

The Tools

In order to use radiosity in your scene, you must first turn it on by clicking the Enable Radiosity button found in the Light Properties Global Illumination panel about halfway down.

Once this is done, you have three radiosity methods to choose from.

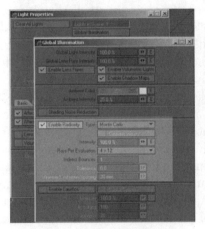

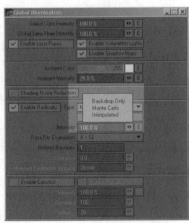

Figure 12.1: Enabling radiosity in the Global Illumination panel.

Figure 12.2: Radiosity type options.

Backdrop Only is at the top of the Type drop-down list. According to Kenneth Woodruff, author of "LightWave's 'Full Precision' Renderer and You," Backdrop Only radiosity works like an "accessibility" plug-in in which surfaces are illuminated based on how much light from the backdrop can reach areas in the scene. This is a relatively quick radiosity solution that provides beautiful, natural, soft shadows in occluded areas. As a matter of fact, it works like a gigantic, ball-shaped area light. The trade-off is that Backdrop Only does not calculate any bounces and subsequently does not "pick up" any color from bounce surfaces. But there are ways to fake colored bounces, and the soft shadows really make the extra render time worth it.

Monte Carlo is the best quality radiosity available in LightWave. The primary difference between Backdrop Only and Monte Carlo is that the light is actually bounced from one surface to another along with the surface color. In LightWave 3D 7.5 NewTek gifted us with the ability to bounce light as many as eight times where previously Monte Carlo would calculate only one bounce. This makes a dramatic difference in quality and also in render time. I find it difficult not to justify the extra render time considering the final render is exponentially better looking with multi-bounce radiosity. Fortunately, those brains at NewTek provided us a way out of this conundrum. It's called Interpolated Radiosity.

Interpolated Radiosity provides you with two additional settings that allow you to tweak sensitivity and speed up renders. Higher Tolerance settings speed up render times but come at the expense of accuracy, so there may be differences from one frame to the next. Minimum Evaluation Spacing determines how close the closest evaluation rays will come to each other. By setting a higher value, there are fewer rays in the scene and, therefore, faster rendering times. The trade-off of faster rendering times is decreased accuracy and a higher likelihood that the radiosity solution will be calculated differently from one frame to the next, resulting in a "crawling" artifact effect. But I have found that there is usually a certain amount that each of these settings can be pushed. Also, keep scale in mind. If you are calculating a radiosity solution for a very large scene, make the Minimum Evaluation Spacing proportionately larger. For example, if you are rendering a cityscape, it hardly makes sense to set minimum spacing to 20 mm. Start with something much larger like 1 meter or so. Twiddle with settings until you get the fastest possible rendering time with acceptable lighting quality. More complex textures will also help. If, for example, you are rendering with radiosity on an untextured, white plane, you are likely to see every artifact and miscalculation. On the other hand, if your plane is covered with a dirty, complex asphalt texture, you are much less likely to see any errors at all. Keep this in mind. Hiding radiosity artifacts is as good as not having them at all.

The following image demonstrates all three radiosity types including render times. You can see that the two-bounce Monte Carlo and the two-bounce Interpolated are pretty much identical, yet the Interpolated took just over half the render time. That's a very significant saving.

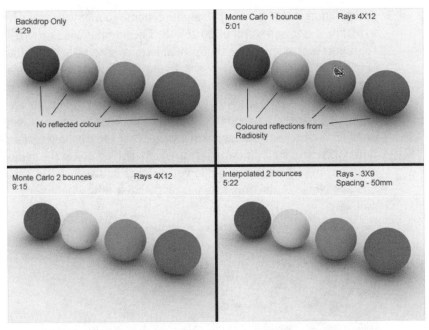

Figure 12.3: Radiosity types. (See color image.)

The LightWave manual contains an excellent explanation of how radiosity is calculated within LightWave, so feel free to read that document for a detailed explanation. Suffice it to say that a theoretical hemisphere (half a ball) is placed on the surface of an object that receives light. The normals (polygon faces) of that theoretical hemisphere are used to project light rays that represent the diffuse reflected light of the real world. It is important to understand this concept because all three radiosity types have a pertinent setting that can help speed up render times: Rays Per Evaluation.

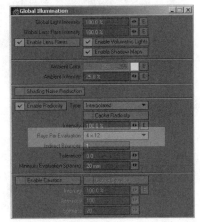

Figure 12.4: The Rays Per Evaluation setting.

You will notice that rays per evaluation come in many sizes such as 1x3, 2x6, 3x9, 4x12, and so on up to 16x48. These dimensions represent the segments and sides of the theoretical hemisphere or half-ball that is being used to project the radiosity light rays. The default setting is 4x12, but you can set this higher or lower as you see fit. Lower settings will improve render times. Try it. Often you can get away with lower settings. Sometimes, for detailed work or very smooth textures, you will need to use higher settings. Don't forget that the Shading Noise Reduction option will smooth out many artifacts and errors in the radiosity solution, so you can often use lower, quicker settings just by turning on Shading Noise Reduction. I turn it on by habit now whenever I use radiosity.

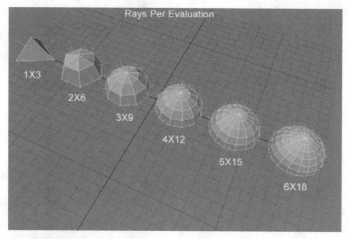

Figure 12.5

As you can see, higher "resolutions" in calculating the number of rays per evaluation will obviously provide a smoother, more uniform radiosity solution. Higher settings, however, mean higher rendering times. For each "ray" that is shot out of a normal, a new evaluation is spawned for each bounce, so you can see why higher bounces become exponentially longer to render.

The purpose of the Intensity box is pretty self-evident. The default level is 100%. If you find the radiosity lighting too bright or too dim, simply adjust the level.

The images in Figure 12.6 balance quality with rendering time. In general, better quality means higher rendering times and vice versa. But there is always an upper and lower limit to this depending on your scene. You must know what the scale is, how detailed it is, how close to photo-reality you wish to be, how much motion blur and camera movement are there to hide artifacting, and how much texturing is apparent. In general, more detailed textures hide the artifacting of lower-quality radiosity solutions. Flat, monochromatic surfaces generally require the highest quality radiosity solutions. Notice the blotchiness that is very noticeable on the ground plane but not on the aircraft. This is due to the aircraft's irregular texturing, which is already blotchy and helps hide the lighting inconsistencies.

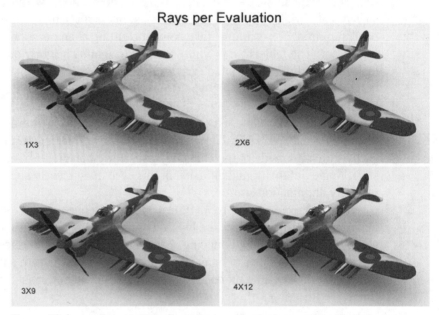

Figure 12.6

Note that while higher Rays Per Evaluation settings are available, a setting of 4x12 has rendered quite adequate results. Higher settings are not required. If the ground plane were textured rather than flat and white, a lower setting would have been acceptable, resulting in faster render times. You will notice that even in the 1x3 render, while the ground plane looks terrible, the aircraft looks pretty much the same as the higher quality renders.

When and Where to Use Radiosity

Radiosity can be a subtle and tricky effect. This works to our advantage because the untrained eye cannot always distinguish between physically accurate radiosity and some of the cheesy, dirty tricks we've come up with to shave minutes off a render.

The first question you must ask yourself is whether or not radiosity is actually required in the scene. Most often the answer will be "no." Radiosity is most apparent and necessary in shots where two adjacent surfaces are brightly enough lit that at least one light bounce is obviously required. For example, take someone sitting at an outdoor restaurant. The tablecloth is white, the sun is shining brightly on the table. This lighting situation clearly calls for some sort of radiosity solution to simulate the light that would bounce off the table and onto the underside of the person's face and onto the clothing. It is obvious that the sunlight would reflect off the tablecloth and up onto the person sitting at the table, probably illuminating any downward-facing surfaces such as the underside of the chin and nose, as well as the front of the shirt. Angle, intensity, and diffusion in this case must clearly show a radiosity illumination source.

A typical example is a room interior that has a beam of light streaming in through the window. The light hits the floor, bounces onto the nearby walls and ceiling, bouncing again onto other nearby surfaces, and so on. A higher number of bounces is more physically accurate and generally looks better but comes at the price of drastically increased render times.

Figure 12.7: Example of radiosity.

As a matter of fact, the best way to understand radiosity is to observe. As with any other art, if we observe and strive to understand nature's work, we can incorporate that knowledge into our own artwork.

Radiosity can be a subtle and convincing effect, adding unparalleled realism to your work. In fact, there is only one good reason not to use radiosity, and that is the high render times associated with radiosity calculations. Since radiosity occurs everywhere in nature all the time, it is only natural to wish to include it in a lighting setup. Unfortunately, until CPU speed increases drastically, radiosity will be a luxury tool. In the meantime, we rely on many cheats and tricks to create lighting that "looks" similar to radiosity in order to fool the viewer.

Radiosity Cheats and Tricks

Cheating, faking, tricking, outright deceit: These are the gems that make us great CG artists, not because the art is good but because it renders fast and fools the eye. In a production environment, one thing you will hear time and again is that your render is taking too long, that there are other artists who would love to use the farm if Your Highness is through with it. You'll be called names like Render Hog, Farm King, and other expletives that cannot be printed here (not that I, personally, have ever been called such things). Worry not. There are many ways to fake radiosity, speed up those render times, and rid yourself of the pesky villagers with pitchforks and torches.

LightWave creates a radiosity solution by calculating light bounce from one surface to another. Rather than giving your CPU all those extra calculations, try turning off radiosity and instead place a lighting instrument where the bounce would occur and pointing in the direction in which the bounce would go.

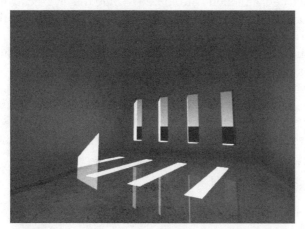

Figure 12.8: Using an area light and falloff to simulate radiosity.

In Figure 12.8, radiosity has been turned off. An area light has been placed at floor level pointing upward where the light beam hits the floor. A theoretically accurate falloff was used to give the corners of the room the illumination characteristics of radiosity.

The final render is not as accurate as the radiosity render, but because Interpolated was used for the radiosity render to keep render times down, that image has splotchy lighting, while the area light solution is clean and smooth. Further, while the radiosity solution took over 7 minutes, the area light solution took just under 1 minute. Following is another solution.

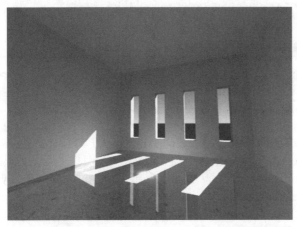

Figure 12.9: Using a point light to simulate radiosity.

In this solution, a single point light was used in place of the area light. The problems are that the lighting is yet again less accurate than a true radiosity solution, and a bright spot is visible on the floor near where the point light is located, although I attempted to hide this by placing it within the square of light from the exterior source. But there are times you may need a very cheap solution to provide some apparent bounce in your environment. This render took 11.7 seconds. A radiosity solution takes 35 times longer.

Every light in the toolbox can be used as a fake radiosity bounce source. You need only to know the qualities and properties of that bounce, where it originates, what color it should be, and what direction it is going. Just treat the bounce as though it were a lighting instrument and proceed accordingly.

Baking Radiosity

One of the best lighting tools in LightWave is the Surface Baker. What this great gadget does is take all the layers of painstakingly painted textures you have created and mash them flat into one layer that you can then apply back to the surface. This new surface takes less time to render because, well, because it is only one texture instead of many.

"So why does this make my lighting better?" you ask. Simple; you can also bake lighting information into the texture. This means that you can create a detailed radiosity or HDRI lighting solution, render a single frame to bake the textures, then apply the new texture, lighting information included, back onto your surface. You set your surface luminosity to 100% and your surface diffuse to 0% and voilà. You can also bake *only* the illumination data into the map and apply that on the illumination channel of the texture if you don't want to lose the advantage of having separate channels of control in your Surface Editor.

> **Note:** Don't forget to then turn off radiosity and disable the Surface Baker before continuing.

The drawback to this is that any surface-baked surfaces must not move during the animation; otherwise the shadows will not move with the object—the lighting and shadows are baked into the texture, right? Also, because the luminosity is up and the diffuse is down, you will not be able to cast shadows onto the baked surface. There are ways around this, of course, such as rendering separate elements and then compositing them, but it is good to be aware. You can also have the diffuse value higher than 0% to receive shadows, but then the texture will be brighter than it originally was. This is fine, provided you plan for it when creating your textures.

If you have a scene in which you can use this technique, it will save many hours of render time and afford you the beauty of radiosity at a fraction of the cost. For example, if you have a character walking down a street with buildings on both sides of the street, the character's shadows never touch the buildings, and the buildings never move, then you can bake a beautiful radiosity solution into the buildings' surfaces. You leave the ground alone so it can receive shadows from the walking character. Turn radiosity and the Surface Baker off and render the sequence. You will get radiosity lighting on your building walls and still have shadows from the character without the render times of radiosity. For more information on the Surface Baker and for details on its use, see the

LightWave manual. Chapter 23 also has a short discussion on creating UV maps and baking illumination into your textures.

A Note on Radiosity's Natural Falloff

I have been asked why radiosity does not include a falloff control like other lighting tools. In the real world, falloff occurs because a light source is emitting a particular density of photons. Those photons spread out in space because the light is emitted omnidirectionally; therefore the density decreases. A lower density of photons means that fewer photons will reach any particular surface. When a bunch of photons reach a surface from a light source, some of them bounce off, diffusing yet again into more directions. Over time and over the course of diverging photons there is just less light there to see. This is what falloff is. It is very similar to the reason noise seems quieter as you get farther away from the source. Radiosity calculates by spreading out light rays from surfaces. They diverge in the same way and therefore, over distance, there is less light per square centimeter. So no falloff control is needed for radiosity because it occurs naturally as a part of the radiosity calculation.

• • •

You should now have a good reasonably good understanding of what radiosity is, and you should be able to make decisions about when to use it and when not to use it. You should also have a few good ideas about how to improve render times while still using radiosity. The clever artist will now spend some time devising new ways of reducing render times with radiosity.

Chapter 13

HDRI and Caustics

This chapter covers HDRI, or High Dynamic Range Images, and caustics. In addition, you will learn some methods of employing these tools in your scenes.

> **Note:** Be aware that these are both advanced lighting options and are seldom used in a production environment due to the high rendering times and the fact that the technology requires further maturing. To date, HDRI cannot be justified as its increased quality comes with increased render times. HDRI lighting cannot create quality superior to other, less expensive techniques used by a skilled lighting artist.

The universe contains a wide range of visible illumination. The human eye can detect extremely low levels of light but has an upper threshold. Light above this threshold can cause pain and even retinal damage. Enter the iris. The iris opens very wide under low-light conditions to allow as much light as possible into the eye. In brighter conditions such as a plainly lit office, your iris will close somewhat, allowing less light in so that the pain threshold is not exceeded. There is enough light so that you can see clearly, but not too much. If you step outside into direct sunlight, the iris will become very small, allowing even less light in. The sun produces much more light than the eye requires to see clearly and the iris cuts out most of the light to prevent eye damage and pain.

If you step out of the sunlight and into a dark room, you will at first be unable to see. This is because the iris is contracted to a small circle and is allowing in very little light. Over time, the iris will open, allowing more light into the eye. As your eyes "adjust," more detail in the room will become visible.

Now that we understand that the range of light in the universe is much higher than the range of light that the human eye can process, we can look at HDRI.

What Is HDRI?

HDRI refers to High Dynamic Range Images. These are images that contain more illumination information than is visible at any one time — more illumination information, for example, than can be displayed on your computer monitor. The *dynamic range* is the difference between the lightest and darkest points in the image, also known as the *contrast* of the image. *High dynamic range* means that the range from the lightest to darkest point in the image is greater than a human eye or a computer monitor can process at any one time. This high range of information rendered out in LightWave is available to the user through image manipulation and post processing. The extra information cannot be stored in regular RGB image file formats, however, and requires its own formats such as LightWave's own .flx format or ILM's great new OpenEXR format. The full range of HDRI illumination information is not viewable on standard output devices.

So if you can't see the information, what's so great about HDR images? Well, the most obvious advantage comes when you render out your CG elements in an HDR format and hand it over to a compositing artist. That compositing artist now has much more flexibility when it comes to manipulating the image. For example, if the CG element is rendered very dark, and there are areas of complete darkness, the compositor would not be able to "pull up" any information in the black areas, but with an HDR image, all the geometry information is still in there and can be accessed. This means that the compositor does not have to ask the CG artist to relight and re-render the CG element brighter. The compositor can brighten the image without any image loss or "clipping."

Let's take a look at a normal RGB format like a TGA image. Each pixel is colored within a range from 0 to 16 million. The RGB (red, green, blue) information is stored as ranges from 0 to 255. So an RGB color of black is 0, 0, 0, and an RGB color of white is 255, 255, 255. Red is 255, 0, 0, green is 0, 255, 0, and so on. This is a fairly accurate way of mixing colors. The problem is that in the real world the high range of natural light acts on colors more broadly than is possible in a straight RGB image. Colors appear to shift in saturation and value when subjected to high or low lighting conditions. For example, the visual perception of a sunlit scene is completely different from the visual perception of a moonlit evening. The color of the ground is the same at night as in the day, but the illumination environment will change that perception.

If, for example, you had a bright spotlight shining on a white wall, you would conclude that the wall is colored 255, 255, 255, or pure white. What if we then shine some sunlight on that wall. Clearly the sun is much brighter than a spotlight, so the illumination conditions should change, but we have already "maxed out" our RGB values. What we need is a higher range of values. That is why HDR was invented. Artists needed a way to deal with the widely variable lighting conditions that they come across in photo-real work. The simple coloring and texturing of surfaces requires only the colors found in an RGB image, but lighting a scene brings in a whole new level of reality. HDR images allow us to tap into that reality by using "floating-point" values instead of the old, limited RGB value range of 0 to 255. Floating-point values are equivalent to RGB values in that 0 in RGB is the same as 0 in floating point (FP), and an FP value of 1.0 is the same as an RGB value of 255. But FP is not limited to an upper maximum value of 1.0; you can go as high as you want. This is where the higher range comes into play, providing you with virtually unlimited lighting levels.

Why Should I Use HDRI?

There are many good reasons for using HDR image file formats, not the least of which is that all the lighting information is retained in the file, regardless of whether most of the image is in black shadows or blown out with blinding light. This means that an artist, be it animator, compositor, graphic designer, whomever, can brighten up or darken down the image *after* it is rendered to bring out the detail that would have been completely lost in a regular RGB format file. How many times have you rendered a sequence, then wished it were a touch lighter or had the client come and ask for an intensity change that made you have to re-render the sequence? No more. Post-render image manipulation is now the answer to most of these problems.

As far as lighting a scene, HDRI has its pros and its cons. The great thing is that you can load up an HDR image into your scene using the

Figure 13.1

Textured Environment plug-in, which can be found in the Effects panel under the Backdrop tab.

This essentially wraps the HDR image around your scene like a spherical map. When you enable radiosity, the color and high dynamic range illumination information is used to light the scene. If you can imagine that each pixel in the HDR image is a different color and illumination value, HDRI is somewhat like placing a spotlight at each pixel with the right color and illumination value. So if you have an image of a blue sky with a sun on one side, the key light will be the sun, which is illuminating the scene, and the fill light will be from all of the blue sky in the image. There are no actual lights, but the camera has recorded the illumination of the sun very high on the scale, so a majority of the scene's illumination will be coming from the area of the image where the sun is located.

The result is very complex and theoretically very realistic lighting. Even using Backdrop Only radiosity the lighting will be much more natural due to the complex colors and shapes of the lighting.

In feature production, this method can only be used well if HDRI Light Probe (360 degree) images are taken on set so that your CG lighting will closely match the real lighting used there. However, if you are doing all-CG work, you can use whatever HDR images suit your fancy, since you're designing all the lights, rather than trying to replicate someone else's lighting.

Figure 13.2: Render on left with HDR image on right. (See color image.)

In Figure 13.2, the tiger head and a complex surface were lit using HDR images only. The only difference between the two renders on the left is the HDR images to the right. Note that the HDR images are "fish-eye." This is to compress the entire 360 degree world into the image so that the whole environment is retained without stretching when the image is placed in your spherical environment.

How Do I Use HDRI to Light a Scene?

To start with, you will need some HDR images. There are a number of HDRI references on the web. Using your favorite search engine, type in HDRI and you should get several pages of listings. Not only is there a wide selection of free HDR images available, you can also find free tools to build your own HDR images such as HDR Shop.

Using LightGen

There is also an HDR Shop plug-in called LightGen. Both HDR Shop and LightGen are available on the web at http://www.debevec.org/HDRShop/. According to the documentation, LightGen "generates a list of directional light sources to approximate the lighting from a lightprobe image." A LightWave Lscript called LightGen2LW then takes the data from the list and converts it into an array of lights within LightWave using the appropriate positional, directional, intensity, and color data for each light. LightGen2LW is available on the Internet. Just do a search; you'll find it.

It probably sounds more difficult than it is, but if you follow the instructions on the HDR Shop web site, you'll find yourself creating colored light arrays in no time. It took me about ten minutes to locate and download an HDR image, locate and install both HDR Shop and LightGen, and create a text file. A few minutes later I had a nice light array in LightWave's Layout and rendered the following image.

Figure 13.3: LightGen render. (See color image.)

This technique renders in much less time than HDRI and radiosity; however, it is unlikely that you will achieve the subtle complexities of image-based lighting unless you add a very large number of lights. Figure 13.3 used 20 distant lights. The drawbacks to this method are as follows:

- Distant lights mean you'll have ray-traced, hard-edged shadows while HDRI and radiosity provide soft, diffuse global lighting. You can use any light type you wish. I would recommend spotlights because you can use shadow maps and soften the shadows.

- Multiple lights mean multiple shadows. Most lighting environments do not cast multiple shadows, unless you are in a room with multiple competing light sources. Outdoor lighting rarely exhibits multiple shadows except the relatively hard shadow from the sun and the soft shadow from the sky. If you are using 20 or more lights, as I did, you will end up with 20 or more shadows. To my eye, this just doesn't read correctly.

As with any other technique, there will be situations where these points are moot. Shots with high motion blur, for example, can hide the stepping effect of multiple shadows. It is a cheap way to achieve more complex lighting than you will get from basic lighting techniques and sometimes it will be very valuable to you. If I had the choice, the reference images, and the render power, though, I'd use HDRI and radiosity all the time.

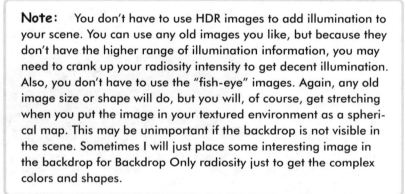

Note: You don't have to use HDR images to add illumination to your scene. You can use any old images you like, but because they don't have the higher range of illumination information, you may need to crank up your radiosity intensity to get decent illumination. Also, you don't have to use the "fish-eye" images. Again, any old image size or shape will do, but you will, of course, get stretching when you put the image in your textured environment as a spherical map. This may be unimportant if the backdrop is not visible in the scene. Sometimes I will just place some interesting image in the backdrop for Backdrop Only radiosity just to get the complex colors and shapes.

Using Textured Environment

On the Effects panel Backdrop tab, click the Add Environment button and select Textured Environment from the drop-down list.

When you double-click Textured Environment, additional information will appear on the panel.

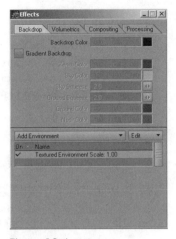

Figure 13.4

Figure 13.5

Make sure Y is the axis, then click the Texture button. This will open up a new panel just like the Texture Editor you find in the Surface panel.

Figure 13.6

You are simply taking a spherical image map and wrapping it around your environment just as if you were wrapping a picture around a ball. The only difference for us is that it is an HDR image and that means it has additional illumination information embedded in it. When you turn radiosity on, this information will come into play and illuminate the scene.

For more information on how to apply spherical image maps, see the LightWave 3D manual.

> **Note:** You don't have to use an HDR image in the textured environment. You can use a regular RGB image, a colored gradient, or a procedural texture just as well. The great advantage to HDR images is that they contain very natural, high dynamic range lighting information that will provide your scene with realistic and natural lighting.

Using Image World

Textured Environment provides you with the option to use procedural textures, gradients, or image maps. If you know you only need to use a spherical image wrapped around your environment, Image World is a real shortcut. You apply Image World just the same as Textured Environment in the Effects panel, Backdrop tab.

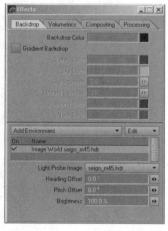

Simply load the HDR image, also known as a Light Probe image, add a heading and/or pitch offset if desired, and tweak the brightness if necessary. The heading and pitch offsets are useful if you wish to reorient the background image for some reason such as an image seam in frame.

Figure 13.7

Brightness is another way of adjusting the luminance of the background HDR image without having to crank up the radiosity intensity. An Image World Brightness of 200% and a Radiosity Intensity of 100% will light an object in the scene exactly the same as an Image World Brightness of 100% and a Radiosity Intensity of 200%. The difference is that a higher brightness in Image World will show as a brighter background image.

Unlike Textured Environment, Image World is exclusively for HDR, or Light Probe, images.

Caustics Defined

Caustics in the real world refer to substances that burn or corrode in a certain way. Like so many other words of our profession, an entirely new definition has been devised to describe a new effect that does not exist in the real world. This is not to say that the visual effect we call caustics does not occur. It does. It is just not a fancy, render-expensive, and luxurious frill that is separate from the rest of the lighting.

Caustics is the focusing of light due to reflection or refraction onto another surface so as to cause areas of intense illumination. Let's examine how this occurs.

If light is reflected onto a curved surface, and the curved surface causes light to focus and intensify onto an area, we call that caustics. But we also call it specularity because that is exactly what happens for specularity also. The only difference is perceptual. In the case of specularity, the light is focused and concentrated from whatever our point of view is. In the case of caustics, the light is focused and concentrated onto another surface. The principles are exactly the same. In the real world, in fact, caustics, specularity, reflection, and diffuseness are all pretty much the same effect. But here in the wonderful world of CG, we can separate and individually adjust each element of that effect.

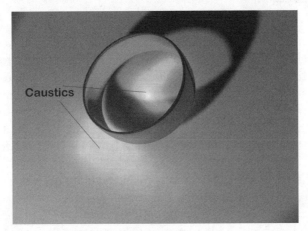

Figure 13.8: Example of caustics.

Caustics also occurs when light enters a material of a density higher than air and is refracted in such a way that the light focuses onto another surface. For those not familiar with refraction, here is how it works: Light bends when it passes from a substance of one density into a substance of another density, provided the light reaches the new substance at an angle. If the light approaches the new substance squarely, it will not bend.

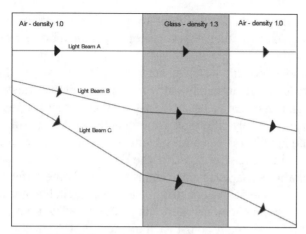

Figure 13.9: Refraction

In the above image, we are using glass as a common example of a substance with a higher density than air. The same principles apply to water or any other transparent substance, although the diffraction value may be different. You can see that as light approaches a substance of higher density at a more obtuse angle, the angle of refraction is also more obtuse. If both the entry and exit points of the substance are parallel, the light will exit at the same angle that it entered, but the position will be altered.

This is the effect that occurs when you stand knee-deep in water and it looks like your legs are bent.

To remember which direction the light rays bend, think of an SUV leaving a paved road and driving into a muddy countryside. If the SUV drives straight into the mud, the angle will not change, but it will be slowed somewhat. If the SUV enters the mud at an angle, the side that enters the mud first will slow down first so the SUV will angle in that direction. The same principle applies to the exit. Whichever side of the SUV exits the mud first will speed up first, causing the vehicle to speed up on that side first. For example, if the left tires reach the mud first and slow down, the vehicle will angle to the left. If the left tires then exit the mud and speed up before the right tires, the vehicle will angle to the right.

Why do you care about this? It's true that LightWave calculates all this automatically, but you may find yourself trying to fake this effect one day. Understanding exactly how refraction works will help you.

The following image demonstrates how parallel light beams are affected by a convex lens. Remember the truck-in-the-mud analogy and you will see that the light's behavior is highly predictable and obvious.

The focusing demonstrated in this illustration is the effect that causes the caustic areas of intensity to occur when light is focused and intensified by a convex lens such as a glass of water.

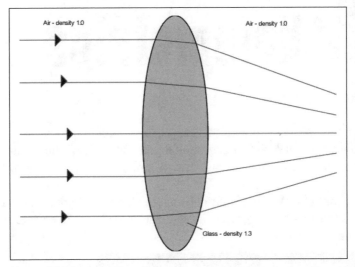

Figure 13.10

When and Where to Use Caustics

As attractive as caustics sounds and as physically accurate as it may be, I have found little practical use for this effect. To be sure, artists can create beautiful still images with glowing caustics, but the caustic calculation seems to differ with each frame, making it impractical for animation. Also, the controls seem not to be entirely predictable yet.

Caustics is a relatively new tool, however, and will no doubt undergo refinement until it becomes yet another strong, predictable tool in our LightWave toolset.

Still, it is a beautiful effect once you have sorted out the settings for your particular need. This effect is probably currently confined to use in still images, but don't let that stop you from trying to make it work in animation. And if you have success, I would love to hear about it.

• • •

You should now clearly understand what HDRI and caustics are and how to use them in your scene setups.

Carry on.

173

Chapter 14

Volumetrics

When you are finished with this chapter, you should have a basic understanding of LightWave's fog, ground fog, HyperVoxels™, and volumetric lighting effects. We also discuss how volumetrics and lighting can interact.

Within LightWave, all our objects are made up of hollow surfaces. That is to say, all the surfaces are just flat, thin sheets like paper with nothing in between.

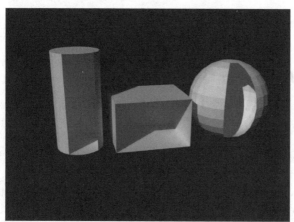

Figure 14.1

Note in the above image that a cylinder, a box, and a sphere created in LightWave's Modeler have no substance. They are just hollow shapes. But we note that in lighting some scenes, there are atmospheric effects that do have volume, or depth and substance, all the way through. Clouds are a good example of a material that must have volume. And so the tool called volumetrics was invented.

It may be argued that volumetrics are not a lighting effect, or that some of the volumetric tools have less to do with lighting than they do with materials and surfaces. This is true, but volumetric effects and lighting often interact in a way that provides unparalleled realism to your render. There is no doubt that a discussion of volumetrics is just as important in a lighting book as it is in a texturing book, especially considering there is a special type of lighting tool called *volumetric lighting*.

Volumetrics allow us to create, for example, a cloud that the camera can fly through. If we created a cloud out of polygons and attempted to fly the camera through, the camera would "pop" through one surface, there would be no cloud inside, and the camera would "pop" out the other side. Volumetrics actually calculate a continuous volume of substance that the camera can see.

So why is this important to lighting? Simple; atmospheric conditions play an integral part in lighting a scene. How many movies or television shows have you seen where the hero is creeping down a dark hall with a bright flashlight illuminating the mist wherever the light beam points? This is a classic example of volumetrics. The sun shining through trees on a foggy day creating that beautiful "God light" is a good one too. Sometimes you don't need those illuminated "rays" but you may require your CG elements to fade into the fog over distance. Regardless of the particular need, volumetrics play a very important part in lighting your scene.

Fog

Under the Effects panel Volumetrics sub-tab you will find fog settings occupying the top half of the panel. This is a fake fog, not a real volumetric effect, but it is often very effective and is very quick to render. It works by creating a "circle of fog" that centers on the camera and remains centered on the camera even if it moves around.

There are four settings in the Fog Type drop-down list. The choices are Off, which disables fog, Linear, which provides a straight

Figure 14.2: The Volumetrics sub-tab.

linear falloff between the minimum and maximum distances, and two choices of Non-Linear curves. In the small square graph to the left, you will see the effects of whichever curve type you choose. The left side of this graph represents the minimum amount of fog and the right side represents the maximum amount of fog, while the height or vertical measurement represents the range from 0% to 100% fog. 0% means there is no fog visible and 100% means that the fog is 100% thick and you cannot see anything beyond it.

Min Distance refers to the distance from the camera to where the fog begins, while Max Distance refers to the distance from the camera to where the fog ends. Min Amount determines the percentage, or "thickness," of the fog at the Min Distance, and Max Amount determines the percentage, or "thickness," of the fog at the Min Distance.

For example, if you set a Min Distance of 1 meter, a Max Distance of 10 meters, set a Min Amount of 0%, and a Max Amount of 90%, there will be no fog at the camera. There will be no fog 1 meter from the camera, but then the fog will slowly increase until it reaches 90% thickness 10 meters away from the camera. How quickly the fog goes from 0% to 90% will depend on which curve you choose. Try them all out and see which suits your purpose best.

Fog Linear   Fog Non-Linear 1   Fog Non-Linear 2

Figure 14.3

As you can see in Figure 14.3, a linear fog ramps up more slowly than either of the curves. The Non-Linear 2 setting adds the most fog closest to the camera.

The one disadvantage to LightWave's fog is that it will not react to lights as though it were a real volumetric effect. Note in Figure 14.4 that there is a spotlight illuminating two of the cylinders, but you cannot see the light beams coming in from the light. If this were real fog, you would be able to see the whole cone of light, but since this is not a real volumetric effect, the light cone is not visible.

Figure 14.4

One interesting advantage to fog is that, even with no lights or ambient intensity, the fog itself still provides illumination to the scene as though it were a diffuse light source itself. Used properly, this can be a stunning and subtle effect that adds great realism to your scene with very little impact on overall render time.

Figure 14.5

Figure 14.5 uses no illumination sources. Only the fog is illuminating the scene.

You can set your fog Min and Max distances more interactively by enabling Show Fog Circles in the Display Options panel. If you then view the camera from one of the isometric views (Top, Bottom, Back, Front,

Left, Right), you will see the size of the fog circles change size as you slide the values up and down.

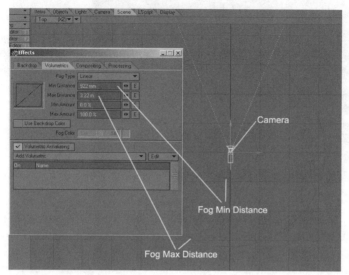

Figure 14.6

You can also change the color of your fog using the usual color selection methods.

Ground Fog

The Ground Fog plug-in is available in the Effects panel Volumetrics sub-tab under the Add Volumetric drop-down. To alter the default settings, simply double-click on the plug-in in the list and an options panel will open.

Figure 14.7

Figure 14.8

Note: In the Volumetrics sub-tab, the Volumetric Antialiasing button is enabled by default. If your volumetrics are taking a great deal of time to render, you can speed up render times by disabling this feature. Most volumetrics don't seem to require antialiasing anyway unless motion blur is required. So keep it off unless you need it.

Ground fog is very similar to the normal fog that was discussed in the previous section, except that this fog is independent of the camera, is actual 3D fog, and interacts with your lighting. You can choose between Fast Fog, which is linear and smooth, or you can choose Ray Marcher fog, which renders more slowly but has the added bonus of being able to texture the fog to make it more realistic with changes in density and shape, just like real fog.

Figure 14.9: Ground fog.

Ground fog doesn't have to be pea-soup thick. It can be a subtle effect in your scene, adding visual impact and environmental information to the picture. For full details on the controls and operation of the Ground Fog plug-in, consult the LightWave manual.

HyperVoxels

HyperVoxels are virtual blobs of material that form around points or particles in your LightWave scene. They come in two main flavors: surfaces and volumes. We discuss volumes here, since this is a volumetric section.

You can use HyperVoxels for an incredible array of different effects from foliage and sandstorms to fire blasting out of a rocket engine and cigarette smoke drifting upward. HyperVoxels can be snow, rain, or a bowl of water. The possibilities really are endless. In this case, we are looking at HyperVoxels as a potential tool for use in lighting our scene.

HyperVoxels can be used to create volumetric fog in the scene and, since your lights will interact automatically with HyperVoxels, they can provide a very nice atmospheric solution. One great thing about HyperVoxels is Sprite Mode. In this mode, rather than calculating the entire volume of a HyperVoxel, a slice or a number of slices is taken from the HyperVoxel and only that slice or those slices are calculated. It is not as beautiful and accurate as the true volume but can often suffice.

Take the example of the blasting rocket engine. One could apply a high luminosity to the HyperVoxels emitting from the rocket, then turn on radiosity. Now, with both radiosity and HyperVoxels on, chances are the frame will take a long time to render, but sometimes you just have to do it for the fun of it. Imagine the beautiful illumination near the launch pad. Sure, there are way cheaper, easier ways of doing this, like placing a lighting instrument to fake the rocket illumination, but they're not nearly as fun!

Figure 14.10: Using HyperVoxels and radiosity. (See color image.)

Here's a little trick I discovered. If you have ever found yourself in a situation where you need an array of lightbulbs, such as in a warehouse or an aircraft hangar, you don't need to create the geometry for the lightbulbs. Just create points, add HyperVoxel surfaces, and turn up illumination. In Figure 14.11, I applied HyperVoxel surfaces to a plain box.

When the HyperVoxels render, there is one at each point of the box. I turned on radiosity just for fun and added a high luminosity to the HV surface. Instant lightbulbs!

Figure 14.11

Volumetric Lights

There are many different volumetric effects in LightWave. Where lighting is concerned, I find volumetric lights to be the most useful and most used of them all. What is a volumetric light? Let me explain it this way: When you are in a smoky or steamy room, you can see the smoke or steam mainly in areas of high illumination. For example, if there is a spotlight in the ceiling shining a light beam down at the floor, you can see the smoke or steam because it is being illuminated, and the area of illumination, naturally, is exactly the size and shape of the light beam. Wherever there is illumination, you see smoke or steam. Now there is still smoke or steam in the rest of the room; it's just not as apparent as the illuminated smoke or steam. So some brainy programmer got the idea to put this smoky effect only in the light beam. Why put it in the rest of the room and waste all that computing power if you can't even see it? Thus, volumetric lights were born. When you turn on volumetrics for a light, a virtual volumetric haze will appear in the light beam.

In Layout, you can see the volumetric shape in the OpenGL interface by way of a gray shape that becomes visible when you enable volumetrics for a distant light, a spotlight, or a point light.

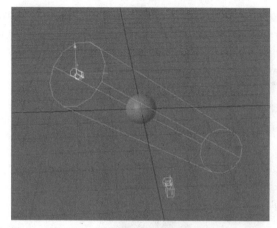

Figure 14.12

Figure 14.13: A distant light with volumetrics enabled.

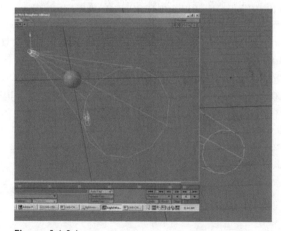

Figure 14.14

Figure 14.15: A spotlight with volumetrics
enabled.

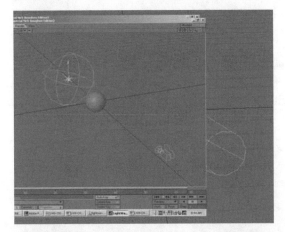

Figure 14.16

Figure 14.17: A point light with volumetrics
enabled.

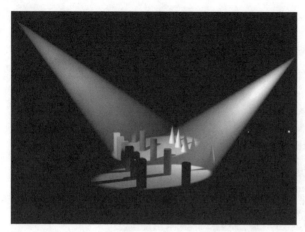

Figure 14.18

As you can see in Figure 14.18, two spotlights are illuminating the objects in the scene. Both lights have volumetric lighting enabled. This button is found on the Light Properties panel.

Once you have enabled volumetric lighting on a light (this feature can be enabled or disabled on each individual light), the Volumetric Light Options button will be enabled and you will have access to a panel of settings as shown in Figure 14.20.

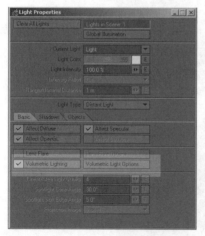

Figure 14.20: Volumetric Options panel.

Figure 14.19: Volumetric Lighting options.

All of the controls in this panel are self explanatory and relatively intuitive. As this is not a book on volumetrics, and as all the information regarding the controls in this panel is available in the manual, it is not

covered here. But get to know the controls, if you don't already. Volumetric lighting can add a great deal of atmosphere to your shots.

Additive and Subtractive Volumetric Lights

Volumetric lights in LightWave behave just the same way as
nonvolumetrics when it comes to positive and negative intensities.
When you shine two volumetric lights in such a way that their beams
overlap, the intensity (and therefore the volumetric density and brightness) is doubled.

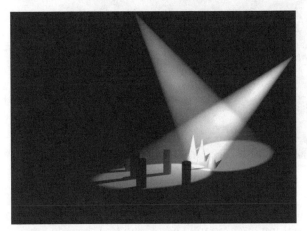

Figure 14.21

And for another trick, if you were to give the first of the two lights a negative intensity, that light will subtract volumetrics from the second light
as in Figure 14.22.

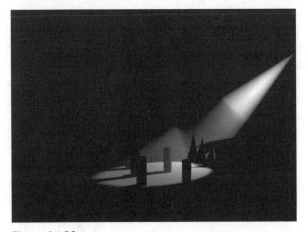

Figure 14.22

As you can see in Figure 14.22, a portion of the volumetric from the light on the right has been removed. This is because the intensity of the left light has been set to –100%, thereby removing 100% of the intensity and volumetric from the right light. In Figure 14.23, the intensity of the right light is set to –40%, so only 40% of the volumetric is missing from the right light.

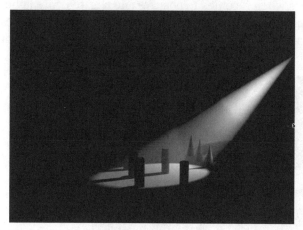

Figure 14.23

I have yet to use this effect in any production lighting scenarios. However, I imagine it might come in handy if one found oneself in a situation where the shape of a volumetric light needed to be sculpted.

A Cool Volumetric Light Trick

We all know that volumetric lighting is disabled for linear and area lights. I'm not sure exactly why this is. It probably has something to do with render times or strange behaviors, but here's how you can get it to work — at least in still images.

Make your light a distant light (or point or spot), set your volumetric settings, and then switch the light type to Area. You'll see volumetrics in the shape of the light you first chose but with the shadow properties of an area light (at least within the volumetric). I'm not sure exactly what practical use this trick has, but it's good to have in the bag-o'-tricks. This also works for linear lights.

Figure 14.24: A simple distant light with default volumetrics.

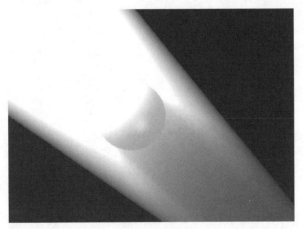

Figure 14.25: The same as above, but with the light type switched to Area.

Creating "Atmosphere"

One of the dead giveaways of CG work is the clean, crisp, fresh renders. They are usually too crisp, too clean. Adding a little atmosphere in the form of volumetric lighting or overall fog can have several effects. First of all, atmosphere in your scene will hide any number of sins such as shoddy texture mapping, marginal camera tracking, and lower detail. But those are not great reasons for using fog. Fog can add mystery and suspense to the scene, or it can describe local atmospheric conditions, whether it's thick London fog or a smoky bar at midnight.

● ● ●

Volumetrics in LightWave can be any number of powerful tools that add an organic realism not found in any of the other tools and enhance your lighting setup. Volumetrics goes far beyond the few uses we have discussed here, however. For a complete description of LightWave's HyperVoxels, see the manual and take a look at the numerous tutorials available on the web, some of which can be found at www.newtek.com.

You should now have a basic understanding of LightWave's fog, ground fog, HyperVoxels, and volumetric lighting effects. You should be able to create volumetrics that interact predictably with your lighting tools. For further discussion on volumetrics, volumetric lighting, and fog, please see the LightWave manual.

Chapter 15

Lens Flares

This chapter briefly covers the purposes and use of lens flares. By the time you have finished this chapter you should be able to create lens flares in LightWave and find useful purposes for them.

Lens flares are another real-world lighting effect that has a corresponding tool in LightWave. Strangely, this tool is less often used to simulate its real-world counterpart than it is to create other, completely different effects.

Lens Flares Defined

A camera lens is really a tube filled with a number of different lenses. Each of these lenses has a highly polished optical glass surface. Because the glass is highly polished, it is also highly specular and, therefore, highly reflective as well. Camera and lens manufacturers go to great lengths to prevent reflection from occurring within the lens housing. They paint the inside of the tube black and apply anti-reflective coatings to the lens, but these measures are of little help when a very bright light source like the sun or a car headlamp shines directly into the front of the lens. When this happens, bright light will reflect back and forth between the lens surfaces, creating visible reflections called a *lens flare*. You have probably seen many lens flares on television and in movies whenever the camera pans past the sun or when a car drives by at night with its headlights on.

Figure 15.1: Lens flares. (See color image.)

Figure 15.1 was created in LightWave using the lens flare tools available in the Light Properties panel. This phenomenon is common in outdoor shots where the sun is in frame.

Why Not to Use Them

When lens flare tools were first added to LightWave it was thought that this effect added a new, unparalleled realism to CG renders. Since the main problem with CG renders is a lack of errors, it was thought that these lens flares would add a natural error into the shot, making it seem to be real photography. At first this was true. There was a very high "cool" factor attached to the use of lens flares. The problem was that this tool became seriously overused both in intensity and in frequency.

LightWave lens flares soon became cliché. They clearly identified shots as CG, creating the exact opposite effect that the artist desired. Less-experienced artists began to use lens flares all over the place, at intensities much too high to be real. A dead giveaway of an inexperienced artist is overuse, or even any use, of lens flares on the demo reel.

Good Uses for Lens Flares

Just because a lot of artists over the years have made lens flares cheesy and obvious doesn't mean you can't use them in other great, less obvious ways. Of course, sometimes you will actually have to use a lens flare for a real lens flare effect.

Lens flares should be used judiciously. First of all, there absolutely must be a valid and pressing reason to use a lens flare such as our example of the sun crossing the field of view. If this happens, lens flares should be subtle. Don't overdo it.

Any light type can have a lens flare. Simply open the Light Properties panel, select the light to which you wish to add a flare, then under the Basic sub-tab, click the Lens Flare button. This will enable the Lens Flare Options button to the right, which gives you access to all the lens flare controls.

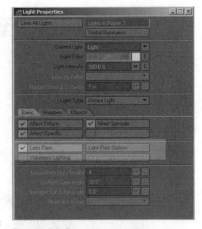

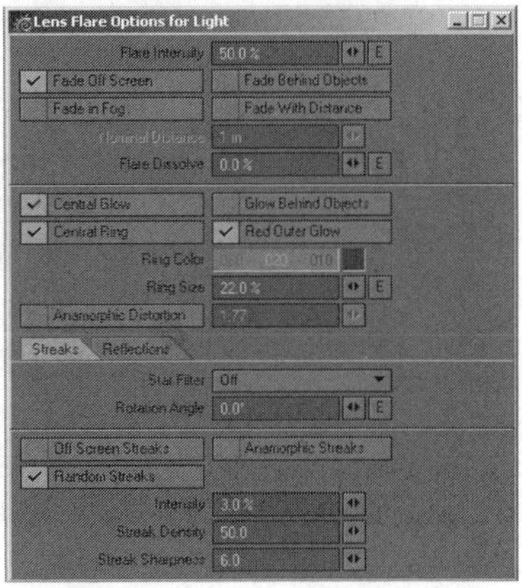

Figure 15.2

Within the Lens Flare Options panel are myriad controls that allow you to precisely match lens flares from any given lens. If you wish to get into the gruesome details of every facet of a lens flare, I urge you to check out the LightWave manual. I will not devote my writing time to or take up your reading time with an effect that is so infrequently used and has almost nothing to do with lighting your scene; it's all well covered within the pages of the manual.

Figure 15.3

In truth, I have never had the need in production to use this tool for creating lens flares. That is not to say that I have never used the lens flare tools in production; it's just that I have never used them for lens flares.

I have found lens flares to be an extremely useful tool, not as lens flares, but instead as small, distant light sources such as those warning lights you might see at the top of an antenna so that aircraft don't come too close. You see, lens flares create a small area of intense brightness right near the light source. So you may, for example, take a point light, stick it to the top of your antenna, and turn on lens flares. Turn off Lens Reflections (found in the Reflections tab) and Central Ring in the Lens Flare Options panel, and you will find that your point light is now a visible light source.

191

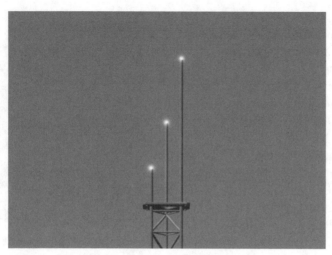

Figure 15.4: Using lens flares. (See color image.)

When using this technique, the lens flare takes on the color of the light. In this case I used point lights with a color of 255, 0, 0. One of the great things is that the lens flare intensity is independent of the light intensity. So you can turn the light intensity off and still have a great lens flare. It is a very versatile little technique that can be used in innumerable ways. Picture street lamps as viewed from a helicopter. Or imagine how useful this effect might have been in the days of *Blade Runner* when a night-time cityscape was composed mainly of bright point source lights just like this.

This technique is by far the best use I have found for lens flares in LightWave. But you may very well find a place where you need a real lens-reflection type lens flare. Go ahead and use it. But remember, as with all effects and techniques, subtlety is usually the key to success.

Recently I set up a scene with 15 lens flares interacting with five render passes of particles to create a magical effect. The lens flares were nothing more than drifting light sources floating around in space. One of the double-edged swords in LightWave is that the light sources themselves are not visible. This is good because it means you can place a light anywhere on the set, including directly in front of the camera, and not worry about seeing it. On the other hand, when you want to see the light source, you're out of luck. This is where lens flares come in handy. If you turn off all the rings, streaks, and whatnot, you are left with a single intense point where the light's pivot point is. This is a great visible light source that is useful for all sorts of effects and situations.

My last piece of advice about lens flares is to use them sparingly and wisely. Overuse of this effect is a dead giveaway that the work is CG.

• • •

You should now understand the use and purpose of lens flares in LightWave. Remember, it is usually the creative and uncommon uses of these tools that get you noticed as an artist.

Lighting Plug-ins, LScripts, Pixel Filters, and Image Filters

This chapter discusses a few of the more popular tools used in Light-Wave for lighting and shading. There are many more out there. Some are expensive, some are cheap, and some are even free. If the tool you need isn't listed here, it is almost certainly out there somewhere. Do a web search, but first check www.Flay.com.

Because of LightWave's open architecture, there seems to be an endless stream of new plug-ins and LScripts for artists to explore and employ in their work. Of course, these new features go far beyond lighting, but the mere possibilities in lighting alone are mind-boggling. Usually a discussion starts on one of the mailing lists between a few artists experiencing the same problem under similar circumstances. Next thing you know, some programming brainiac has come up with some solution. Nine times out of ten it's a freebie too! That community spirit is one of the things that makes LightWave great and guarantees its continued presence in the world market of prime animation software packages.

There are a number of tools available — some are commercial, some come with LightWave, and some are freely available on the web. I'll go through a few of the most common and best-known ones here. Don't let that stop you from discovering others. If there's one thing I've learned about LightWave it's that there's always something new and different to learn just around the corner.

I do not go into detail on the use of most of these plug-ins but I do provide brief descriptions and example renders where I can. These tools can all be researched on the web at www.Flay.com and elsewhere, and in the LightWave manual and on the LightWave web site, www.newtek.com. It's also worth your while to keep an eye on Worley Labs at www.worley.com. Worley always seems to be coming up with handy, rather mind-blowing lighting tools these days. It is worth your time to check out all these sites and any others you can find; they may save your bacon.

Bear in mind that most lighting plug-ins are post-process filters that alter the rendered image. After you've done your lighting, set positions, intensities, colors, and whatnot, you can still work on your image. Because the final render is just a two-dimensional image made out of pixels, you have all the tools of a painter and many, many more. Learn them, love them, use them. These are some of the details that separate good artists from great ones.

Also, some of the tools mentioned here are free and available on the web. Others have a commercial cost, sometimes too great for hobbyists, freelancers, or small houses. All I can say about the expensive ones is that if you're doing a job where you really need this tool, you should be able to justify it within your budget. If your client isn't paying you enough to comfortably acquire the tools you need for the job and still make a profit, then your client isn't paying you enough.

Shadow Designer 2

Shadow Designer 2 by evasion 3D (www.evasion3d.com) was designed to simulate soft real-world type shadows that are difficult or even impossible to simulate using simple ray-traced lighting instruments like spotlights, point lights, and distant lights. Evasion states in its documentation that this plug-in is intended to be used for subtle, soft lighting effects, although it can produce hard shadows if necessary. One of the greatest advantages to Shadow Designer is that you can apply it on a surface-by-surface basis so that unlike radiosity or area lights, the soft shadows are only calculated in areas specified by the artist. SD also provides the capability of applying multiple shadow layers from multiple lights, allowing you to "paint" with your shadows and making it possible for you to achieve very custom lighting and shadows not possible within LightWave alone. While the first version of Shadow Designer did, in fact, produce very nice soft shadows, it was often slower than a beautiful soft shadow created using an area light. Evasion boasts a speed increase in

the current version (2) of 300% to 2000%, which would make it faster
than area lights and much faster than radiosity. For a soft shadow solution, this software is worth a look. It doesn't come cheap, though,
especially if you are a small operation.

Figure 16.1: An image created using Shadow Designer. (See color image.)

Figure 16.1 was rendered from the Shadow Designer 2 tutorial files sup-
plied with the plug-in. The render using Shadow Designer took 18
minutes and 18 seconds. Figure 16.2 is the same scene using an area
light and ray tracing instead of Shadow Designer. While the final results
are comparable, the LightWave-only render took 31 minutes and 53 seconds. That's 74% longer. Shadow Designer takes a little time to tweak,
but the render time savings are significant enough to make the front-end
time investment well worth it for a long render.

Figure 16.2: An image created using area light and ray
tracing in LightWave. (See color image.)

G2

G2 from Worley Labs is a tool that will change your lighting process. With its interactive preview, you will be tweaking lighting and texture settings on the fly and watching them update near real time in the preview window — sort of like Viper on steroids. If you haven't already heard of G2, you must be dead. If you haven't tried it, you really, really should, if you can afford it. As with other Worley Labs plug-ins, it comes at a high price for small houses or freelancers. But the logic is, if you really need it for a project, you should budget for it. It's worth it and will pay for itself in time saved on your first project.

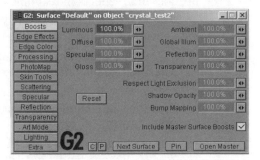

Figure 16.3

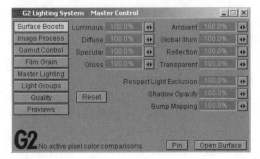

Figure 16.4

G2 features the following:

- Sub-surface scattering
- Optimized human skin shader
- Interactive compositing
- Output gamut and color adjustment
- Light grouping
- Noiseless area light shading
- Radiosity adjustment
- Proper glass refraction without duplicated backside polygons
- Edge effect tools
- Anisotropy
- Photo "shading de-baking" for mapping

According to the web site, all of these features show their exact pixel-accurate effects in real time using the new G2 preview system. (Sounds like what Viper was supposed to be.)

Steven Worley of Worley Labs describes G2 this way:

"G2 is a different beast. It's not a shader like Gaffer; it's a system of plug-ins that kind of interlock into LightWave to become symbiotic with it. There are Master class plug-ins to 'run' everything, Generics for commands, a shader for flagging surfaces, and a pixel filter for applying effects and post-processing. The goal of G2 was beyond Gaffer; it was more of 'LightWave needs an improved inter-face for lighting, and it needs to do things totally differently. Can we make it happen?' As an experiment I experimented with a texturing preview system in 'Disgust' a year ago, and that worked well. So I spent months and months planning a whole system for replacing LW's system. And that's what became G2. The name 'G2' is unfor-tunate in many ways; it's more of my laziness since I didn't know what to call it. :-)

"But the cool thing about G2 is that it's a whole FRAMEWORK for dealing with rendering, lighting, and shading effects, and one that's turned out REALLY well. This is cool because now, starting with this framework which is powerful and accurate, I can add more and more capabilities into it, like new light types, new shading mod-els, new processing effects, new rendering methods, and so on. The current lighting and shading tools are just sort of the default obvious extensions and what I do with G2 UPDATES will be very interest-ing.

"I'm especially eager to merge G2's system with Sasquatch, allowing for a Big Change in how users interact with fur and hair. I haven't even started that yet, but I'm looking forward to that."

After using G2 for feature work I can attest to the fact that this tool has completely changed how I work. The "old" way of achieving final looks for the render was to approximate your settings, hit F9 to render out a test render, examine it, make some adjustments, hit F9 to render out another test render, and so on. If your frames take any significant amount of time, you can imagine how the artists' time soon becomes spent mostly waiting for frames to render so they can make a quick adjustment, then sit there waiting for the next render. With G2, you ren-der out your frame once, and then make all your tweaks and adjustments in G2. As you are making the adjustments, they are interactively updat-ing in the G2 preview window.

One of my favorite features of G2 is its area light shadows. G2 uses its own rendering engine to calculate area light shadows, and you have complete control over the shadow quality. G2 area light shadows are much cleaner than those from LightWave alone, although they take slightly longer to render at higher quality settings.

Check out the Worley web site at www.worley.com if you haven't already, and take a look at the session videos — they will blow your mind.

Overcaster

> **Note:** At the time of publication, Eki's PlugPak for LightWave 8.0 was still under construction. The most current version of Eki's PlugPak can be downloaded from www.kolumbus.fi/erkki.halk-ka.plugpak. We decided not to put the PlugPak on the CD this time since Eki will have added new, amazing features by the time you read this, and the one on the CD would then be out of date. So why waste the space? Please download Eki's PlugPak if you wish to follow along with the tutorial.

Overcaster originated when a LightWave artist named Eki Halkka decided to automate the "spinning light trick" by writing an LScript. It is now a sophisticated set of LScripts that you can use to simulate global illumination. The results of Overcaster are often of sufficient quality to replace Background Only global illumination while rendering many times faster.

For those unfamiliar with the spinning light trick, the idea was born out of the inadequacy of distant lights' ray-traced shadows, which are much too hard-edged to be realistic. A number of artists have been credited with inventing this technique. The principle is that if you spin a light one whole rotation per frame with motion blur on, then the light will behave like many lights from many directions. Here's the LightWave manual's description of how it handles motion blur:

> "LightWave simulates motion blur by producing a number of semi-dissolved images of a moving object. In the Normal mode, the number of images is determined by the number of antialiasing passes. In fact, you must have some level of antialiasing in order to use motion blur. The Dithered mode greatly enhances the quality of the effect by doubling the number of images."

To fully understand how motion blur works, please see the LightWave manual. For more on Overcaster, I turn over the quill to Eki himself, who was kind enough to take time out of his schedule to write a description of his great tool as well as a short tutorial on its use.

Overcaster and Spinning Lights

Overcaster scripts, which are a part of Eki's PlugPak, rely on three lighting tricks that are rather well known by experienced LightWave users.

First and most important is the spinning light trick. The others are the use of morph mixer and channel follower for controlling light properties with sliders and the use of duplicated lights with different properties for semitransparent shadows. Each scene that's created with Overcaster or any other script from Eki's PlugPak could have been just as well made manually by the user. The scripts only automate the setup.

LightWave calculates motion blur by rendering a different time step at each antialiasing pass and combining these to a single image. If the antialiasing setting is low and there's fast motion in the frame, a series of ghost images can be seen. The spinning light trick uses this phenomenon to multiply the apparent number of lights in the scene. When a high enough antialiasing setting is used, the shadows from the lights are blended together, giving the appearance of a single soft shadow.

Figure 16.5: Chastity model lit with Overcaster spot. Medium antialiasing with dithered motion blur.

With a basic spinning light setup, the goal is to make the light rotate a full revolution, 360 degrees, during the antialiasing passes. LightWave's default motion blur length is 50%, so to get 360 degrees of rotation the light has to turn 720 degrees each frame. When the user runs an

Overcaster script, the script first reads some parameters from the scene. The most important is the motion blur length of the current camera. If the user has set the motion blur to 5%, for example, the amount of spinning must be increased to 7200 degrees to get a full revolution during the antialiasing passes, as the desired 360 degrees is 5% of 7200.

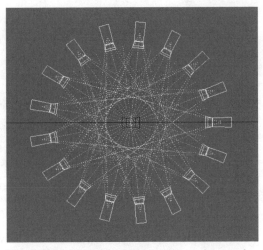

Figure 16.6: With high antialiasing and normal motion blur, a single spinning light will shine from 17 different positions. There's no difference in render time compared to a regular light.

Overcaster automatically creates the spinners according to the current frames per second rate and motion blur amount. If the user changes these after applying Overcaster, nasty flickering errors may occur. To enable field rendering, Overcaster actually creates the spinning keyframes at frame 0.5, which causes both fields to get an equal amount of motion. However, with field rendering enabled, the Overcaster lights will by default rotate only half a circle. This phenomenon can be fixed by halving the motion blur length temporarily before applying the Overcaster lights when field rendering is used.

Most Overcaster setups come in multiple resolutions. The Overcaster EZ rigs are the most basic form of spinning lights. The script adds the necessary spinner nulls with correct settings to a single light, and all the light's properties are set up as if the light was a regular, non-spinning light. There's usually only one slider control, for the softness of the light. The normal resolution Overcaster setups are exactly the same as the EZ versions as far as the spinning light trick is concerned, but they incorporate the other Overcaster niceties, such as semitransparent, colored shadows. The dual and quad rigs multiply the number of lights, giving better results especially at lower antialiasing settings. The drawback is a hit in the render times.

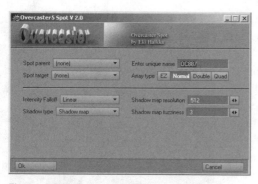

Figure 16.7: Overcaster Spot interface. The user can select various options for the spinning light setup.

In these rigs, each light is broken down to its base components. There are separate lights for at least diffuse and specular shading, as well as lights that only affect the shadows. The principle of the shadow trick is simple: If we have two lights that are identical except that one has its intensity set to 100% and the other to –100%, they cancel each other out, having no effect on the scene whatsoever. If we turn shadows on for the positive light, the lights cancel each other out everywhere else except in the shadow area, which gets darkened by the negative light. These two lights would now create only shadows and have no effect on diffuse or specular shading. If we set the light intensities to 50% and –50%, the shadow will become half transparent.

All these separate lights are controlled with sliders. Each setup has a control object that has multiple built-in endomorph targets. These morph targets do not actually deform anything, but they give access to designated morph mixer channels. These can be controlled with Light-Wave's slider banks or by adjusting them directly in the endomorph mixer.

When the user adjusts a slider for specular shading, a channel follower applied to the specular light's intensity channel will modify the specular light's intensity envelope. In practice, the user will see the specular shading change its intensity.

Depending on the type of light that's emulated with Overcaster, various things may happen when the user modifies the Shadow Softness slider. With Overcaster Sun, the slider actually modifies the pitch of all the lights in the rig. The lights are parented to a spinning null object. The more the lights are rotated relative to the spinner null, the softer the lighting and shadows will appear. As all the lights in the setup are distant lights, their position does not matter, only rotation.

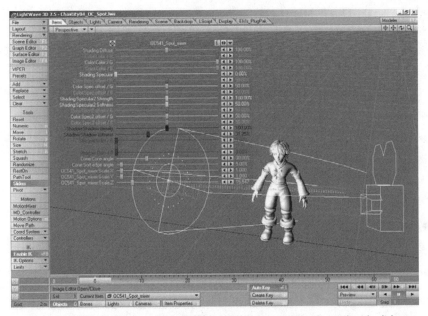

Figure 16.8: The properties of the spinning light rig can be adjusted with sliders. A rough estimate of the result is seen in the OpenGL preview.

With Overcaster Spot, the slider controls the light's distances from the spinning null. The lights are targeted to another null and will form a torus-like light source, pointing toward the target null, when motion blur is applied.

Many variants of the spinning light trick do not actually use spinning motion. Overcaster Tube, which attempts to emulate a fluorescent tube similar to LightWave's linear lights, moves the lights on a linear path during the antialiasing passes. Overcaster Ambimage has up to 24 lights that rotate, but only a few degrees each. For more in-depth info about Overcaster, see the Overcaster documentation on the PlugPak web site (http://www.kolumbus.fi/erkki.halkka/plugpak).

Overcaster Tutorial

Load the scene called Chastity01.lws from the companion CD. This is a scene with a character standing on the ground, with default LightWave lighting. The Chastity model was created by Jeff Greulich. (Thanks, Jeff!!)

Motion blur is set to dithered with low antialiasing, and shadow ray tracing is turned on.

Let's start lighting the scene by replacing the dull LightWave default ambient light with Overcaster Ambimage. In many cases you may wish to run the Overcaster HUB LScript to run multiple subscripts at once, but for clarity's sake, we will run the scripts separately this time.

Figure 16.9: Overcaster Ambimage interface. There are settings for defining the quality of the array, as well as settings for the method to retrieve colors for the lights.

Run the OC_Ambimage LScript. The PlugPak setup should have added a button for this automatically. Select Manual Gradient as the method. The other methods can be used to automatically match the background, but that's not necessary in this scene. Set the Array type to Dome 12. This is the same as the default Sphere 24, except that only the Zenith and Sky lights are active.

Figure 16.10: Setting up the gradient for the lights.

In the second dialog, you will define a gradient from which the Ambimage lights get their colors. This time I set up a bluish sky-like gradient. Only the Sky and Zenith colors are taken into an account.

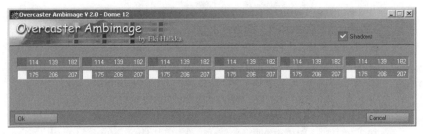

Figure 16.11: Fine-tuning the settings if necessary.

In the subsequent dialog, you will see the colors of each of the 12 active lights in the current Ambimage rig. The color requesters for the 12 lower lights are hidden. You can see that all lights in both rows have the same colors, based on your gradient settings. Click OK. At this point, select the LightWave default light (the one called Light), and delete it. The light couldn't have been deleted earlier, as there always has to be at least one light in the scene. Do a test render by pressing F9. You should now have smooth ambient lighting in the scene. The only thing is, it takes a bit of time to render.

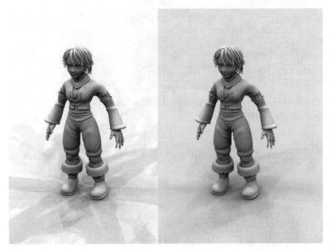

Figure 16.12: Chastity rendered with Overcaster Ambimage lighting.

Notice in Figure 16.12 that low antialiasing was used on the left side and the render time was around 2 minutes. Separate shadows are clearly visible. Ugly. The right side was rendered at dithered enhanced medium antialiasing. The result is decent, but the render time grew to about 7 minutes (both rendered on a 1.7 GHz P4 at 1280 x 920 pixel resolution).

205

Let's get quicker soft shadows. First, run OC_Ambimage again and set the Array type to Dome 12 (you always need to remember which type you used if you wish to modify settings later). Accept Skip as the method and click OK. In the dialog with 12 lights, turn off the Shadows check box. This will disable the ray-traced shadows cast by the OC_Ambimage rig. We will replace them with OC_Shadow.

Run the OC_Shadow LScript. Set Chastity.lwo as the shadow parent, and activate Automatic settings. Accept the defaults for all the other settings. This way the script will try to automatically place and scale the shadower rig so that it covers the parent object as efficiently as possible.

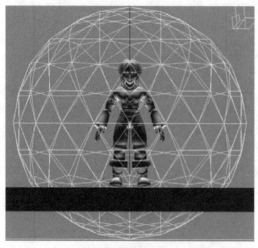

Figure 16.13: Shadow area surrounding Chastity model with automatic settings.

Overcaster Shadower uses shadow-mapped spotlights to do its magic. The spots are aimed so that they affect everything that is inside the Shadow_area object. If you scale the area too large, the shadows will become rather fuzzy due to lack of shadow map resolution, so you should always try to make the Shadow_area surround your main objects as closely as possible. If you run the script again with the current mixer object active, you can modify the shadow map sizes and other parameters — this requires Eki's PlugPak version 2.0 or better.

As we are doing a daylight scene, we will need a sun. You guessed it — we will use the OC_Sun LScript. This time the default settings should work fine. Rotate the Sun_mixer object to aim the light.

I suggest doing a few test renders with different orientations. I finally ended up at Heading 70, Pitch 30, Bank 0.

If you examine the sun's shadow, you can see that the shadow gets softer over distance. You can adjust the softness and many more parameters with the Sun_mixer object's sliders or endomorph mixer.

Figure 16.14: The result of the tutorial. Consider this as just the initial setup. The light intensities and other properties can be easily animated with the sliders.

Color Theory Lighting Designer

Gary Hartenstein wrote this terrific little LScript that helps you put together complementary and related tints for your lighting designer if you don't want to have to think about it. Gary describes it this way:

"It's a generic Layout plug that automates color theory color calculations (complementary, triadic, split complementary, and double split complementary) and assigns the results to lights of your choosing."

When you install and run the script lightdesign.lsc, you'll get a colorful interface.

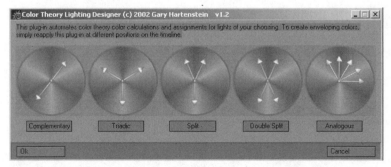

Figure 16.15: The Color Theory Lighting Designer interface. (See color image.)

207

This interface provides you with the option of selecting between five different color selection methods. The colored images above each button describe how each color selection method works. Complementary, for example, will select color for two lights. You pick the color for the first light of your choosing, and the second color is automatically selected from the opposite side of the color wheel and assigned to the second light of your choice. The other four methods work exactly the same: You select the first color and all the other colors are calculated automatically. The colors are added to the lights of your choice.

When you select one of the methods and click one of the buttons, a second interface is presented.

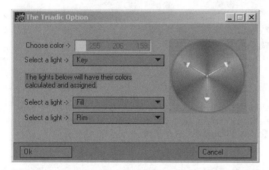

Figure 16.16: The Triadic Option interface. (See color image.)

In this case, I have chosen the Triadic method. As you can see, you select the color for the first light (you can select any light from the drop-down) and the colors for the second two lights will be calculated and added automatically.

> **Note:** You will be notified if you don't have enough lights in the scene for the selected method.

> **Note:** The Analogous method is also known as Related Tint.

Virtual Darkroom

Virtual Darkroom is an image filter plug-in that comes with LightWave.

This plug-in is often ignored by most artists, but it provides serious post-processing capabilities. If you know anything about photography, you'll know that film can be "pushed" or "pulled" if it has been exposed improperly or abnormally so that additional information can be extracted from the photosensitive surface. LightWave's Virtual Darkroom allows you to do the same thing to your LightWave renders.

Also, when the negative is exposed onto paper, a number of exposure techniques can be used to alter the final image. Virtual Darkroom allows for these techniques as well.

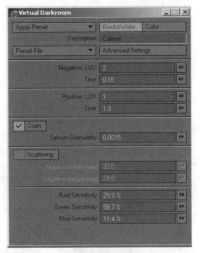

Figure 16.17: The Virtual Darkroom interface.

Quoting again from Kenneth Woodruff's excellent article "LightWave's 'Full Precision' Renderer and You" (see the appendix), you will see that this image filter plug-in is particularly useful for artists rendering FP (floating-point) frames or wishing to make fine "exposure" adjustments to their RGB frames without altering the lighting in the scene.

"This complex plug-in can be used to control the exposure of HDR images, while adding some film artifacts like grain and halo which may enhance the image's apparent naturalism.

"The Virtual Darkroom (VDR) simulates the exposure and printing processes for different types of film and paper. It will introduce color shifting, representing the curves in the image in a way that more closely represents specific film types, going as far as applying sepia tones when the film stock has been designed to do so."

If you're serious (and perhaps slightly anal) about beautiful, perfect lighting, you owe it to yourself to become familiar with this plug-in.

Bloom

Bloom is one of my favorite post filters. It's a simple process that can be very subtle and yet really sweeten an image. Bloom is the phenomenon that occurs when a specular hit or light reflection is too bright for the film and seems to "bleed" a little bit, adding more exposure to nearby areas of the image.

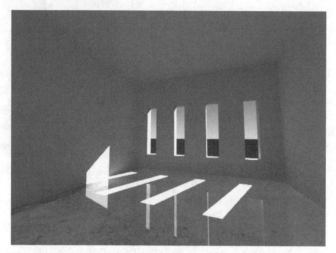

Figure 16.18: Note radiosity on the ceiling and walls.

Remember our old radiosity room from Chapter 12? Here's what it looks like with a little garden variety bloom applied:

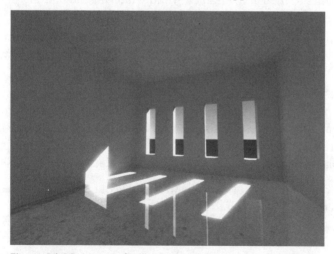

Figure 16.19: Note radiosity on the ceiling and walls with bloom added.

Notice the soft glow around the edges where direct light is hitting the floor and the window ledges. This simulates the overexposure that causes bloom in real photography.

There's something about that softening, bloomy edge that appeals to me. Naturally, this effect is not useful for everything, and if you're working in a production pipeline your compositors will likely add any cool effects like this, but if you are doing your own work or if you're in a small company where you do everything, this pretty little trick can come in handy.

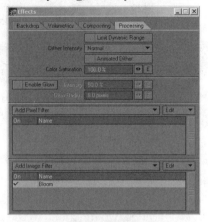

Bloom is an image filter plug-in and is added on the Effects panel.

The three controls, Threshold, Strength, and Size, are simple and obvious. Threshold lets you choose at what brightness the bloom filter is applied to a pixel. Strength, naturally, lets you choose how strong the bloom is, and Size lets you determine how big the bloom becomes in relation to the frame size. It doesn't take very long to become familiar enough with the controls that you'll need to make very few adjustments.

Figure 16.20: The Effects panel.

Figure 16.21: Setting bloom options.

Corona

Corona is another image filter that comes with LightWave. Simply put, Corona is Bloom on steroids.

There is good documentation within the LightWave manual regarding this plug-in, but essentially it allows you to choose exactly how and where to apply the bloom (or whatever other effect you choose) whereas Bloom, being very simple, is also very limited. Check out this plug-in. You can do a lot of crazy things with it.

Figure 16.22: The Corona interface.

BRDF

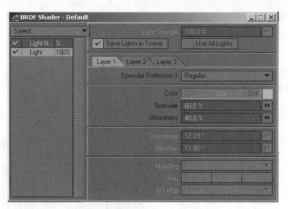

Figure 16.23: BRDF Shader interface.

The BRDF (Bidirectional Reflectance Distribution Function) shader provides two functions to the lighting artist. First, and probably most used, this shader allows you to exclude lights on a per-surface basis. This is very convenient when you don't wish to separate your object into a bunch of objects just to obtain light exclusion using the light exclusion or object exclusion options.

This one feature alone makes BRDF a very handy tool to have in your lighting kit. It's not flashy or expensive in render time. Your geek co-workers won't ooh and aah at your cleverness, but I bet you dollars to doughnuts that most of them have never used it and don't know its great advantages.

The second purpose of the BRDF shader is to simulate a couple of situations where light specularity reflects differently off a surface than "normal" light specularity.

For example, if you had a multilayered surface such as a glass mirror, you might want to use this. Remember, the glass at the front is one reflective surface, and the shiny mirror at the back of the glass is a second reflective layer. Some glass bulb ornaments have paint or silver washed around on the inside, so that the glass surface is one specular surface and the paint or silver on the inside is a second surface. The LightWave manual refers to a car paint job in which the bottom layer is the pigmented paint and that layer is covered with a clear gloss coat. Once again, you end up with multiple layers and therefore would expect multiple specular hits.

Actually, modeling two layers is possible but not desirable, especially when BRDF can simulate the layers for you.

The reflected layers can be either normal or anistropic.

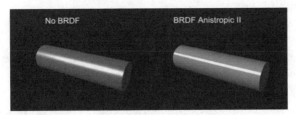

Figure 16.24

An anistropic layer is one that appears "stretched" in one direction because of the grain of the material. Materials such as shiny ribbons, brushed metal, and some silks definitely have specular reflections that appear anistropic. For a full description of the BRDF shader, please see the manual, but be aware that shaders are just as much a part of lighting as are the lights themselves.

Fast Fresnel

Perhaps the most used shader of all time is Fast Fresnel. This shader changes the value of a surface based on its angle to the camera. This shader can be used to great effect in highly stylized work, or subtly to enhance the lighting effect on photo-real objects.

Have you ever noticed that if you look straight at a glass window it does not look as reflective as if you look at the same window at a very shallow angle? The farther you look from the side, the more reflective the window appears. The window is not more reflective at this angle, although that is the perception.

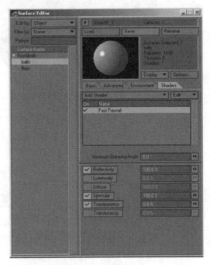

Figure 16.25

Because the area you are viewing is foreshortened by perspective, the apparent density of light is increased. To put it another way, a window that is four feet wide might only look one or two feet wide when you view it from the side. But all the light from the four feet of width is apparently being "compressed" into that apparent one or two feet, making it appear brighter. Get it?

The Fast Fresnel shader helps simulate this.

Take, for example, some balls with the Fast Fresnel shader applied. The part of the balls that are facing straight toward the camera are unchanged; however, the edges that are facing exactly 90 degrees away from the camera are most affected by the shader. You may select between Reflectivity, Luminosity, Diffuse, Specular, Transparency, and Translucency values.

Figure 16.26

Where lighting comes into this picture is usually in the Diffuse and Luminous values (although I'm sure many clever artists out there have thought of many other ways to use this).

If you apply a high luminous value to the surface, it can appear that there is a rim light illuminating the object. Furthermore, this fake rim illumination will always exist around the object regardless of how it rotates or moves in relation to the camera. If you are a fan of modern CG feature films, you may have noticed that this type of effect is used very, very, very, very, very, very, very often to make the CG characters stand out from their backgrounds. Not that there's anything wrong with that.

gMIL

gMIL is a shader-based solution that simulates Backdrop Only global illumination. It is referred to as an "occlusion" or "accessibility" shader. In other words, it measures how much access any portion of the geometry has to a light source and shades based on that information. If, for example, you had a chair sitting on a ground plane and lit with Backdrop Only GI, the top and side surfaces of the chair would be less occluded from the light source than the bottom surfaces. The bottom surfaces have less access to the lighting sources than the top and side surfaces. Get it?

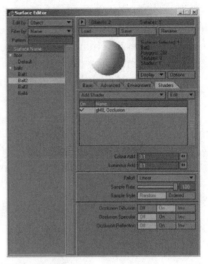

Figure 16.27

Perhaps the single greatest feature of gMIL is that since it is a shader, it can be applied on a per-surface basis, so you need not enable radiosity and also don't have to calculate it for the entire scene. Simply apply the gMIL shader to the surfaces you want to look globally illuminated.

There are a number of other options in gMIL as well, including the ability to invert the occlusion and select between linear and inverse square falloff.

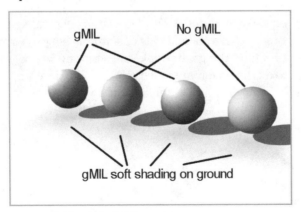

Figure 16.28: gMIL shading.

All the Others

There are numerous other tools available all over the web. Probably the best source for LightWave plug-ins, however, is www.Flay.com. In addition to a massive database of LightWave plug-ins and LScripts, Flay.com covers news, techniques, links, tutorials, and tips. For the new or uninitiated LightWave artist, this web site is an oasis.

Just like anything else out there on the web, the research is up to you. Many times you will find yourself in a situation requiring a unique solution. You can rely, to some extent, on the LightWave community of artists and programmers to help you out. Sometimes the answers (and the tools) will be free; sometimes not. But even if you can't afford a particular tool, there is usually another way to do it — usually a more difficult, painful, and tedious way, certainly, but a way nonetheless.

Rolling Your Own

If you are lucky enough to be a programming wizard, you can just lock yourself in the basement and come up with a dazzling new plug-in or LScript that will change the face of 3D.

On the other hand, if you are like most LightWave artists, you spent all your time learning your art and never bothered with programming. Now there's a solution for artists who want to automate procedures or techniques that they use often. The solution is called LScript Commander.

What Is an LScript?

An LScript is a LightWave Script. A *script* is a series of commands that are executed in order. There are all kinds of scripting languages around for doing all sorts of nifty things. If people had scripting languages, you could get them to do things for you much more easily. Here's an example of what an Nscript (Nick Script) might be if I were run by scripts:

```
Generic
{
Open eyes
Look around
Remove blanket
Put feet on ground
Stand
Open bedroom door
Go out door
```

Turn right
Walk forward seven paces
Turn left
Enter kitchen
Open cupboard
Remove cereal
Pour cereal into bowl
}

An LScript works just like this but commands LightWave to do things instead of commanding me.

LScript Commander

LScript Commander is a Master Class plug-in found under the Scene tab in Master Plug-ins. It is available only within Layout.

Figure 16.29

As a LightWave artist, you command LightWave to do things all the time. You tell it to load an object, and you position the object and maybe rotate it. You add a light and change the position, rotation, intensity, and color of that light. You are executing a series of commands in LightWave. But what if you are a lighting technical director with a series of favorite lighting techniques or special setups that you like to use? You could save your lighting setups in special scenes and then load the scenes, or you could create an LScript to recreate your special lighting setups.

The LScript Commander interface is simple and obvious. The upper half of the LScript Commander interface is a simple text editor where you add all the commands you wish to use in your LScript. In the lower half you have two resources from which you can draw commands for your LScript.

The first tab, Events, contains a listing of all the commands you have executed since you started your LScript Commander session. You can add any command or any sequence of commands from that list simply by selecting (or multiselecting) the command(s) and right-clicking. That will copy the selected commands to the upper half.

Figure 16.30: LScript Commander Events tab.

Figure 16.31: LScript Commander Command Sequence tab.

The second tab, Command Sequence, alphabetically lists all the commands you can use in an LScript so that you can manually add in whatever commands you like. After you use LScript Commander for a while, you will start to understand the syntax and usage of many commands. Who knows? Eventually you may become an LScript guru just by osmosis.

Once the commands are added, from either the Events tab or the Command Sequence tab, you can manually edit them.

When you are finished creating your masterpiece that will alter the face of 3D, you can save the session and execute it from the LScript Commander interface whenever you want. To be really cool, you can convert it into an LScript, give it a name like "3D Revolution," stick it in your LScripts directory, and make it a button on your LightWave interface.

Creating an LScript

Creating your own LScript is really very easy. In this example, we will start with a default scene in LightWave. That means there is a single distant light and a camera already in the scene in default positions. I loaded up the headfroze.lwo file from the companion CD so I could see how my lights looked after I created this simple script. You can load that object too, or you can load any object you wish.

In this LScript, we are going to build a simple three-point lighting setup.

First, I opened up the LScript Commander and pushed it to the side. The purpose of having the Commander open is to make a recording of all the actions you take. Once you have done everything you want to do, you can go back, look at the history list, and selectively copy commands into the text editor to make a nice, clean script. Why select some commands and not others? Not all of the commands you execute will be essential to your script. For example, what if you move a light, then move it a little more? You don't need both movements in the script, just the final position. So you only add the second positional change to the script, disregarding the first. Sure, you could add both if you wanted to, but the first is redundant. It makes the script bigger, which means it takes up more disk space and takes longer to execute. For very small scripts this isn't really a consideration, but keeping your code clean is a good habit to get into right from the start. One day you could be creating huge scripts. You want them to be organized and logical.

So, once I had LScript Commander up and pushed over to the side, I changed the default distant light into a spotlight. I then switched its shadow type to Shadow Map, increased the shadow fuzziness to 2, changed the light color to a light blue, then moved and rotated it into the position I wanted. I then cloned that light, moved the clone to a new position and rotation, and changed its color to a light amber. I then cloned that light, moved it to a new position and rotation, and changed its color to white.

After that, I turned on Low Antialiasing, turned off Adaptive Sampling, and hit F9 to render a sample frame.

After I did all this, I copied all the desired commands from the history list into the text editor by right-clicking each line in the order I wanted them to be executed. The final Commander Script looked like Figure 16.32 in the text editor:

I then cleared my scene, loaded up headfroze.lwo again, then clicked the Execute button on the LScript Commander interface. The script executed flawlessly, making all the changes I outlined in the script.

Of course the true beauty of LScript Commander is that you don't have to know the scripting language in order to make use of the raw power of LScripts. Everything is done for you. You can convert your Commander script text into a real LScript simply by clicking the Session drop-down at the top of the LScript Commander interface and selecting Convert to LScript. Instantly, the text in the editor will be reformatted, all the syntax will be automatically included, and your simple Commander Script file will look something like Figure 16.33.

Figure 16.32

This LScript can be converted back to a Commander script by selecting Convert to CS from the Session drop-down at the top of the LScript Commander interface.

You can save, clear, load, or close a CS session any time using the Session drop-down list. This is also where you can start a new session.

You can have multiple different CS sessions running at the same time. Switch from one session to the other using the Session 1 drop-down list located at the top of the Commander Script interface.

Figure 16.33

Assigning your LScript to a Button

Perhaps one of the most convenient features of the LScript Commander is the Install button found at the top right of the interface. Once your LScript is complete, clicking this button will save the text as an LScript in LightWave's LScript\Macros\ directory and it will automatically be added under the Macros group under Layout's LScript tab. Once the LScript is saved, you can use LightWave's Configure Menus panel to assign a button for this LScript anywhere on the interface you like!

• • •

As you can see by perusing this chapter, there are a multitude of tools, solutions, tricks, tools, and toys that will not only provide you with superior lighting capability, but can also make your life a great deal easier by speeding up or automating those boring, repetitive everyday tasks. If you are working in a production environment, it is difficult to find time to test, learn, and employ most of these tools. You're going to have to trust me on this — they are worth the time! All I can suggest is that you take the best possible advantage of any R&D time you get to work with some of these tools and some of the many others that are available on the web and through commercial purchase.

Chapter 17

Luxigons

This chapter deals with the creation of light arrays using luxigons. By the time you are finished with this chapter, you should have a solid grasp of how to create luxigons in Modeler, import them into Layout, and assign the desired lighting properties to all the luxigon lights.

Perhaps one of the coolest lighting tools to come along in a while is luxigons. I generally assign greatness by a ratio of power vs. simplicity. Luxigons are a perfect example of ridiculous simplicity with terrific power. This tool was added to LightWave in version 7.5. From instantly creating global lighting arrays to building lighting for streets and buildings with a few clicks, it's really an incredibly simple concept very similar to Modeler's Skelegons™. With Skelegons, you can create a skeleton made of special polygons in Modeler, then move the object to Layout and convert all the special Skelegons into bones. With luxigons, you assign light properties to individual polygons or groups of polygons. Then, after importing the polygonal object into Layout, you convert the polygons into lights. The polygons remain and a new light is parented to each polygon, facing in the direction of the polygon normal. Because Modeler's multiply tools are much more sophisticated than those in Layout, large and complex arrays of lights can be created very quickly and easily.

Imagine, for example, if you were building a model of the *Titanic* and had to fill rows of portholes with illumination. There are a number of ways to do this, including using luminosity maps (a very simple way of solving this sort of problem). Or you could load the model into Layout and painstakingly hand-position each light within the porthole. If you find yourself in a situation like this and discover for some reason you really have to use lights in LightWave instead of another solution, then luxigons will quickly become your best friend. You simply select a polygon associated with each porthole (just inside the porthole is best because that's where the light would be positioned), apply luxigons, convert them to lights in Layout, then tweak settings. No hand-positioning of possibly hundreds of individual lights.

A Quick Luxigon Tutorial

In Modeler, create a polygonal object and select some of the polygons. I chose to make a ball and select the upper few rows of polygons. I made sure to flip all the polys so that they were facing inward. The direction of the polygon normal determines the direction of the light when it is created from a luxigon. It may be a good idea to jitter your ball a little before creating the luxigons to guarantee that the lights are not too uniform for a diffused lighting array.

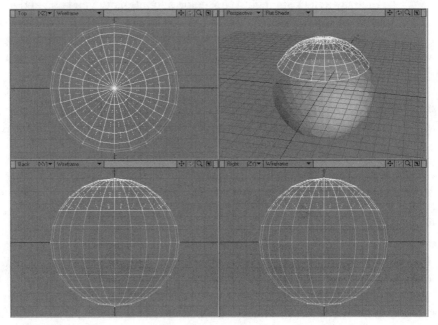

Figure 17.1

On the Setup panel, click the Add Luxigon button in the Layout Tools section.

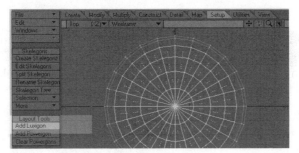

Figure 17.2

You will see the following panel appear.

Figure 17.3

You may select any light type, color, and intensity you wish and it will be applied to all the selected polygons. You may also select whether or not shadows are enabled. If you wish to have lights with different properties, simply select the polygons individually or in groups of similar lights.

> **Note:** The Shadow Type option on the Attach Light to Polygon panel will remain grayed out unless you select Spotlight as the light type, in which case you have the option of choosing between ray-traced shadows or shadow maps.

Once you have saved your object, send it to Layout and switch to Layout. Or, if you do not have LightWave's Hub active, simply open Layout and load your object.

In Layout, make sure you have your luxigon object selected. Select the Additional drop-down in the Utilities tab. (If you are working with luxigons all the time, you probably will have been clever and added a button somewhere in one of your menus. I have a Lighting tab in my Layout interface.) There you will see the ConvertLuxigons command. Select ConvertLuxigons to bring up the following panel.

Figure 17.4

If you have other lights in your scene and you wish to apply the properties of one of those lights to the luxigons, select that light in the Clone Item drop-down. If you wish to keep the settings you set in Modeler, then leave it as [none].

> **Note:** I have discovered, over time, that my best use of luxigons is when I carefully plan their use. This means that I prepare a light in Layout that I want to clone with my luxigon object. There are very few light settings available in Modeler, so naturally it makes sense to create your light in Layout, then import the luxigon object and use the prepared light as the clone source.

When you click OK, all the luxigons will be converted to lights of the type, color, and intensity you specified. In my scene, I converted the top few rows of my ball into luxigons, so now I have a bunch of distant lights all pointed inward toward my object. Hmmm, this looks suspiciously like a clever and cheap replacement for global illumination…

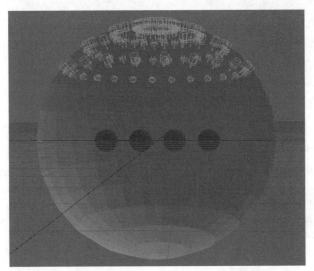

Figure 17.5

Imagine the possibilities. You could apply the famous "spinning light trick" using an entire array of distant lights instead of just one or two. The rendering times will be a little higher, but they will be much faster than radiosity lighting and the results will still be very good. Here is a quick render using my distant light array:

Figure 17.6: A distant light array. (See color image.)

Note: Use this "LightArray" technique judiciously. Too many lights in your array will be redundant and may actually result in *longer* rendering times than radiosity while light arrays with too few lights will result in "stair stepping" in your shadows.

Note: If you are using a large array of lights like this one, keep in mind that the illumination is additive. That is, if you have a hundred lights at 100% luminosity, you have 10,000% illumination where all the lights overlap. You may have to turn your lights down very low. For my scene, I ended up setting all the lights to 1% illumination, which worked out quite nicely.

In other scenarios, you may wish to create a vast array of point lights, not for the illumination but for lens-flare lightbulbs like those discussed in Chapter 15. Simply create the geometry so that you have a polygon wherever you want a light, create the luxigons in Modeler, and then convert them in Layout using a previously set-up point light as a clone item. That way you can convert all your luxigons at once using the lens flare settings of the cloned light.

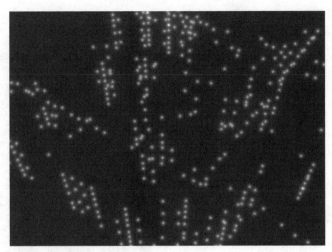

Figure 17.7 (See color image.)

For the image in Figure 17.7, it took me about two minutes to build an array of cubes, randomly select some of the polygons and assign luxigons to them, then import the object into Layout and convert luxigons using a previously made point light as a clone object. With a little work, this could easily be a factory or a city block at night.

Luxigons can really speed up placement of lights as well. Since it is very easy to manipulate polygons in Modeler, you can quickly place a polygon in the precise location where you would like a light, then simply add luxigons and convert it in Layout. Once the luxigon is converted to a light in Layout, the light is parented to the luxigon from which it was created.

Most likely, once your light array is converted in Layout, you will wish to remove polygons that may now be interfering with your lighting. There are several ways to accomplish this. You probably won't simply delete the luxigon polys since all the lights are parented to them. You could add a null object, reparent all the lights to it, and then remove the polygons. This would guarantee that you can still move your array very easily. Or you could replace the luxigon object with a null. Or you could open the Object

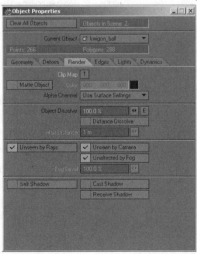

Figure 17.8

Properties panel Render sub-tab and make the luxigon polys invisible by selecting Unseen by Rays, Unseen by Camera, and Unaffected by Fog (if you use fog), and by deselecting Self Shadow, Cast Shadow, and Receive Shadow.

Another method for making the polys disappear is to set Object Dissolve to 100%. This is also found on the Render sub-tab in the Object Properties panel. Or you could switch to the Object Properties panel Edges sub-tab. In this panel, you can set polygon size to 0%, effectively making the polys disappear.

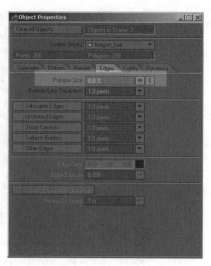

Figure 17.9

This is probably the quickest method for removing the polys from the render, but they will still be visible in the Layout window unless you turn them off in the Scene Editor. If you wish to remove them completely, simply replace them with a null as discussed earlier, or create a small dummy object and use Object Replace.

It is not required that you have your lights parented to anything, however. You can simply unparent the lights from the luxigon polys and delete the polys if you wish.

> **Note:** Remember that if you have Parent in Place turned on (Options panel in Layout) you can unparent an object and have it maintain its position. Parent in Place is also Unparent in Place.

Obviously, this tool immensely speeds up the creation of light arrays in Layout, providing the artist with the full manipulation and multiplication toolset available in Modeler — a powerful combination to be sure.

• • •

You should now understand the process for creating luxigons in Modeler, importing them into Layout, and assigning the light properties you wish for the array. A clever lighting artist will already be thinking up a million new and untried techniques for using this powerful tool.

Figure 1.3

Figure 6.6: McCandless lighting.

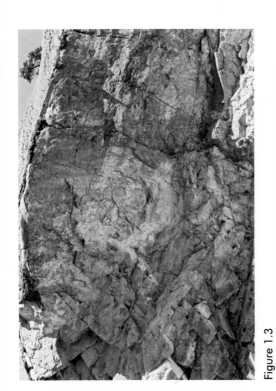

Here is a good example of a highlight in nature. In this example, one could argue that the key light is the highlight, or rim light. Others may say there is no key, just a fill and a rim.

Figure 6.4

Figure 6.8: Three-point lighting.

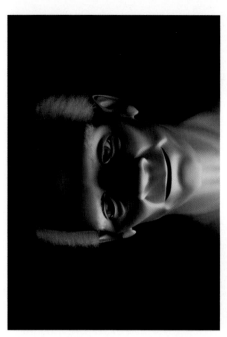

Figure 6.10

In this image, the "bounce" light behaves like radiosity reflected from the floor or road in front of the man, also filling in where lesser experienced lighting artists might be tempted to use ambient intensity — a big no-no in most cases.

Figure 6.12: Footlight.

Figure 6.13: Complementary tint.

Figure 6.11: Sidelight.

Figure 6.14: Related tint.

Figure 8.3: The HSV <--> RGB panel.

Figure 8.4: The Tint & Shade panel.

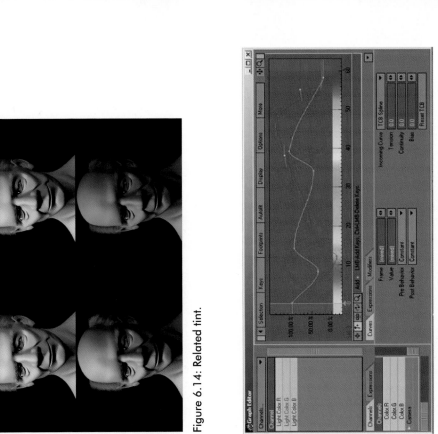

Figure 7.2: The LightWave RGB Color Graph Editor.

Figure 8.5: The Wavelength panel.

Figure 8.6: The Kelvin panel.

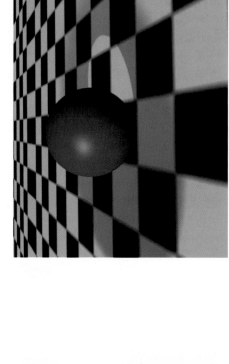

Figure 11.14: If the spotlight had a positive intensity value, the shadow area behind the ball would not receive illumination from the spotlight. Since the spotlight has a negative intensity value, the shadowed area behind the ball is not having light removed and you get a sort of "photo-negative" effect.

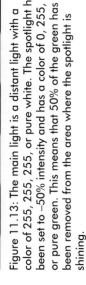

Figure 11.13: The main light is a distant light with a color of 255, 255, 255, or pure white. The spotlight has been set to −50% intensity and has a color of 0, 255, 0, or pure green. This means that 50% of the green has been removed from the area where the spotlight is shining.

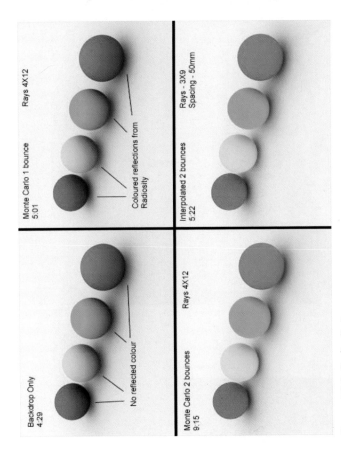

Figure 12.3: Radiosity types.

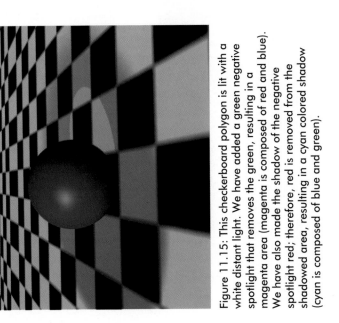

Figure 11.15: This checkerboard polygon is lit with a white distant light. We have added a green negative spotlight that removes the green, resulting in a magenta area (magenta is composed of red and blue). We have also made the shadow of the negative spotlight red; therefore, red is removed from the shadowed area, resulting in a cyan colored shadow (cyan is composed of blue and green).

Figure 13.3: LightGen render.

Figure 14.10: Using HyperVoxels and radiosity.

Figure 13.2: Render on left with HDR image on right.

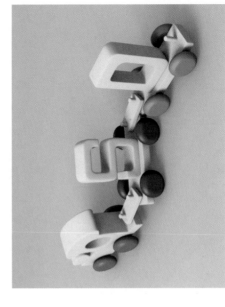

Figure 16.2: An image created using area light and ray tracing in LightWave.

Figure 16.1: An image created using Shadow Designer.

Figure 15.1: Lens flares.

Figure 15.4: Using lens flares.

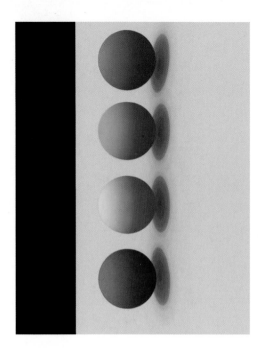

Figure 16.15: The Color Theory Lighting Designer interface.

Figure 16.16: The Triadic Option interface.

Figure 17.6: A distant light array.

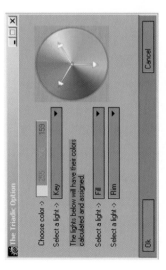

Figure 17.7

C-8

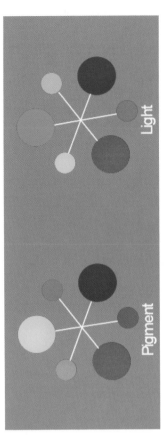

Figure 19.3

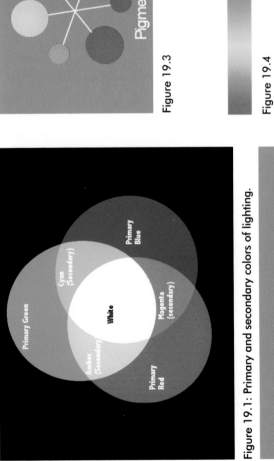

Figure 19.1: Primary and secondary colors of lighting.

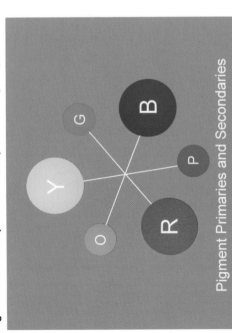

Pigment Primaries and Secondaries

Figure 19.2

Figure 19.4

Low Saturation

High Saturation

Figure 19.5

Low Value

High Value

Figure 19.6

Color model
showing the
interaction of
hue, saturation,
and value.

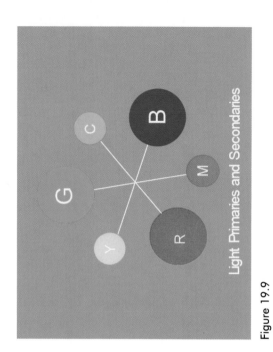

Figure 19.7

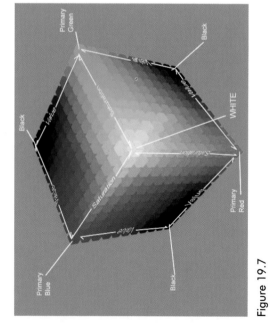

Figure 19.8

Light Primaries and Secondaries

Figure 19.9

Figure 19.10

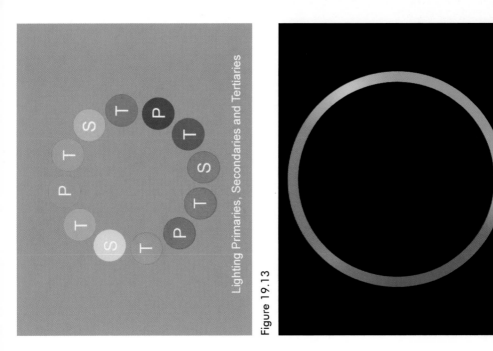

Figure 19.11:
A graphic representation of all three light colors.

% of Transmission

Wavelength in NanoMetres
380   420   460   500   540   580   620   660   700

Figure 19.12:
A typical wavelength transmission graph for a lighting filter.

% of Transmission

Wavelength in NanoMetres
380   420   460   500   540   580   620   660   700

Lighting Primaries, Secondaries and Tertiaries

Figure 19.13

Figure 19.14: Color wheel showing hues.

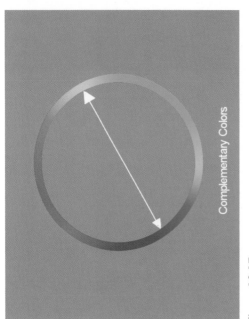

Figure 19.15

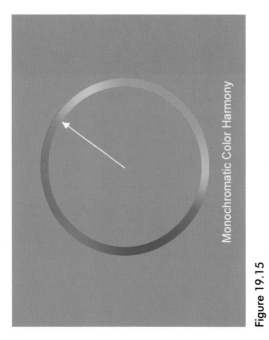

Figure 19.16

Figure 19.17

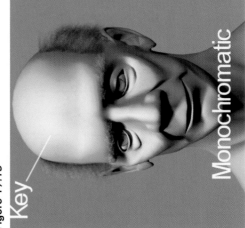

Figure 19.18

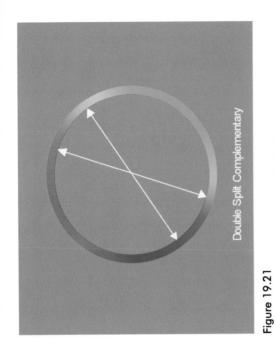

Figure 19.21

Double Split Complementary

Key 1
Key2
Fill1
Fill2

Double Split Complementary

Figure 19.22

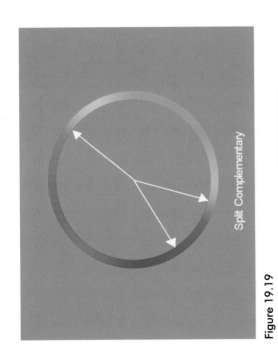

Figure 19.19

Split Complementary

Key
Fill 1
Fill2

Split Complementary

Figure 19.20

C-13

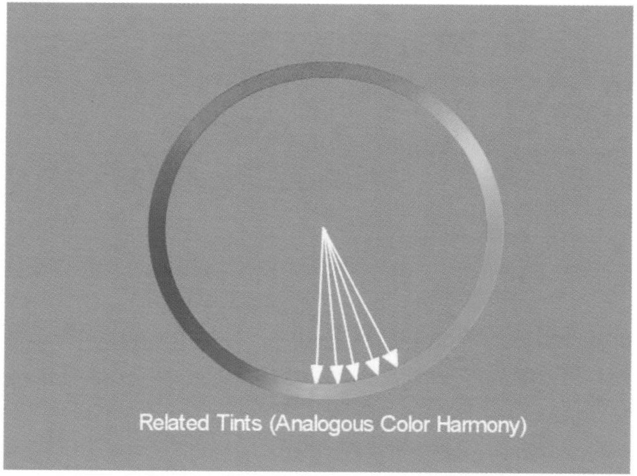

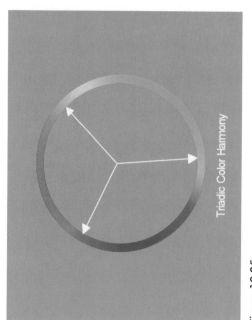

Figure 19.23

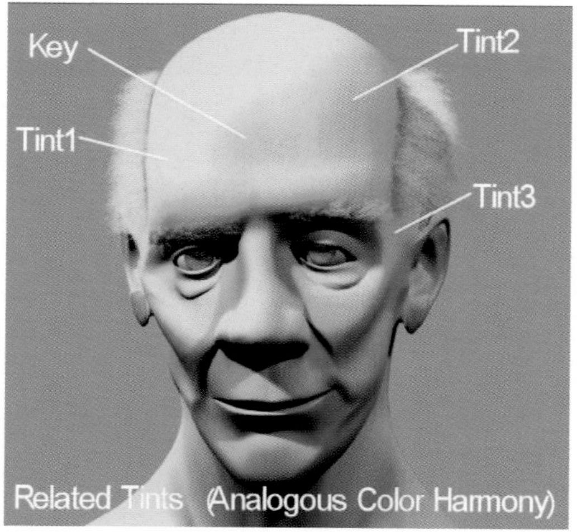

Related Tints (Analogous Color Harmony)

Figure 19.25

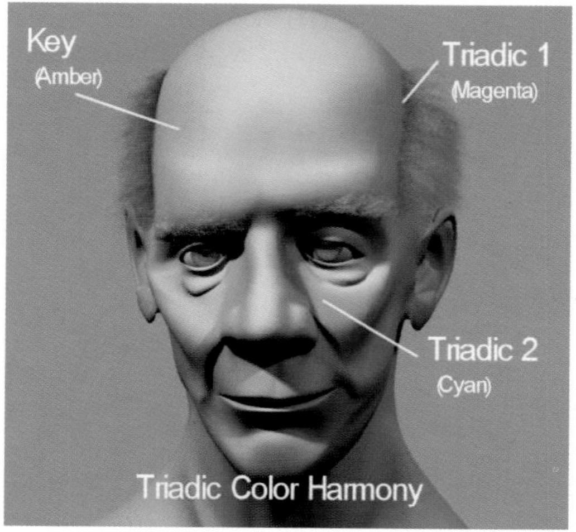

Triadic Color Harmony

Figure 19.24

Related Tints (Analogous Color Harmony)

Key
Tint1
Tint2
Tint3

Figure 19.26

Triadic Color Harmony

Key
(Amber)
Triadic 1
(Magenta)
Triadic 2
(Cyan)

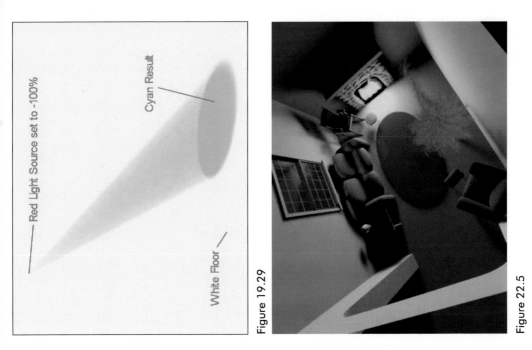

Figure 19.29

Figure 22.5

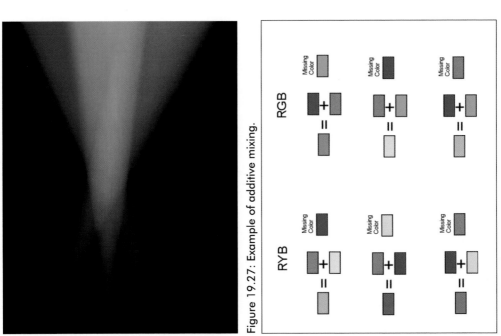

Figure 19.27: Example of additive mixing.

Figure 19.28

Aztec Calendar
(Nicholas Boughen)

Dune Buggy
(Nicholas Boughen)

Part III

Creating Lighting

Cool vs. Real, or "What Separates Hobbyists from Pros"

One of the great things about working in 3D is the instant gratification you get from creating and rendering something cool. No doubt if you are just starting out in the world of 3D, you will spend a lot of time making cool creations, showing your friends, boring your spouse or partner, and forcing your family to say "cool." If you are on the path to an animation career or if you already are a professional, you probably know that mere "cool factor" doesn't usually make the cut anymore. If you are a serious artist, you know that the best creation comes with hard work and a great deal of patience. This means it's time to forget about instant gratification. It's time to realize that your very best work is going to take your very best effort and a substantial chunk of time. But when you're done, the "cool" you hear from friends and family won't be obligatory; it will be genuine. Your mother will start telling her friends about your successes. Your father will tape the first TV series you work on so he can pause the tape on the credits and show his friends your name.

Becoming a professional CG artist is not an easy road. Being a world-class artist is not for the lazy or impatient. But if you have patience and the drive to make it, you will be able to count yourself among the top names in CG.

Design Considerations, Both Technical and Artistic

Designing lights for a shot requires both technical and artistic considerations. If you are lighting a CG element for compositing onto a photographic background plate, your considerations are likely to be more technical than artistic. In other words, you are likely required to simply analyze and simulate the lighting in the plate. But if you are lucky enough to be designing lighting for a full CG scene, everything you know about lighting and art will come into play.

Technical considerations include placement, direction, and color of the lights. You must also consider such things as:

- Camera placement
- What lighting is used in a background plate
- What tricks you can employ to reduce rendering times
- How tolerant the CG element is to lighting cheats
- How much time you have to complete the shot and its render
- What, exactly, the supervisor or director is looking for in your CG element

These things and more are covered in the following chapters. It is my hope that you will acquire not only technical expertise, but also an understanding of the process. This understanding will make you a more valuable artist, enabling you to foresee problems, plan your actions, and bring in your work on the project on time and budget. You see, there is much more to being a good artist than creating good art. Business environments require that we interact with many other people. Your competence as a communicator and a problem-solver are as important as your artistic talent.

This part of the book contains tutorials explaining a variety of techniques. My hope is that the tutorials do more than simply teach, but enable you to see the underlying principles of the techniques. If this is successful, you will be able to design your own techniques as needed. If you can walk away from this book with that skill, then I will consider this work a success.

Chapter 18

Intent and Purpose

This chapter deals briefly with the artistic concepts of intent and purpose. These are less esoteric and more obvious than such concepts as "style" and "art." Intent refers to both the intent of the script or scenario and your intentions to the story as a designer. Purpose refers to the practical justification of your lighting design. Each lighting tool and technique must have a specific design purpose. By the time you finish this chapter you should have a good grasp of the importance of both intent and purpose in your lighting designs.

In a production environment, the first step to lighting design is script analysis. In other words, you read the script, try to find out what story the author is telling and how it is told, then decide how you want to interpret that story or, if you are not the director, find out how the director wishes to interpret the story. Any good lighting designer is going to go into a meeting with a director having some idea of the direction he or she wishes to go with the lighting. An even better designer will enter the meeting with two or three completely different design concepts for the project. Having multiple ideas for the director to choose from is often a good strategy for heading off complete rejection. If a director has only one idea to choose from, you can almost guarantee major changes. If the director has two or three ideas to look at, there is a better chance that she will select one of your directions rather than taking a completely different one.

If you are lucky, you will have a director who wants to hear your ideas before making any final decisions. The obvious bonus here is that you will have real artistic input into the final look of the shot. In another scenario, the director may have an already completed vision of the final product. You may end up simply providing the technical expertise to accomplish someone else's artistic vision. But you still need to know how exactly to do that.

Understanding Artistic and Emotional Intent

When you first read the script, you will need to break it down into scenes, if it is not already done for you. Scenes are all the individual measures of the script, each of which tells a small part of the story. Scenes usually consist of individual time spans during which a specific kernel of information is revealed about the story. For example, the three witches in *Macbeth* have their own scenes, each of which occurs in its own locale during its own time period, and is separate from the other scenes. Each delivers specific information to the audience. Each begins and ends logically and ties to the next and previous scenes in some way. Within each scene there may be a number of different shots. It is likely that most of the shots in each scene will have a similar emotional tone. You will want to make note of whether a scene is happy or sad, gloomy or foreboding, exciting or disgusting. These are the cornerstones of your lighting design. It is your job to assist the storyteller and the audience in experiencing the story as fully as possible.

After you understand the feeling of a scene, your next job is to look at the technical requirements of the scene. Back to basics. Is it interior or exterior? Is it in a basement or on the roof of a 100-story skyscraper?

Now that you have the two key elements of lighting in your grasp — the emotional and the technical — it is your job to find a way to convey the first, without upsetting the second. For example, if I had a very sad, morose scene and I wished to make the audience feel the despair of the characters in the story, I would probably first think of using muted colors, low lighting levels, and perhaps some odd angles to make the whole scene uncomfortable. But what if the scene takes place at midday at a carnival? What if it is on a California beach? I seem to be stuck with the light provided by reality, and there seems to be little I can do to help the story with lighting. But if I put on my thinking cap, I will discover that there are many subtle changes I can make to these two scenarios, especially the carnival scenario, that will add surrealism to the scene. This surrealism will support the negative emotional intent of the scene. If you have ever experienced a real crisis, you will remember the feeling of surreality that accompanied the event. This is easy to accomplish in a carnival. I can choose unusual colors and angles. I don't have to mute colors and intensities. In fact, I can counterpoint the emotion by adding brighter, more colorful lights, creating a deeper gulf between the environment and the tone of the scene. Sometimes going in the opposite direction will have a deeper effect on the scene than trying to create lighting of the same tone as the scene.

The key element here is that you, as the lighting designer, are purposeful with the placement and settings of your lighting tools. You must grasp the emotional intent of the script and implement your lighting deliberately in a way that you feel accomplishes or helps accomplish the goals of the storyteller.

What Is Your Light's Motivation? (Justifying Choices)

The objects in your scene are illuminated by one or more light sources. Each of those sources must be justified. Now in the world of photorealism, this usually means each light source must have a real-world counterpart. In other words, if you're making sunlight the key light in your scene and blue skylight the fill, then the background image should be illuminated primarily by the sun and secondarily by a nice blue sky. The angle of the sunlight on your CG elements should also be the same angle as that in the background image. If there are no additional light sources in the background plate, then there should be no additional lighting sources in your CG scene. Every simulated light source must be justified by the existence of a real light source.

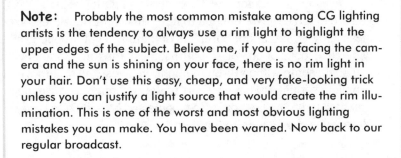

Note: Probably the most common mistake among CG lighting artists is the tendency to always use a rim light to highlight the upper edges of the subject. Believe me, if you are facing the camera and the sun is shining on your face, there is no rim light in your hair. Don't use this easy, cheap, and very fake-looking trick unless you can justify a light source that would create the rim illumination. This is one of the worst and most obvious lighting mistakes you can make. You have been warned. Now back to our regular broadcast.

In the world of practical reality, however, there are numerous problems with such an exacting and unforgiving rule. Often we receive background images (plates) where the existing lighting will not allow us to illuminate our CG elements in a way that will present the story elements we wish to present. Sometimes we need to "beautify" the shot by adding subtle highlights and areas of focus without the physical justification for those light sources. Sometimes your director or VFX supervisor will just tell you to darn well do it (that's justification). Not everyone is

233

concerned with whether or not something is physically possible. And sometimes, it's just not a good idea to argue with your boss.

So, as artists who are paid to do what our overlords wish, we will find ways to stretch reality in an attempt to provide the desired effect without completely rewriting the laws of physics. In general, and where possible, a lighting artist should, however, make every attempt to place light sources only as justified by the plate. Failing that, try to get creative with your justification: "There *could* be a light over there, or up there, even though we don't see it in the plate." That's justification too.

If, on the other hand, you are designing lights for an all-CG scene, then you have a world of possibilities. As the lighting designer, you should have access to the other designers and to the director to discuss, beforehand, where lights will be placed for the best possible lighting. You will likely be able to discuss with the scenic designer, for example, just where a window might be placed behind the action so you can adorn the foreground objects with that magic halo of light (the evil rim light) that almost never happens in reality. Or you might contribute to the story in ways that enhance lighting. Take, for example, a scene on a stormy day. It's raining hard. "Here's a perfect opportunity for effect lighting," you think to yourself. "How about some lightning outside!" you spout. Lightning can be used in a variety of ways to load the scene with tension and foreboding or to surprise us with the skeleton in the dark closet that we didn't see before.

Designing lights for all-CG scenes is a lighting artist's playground. If you are ever fortunate enough to have this opportunity, let loose. Throw ideas in every direction. Sure, lots of them will get dropped and some will evoke looks of horror — but that's half the fun! Some of your ideas will stick, some will go through minor changes, and others will need complete rethinks. That's all part of the challenge. Don't expect your first idea to be the best one. Be flexible and be willing to consider new ideas, even if they aren't your own.

Chiaroscuro: The Use of Light and Shadow

Chiaroscuro is a method of painting invented in Italy during the Renaissance. Artists such as Leonardo da Vinci and Raphael used this method, a defined set of rules really, to determine how light affected the objects in their paintings. The rules were based on light approaching the object from a predetermined direction. The word "chiaroscuro" comes from two Italian words: *chiaro* meaning bright or clear and *oscuro* meaning dark or obscure. My favorite master of chiaroscuro is Rembrandt, whose paintings are made deep and foreboding by the deep shadows and dark backgrounds that make his human subjects nearly leap off the canvas with life. In my opinion, it is Rembrandt's mastery of light and shadow that defines his breathtaking style.

Your use of light can define the entire style of your CG artwork too.

Think about a brightly lit room. Sunlight streams through the tall windows and radiates from the high ceiling. The air is warm and still. The room is silent. Leather-bound books line the walls and an old oak desk sits at an angle in front of a stone fireplace.

Picture this same room at night. Moonlight streams through the high windows. There are no lights on in the room, but the oak desk is in silhouette from the dying embers of an unattended fire. The room is nearly black but for the silver-rimmed, moonlit furniture and the pale, orange glow silhouetting the desk.

Both of these scenes offer interesting lighting challenges. Lighting alone can give strong feelings to these scenes; the day scene makes me think of ages of dust, perhaps particles in the air creating a volumetric effect to the light streaming in the window. I see yellowish, amber radiosity as the light bounces off the natural wood floor and the oak desk. In my mind the room is silent in the afternoon, unused, but warm by the day's sunlight. By night, the room is still warm from the dying fire. The fire tells us the room is not derelict, the house is occupied, and the inhabitants are probably now asleep. The moonlight tells us that the weather is clear, and may be a hint as to the time of year. There is a sense of activity here as we survey in the moonlight the papers strewn across the desk, the work left unfinished, to be completed another day.

Do you see how easy it is to enhance a story with a few simple lights using basic colors?

Some Examples

The following examples demonstrate the most basic interpretation of these scenes. This is by no means the only way, nor the most interesting way, of accomplishing these lighting objectives. My purpose here is to provide a basic understanding that you can use to grow and develop your own much more interesting ideas. Besides, if I wrote down *all* my good ideas, then everyone would probably get to be a better lighting artist than me. And *then* where would I be?

A Pleasant Scene

Typically, a pleasant scene will strike the audience with its warmth, brightness, gentle mood, and familiarity. Take a look at the following image and see if you can pick out the lighting techniques used to make the image more pleasant.

Figure 18.1

Here we have a toy horse sitting in front of a fireplace. The scene is illuminated by a soft glow from the flames. A highlight has been added to both sides of the toy, one side to represent illumination from the fireplace, and the other to represent moonlight entering from the window above the couch to the left. (If this were a color image, you would see that the fire highlight is amber and the moon highlight is blue.) It is a simple scene utilizing only three lights. Both highlights are spotlights and the fireplace light is an area light.

The room feels warm and welcoming. The moonlight adds a sense of magic to the scene. The additional highlights add subtle form and color to enrich the scene.

A Sad Scene

Let's take the same scene and apply a few changes to make it into a sad scene.

Figure 18.2

First, and this is not a lighting thing, I changed the camera angle. Instead of the previous shot, which had a more "toy" point of view, I've raised the camera and pointed it downward for a more "human" POV. This makes the toy seem more alone and lonely in the middle of the floor.

As for the lighting, I removed the warmth from the scene by turning off the fireplace and enhancing the cool moonlight. Now the only lights in the room are the cold, lonely moonlight from outside and its radiosity source, which is softly illuminating the surrounding room. I think it gives a real sense of sadness and loneliness.

A Frightening Scene

Perhaps the simplest way of making a scene tense, strange, or frightening is to use colors, angles, and intensities that immediately strike the audience as unnatural, unusual, or strange.

Figure 18.3

In this image, I added a gobo to the moonlight source to create a window shadow with overexaggerated, or forced, perspective. This, coupled with the long shadows created by the low angle and also by the banking or "Dutch" angle of the camera, serves to make the scene seem quite strange and perhaps even frightening. It is difficult, without the context of a story, to look at this image and find it frightening, but what if the light through the window had been a flash of lightning revealing something other than a toy horse? It could quite easily jolt you out of your seat.

• • •

Any artist, before laying brush to canvas, intends to create a specific image. Within that image, each element has a purpose. Consider these as you are designing your lights and you will sidestep the many pitfalls of lighting design such as clutter, overdesign, and the inappropriate use of light.

If you design with both intent and purpose, your design is likely to be streamlined, elegant, and simple, not to mention illuminating. Good luck with your search for lighting perfection. Let me know when you get there — I hope I won't be far behind!

You should now have at least a basic understanding of the importance of intent in your work and purpose for each of your design elements. While not all of these concepts may be clear to you yet, they will become so as you begin to work on telling your own stories with your design work.

Chapter 19

Color Mixing

In this chapter we discuss what makes colored light and what makes colored pigments. We also look at the relationship between mixtures of light and pigment as well as the color wheel and principles of color mixing. By the time you are finished reading this chapter, you should have a grasp of how color wavelengths interact to create the many colors available for our CG palette.

Two Types of Color

Understanding color mixing begins with understanding two distinct principles:

- Light such as the color of sunlight, neon signs or fireworks. You must understand what makes a particular color of light appear to be that color.
- Pigments such as paints, dyes, fabrics, stone and wood. You must understand what makes pigments appear to be the color that they are.

The Color of Light

Light is composed of a wide range of electromagnetic radiation from heat sources. Most light radiated by these heat sources is not visible to the human eye. There is a very small range of light between about 0.4 micrometers and 0.7 micrometers that is visible to the human eye. Light at the top of the visible range with wavelengths shorter than 0.4 micrometers falls into the ultraviolet range. Light at the bottom of the visible range with wavelengths longer than 0.7 micrometers falls into the infrared range. Neither ultraviolet nor infrared light is visible to the human eye. Below infrared light lie the ranges of microwaves and radio waves. Above ultraviolet lie the ranges of x-rays and gamma rays. Lower band radio waves can be found in the frequency range of 300 meters or more while gamma rays are in the frequency range of 0.003 nanometers. So you can see that the range of light in the universe is incredibly large, and of that enormous range, the bit that we can see is very, very small.

Within the human visible range of light, the color spectrum extends from red to violet going sequentially through orange, yellow, green, and blue respectively. Remember your elementary school lesson about rainbows? ROYGBIV: red, orange, yellow, green, blue, indigo, and violet. The rainbow is simply white light that has been refracted and split up into its component light frequencies. Or, to put it another way, when you take all of the frequencies of visible light and mix them together, the result is pure white light.

So what does this mean? Well, to start with, there are three primary colors in light: red, green, and blue. By mixing these three colors, you should be able to create any color shade visible in the world.

There is a very easy way to visualize why colored light is colored. First, think of white light as "whole" light. It is made up of a mixture of every color or wavelength in the visible spectrum. Any individual color like green, pink, or blue is that "whole" light with some wavelengths or colors missing.

Pink light, for example, is white light with most of the green ranges missing. Only red and blue ranges remain, and when you mix red and blue light, you get pink. If you were to put a red colored filter, or "gel," in front of that pink light, the light coming out the other side of that gel would be mostly red. The gel filters out most of the light in the blue range of the visible spectrum.

This is called *subtractive* color mixing. It may take you a while to get your head around exactly how it works, but once you do, you will be able to easily mix any colors you desire, not only on the color palette but by shining the light from two or more lights together, including lights of both positive intensity (for additive mixing) and negative intensity (for subtractive mixing).

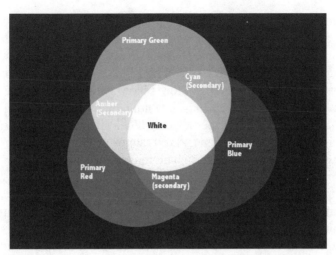

Figure 19.1: Primary and secondary colors of lighting. (See color image.)

To create the image in Figure 19.1, I placed three spotlights over a white polygon and aimed them so that they would overlap. One light had an RGB value of 255, 0, 0 (pure red) and the other two were 0, 255, 0 and 0, 0, 255 (pure green and pure blue, respectively). Where any two of the colors mix together, a secondary color is created. In lighting, the three secondary colors are amber, cyan, and magenta. In the center area where all three primary colors overlap, the light is white because all the ranges of visible light have been mixed back together. Remember, we get closer to white by adding missing colors. We make a color more pure by subtracting colors.

The Color of Pigments

Pigments are colors that apply to materials. Paint, for example, is a pigment. So is color dye and ink. Every material in the world — rocks, cloth, leaves, metal, paper, everything — has at least one pigment. Materials absorb some wavelengths and reflect others. Different materials absorb and reflect different wavelengths. This is why different materials have different colors.

Where light colors are identified by the light *wavelengths* transmitted, pigments are determined by which wavelengths are absorbed and which wavelengths are reflected.

If, for example, you shine white light onto a piece of white paper, the illuminated area of the paper appears white. This is because the full spectrum of visible light is being shone at the paper and the paper is not absorbing any wavelengths but reflecting all of them. Materials that are white absorb very few or none of the visible wavelengths of light.

If, on the other hand, you shine a white light at a blue piece of paper, the illuminated area of the paper appears blue. This is because the paper absorbs all or most of the green and red ranges of the visible light spectrum but reflects all or most of the blue range of the visible light spectrum. Since only blue light is reflected, your eyes only receive the blue portion of the white light that is being shone on the paper.

If you shine a blue light at a white piece of paper, the illuminated area, again, appears blue. Although the white piece of paper reflects all wavelengths, the only ones being shone on the paper are blue, and therefore only blue light is visible.

This means that different materials appear to be different colors to us because different physical materials tend to either absorb or reflect certain visible wavelengths. Our eyes perceive these different wavelengths and interpret them as different colors.

One would not expect that there are two kinds of pigments. But in fact, pigments in the real world behave one way, while pigments in the computer world behave a different way.

Pigments in the Real World

In the real world, pigments have three primary colors: red, yellow, and blue. If you mix red and yellow paint, you will get orange. If you mix yellow and blue paint, you will get green. If you mix red and blue paint, you will get purple.

In other words, pigment secondary colors are orange, green, and purple, where secondary colors in lighting are amber, cyan, and magenta.

If you have ever tried to mix paint colors, you are probably familiar with these simple color mixes.

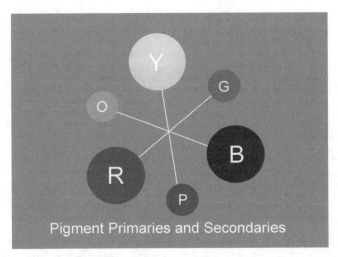

Figure 19.2 (See color image.)

Figure 19.2 shows a color wheel displaying the three primary pigment colors (the large circles) and the secondaries that can be achieved by mixing the primaries in equal proportions. So we know that pigments in the real world mix very differently than light does. Take a look at both color wheels side by side.

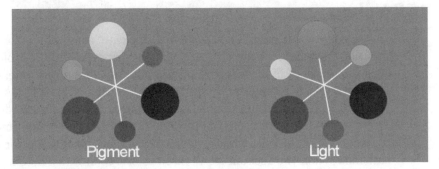

Figure 19.3 (See color image.)

Pigments in LightWave

One might expect that mixing pigment colors and mixing lighting colors in LightWave would adhere to the physical realities of the real world as much as possible. But there is a problem inherent in trying to mix pigment colors on a computer monitor. The problem is that computer monitors, and television monitors for that matter, create colors by mixing red, green, and blue picture elements, or *pixels*. So any color mixed on a computer is going to be created using the RGB lighting color model as opposed to the RYB pigment color model.

"Why then," you might ask, "bother learning about the RYB pigment color model?" Because you will be mixing colors with pigments in the computer. You may be trying to mix colors to simulate a background plate if you are working in visual effects. It is essential for you to understand the physically correct relationships between light and pigment.

What you must keep in mind is that "real-world" pigment primaries are red, yellow, and blue, and "real-world" lighting primaries are red, green, and blue.

LightWave's pigment primaries are red, green, and blue, and LightWave's lighting primaries are also red, green, and blue.

It's a funny way of creating pigment colors, but at least this way you only have to think about one way of mixing colors and one set of primaries.

Those of you who have experience mixing paints will understand exactly why I feel this is kind of strange. Those of you who have only mixed colors using computer software will probably wonder what planet I'm from. The bottom line is that if you can mix the color you want for your surface textures, and if you can mix the color you want for your light, and if your light and your texture interact in the way you desire, then there's really no problem, is there?

RGB Values

Any color you choose in LightWave's color picker, whether it is for a lighting instrument or for a texture, will be composed of three 8-bit values, one for each of the three primary colors, red, green, and blue. 8-bit values are used because, in binary language, a value of 1111 1111 is equal to 255. If you count from 0, an 8-bit range accounts for 256 discrete values. Now, for each color, a value of 0 means there is no amount of that color in the mix, while a value of 255 means all of that color is in the mix. When you account for all three colors, each with a potential value in the mix ranging from 0 to 255, the number of possible combinations is calculated by multiplying 256 x 256 x 256, resulting in 16,777,216 possible combinations of color. This is why modern computer monitors and video cards are advertised as being capable of displaying over 16 million colors.

Following are some typical RGB values and their associated colors:

R	G	B	Color
0	0	255	Blue (primary)
0	255	0	Green (primary)

R	G	B	Color
255	0	0	Red (primary)
255	255	0	Yellow (secondary)
0	255	255	Cyan (secondary)
255	0	255	Magenta (secondary)

It is easy to see how so many different colors can be mixed so quickly using this method.

Floating-Point Color Values

Using 8-bit values for lighting color has its limitations. Since the ranges exist only from 0 (no color) to 255 (full color), there is no ability to access values below or above that range. Imagine, for example, you have a red Ferrari model and you have colored it with an RGB value of 255, 0, 0 (pure red). You put it in a showroom and shine some nice track lights on it. You want the car to look well-lit, so you turn up the light values to 100%. The lighting intensity level is a multiplier of the car's color. In other words, if the light is at 100%, then the surface, which is pure red, is showing its natural, pure color.

So what happens if you decide to put the car outside in the sunlight? Say your sun's intensity level is set to 150% or even 200% or more. You can't see more light than fully lit, can you? Well, now that floating-point values exist, you sure can. Instead of using a limited range from 0 to 255, decimal-based values are used, ranging from 0 to 1.0 where 0 is no color and 1.0 is full, pure color. The beauty of this value system is that you can also have a value of 1.5 or 2 or even 4 or more if you like. Also, with 8-bit values, you can have a value of 75 or 76 but not 75.5. There is no intermediate value. With decimal ranges, you can make much finer adjustments to your RGB values. Furthermore, the color value will not become "clipped" or washed out, thereby losing image information.

LightWave's full precision rendering engine maintains all the lighting and texturing information for every pixel without clipping. Unlike the "old" RGB values containing only 8 bits per channel, you now have 32 bits of data for each RGB channel and the alpha channel as well. Images using full precision rendering contain so much information that only a small portion of it is visible at any one time on your monitor. Using post processes, you can choose later what range of the data you wish to use, provided you save your images in an FP format. For more information on full precision rendering and LightWave's full precision formats, see the LightWave manual or read Kenneth Woodruff's "LightWave's 'Full Precision' Renderer and You," included in the appendix.

Hue, Saturation, and Value

Using the Hue, Saturation, and Value, or HSV, method of mixing colors can give us a different understanding or a different way of looking at color and how it mixes.

You can mix any color using the HSV method that you can mix using the RGB method. If you have taken some time to play with the LightWave HSV<- ->RGB Color Picker you will notice that as you change any of the H, S, or V values numerically, the RGB values also change. This is because that while HSV and RGB are different types of values, they are linked together.

Hue

Hue refers to the pure color that is being chosen. Any color along the visible spectrum of light is considered a hue, whether it is a primary or a mixed color. Figure 19.4 demonstrates the range of hues available to the human eye.

Figure 19.4 (See color image.)

You can see all the colors of the rainbow in this spectrum. Each of these wavelengths is a component of white light. In other words, if we were to mix them together again, we would produce white light.

But we are able to mix much lighter and much darker colors than just those visible on this spectrum.

Saturation

When we think of *saturation* we think of how *much* of a color is incorporated. We think of a highly saturated color as being pure and deep. For example, if we say that the light coming from a lighting instrument is a highly saturated red, then we think of a deep red, perhaps even primary. We think of less saturated colors as being paler and closer to white. A very light pink, for example, would be considered a low-saturation red. This is exactly how saturation works in the HSV model of color picking.

This is a very interesting way of demonstrating saturation, since it is actually opposite to how it really occurs. We know, for example, that white light is "whole" with all the primaries at full saturation. If you remove all the green and all the blue, then you have primary red. Certainly the final color is a highly saturated red, but is primary red a more saturated color than white? White is actually a highly saturated mix of the primaries.

However, for the purposes of individual hues, we will accept that any color that moves toward white is less saturated.

High Saturation   **Low Saturation**

Figure 19.5 (See color image.)

Value

Value works similarly to saturation except that instead of the hue moving toward white, the hue moves toward black. A higher *value* color is considered to be closer to the pure hue. For example, a pure cyan is considered to be a color of a very high value. If that color were to become very dark, getting closer to black, then that color would be considered to have a very low value.

High Value   **Low Value**

Figure 19.6 (See color image.)

In the business of lighting, value is tied to light intensity, as we know that a light that is colored black emits no light. As a matter of fact, if you set a light to 1,000,000% intensity, set that light's color to a value of 0, and shine it on a white, 100% diffuse surface, there will be no illumination on that white surface.

So, in fact, there is more than one way of setting a final color value. You can set the value in the HSV color picker, you can change the light's intensity, or you can even change the diffuse value of the surface that the light is shining on. The diffuse value of a surface is a multiplier of how much illumination is applied to a surface. Less illumination means less color transmission to the surface. Less color transmission means a lower final value.

How Hue, Saturation, and Value Interact

Hue, saturation, and value are not completely independent values. They are interlinked through axes. Just like there are x, y, and z axes in LightWave's Layout and Modeler, there are H, S, and V axes in the HSV color selection model.

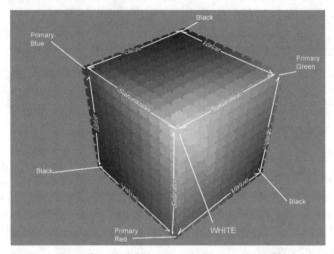

Figure 19.7: Color model showing the interaction of hue, saturation, and value. (See color image.)

As you can see in this "color cube" model, color hues that tend toward black have low values, while colors that tend toward white have low saturations. Colors that are closest to their original hues have high saturation and high value.

Recapping HSV

To be clear, hue is simply the base color, the pure wavelengths, whether it be orange, green, purple, or whatever. Saturation is how pale a hue is, with lower saturations being paler and higher saturations being more vivid. Value is how dark a hue is, with very dark colors having a low value and very vivid colors having a high value.

The Additive Color Wheel

There are a number of different ways of describing what is called the "color wheel." Some color wheels display only primary colors and their mixes, some display primaries and secondaries, and others run the full spectrum including variations of hues, saturations, and values.

The *additive color wheel* is a simple circle of colors in which a color mixture is created by adding light colors or wavelengths together. This is different from subtractive color mixing. Subtractive color mixing applies to pigments instead of light and refers to what light wavelengths are absorbed by the pigment. By adding pigments together, more wavelengths are absorbed and are therefore subtracted from the total reflected light. For more on this, read the sections on additive and subtractive color mixing later in this chapter.

Figures 19.8 to 19.10 are different examples of color wheels. Each displays the correct orientations and relationships between the colors.

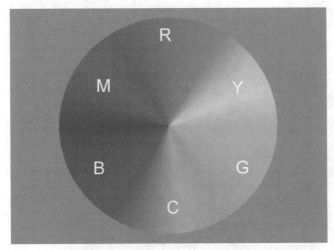

Figure 19.8 (See color image.)

The color wheel in Figure 19.8 shows the three primary colors — red, green, and blue — and the secondary colors — magenta, yellow, and cyan — that are created by mixing combinations of the primaries. Where red and green mix, we get yellow, where red and blue mix, we get magenta, and where green and blue mix we get cyan. This is a good way to begin to understand how basic color mixing works when choosing different light colors for your scenes.

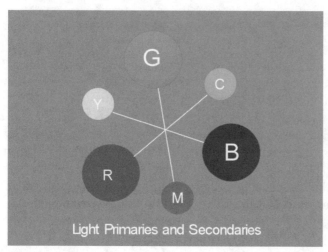

Figure 19.9 (See color image.)

A more traditional color wheel, like the one shown in Figure 19.9, also represents the three primaries and the three secondaries, although I prefer a color wheel that shows the mixing as it actually occurs.

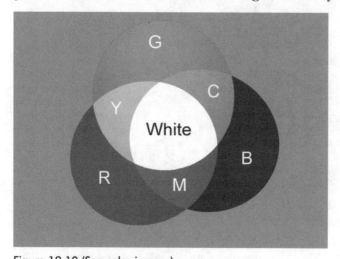

Figure 19.10 (See color image.)

For a color wheel that demonstrates all the primaries and secondaries, the one in Figure 19.10 is my favorite. This color wheel not only shows what happens when you mix primaries but also what happens when you mix secondaries together. This color wheel gets to the heart of what light is made of. In the center of this wheel, we see white. White is what I call "whole" light. White light contains all the wavelengths, or colors, in the visible spectrum. Each of the primary colors is an individual part of that whole. So if you mix a secondary color like magenta (which contains red and blue) with a secondary like cyan (which contains green and blue) then you have all three pure primary colors. Mixing all three pure primary colors will result in white, providing all three primaries are at full saturation and full value.

Primary Colors

Considering this is a book about lighting in LightWave, and considering that LightWave does not use the "real-world" RYB pigment model of primary colors, this section deals exclusively with the RGB color model.

Primary colors are those colors in the visible light spectrum from which all other colors can be derived through mixing. Primary colors are not divisible into other colors.

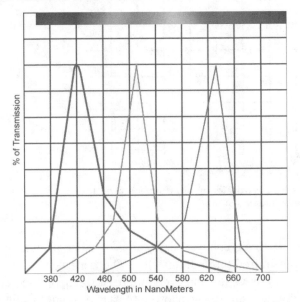

Figure 19.11: A graphic representation of all three light colors. (See color image.)

The graph in Figure 19.11 illustrates the three primary colors in the RGB lighting model and how they might appear in a color transmission graph. The horizontal axis represents the wavelength, shown here both in nanometers and as a color representation. The vertical axis represents the amount of all wavelengths that is mixed into the color.

In theory, primary red, primary green, and primary blue would be only a single spike exactly on a single wavelength; however, in reality it is extremely difficult to produce physically precise primary colors.

If you find yourself in a situation where you are mixing primary colors for a scene, be aware that "real-world" lighting and "real-world" pigments almost always have mixes of other wavelengths within them.

A typical wavelength transmission graph for a theatrical lighting filter (gel), for example, will look something like Figure 19.12.

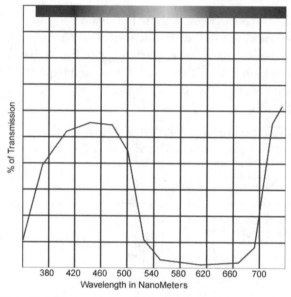

Figure 19.12: A typical wavelength transmission graph for a lighting filter. (See color image.)

As you can see in this graph, primary blue is only one portion of all the light that is transmitted through this filter. There are related wavelengths such as cyan, violet, and even green. At the upper end of the spectrum, some red light is also allowed to pass through this filter. In the world of stage lighting, this is known as a primary blue filter. But how can it be primary blue if it contains so many other colors? There are two main reasons. One is that all the colors you use in your design are relative. They are relative to each other and to the scenery. Also, the human eye can easily be fooled into believing this is primary. This filter is close enough to primary blue and contains enough of the blue range of wavelengths to pass for primary blue by completely overpowering the traces of other wavelengths.

What it comes down to is this: One of the main problems with computer-generated work is that it often looks computer generated. You can add some error simply by taking care never to create colors, like primaries, that are practically impossible in the real world. Don't be afraid to fudge around with the colors. You will find it adds a great deal of dimension to your lighting.

Secondary Colors

Secondary colors are created by mixing primary colors in equal proportions. If you look back at Figure 19.3, you will see how the primary colors (the large circles) mix equally to produce the secondary colors (the small circles).

Tertiary Colors

Tertiary colors can be created by mixing secondary colors with their primary colors on either side in the color wheel. You can see now that there are three primary colors, three secondary colors, and six tertiary colors.

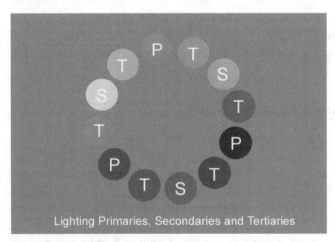

Lighting Primaries, Secondaries and Tertiaries

Figure 19.13 (See color image.)

Intermediate Colors

Intermediate colors compose all the other hues that come in between the primary, secondary, and tertiary hues on the color wheel.

Figure 19.14: Color wheel showing hues. (See color image.)

I find it much more natural and intuitive to view a color wheel like the one in Figure 19.14 as I work. This color wheel demonstrates color mixing in action, rather than displaying the individual colors arranged in a pattern, although those examples are good for illustrating the basic examples between primary colors and their mixed results. This color wheel also shows the full spectrum of hues, rather than only specific mixes.

Color Harmonies, or Schemes

When we think of the word "harmony," we probably think first of musical notes that sound agreeable together. Color harmonies follow that logic. They are a way of finding colors on the color wheel that will work well together. There are a number of standard harmonies that you can use in your lighting design to create vivid, pleasing, and stylistically strong work. This does not, by any means, imply that you are confined to a set of rules for selecting your colors. These harmonies are principles that can help guide you in your color choices. If you wish, you can discard these completely; however, color harmonies are known as effective color selection tools that can greatly speed up your color choice process and at least get you into the ballpark of where you want your final colors to be.

Monochromatic Harmony

A *monochromatic color harmony* simply means that you have chosen to use a single hue alone. Any choice of only one hue constitutes a monochromatic color harmony. You may, for example, choose a single amber light as room illumination. If you have a basement room with no exterior illumination and only a single, bare lightbulb in the ceiling, a monochromatic color scheme may very well fit the bill. This is not a very exciting, vibrant, or interesting way of lighting, but that does not make it any less valid a color scheme. Your scene may call for drab, dull, boring. Monochromatic color schemes are an excellent way of conveying this sort of feeling to the viewer.

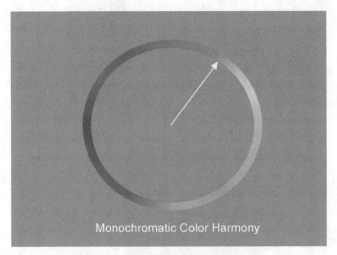

Monochromatic Color Harmony

Figure 19.15 (See color image.)

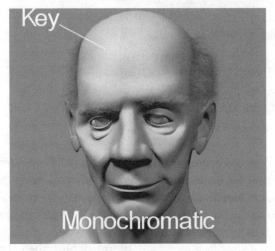

Figure 19.16 (See color image.)

Complementary Colors

Complementary colors are two colors from the color wheel that are directly opposite each other. If, for example, you chose primary blue as one of your colors, the complement to that color would be yellow.

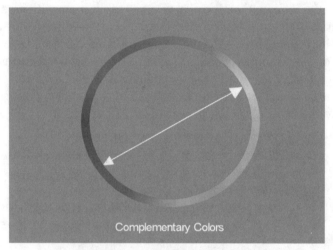

Complementary Colors

Figure 19.17 (See color image.)

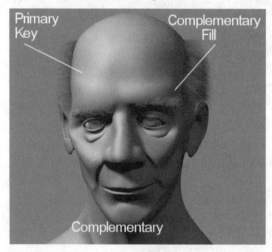

Primary
Key

Complementary
Fill

Complementary

Figure 19.18 (See color image.)

Complementary colors have a high contrast that makes them vibrant and exciting. This system of color harmonies, along with split complementary, is, perhaps, one of the most used color selection systems used in lighting. If you are outside on a sunny day, you are lit with complementary colors. The sun has a yellowish hue that illuminates your face. Within the shadows of your face, however, there are blue hues. This blue illumination comes from the sky that is acting as the fill light source. So complementary color illumination exists everywhere and is extremely natural and pleasing. You are free to exaggerate this relationship by selecting more vibrant and more saturated colors if you wish or by selecting less saturated colors.

Split Complementary

One of my favorite color selection methods is *split complementary*. What this means is that one color is chosen as the key color. Two complementary colors are chosen, which are the colors on either side of the color that is directly complementary to the key. Because the color scheme is based on a key color with a pair of complementary colors slightly off of opposite, there is a pleasant color variation rather than a garish or clashing scheme like triadic color harmony, which is mentioned later in this chapter.

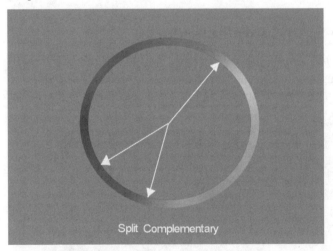

Split Complementary

Figure 19.19 (See color image.)

Split complementary allows the designer to build a color highlight into either the key or fill light sources (or whatever light source you choose, really) by adding a second complement that is a related hue.

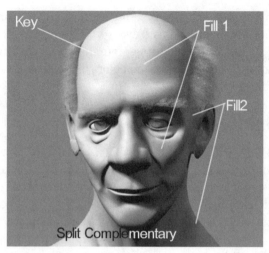

Figure 19.20 (See color image.)

Double Split Complementary

Double split complementary is simply two related hues with their respective complements across the color wheel. You can use this color selection method to find the appropriate color highlight for both key and fill sources, for example.

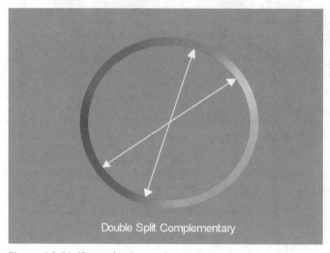

Figure 19.21 (See color image.)

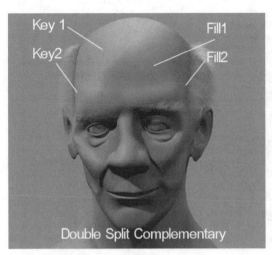

Figure 19.22 (See color image.)

In Figure 19.22, a key light and a fill light were added to the scene using complementary tints. A secondary key and a secondary fill were then added using the double-split complementary tint color selection method. The secondary key and fill lights were used to create pleasing color highlights on the subject, adding a richer and more three-dimensional look to the lighting.

Analogous Color Harmony, aka Related Tints

Analogous color harmony, or *related tints*, means a selection of colors that are in a similar hue range. Orange and yellow, for example, would be considered related tints. So would orange and red or red and crimson. Red, magenta, and blue would not be considered related tints because, although red and blue are both related to magenta, they are not related to each other. Color selections must be closer to each other than the distance between primaries.

There can be any number of color selections in a related tints color scheme. Unlike complementary, which is limited to two selections, and split complementary, which is limited to three, related tints really has no such limitation. You can select any number of primary, secondary, tertiary, or intermediate colors, provided they all fall within a related hue range.

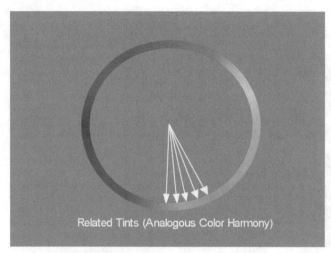

Figure 19.23 (See color image.)

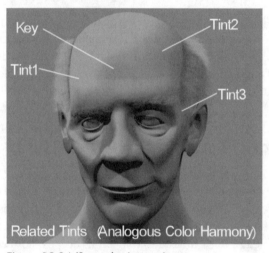

Figure 19.24 (See color image.)

Related tints tend to be more calming than the vibrant complementary schemes.

Triadic Color Harmony

Triadic color harmonies are similar to split complementary. They are composed of three colors on the color wheel, two of which are nearly opposite the third. In triadic color harmonies, however, the three colors are evenly spaced about the color wheel. If you selected the three primary colors, for example, that would be considered a perfect triadic color harmony.

Triadic color harmonies tend to be bright, vibrant, and rather garish and unsophisticated. If you were painting a child's playroom, you might select a triadic color harmony. You might also use this type of color scheme if you wish to grab attention or if you wish the scene to seem edgy and disturbing.

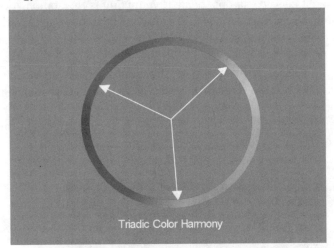

Figure 19.25 (See color image.)

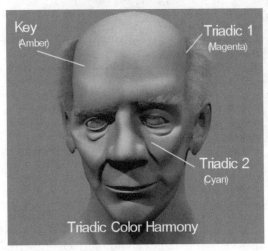

Figure 19.26 (See color image.)

Additive Mixing

Additive mixing refers to a color mixing method in which light wavelengths or colors from one light source are combined with light wavelengths or colors from one or more other light sources. The combined sum of all the wavelengths and intensities from all the light sources results in a final color.

The most classic example of additive mixing is the combination of all three primary lighting colors at 100%. If you color three lights red, green, and blue, set them each to 100%, and aim them all at the same spot on a surface that is set to an RGB value of 1.0, 1.0, 1.0 or 255, 255, 255, and the surface is 100% diffuse, the resulting color on the surface will be white. The three primaries combine to make white on a surface that absorbs no light wavelengths.

Regardless of the surface color, however, the light from the three lighting instruments combines to create white light at 100%. This can be demonstrated if we can see the light beams by using volumetrics.

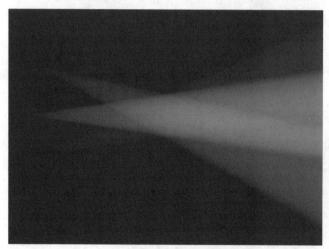

Figure 19.27: Example of additive mixing. (See color image.)

Additive mixing occurs any time you are using two or more lights of different hues on the same surface. Knowing, or at least being able to estimate, the final hue is critical to lighting your surface properly. Have you noticed how on a bright, hot, sunny summer day, the light seems very white? This is not because the sun emits a very white light. As a matter of fact, sunlight is rather yellow. But once you mix the blue from the sky into the sunlight, the light appears very white. Why is this? If you look at your color wheel, you will see that yellow light such as sunlight is composed of the primaries red and green. If you add blue light into this, you then have all three primaries in the mix to some extent — red, green, and blue. Mixing these three lighting colors always results in a whiter light color.

By examining the component colors of any color you have selected, you should be able to guess what the final color will be if mixed with another light.

We are only talking about light color here. Once the light reaches a colored surface, there are many other considerations that can change your expected results. If, for example, you have a red light and a green light and you combine them by aiming them together at a blue surface, you know that you have a combined yellow light shining at the blue surface. But what will the surface color be when it is illuminated by the yellow light?

The following chart shows examples of some mixing results:

Color 1 +	Color 2 =	Color 3
Red	Green	Yellow
Red	Orange	Bright Orange
Orange	Green	White
Blue	Magenta	Purple

Try throwing a couple of lights together, point them at a white surface, and start fiddling with the colors. If you don't already have a handle on light color mixing, you soon will.

Missing Color

One good way of estimating the final color of a lighting mix is to try to determine a "missing color." If you were to mix an orange-colored light with a green-colored light, for example, what would the missing color be? Well, we know that green is a primary and so it cannot be broken down into component primary colors. An orange light color is mixed out of red and green. So we now know that red, green, and green are the components of the two lights. The missing color is blue. We know that the final color of the two mixed lights will not contain any blue light. This tells us that the final color is probably in the yellow-orange range of the color wheel, nearly opposite the blue range.

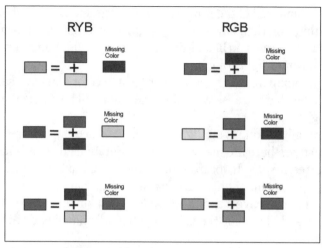

Figure 19.28 (See color image.)

Subtractive Mixing

In the real world, we usually refer to *subtractive mixing* when we are talking about mixing paints together. This is because, unlike lights which get whiter as you mix more colors together, paints get blacker as you mix more colors together. In theory, if you could mix true primary red, yellow, and blue paint together, the result would be black paint. In reality, paint pigments are never true primary colors. Primaries are extremely difficult to produce and impractical for paint pigments. Besides, most people will never be able to tell the difference.

But what is it that makes this *subtractive* color mixing?

Simply put, pigments appear to be a certain color because they reflect the wavelength's component to that color. Orange paint, for example, reflects red and green light wavelengths while absorbing blue wavelengths. The blue wavelengths do not reach your eye; they are absorbed into the paint and do not, therefore, mix into the reflected light that makes up the color of the surface. Blue paint, on the other hand, reflects mostly blue wavelengths and absorbs most red and green wavelengths. So what would happen if we mixed the blue paint with the orange paint? The blue paint would probably subtract most of the reflected red and green light wavelengths that the orange paint had originally reflected.

By adding more colors to the paint, we are subtracting the number of wavelengths that are being reflected by the pigment. This is why paint mixing is called "subtractive mixing."

Subtractive Mixing Lights

I know, I know. I just finished explaining how light mixing is additive and pigment mixing is subtractive. Here is where we step off the tracks of physical reality and into the world of computer-calculated light intensities.

One of the coolest tools available to the CG lighting artist (which is not available to real-world lighters, I might add) is the ability to create negative lights.

You make a negative light by loading it up and setting its intensity level to a negative number like –100%. Not only will this make the light decrease illumination intensity wherever you shine it, but it will also subtract color from wherever you shine it.

Say, for example, you have a white floor lit by a white distant light. If you shine a spotlight on that floor, make the spotlight intensity –100%, and set the color to red (255, 0, 0), that spotlight will remove 100% of the red light from the white floor. This means that only green and blue light will remain in the area where the spotlight is shining.

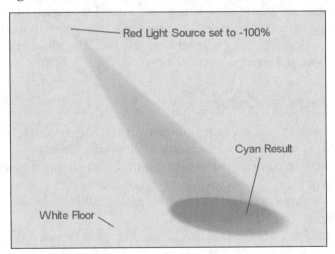

Figure 19.29 (See color image.)

Subtractive mixing can take many complex forms, resulting in unusual permutations. You can use subtractive lights to create negative shadow colors, for one. You can surgically remove intensity or color from specific areas. In short, subtractive mixing of intensity and color is a precision tool that gaffers worldwide wish they had at their fingertips.

Mixing Light with Pigments

Once you get down to lighting colored surfaces, you will have to understand exactly what light is absorbed and what is reflected by the surface. Lighting a yellow piece of paper with a blue light, for example, is not likely to result in very much illumination. Why is this? Yellow paper absorbs blue light and reflects red and green light. If you only shine blue light at the yellow paper, it will absorb the blue light. There are no other (or few other) wavelengths left to reflect. The likelihood is that the yellow paper is going to appear black or, perhaps, very dark green, depending upon how close both the light color and the paper color are to their respective primaries.

Try to keep these simple rules in mind:

- Pigment reflects its color and absorbs all others. So red light on red paper will show red paper.

- Light is absorbed by pigments if it is a different color than the pigment.

So if we shine a white light on pink paper, we will see pink paper. If we shine a blue light on pink paper, the paper will appear blue. If we shine red light on pink paper, the paper will appear red. If we shine green light on pink paper, the paper will appear black.

The Psychology of Color

It is quite simple, really. Certain colors tend to make people feel certain ways. That is not to say that a single particular color should always be used for a single particular emotional intent. In fact, artists throughout history have made yet more poignant statements by juxtaposing scenes with color choices that might, at first, be considered completely inappropriate.

It comes down to the first rule of art: There are no rules. With this section, I hope to provide you with a starting point, a beginning way of thinking, so that you can take your art to the next level. Don't hesitate to experiment with completely outlandish ideas or with color selections and lighting methods that you might think at first are completely wrong. Go for it. Sure, it might look awful, but you can always change it back.

Mixing color is partly about finding pleasing, relevant color combinations for your scene. The color mix must be relevant in that the colors are appropriate to the design and practical considerations of the scene. Red neon lights, for example, produce a red glow on nearby walls. If it's sunny, and the sun is the key light source, the light should probably be somewhere in the yellow range of the visible light spectrum. Relevance is the first technical consideration of your lighting design.

Following relevance, your lighting must be pleasing. I am not inferring that it must be rosy and pretty. When I say your lighting must be pleasing, I mean it must please you, the designer. It must convey those meanings you wish it to convey. If you want a scene to appear morose, and you achieve morose lighting or some lighting effect that contributes to the feeling "morose," I imagine that you would be pleased. Understanding the psychological effects of certain color ranges and mixes can assist you in presenting a pleasing and effective lighting design

The following sections will offer some basic ideas about how color selections tend to affect most people. Use this as a guide or a starting point. Remember, this is only the very basics. How much further you go is completely up to your imagination.

Warm Colors

Warm colors include those that are in the red, magenta, or yellow side of the color spectrum or color wheel. Colors that are warm tend to give us feelings of warmth and coziness because we associate reds, yellows, and oranges with heat, such as that from a fireplace.

Red

Red is one of the most powerful and aggressive colors. It can represent blood, heat, fire, emergencies, warmth, love, and excitement, to name a few. Alone, red can be overpowering. Using red as an accent can draw attention to specific areas of a scene.

Orange

Orange can represent strength, generosity, and warmth. Although not as powerful as red, it has a wider appeal and can be used to subtler effect.

Yellow

Bright yellows can be cheerful, but they can also be irritating. Because yellow reflects so much light, it can become tiresome for the eye and may lead to discomfort or even annoyance and distraction.

Cool Colors

Cool colors include those in the blue, green, and cyan side of the color wheel. We associate these colors with ice and water. These colors can be associated with feelings of peace and serenity or even sadness and withdrawal.

Green

Green has long stood for renewal and rebirth. For thousands of years, primitive tribes initiated the rites of renewal at the winter solstice, half of the tribe blackened with charcoal, the other half adorned with green leaves. The two halves of the tribe fought in mock battle, the green side always winning. This sympathetic magic was used to ensure the return of spring and growth to the world. Since those ages long past, green has always been strongly associated with fertility and life.

Blue

Blue can be a calming and trustworthy color. Blue is the favorite color of most people. But it also denotes sadness and depression. Have you ever felt "blue"? In its purer forms, blue can indicate wisdom and trustworthiness. In its paler forms, it can give a sense of loss and helplessness.

Purple

Purple is often associated with royalty and wealth. Royal purple is one of the favorite shades of purple. It indicates wealth and sophistication, containing both the loyalty and trust of blue with the power and excitement of red.

Black

Black can be associated with evil such as black magic and fear or it can denote strength and power. Many people prefer black clothing because it gives them an air of control and serenity, others because it can be intimidating. On the other hand, black is often associated with personal loss, death, despair, and mourning.

White

White is often associated with cleanliness, purity, chastity, innocence, honesty, and other human traits that are thought to be good and desirable. A bride may wear a white dress to denote virginity and/or chastity while an angel is clad in white to represent pure good. And we all know who the good guy is if he is wearing a white cowboy hat.

Other Colors

Of course there are millions of other colors distinguishable to the human eye. Most of them fall into a range near at least one of the colors discussed above. These definitions are only part of how color can be interpreted. How you choose to use colors in your design is up to you. Whether or not your color choices work will be up to the judgment of hindsight. But you've got to start somewhere. Let's take a look at how some colors may mix to create emotional responses.

Related Tints

Related tints is also known as *analogous color harmony*. It refers to two or more colors selected from a similar range of the visible color spectrum. Olive green and forest green, for example are considered related tints. So are pink and purple. Sand and orange are related as well.

Related tints tend to have a calming effect. This is true not only of lighting colors but of pigment application as well. If you wish your viewer to maintain a serene vision, avoid clashes or strong complements and go with a key and its relatives.

Complementary Colors

Complementary colors refers to colors that are opposite or close to opposite on the color wheel.

At this point, we must bear in mind and understand the key difference between primary pigments in the real world and primary pigments in the computer world. In the computer world, the three primary colors are red, green, and blue, whether you refer to lighting or pigments. In the real world, however, pigments have a different set of primaries. (For more details on this, see "Primary Colors" earlier in this chapter.) The "real-world" pigment primaries are red, yellow, and blue.

This is an extremely important distinction when mixing colors because even though computer-generated pigments are mixed using RGB primaries, you must mix them *as though* their primaries were RYB.

In the RGB world, the complement of red is achieved by mixing the other two primaries, in this case green and blue. The complement of red, therefore, is cyan.

In the RYB world, however, the complement of red is achieved by mixing the other two primaries, yellow and blue. The complement of red, therefore, is green.

So when you are creating complementary colors in your lighting design, you must consider that the complement to your key is achieved by going across the RGB color wheel. If you are creating pigment complements, however, you should mix using the RYB primary system for pigments; otherwise your complementary, secondary, and tertiary colors will come out differently than they would in the real world. LightWave does not support RYB color mixing, so you'll just have to keep an RYB color wheel handy or make one up yourself. There are also many color mixing references available on the web that will help you understand pigment primaries and color mixing, if you don't already have a handle on them.

That said, let's get to the psychological effect of complementary colors, regardless of the primary system you are going to use.

A key color next to its complement can be very vibrant and exciting. If you wish to maintain a vibrancy to your scene, using a complementary color scheme is a good place to start. Standard McCandless key-fill lighting uses complementary colors. Even a sunny day uses this color scheme. The sun is your key light in the yellow range, while your fill light source, the sky, is blue. Blue is directly complementary to yellow in the RGB system we use for lighting.

Complementary coloring is arguably the color selection method used most often in lighting and, perhaps, in pigment selection as well. It is very simple and very effective, producing interesting and usually visually pleasing results.

Triadic Colors

Perhaps the first, most obvious use of a triadic color harmony is the use of all three primary colors in a coloring scheme. How many children's toys have you seen that make use of red, yellow, and blue, or of red, green, and blue? Triadic color harmonies tend to go beyond the vibrancy of complementary coloring schemes and take the excitement to a new level. Some selections can be shocking or even odd.

Imagine what your scene would look like lit with three-point lighting using one each of the three primaries.

Monochromatic Colors

Monochromatic lighting designs are usually used with the express purpose of conveying boredom, drabness, and plainness. Monochromatic color schemes, using one and only one lighting color, have been used many times to denote unpleasant office environments, poor, shabby homes, or drab, boring, rainy afternoons. They're also used effectively in real-looking space shots, as the only light source often is the sun.

While it seems at first that this would be a very strange and mainly useless design tool, one must consider the viewer reaction if such a drably lit scene were juxtaposed with a scene lit using bright complements or even triadic color selections. One may use this tool to counterpoint a severe disparity between two peoples' lives or between two environments.

Monochromatic design is really a very powerful design tool and can, if used effectively, punch home a design concept.

High-Saturation, High-Value Colors

High-saturation, high-value colors tend to be more vivid and exciting than those of lower values or saturations. Toys for infants and children often use these colors in order to stimulate the less-developed optical senses of the child. We understand, then, that these colors tend to be more noticeable and tend to hold attention longer than the softer, gentler colors created by using lower saturation and value.

Low-Value Colors

Lower value colors, as discussed earlier, are colors that tend toward black. A dark crimson, for example, is a lower value shade of red. These colors tend to have mysteriousness about them. They can also be interpreted as having a "rich" quality as in the colors dark emerald and royal blue. Dark wood colors such as those found in oak, cherry, and walnut are considered to be more expensive and luxurious than light wood such as pine, fir, and maple.

Low-Saturation Colors

Colors with lower saturation tend toward white. Pink, for example, is a lower saturation shade of red. Many low-saturation colors are referred to as *pastel* colors, named after the oil chalks. These low-saturation colors are often associated with serenity, calm, and softness.

High-Contrast Colors

High-contrast colors are those usually found on opposite sides of the color wheel. Whether you are mixing with light or pigment, pick a color, find the color on the opposite side of the color wheel, and you will have a high-contrast color. Yellow contrasts highly with blue, for example. If you use high-contrast colors together in your design, you are likely to come up with a vibrant, exciting result. Here are some other high-contrast combinations:

RGB		
Red	-	Cyan
Green	-	Magenta
Orange	-	Aqua
RYB		
Yellow	-	Purple
Green	-	Red
Orange	-	Blue

Low-Contrast Colors

Low-contrast colors tend to be near each other on the color wheel. They usually offer the viewer a sense of calm and order as opposed to the vivid excitement of their high-contrast counterparts. Lower contrast examples include:

RGB		
Magenta	-	Blue
Green	-	Yellow
Red	-	Orange
RYB		
Green	-	Blue
Purple	-	Red
Yellow	-	Orange

Designing with Color

There is no way to set out the ABCs of color use in your design. The attempt of this chapter has been to give you a theoretical background, a basic understanding so that you can use whatever colors you wish to achieve your desired effect.

You do not need a tutorial to explain where to place a light, what color to make it, and what intensity to set. You need to equip yourself with a base understanding of color and the effects it has on your scene.

You need to understand how the light plays in your scene and what a colored light does to a colored texture. You should have an understanding of what different colors and intensities do to your scene to bring about a desired psychological or emotional response from your viewers.

There is only one way to achieve this knowledge and understanding and that is by practice. Practice your lighting and trust your eye. When you choose a color, look at how it plays on the scene and ask yourself how it makes you feel, what, if any, emotional response you have to it, and what sort of mood you think the light brings to your scene.

If I were an audience member and was shown a scene brightly lit with warm hues of pink and orange, I might expect that the scene will be happy, invigorating, joyful, or even comedic. If the scene were lit dimly, on the other hand, using the cool hues of blue and green, I might be expecting a darker tone to the scene, a morose theme, or perhaps black comedy.

This is not to say that you might not light a death scene very brightly with highly saturated colors and multiple highlights. Such a contrary set of color choices may serve not to dilute the emotions of loss and grief but to enhance and complement them, perhaps even to punctuate them by virtue of their complementary and contrasting nature.

You are the designer. The choices are yours.

• • •

Now that you have come to the end of this chapter, you should have at least a basic understanding of color primaries, secondaries, and tertiaries as well as how light and pigment interact and relate to each other. As an exercise, you might try imagining what color will result if you shine a spotlight of color "A" on a surface with color "B." Fill in the A and B with whatever color you like. Once you get every answer right, you've pretty much got color mixing down.

Chapter 20

Mood Setting

This chapter describes yet another esoteric and debatable topic: mood setting. It may very well be that you disagree with everything written here. Storytelling does, after all, take infinite forms. But I hope, at least, that this will help you think about how you go about setting the mood of your scene and that you accomplish it intentionally and with planning and art.

Every scene has a mood. Every mood can be defined by any number of criteria, not the least of which is lighting. Design style can set a mood, as can music, characters, scenery, or even odor.

What is it about lighting that helps define a mood? Some say that millions of years of evolution are to thank (or blame) for our emotional response to certain lighting qualities. Some say that it is social conditioning or even traumatic experience. Probably the truth involves some or all of these for each of us, and that our specific reactions tend to differ depending on our cultural, social, and personal backgrounds and experiences.

There do seem, however, to be general trends that apply to most people. If, for example, we choose to illuminate a scene with blue lighting, the audience is likely to presume a morose scene, a nighttime scene, or a very cold scene. If, on the other hand, we choose to illuminate the scene with bright, white light from below, our audience will likely experience a sense of foreboding, evil, or drama. If we light with green, the audience is likely to be ill at ease or, in the absence of any other signals, presume the setting is in a forest or under water.

These responses occur because we, as human beings, make certain associations with certain lighting properties. Predominantly dark blue lighting, for example is never experienced during the day. A hot fire is not blue. Happy evenings at home are not generally experienced in dark blue environments. These may seem like obvious statements, but they are key to understanding why dark blue lighting makes us react a particular way.

Lighting a scene from beneath seems dramatic or evil simply because the primary natural light in our world comes from above. It has always come from above, even since long before life graced our little blue marble. Our response, therefore, is that lighting from beneath is odd, off, strange, unusual, unnatural, and weird. This response has been used to great effect by artists of every ilk for millennia.

Angle and color are only two of the lighting properties that can evoke an emotional response from the audience. Let's look at some more.

Angle and Shadow

Angle and shadow, like many light properties, are linked together. Certain lighting angles produce certain types of shadows. Sometimes the shadow is dependent on the orientation of the light relative to the object, and sometimes it is dependent on the orientation of the light relative to the camera.

Let's look at a few examples.

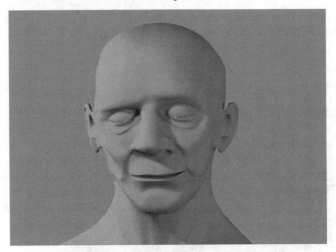

Figure 20.1: Typical key and fill lighting.

This is a fairly typical render, one in which we use a variation of a simple McCandless lighting setup. Key and fill lights coming in at roughly 45 degree angles illuminate the full figure with additional highlight instruments placed for warmth and, of course, highlights. These angles are selected because they represent a natural light source. They make the viewer feel at ease and familiar.

We can change that very easily simply by applying an unnatural or unusual angle to our key light.

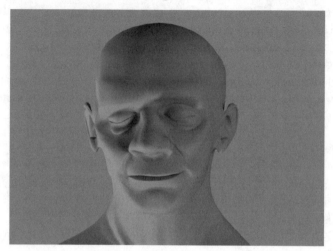

Figure 20.2: Key light from below.

All the other lights remain where they were. Only the key light has been moved to a position in front of and below the subject, yet the image already looks a little odd.

What happens if we turn the other lights off and leave only the single light from below?

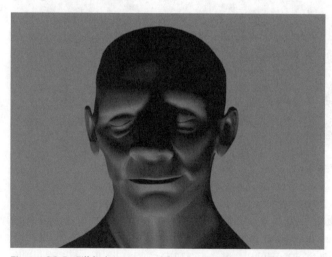

Figure 20.3: Fill light removed for more dramatic effect.

The image in Figure 20.3 is very strange and unnatural, even frightening if the context makes it so.

We can also light the subject from directly above, providing deep, unusual shadows.

Figure 20.4: Top light only for dramatic effect.

These deep shadows provide the figure with a sinister appearance, hiding the eyes and making the subject feel untrustworthy.

Lighting subjects from the side can help define subtle shapes in the subject.

Figure 20.5: Side light only for softer dramatic effect.

This angle is serene, yet still hides part of the subject. It can be used to great effect for many different scene types, primarily where the artist is interested in drawing attention to shapes and forms in the scene.

Mixing these lighting angles with each other, with fill lights, or with anything your heart desires will help you define the mood of your scene. Your lighting angles are an easy way to make your audience either comfortable or ill at ease. Play with a bunch of lights and angles. When you render out a frame, look at it and ask yourself how it makes you feel. Chances are your audience will feel the same.

Contrast

Contrast in your scenic lighting can help set a mood for your scene. Where low-contrast images tend to give viewers a serene, low-energy feeling, higher contrast lighting is likely to energize your shot. Imagine how you feel on a cloudy or rainy day. On those days, the sun is hidden. The clouds are diffusing most of the light, which results in a low-contrast lighting environment. People feel down and tired. On a sunny day though, bright sunlight and dark shadows result in a high-contrast lighting situation. People generally feel energized and happy on sunny days.

Figure 20.6: High-contrast image.

Figure 20.6 is a high-contrast shot. Notice that there is a high range between the whitest and the blackest points in the image.

Figure 20.7: Low-contrast image.

Figure 20.7 is a low-contrast shot. Notice that there is a low range of difference between the whitest and the blackest points in the image.

Intensity

Light intensity is another of the more subtle ways of weaving mood into your scene. Subtle variations in light intensity from one scene to the next can serve as a dynamic thread that leads the viewer through a range of moods or over a gradual change from one mood to another.

Very dim intensities are usually associated with night or evening and can be associated with somber, serene, or unhappy events. Very bright intensities are usually associated with high energy, happiness, activity, and heat. Intensities of medium or "normal" levels tend to make an audience feel relaxed, at home, and familiar.

Of course, that is not to say that you are forbidden from using very bright lights for a very sad scene or very dim intensities for a very happy scene. Once again, sometimes lighting a scene exactly opposite of what is expected can serve to silhouette and intensify your mood message.

The best thing as a designer is for you to experiment, render out frames, and see how they make *you* feel. Trust your instincts.

Motion

Motion is not usually associated with the mood of a scene, but I have observed that it can have a profound effect on an audience's mood. Take, for example, the typical mirror ball. It produces tiny illuminated reflections that move in graceful arcs throughout a room. This lighting gives a sense of wonder and magic to most environments. On the other hand, the rushing lights of speeding traffic tend to heighten stress and awareness, giving an edge of fear and chaos to a scene.

Motions can vary from nearly imperceptible to wild and seemingly uncontrolled. It is up to you to use motion in your scenes as you see fit. It is up to you to decide whether or not lighting motion achieves your objectives or obscures them. The best way to find this out is to experiment with motion.

Weather

In the world of CG, weather is definitely considered to be a lighting condition. Take, for example, lightning. These intensely bright flashes of light can bring fear or even panic into your scene very easily depending on the proximity, and therefore the volume and intensity, of the lightning. Distant lightning can be foreboding, brooding, broiling, and forewarning, while immediate lightning can signal imminent disaster and complete chaos. Mother Nature can be an extremely powerful way to evoke emotions in the viewer. Use it wisely and do not overuse.

Rain on the windowpane can also be considered a lighting effect. I would probably find some footage of a rainfall and project it through a spotlight. This is more of a special effect than a regular lighting effect, but it can be quite persuasive in lending mood to the scene.

• • •

Setting the mood in your scene is not about a single light source, a single color, or a single effect. It is about the web that you weave to draw your audience into the story. The most successful web is woven of multiple subtleties tied together with a thread of style. If you are new to lighting design, your immediate challenge is to know the tools and understand what they can do. Subsequent to that, you should experiment with your lighting as much as you can, as much as you have time for. If you are intimidated by the thought of weaving these careful webs of illusion, my best advice to you is to just throw caution to the wind and do it! Forget about criticism. Be wild. Sooner or later you will get the feel for setting moods. And most of all, observe the world. Reality is, after all, far more strange and unlikely than our best-told stories.

Hopefully by now you have some idea of the importance of deliberately setting the mood of your scene. Certainly you could light a shot simply based on the technical requirements of the scene. But with a little forethought, planning, and imagination, you can change the lighting from mere illumination into a tool that illuminates the story line as well.

The clever artist will now build some scenes with specific emotional intentions in mind, then ask their bored friends, mothers, aunts, or whomever for an emotional response. Hopefully it will be more constructive than "You're such a geek!"

Chapter 21

Style

This chapter briefly discusses the rather esoteric concept of style. You may or may not agree with some of the discussion here. That's okay though, because if you already have your own concept of style, you don't even need this chapter.

Style. There really isn't that much that can be unequivocally defined about style except that it's a very important part of lighting design. The problem is that style can't really be taught. Furthermore, that which one person considers style may not be considered style by another. It's a slippery concept, yet it exists.

So I can't teach you style, yet it is very important for a lighting designer. What, then to do? In the absence of any empirical fact, I'll include herein the few tidbits I have learned about style over the years. Maybe they will help you in some way to find your own style.

What Is Style?

Style can be defined as a distinctive combination of features, either in literature or in visual or performing arts. These features can be characterized through design, execution, performance, or expression and define a particular era, person, or school. In other words, there are a bunch of different ways to define style. In our case, we are discussing the execution and look of the final lighting as defining a style that is distinctly yours.

Sooner or later, if you find yourself designing, you will discover that you wish to explore your own creativity, combining elements from the works of artists you admire, and adding your own ideas and interpretations into the mix. You will try many new things, adapt the old tricks of the Masters to your own use, and mix in the technical requirements of the shot or show. One day you will be able to look at your work on a television monitor as you walk past it in a mall and instantly recognize it as your own. You will recognize it not because you worked on it tirelessly into the wee hours and the shot is burned permanently into your retinas but because you can immediately see that it is decisively *yours* in a way that transcends technical requirements. You will discover that you know your own style.

Your style is not about the show. It is about you. You are an individual with individual experiences and interpretations. You bring these experiences and interpretations to the design table with you because when you read the script, you react to the dramatic situations of the script in a certain way. Your emotional reactions to a scene or to the script in general are based on your life experience, your opinions, and your interpretations. You anthropomorphize non-living characters on a page. You make notes about your reactions and feelings. After you have read the script a couple of times, you have to start thinking about how you are going to make the audience experience those same feelings and reactions.

So What Do I Do?

First you must ask yourself what you want your work to say. Do you want your audience to be shocked or delighted? Do you want to disgust them or please them? Would you prefer to grab attention with a shock or allow your audience to slowly discover your messages? Do you wish them to be comfortable and familiar or uneasy and on edge?

Each of these decisions will have a direct impact on the lighting you choose for your scene. Exactly how you choose to implement those lighting goals is where style comes into play. You can carry a single style through many different types of scenes, or you can choose to vary it, drawing on many different resources and styles.

Style is really a method of making aesthetic choices. For example, a designer may prefer muted earth tones. There is no reason the designer can't use muted earth tones in joyous scenes as well as depressing ones. So the lighting elements will have a common tonal thread running throughout. The scenic designer, however, may handle these scenes in any number of very different ways.

If you wish, every scene can have a completely different look, a completely different style, but exactly the same message. Are you starting to see? There are no rules to style. You can mix and match as you please, provided that in the end you have attained your goals. If your goal was to confuse and upset your audience but they leave angry and want their money back, you may have to revisit your methods or your goals. If your goal was to frighten and delight your audience and they are frightened and delighted, then nobody has an argument with your methods and style, whatever they may be. Be aware, however, that it is easy to clutter and obscure the story with too much style, too many different elements, or too many changes.

Less Is More

If we examine great works of art throughout history, whether it be a marble sculpture, a painting masterpiece, a classic automobile, or a great work of architecture, we see that these great works have one thing in common: simplicity — simplicity of line and form, of design and function. You have probably heard the expression "less is more." In the world of art, nothing could be more true.

I have heard CG lighting artists brag about using 72 lights to illuminate an exterior shot as though more light is better, as though an immense amount of work and a huge number of lights somehow characterizes the technical prowess of the artist. Let's be clear about this: A massive number of lights does not guarantee a superior result.

It's not how big your array is, it's how you use it.

While there will indeed be situations in which you will need to employ a large number of lights for practical or technical reasons, you will find over time, if you don't know already, that the best lighting solution is usually the simplest and the most elegant. Too many light sources are unnatural and unnecessary. The results are likely to be less than satisfactory.

Consistency between Shots

If you are the director, the piece is experimental, and you wish to create a completely different look for each shot, that's your prerogative. Chances are that your audience will be confused and spend so much time struggling to understand your wild changes and design choices that the real story will be lost. That may be your intention. Probably not, though.

As storytellers ourselves, we usually don't want our lighting to be so intrusive that it detracts from the story. We want a smooth, flowing design style that assists the story from behind, never quite getting in the audience's face. Lighting should usually be like the steel or wooden pilings deep in the ground beneath the skyscraper. They're there for support, to help keep the building level and straight. Without them, the building would fall down. But nobody who enters the building ever sees them or thinks about them.

By maintaining some sort of style consistency between shots, the audience is less likely to notice the lighting, which means they are more likely to be thinking about the story. I call that a success. Not everybody does, but I do.

. . .

Style can be a slippery topic to talk about. Debate often rages about what is considered style and what is considered technique. An artist may consider that he has a wildly successful and distinctive style. His art may speak to him, portraying the precise message he wished to portray. On the other hand, others may consider the very same work to be trash, perhaps self-indulgent and meaningless. That certainly does not necessarily validate either position.

This is the subjective nature of art and style. The only advice I can offer is this: If you set out to achieve a particular look for a set of particular reasons, and you achieve that look, then you have been successful. Whether or not others respond to the work in the way you would prefer is not necessarily relevant. You have demonstrated that you can achieve the look you desire when you desire it. It means that you know how to get what you want out of the tools. That's a success in anyone's book.

All that is required is that you simply keep doing that over and over. One day you will realize that you have developed a style all your own.

If you wish to understand style in greater detail, there is no better way to learn than to study the work of great artists throughout history. When you hear a particular piece of music, you may be able to identify the composer. When you see a painting, you may know right away whose masterpiece it is. These are the paths that lead to understanding style.

If, after this chapter, you don't have any clue what style is, don't let it bother you too much. Neither do most people. It's such a personal and subjective thing, that its definition can be argued from many different perspectives. On the other hand, style may be completely unimportant to you, in which case my congratulations for reading all the way to the end of the chapter!

Chapter 22

Designing Lighting

The Design Process

We are artists. Most of us became CG artists because the computer environment affords us the ability to be every kind of artist we ever dreamed of. We can be sculptors, architects, painters, directors, and designers, to name but a few. Many of us would rather stay away from really structured processes. If this is the case with you, you may be disappointed, annoyed, or downright shocked to discover that design can be a rather administrative process with many steps. Each of these steps has a specific order and a specific purpose. That's not to say that there is only one process and everybody must use it. Over time you will, if you have not already, develop your own process, a method that works best for you. No matter how you go about it, however, your process is going to include several key steps. Among these steps will probably be:

- Script analysis
- Research
- Discussion
- Planning
- Implementation
- Evaluation

Script Analysis

Script analysis conjures images of college literature classes, stuffy professors, and long, boring essays. You could get the Coles Notes (or Cliff Notes) or ask someone else what the story was about, but that wouldn't really provide you with the immensely detailed information you will need to successfully complete your lighting design. The best way I have found to analyze a script is a method used by designers for the stage. It's a systematic analysis of the script for story elements, technical requirements, and other considerations such as mood and foreshadowing. It is not as boring and drawn out as you might expect, especially considering you will have direct artistic input into the final look of the project. It's an exciting time filled with possibilities, but it begins with a bit of background work that prepares you very well for the tasks ahead.

Understanding the Story

The real key to an attractive, successful, and cohesive lighting design is the ability of the designer to understand what story is being told by the author and then how to interpret and retell that story using lights. This begins at the beginning, when you are first handed a script and asked to read it. With that unopened script in your hands, your design is a carte blanche, an empty page. How you fill in that page depends on how you approach the script. There are many ways to analyze a script and derive a deep understanding of the story. I prefer the method outlined in the following sections.

First Reading

The first time I crack open a new script, I like to find a quiet, relaxed space where I can indulge myself and enjoy the story. There is no work to be done here. The goal is to familiarize yourself with the story, to gain a general, overall understanding of all the elements before you get into the nitty-gritty, before you start trying to answer all the questions that will inevitably come up during the production and design process. Of course, just because you are reading for pleasure doesn't mean it might not be a good idea to keep a pen and notebook handy just in case a brilliant idea pops into your head. If one does, take the time to jot it down. There is little more infuriating than having a great idea but deciding that you want to finish reading the scene first, and then when you've finished reading the scene, the idea is gone. Design ideas can come out of nowhere or can be triggered by the simplest things. Sometimes the inspiration can be a few words by a character or a brief setting description by the writer. Sometimes it is where you were on vacation last summer. Sometimes unrelated ideas just click with something in the script. I have often found that first reading, spur-of-the-moment ideas tend to be the strongest and clearest of all the design ideas I have. It is, after all, the first impression that holds the longest. Chances are that if an idea really catches you it will really catch your audience as well.

Second Reading

It is probably a good idea not to do your second reading immediately. Put the script away for a day or two and let the story percolate around your brain for a while. Once you've had plenty of time to think about the story, about things you liked or did not like, find that quiet spot again to begin your second reading.

This time, with the story under your belt, with a few glimmers of ideas brewing in the back of your head, try to find ways to build up concepts for scenes. Jot down quick notes either on a notepad or, better yet, in the margins of the script where you won't get notes from Act 1 Scene 4 mixed up with notes from Act 4 Scene 1.

While you are reading, take time to stop and think about scenes and make note of technical requirements for each scene such as time of day, weather conditions, and light sources. Make quick notes and move on. Try not to lose the momentum of the story. Don't forget to jot down any other thoughts or ideas you may have about a scene's mood or foreshadowing opportunities.

Third Reading

When you read the script for a third or even fourth time, you are looking for all the minute details that may come up in the course of your design. If the apartment is messy, for example, you might want to know something about that mess. Are socks hung on the floor lamp? Is the window grimy? Are there burnt-out lightbulbs in the hallway that have not yet been replaced? All these elements are lighting design considerations.

There will be specific technical requirements, such as placement of lighting sources like lamps and windows, and placement of foliage or a clothesline full of clothes, that may have an effect on light sources. There will be specific design elements and ideas such as the light shining through a stained-glass window in a cathedral, or the light through a high, small barred basement window and the volumetric light shining into the dusty basement.

Each scene is likely to be loaded with these details, each one of which must be taken into account while creating your lighting design.

The margins of the script are not likely to be sufficient to house and keep organized all the notes and ideas you are likely to come up with. It is time to do some administration. Get a binder and some page separators. Make a section for each act and, within that, a section for each scene. Keep the right notes with the right scene. You'll be adding a lot more information to each of these sections later on.

Research

Any designer worth her salt is going to take the production seriously enough to engage in some research. How much research is done depends upon the nature of the project and also upon the tenacity of the designer. It's pretty tough, for example, to research the lighting properties on the surface of Planet Xargon Seven or to find photo references for the size and shape of the rocket flame from the good ship *Rescue Team Alpha*. On the other hand, there is a good deal of reference material on real planets and real rockets. You don't have to make your scenes look the same as the real thing, but they could trigger a few interesting ideas way in the back recesses of the brain cavity, and they could help you add a sense of realism to your design work, fantastic as it may be.

Research can take a number of forms. These days most research seems to take place on the Internet. There is a wide variety of written and visual information that is available to the web searcher. You'll want a high-speed connection, though. The quantity of irrelevant information you're likely to have to sift through is not for the faint of heart.

There are also libraries. Remember libraries? Local libraries are a great place to do fairly run-of-the-mill research; however, for more obscure topics you may have to find a large regional library. Colleges and universities generally have good book selections as well. If you are researching period looks, your best bet is to find a college or university with a theater and film design program. These programs maintain large selections of tomes specifically for the use of their design students.

Historical

If you are doing a period piece (a work in a historical context), you are going to find yourself knee-deep in some serious historical research. What if you find yourself lighting a foggy London street in 1849? Do you know what gaslight lamps look like? Do you know the real qualities and properties of the light they produce? Probably not. But there is plenty of reference material available on that era.

What about life in Egypt in the third century B.C.? Do you know how they illuminated their hallways at night? Better find out if you're doing a piece on Pharaoh Ramses III. How about the reflective properties of the material used in pyramids? Pyramids were very large structures covered with white limestone. No doubt there was a great deal of diffuse reflected lighting nearby.

Visual

When we talk about visual research, we are referring to the setting and its surrounding environment. What does the place look like? Is it a smoky bar? Is the only sunlight through cracks in the window shutters? Is it afternoon or nighttime? Is the setting filthy or antiseptic? Are the lights fluorescent or are they candles? What about the scenic textures? At some point any lighting designer is going to get involved in certain aspects of surface textures. Visual elements will include such items as specularity, glossiness, diffuseness, and reflectivity. Is the toilet seat highly specular? Is it plastic or porcelain? Is it stainless steel? Is it highly polished oak or is it one of those furry covers? If you are trying to light a scene and you don't see the specularity you think you should, there may be some surface tweaking to be done. You may find yourself having to correct some of the other surface attributes as well. The artist who built the model, even if it was you, could not know exactly what the model was going to look like within a particular lighting environment. It is probably a good idea to save scene-specific versions of your model as the surface attributes may change from scene to scene.

Technical

Technical research, also referred to as R&D, is the research you will have to do to develop the specific lighting techniques you will need to accomplish all the fancy-pants ideas you have conjured up with the director and the other designers. The design of lighting techniques ensures not only that the look you are seeking is achievable, it also determines early on what sort of render power you are going to require to get all the frames rendered on time and on budget. If you have planned an effect that is going to take ten hours per frame to render, you might want to consider either finding a way to pare down the render time or scrapping and redesigning the look or the technique. Some techniques are just not practical.

Technical research takes place primarily during the early phases of a project; however, ideas change, mature, and evolve as the project grows from an idea into reality. Research and development is likely to continue in some measure until near the end of production.

As an example of R&D, imagine that your project involves a cataclysmic event on the earth such as a comet striking the planet or a massive volcanic explosion. What are you going to do to accomplish the obvious pyrotechnical lighting effects required for the hero shots? A comet shooting through the atmosphere overhead is burning up and is sure to cause some sort of lighting effect. The impact and subsequent explosion of billions of particles of molten rock will certainly be a serious lighting consideration. Many of those molten particles are raining down around your characters. What effect will this have on the local lighting environment? Next, how are you going to accomplish these effects? What light types will you use? Or perhaps you will not use lights. Perhaps you can project an image sequence on the background and use global illumination. That sounds very render intensive, but it might be worth a try. It might look fantastic enough to justify the extra render time. It might make all the difference between your film and some other film. It is probably a good idea to sketch out a number of approaches to each problem and try them out. You'll come to the right balance sooner or later, or perhaps during the course of experimentation you will discover an entirely new, untried technique. Either way, you can see that technical research will be a keystone in your design and development phase.

Dramatic

Dramatic research goes to the very heart of the story and characters. By striving to understand the story, by seeking the emotional truths that lie at its heart, and by seeking to understand all the characters in their fullness, you will be better able to make decisions about how to light specific scenes. Many well-written stories contain much more than the surface story elements on the page. They are also filled with metaphor and symbolism, perhaps pointing from the veneer of the story to an underlying social, political, or emotional truth. By analyzing the story and the characters, the designer is much more likely to understand what the writer is really trying to say. That understanding will bring you, the designer, to a new level of consciousness regarding the story. You will find yourself understanding symbols in the story in a way that is separate from the base story itself. You will be better equipped to provide a more truthful interpretation and, therefore, more truthful lighting.

Take the time to know the story. Discuss it with the other designers and with the director. It may be that the story is a simple, light comedy. If you are lucky, however, you will find yourself working on a project with much deeper meaning, requiring a much deeper understanding on your part.

Discussion: Working with the Design Team

Art is often a solitary business. Many artists prefer to work in complete seclusion, never showing their work until it is complete. There is no reason you can't maintain this attitude with your own CG stories, but it may take you a while to complete all the work yourself. If you are work-ing with a design team, on the other hand, you must realize that there is automatically a teamwork approach to the project. Sometimes a head-strong director will have a single vision and will work toward that vision with little or no regard for the creative processes of the rest of the design team. Sometimes this results in a single, unified look to the fin-ished product, but more often it simply results in disgruntled artists who have not been allowed to exercise their creativity. A director is wise to listen to the ideas of the design team, whether or not she chooses to incorporate them is something else entirely; however, many brilliant ideas have come out of brainstorming sessions with all the designers throwing wacky, strange ideas onto the floor. If you have ever been in one of these meetings and been witness to the birth of a brilliant idea, it is likely that you have never forgotten it. It is one of those memorable moments when everybody stops and stares at each other with excite-ment. They all know that *this* is the idea that will make everything work. Every person is on the same page, everyone is thinking the same thing. All the designers leave the meeting excited, ready to build on the foun-dation that has just been laid. All the designers are now working toward a common goal. Where I previously believed that my artwork was always solitary and that others had little or nothing to do with my artistic successes, I have found team experiences like this to be the most cre-atively fulfilling of my life. It doesn't always happen, to be sure. Sometimes the director and all the designers remain at cross-purposes from one end of the project to the other. Sometimes even this tangled mess creates stylistically and dramatically strong work. Some artists are driven to excellence through harmony, others through tension and strain. In any case, each production team is unique and the interrelation-ships within that team are certain to be interesting to observe.

What it comes down to is that you can never tell at the beginning of a production if that magical team is going to form, if the diverse ideas are going to form into a collective whole, or if the whole thing is going to be a disaster. For the record, very few projects turn into disasters as long as each member of the creative team is willing to do a good job.

The best you can do is review the script and come to the first meet-ing with as many different ideas and with as open a mind as possible. Bring your best ideas to date and present them like a salesman trying to sell a car. You have got to sell your ideas to the rest of the design team. There is a possibility that you will be outvoted, that the rest of the team has completely different ideas. On the other hand, if your ideas are really good, the rest of the team may be willing to look at new ideas themselves.

Bear in mind that, as part of a team, it is your duty and obligation to marry your design ideas with the work of the scenic and costume designers, whatever those ideas might be. To hold onto a single design plan, even if it is at cross-purposes with the other designers, is a disservice to the project and will most likely get you fired. Pride hath no place on a team.

Once you have some experience under your belt, you will probably discover that the challenges of working with a team, of building a collaborative whole, is just as challenging and creatively interesting as solitary work — perhaps even more so.

Planning

Once you're on the same page as the other artistic brains on the team, you have the task of planning just how you will achieve the lighting goals you have set for each and every shot. This means it's time to create a lighting bible.

Depending on the size and scope of the project, the lighting bible may be a few pages attached with a paperclip or a three-ring binder with separators. If you are talking about a feature-length project, you are definitely going to have to be organized. That means you must keep sketches for each scene in addition to storyboards, drawing up magic sheets (described later in this section) and, if you have a team of lighters implementing the show for you, probably some sort of drawn lighting design and lighting schedule.

Sketches and Drawings

Whether you are the sole lighting artist implementing all of the lighting yourself or the lead lighting artist coaching a team of artists of widely varying skills and experience, it is probably a good idea to plan out your lighting design scene by scene, not only with notes, research, and discussions but also with sketches and drawings. If possible, get a hold of the scenic design drawings. Make sure you can keep them and scribble all over them. Plan out each light position and purpose. You might even work out a lighting schedule for each scene if your design becomes complex enough to call for it. You don't have to start out at a drafting table. Start with scribbles on napkins. Take some serious time to forget about the whole project and relax — it might help the ideas flow. When the ideas come, write them down, sketch them out, tell them to someone — just don't let them get away from you. All these scraps of paper, napkins, and whatnot go into your bible for later conversion into useful information such as the magic sheet.

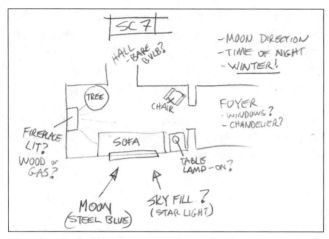

Figure 22.1: Quick sketch of a lighting design.

For this particular sketch, I just did a quick drawing of what I thought the set might look like for the scene, then added elements I thought would affect my lighting design. I had a number of questions about the scene such as whether or not certain lights in the house would be on.

- This scene takes place late at night. There is a child sleeping in the house, so the parents might leave a light on. If so, which lights?
- Perhaps the parents have only just gone to bed. Did they leave a fire burning in the fireplace?
- Is it a wood-burning fireplace or a gas one?
- Is the fireplace ablaze or just dying embers?
- Which direction should the moonlight come from?
- Has the moon's direction been established in previous shots?
- If the light in the foyer is off, there might be moonlight if there are windows.
- If there is no moonlight, will we be filling with an ambient starlight?
- Does the camera see the foyer during this shot? (Make a note to check the storyboards.)

The Magic Sheet

A *magic sheet* is a representational sketch or drawing of a lighting intent. Initially there is no need to be specific about light types, specific colors, or specific techniques. Just take a plan view of the scene and sketch in general directions and purpose. Take the following drawing, for example:

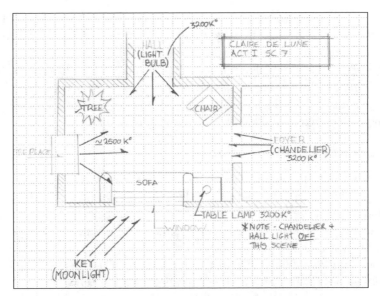

Figure 22.2: Magic sheet reflecting a more formal version of the sketch in Figure 22.1.

The magic sheet is a more formalized version of the napkin sketch. This is drawn once all the questions from the first sketch have been answered. In this drawing, I have roughed in some color temperatures as a guide to the lighting TD (technical director). Actual placement of lighting elements such as lamps and lightbulbs will be a collaborative decision between the scenic and lighting designers and the director. All three are striving to achieve the most effective look with as few compromises as possible. There are likely to be disagreements along the way. If, for example, the scenic designer called for an ornate and detailed chandelier and the modeling department spent a long time building it, they might not be very pleased to discover that it spends most of the time in the dark and is almost unseen. The lighting department, on the other hand, which spent a month researching how best to simulate light from a roaring fireplace, may be annoyed to find that the fire is mere glowing embers. While it is likely that many of these details will be decided upon before the serious work begins, the likelihood of this type of communication snafu is directly proportional to the scale of the project. A production with hundreds or thousands of scenes is almost certain to have any number of these problems, while a short with less than a hundred scenes is much less likely to experience them.

Having regular meetings with the rest of the production team and participating actively in your department's updates and activities discussion is crucial to keeping everybody on the same track. Presenting magic sheets at these meetings as soon as they are available will let everybody know exactly what you are planning and exactly where you are going with your design ideas.

By the way, you don't have to sit down and draw out your sketches and magic sheets the old way with a pencil. You are allowed to use any medium you like, including drafting or drawing software or even crayons, if you like, provided the documents are legible.

A Formal Lighting Plot

Formal lighting plots are by no means a necessary part of your production, unless you find yourself saddled with a huge job in which you wish to convey large amounts of information very precisely. The fact is that most lighting TDs will be tweaking and repositioning lights once they start working on a scene, but a formal lighting plot is a good way to convey your complete design data to the lighting TDs. You will need to develop a symbol system. If you are very anal retentive about cross-referencing your information, you can even write up a lighting instrument schedule, although I have not found this document to be very useful once the lighting implementation has begun since so much of the information becomes obsolete as soon as adjustments begin.

A formal lighting plot is not as stuffy as it sounds. It can be as simple as a set drawing with specific light placement and general direction sketched and notated over the plan.

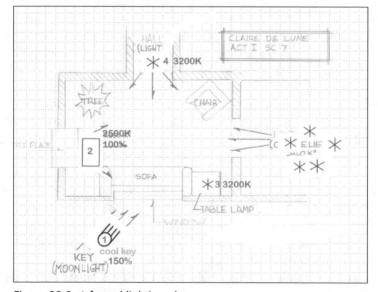

Figure 22.3: A formal lighting plot.

Symbols and Notations

You will be working with a number of different lighting instrument types. Rather than writing in longhand what each light type is on a plot or magic sheet, it is much easier to have a symbol system for your light types. It doesn't matter what the symbols are, just as long as you and the rest of your team can identify and understand the symbol system. Here is a list of symbols I like to use:

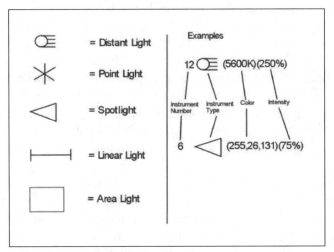

Figure 22.4: Lighting symbols.

In the left column, I have listed all the light types available in LightWave. I find these symbols easily recognizable, easy to remember, and quick to sketch, although you will probably come up with your own set of symbols.

The right column demonstrates usage of the symbols with notation. Each lighting instrument has an instrument number that corresponds with its place on the lighting schedule. Once again, if you choose not to use a lighting schedule, you will not really need to assign a number to each light, although if you are manipulating a large number of lights it might be very useful.

While you are assembling the paperwork, you will not likely know the exact color or intensity you need a light to be. In cases like this it is just as easy, rather than writing in a color or color temperature, to write in "C" for cool or "W" for warm, or you can write in a color name such as "orange," "steel blue," or "hot pink."

The type and number of symbols and notation you use is entirely up to you. Some designers use very little paperwork, while others are manic about it. It is your choice. Whatever works best for the production team is what you should use.

A Formal Lighting Schedule

A *formal lighting schedule* is a numerical listing of all the lights in your scene or act. The page contains a number of columns or fields containing data for each individual lighting instrument. A lighting schedule is a good idea if you are dealing with a large number of lights or a very large lighting project. It is also particularly helpful if you are reusing one setting in many different scenes. You can create a single lighting plot, if you wish, and turn the lights on and off as you require them. A lighting schedule is very helpful, in this case, for keeping track of all the various lights for the various scenes, although it seems to be more efficient and easier to work with a scene if it is pared down to include only the lights required for the scene. Once again, the choice is yours. The best method is the one that works best for you and the rest of the production team.

Instrument Number or Name

Each lighting instrument needs to be identified in the lighting schedule either numerically or with a unique descriptive name. If you choose the numeric method, you will simply list out all the lights in your scene and then number them. If, for example, there are 26 lights illuminating the scene, your lights will be listed on the page from #1 to #26. Finding a numbered instrument on a lighting plot is much easier than finding a descriptive name among 25 other descriptive names. Further, you may run out of really unique descriptive names if you have a large number of lights in the scene. I would recommend descriptive names for scenes with few lights and a numbering system for scenes with many lights.

Descriptive names might be something like *Key, Sunlight, Floor Lamp,* or *Chandelier*. If your chandelier has 20 individual lightbulbs or candles in it, you might give them a descriptive name followed by a number, such as: *Chandelier #12*. Whichever method you choose, you should name or number your light in LightWave the same way you have them in the lighting schedule.

Light Type

Light types need to be identified in the lighting schedule as well as on the lighting plot. It would certainly not do to place a point light where there ought to be an area light. In this column you simply write the type of light such as *area* or *spot*.

Intensity

Naturally, light intensity is key to the final look of the shot. When designing lights, you are likely to have a "ballpark" idea of what you think the intensity will be. Write that number in this column.

Color

Once again, you may not know the exact color. You may simply know whether you want a light to be warm or cool, or you may know roughly where on the color wheel you want to start. On the other hand, you may know the exact color temperature. Color temperature is a very precise way of determining the color of a light source. We know, for example, that most incandescent lightbulbs burn at around 3200 degrees Kelvin. So if you have a lightbulb in your scene, that's a good place to start. You may have to adjust that color later due to the relative color of the other light sources in the scene or because the director wants a dirtier, warmer look, but it can't hurt to start with physically correct measurements.

Position and Angle

You may wish to record the exact final position and direction of the light for archiving and recordkeeping purposes. If this is the case, you can include a column for position and angle. Leave these columns blank, however, until the lighting artists have finished lighting the scene.

Notes

If you are an adamant recordkeeper, chances are you will want some additional space to keep notes about each light. Notes as to the light's purpose are often helpful when leafing through a long lighting schedule looking for a particular light. Notes are especially helpful if you have chosen to number your lights rather than give them descriptive names. It is a good method of cross-referencing your lights.

Following is a sample lighting schedule. You don't have to do it this way. You don't have to include all of the columns listed here, and you can certainly add your own if you like.

Inst#	Type	Int	Col	Pos	Angle	Notes
1	Area	E	E	A	0,90,0	Fireplace 1
2	Area	E	E	A	0,90,0	Fireplace 2
3	Area	E	E	A	0,90,0	Fireplace 3
4	Dist	175	Steel	5.277,5.07,1.2877	56.3,54.8,0	Moon
5	Point	100	3200K	0,756mm,0		Table Lamp

Inst#	Type	Int	Col	Pos	Angle	Notes
6	Point	45	3200K	TBD		Chandelier1
7	Point	45	3200K	TBD		Chandelier2
8	Point	45	3200K	TBD		Chandelier3
9	Point	45	3200K	TBD		Chandelier4
10	Point	45	3200K	TBD		Chandelier5
11	Point	75	3200K	TBD		Hallway

The first three lights have intensities and colors listed as "E." This means that the color and intensity is *enveloped*, changing over time, as one would expect for light emitted from the ever-moving and lapping tongues of firelight. The position is listed as "A," which means *animated*. Animated is the same thing as enveloped, really, but while motion is considered "animation," where position, rotation, and scale change over time, such things as color and intensity changing over time is called an "envelope." For more details about envelopes, take a look at the Light-Wave manual or ask your local LightWave guru. TBD is shorthand for "to be determined."

Implementation

If you are working in a small production environment or if you are a lighting TD in a large production environment, you are going to be the one implementing the lighting design. There are several steps to implementation, usually beginning with a rough "blocking out" of light placement and direction, followed by the roughing out of light intensities and colors. After this, you can start rendering out frames to see exactly what the lights are doing, then move on to the last stage, which is fine-tuning. If you are working in consultation with a director and/or lighting designer, you will be presenting frames for evaluation and further implementing lighting changes as directed by the designer and/or the director. This final phase can go back and forth many times, sometimes indicating that a new approach or an evaluation meeting may be necessary.

Block Placement

When you are in the *block placement* phase of implementation, don't worry too much about exact position. Get the light somewhere you know it's going to roughly do the job. You can fine-tune it later. Make sure the light is not behind any geometry that will prevent it from illuminating the scene once Shadow Type has been set to Ray Trace or Shadow Map. Other than that, it's just placement by eye.

Roughing Out

During the *roughing out* phase, you will look at the properties of each light in your scene and assign it a base intensity and color. The intensities and colors you choose to start with may very well change in the *fine-tuning* stage, but you have to start somewhere, so make your best guess. If the designer has given you a lighting schedule, you should apply any color and intensity data available to you from that resource.

Fine-Tuning

Now that you have your lights roughly in place and you have a starting point for lighting intensities and colors, you can start making test renders to evaluate the lighting in the scene. You would be very lucky indeed to have the lighting work out perfectly the first time around. If you are a meticulous artist with a very specific image in mind, you may find yourself spending a good deal of time going through the evaluation loop of adjustment-render-evaluate again and again until the lighting is satisfactory. Sometimes this process will reveal basic flaws in the lighting design. Don't be afraid to suggest major changes to the design if you think it will provide a major improvement to the scenic illumination. If, however, you are a lighting TD and not the designer, it would be best to seek approval before making any major changes to the design, as your alterations could impact other design elements you are not aware of.

Figure 22.5 (See color image.)

Figure 22.5 shows an early test render for a shot from an animated short. You can see that there have been some scenic design changes since the original sketches and drawings. The hallway has been moved out into the foyer and a rocking chair has been added in the corner by the fireplace. This early test render is not yet textured. This is one frame of a fireplace R&D sequence.

Working with Surfaces

At some point, you will have to start working with surface attributes since lighting and surface attributes are inextricably linked together. Alteration to the surfaces will depend on a number of factors including how segmented the production departments are. In my opinion, the best, most efficient relationship between modeling/texturing departments and the lighting department is for the model to be provided built and shaded. Then when the lighting department takes over, a scene-specific copy of the model is made so that the lighting department can make shading changes as necessary without altering the original "master" model created by the modeling and texturing departments.

If your level of experience and expertise does not include shading and texturing, then you should consult with the texturing artist who originally shaded the model. As a lighting artist, it is your responsibility to learn the crafts of shading so that you can make informed decisions about making surface alterations without seriously impacting other departments or design considerations.

Evaluation

CG lighting designers have an enormous benefit not available to stage, video, or film lighting designers or gaffers. On the stage or the sound stage, lighting designs are implemented at immense cost. Equipment is rented, the crew is hired, the lighting plot is hung and focused. Usually evaluation is the last step — the step where the designer critiques her own work and tries to learn from it, to remember the design elements that really worked, and to scrap or rework elements that may not have been entirely successful. Evaluation for theatrical lighting designers will begin with technical rehearsals where the designer gets to see the lights in action, to see how they affect the scenic elements and the performers. The designer then has a limited number of days to make changes, alterations, and additions and to continue evaluation until opening night. There is an enormous cost associated with these changes, revolving mainly around union wages for the lighting crew and possibly including lighting rental and materials costs.

But in the beautiful, versatile world of CG, usually a single operator or artist implements the lighting design, tweaks and adjusts it, and examines the results within a rendered frame — and all this before lunch! A single rendered frame can provide enough feedback about whether it is necessary to tweak the design or even to completely redesign a scene if necessary (provided the artist time is available and within budget, of course). Regardless, it is much, much simpler to relight a CG scene than it is to relight a stage. Once you have rendered a test frame, you will probably know right away whether or not adjustments are required. You will likely spend time working in the render-evaluate-adjust loop before moving on to the next scene.

Balancing the Scene

Balance can mean a lot of different things. For example, when thinking of balance, one may envision a set of level scales, balancing perfectly. This is the classic image of balance, perfect and very, very cliché. When you are designing lights for your stage, whatever that stage may be, you may want your lights to be balanced in that way, or you may wish them to be balanced in an entirely different way. You may have your lights heavily emphasizing one side of the frame. This is also balance. It's just not balanced in the center. Choosing the balance can also mean choosing to be unbalanced. Unbalanced lighting can seem odd or off to an audience. It can set them on edge and give them the sense that something is not right. Look at the two following images. One of them appears to be right and the other appears to be wrong. But who is to say which is right and which is wrong?

Figure 22.6

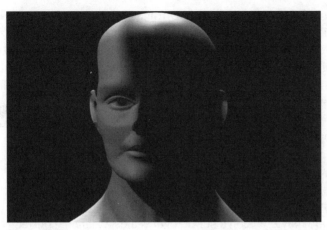

Figure 22.7

Figure 22.6 appears normally lit, as one would expect, while Figure 22.7 seems somehow mysterious. The character may be hiding something or hiding from something. We suspect that there is more to the story than we know and we wish to know more.

Do you see how a simple tool like this can either bore or excite your audience? You choose whether your stage is balanced or unbalanced, whether your lighting will be shocking and outrageous or subtle and keen. You decide whether the audience will be comfortable in their seats or crawling out of them. A simple tool like this can bring an audience laughter, anticipation, horror, fear, or any other emotion.

Focus and Emphasis

You get to decide where the audience looks.

When you are designing lights, there are certain things you and the director wish the audience to notice. There may be things you wish to be unnoticed at first. With lighting levels and a few simple tricks, you can lead your audience's eyes from one shot to the next and place them exactly where you wish them to be in the frame.

It is not necessary for you to be obtrusive in focusing the attention of your viewers onto a particular area of your scene. You can add emphasis through intensity and color, through movement, or by using an unusual lighting angle that makes a particular area stand out from the rest. In the previous test render from our animated short (see Figure 22.5), our eye is first drawn to the fireplace. It is the most brightly lit area of the room. Our eye follows a sweeping curve around the room noting the sofa and window, the rug, and finally the Christmas tree. The picture is painted, the scene has been established in just the way the artists desire.

Designing with Light and Shadow

Everybody knows about designing with light. You place a light so that a desired area is illuminated in a certain way. It may be a soft key light playing across a face, or it may be a brilliant rim light that makes your character stand out from the background. This is a given. Lighting designers design light.

There's more, though. We must also know how to design with shadow. If we can learn where to strategically place shadows just as we instinctively know where to place light, we have effectively doubled our lighting toolkit, for shadows are just as useful, just as good at telling the story, as lights are.

Designing with Light

By illuminating one area more brightly than another or by applying a more vibrant color in one area than another, we can shift focus. We can spread the visibility homogeneously around the scene if we wish or we can punctuate certain symbols or moments within the scene. We can offer clues as to the time of day, the atmospheric conditions, and the setting by use of color, angle, and intensity of light. We can change the lighting during the scene to signify the passage of time or the change of environment. In essence, anything that happens on the stage can be punctuated, supported, or counter-pointed by the deliberate and artistic use of lights in the scene.

Designing with Shadow

Designing with light is only half of the toolset. You can design with shadow as well. That which we choose *not* to light is equally as important as that which we choose to light. We may wish to hide some information until later, perhaps only allowing information to leak subconsciously into the scene. We may wish to be more deliberate than that, excluding important information so that the viewer will wonder why and will focus more on that missing information. There is little that draws a viewer into your story better than genuine curiosity.

Take a man standing half in the shadow of a dark, dead-end alley.

Now that you have that image in your mind, what are you seeing? Are you seeing the half-illuminated face of a man or are you seeing the dark, silhouetted shape that resides in shadow? Certainly the illuminated half tells us that there is a man in the alley. We are given that piece of the story up front: There is a man in the alley. Then the questions start to rise: Why is there a man in the alley? Why is he half in the shadows? Is he trying to hide from something? Or maybe he's stepping into the light on purpose, maybe he's trying to make himself more visible so the old lady walking home won't be frightened of him.

There are many different ways you can use shadow to accentuate elements in your scene, to draw the audience's eye toward, or away from, scenic elements.

Lighting a Scene vs. Lighting an Object

In the world of visual effects, CG artists often find themselves creating and illuminating individual elements to be composited onto photographic background plates. In a case like this, the artist will be attempting to simulate the lighting environment found in the plate. If, on the other hand, you are the designer and your scene is entirely, or even largely, CG, then the design becomes infinitely more complex and infinitely more rewarding.

Lighting a scene means understanding the story and the technical requirements. It means being able to interpret the emotional intent of both the writer and director. It means being able to implement a lighting design that supports that intent. If you are a lighting TD or a lighting artist with experience in visual effects and you wish to move on to lighting all-CG scenes, be aware that lighting individual CG elements for visual effects composition bears very little resemblance to all-CG lighting design. If you have read this chapter in full, you have a good idea of what can be involved in lighting design for computer animation. Don't be discouraged. There is no better way to learn the process than to work your way through it. If you are not lucky enough to be assigned such work, I would recommend taking some time to create your own short. Once you have demonstrated your design abilities, it won't be too long before a suitable opportunity arises.

Putting It All Together (Making a Pleasing Picture)

If you started thematically, with a single vision, then you should not have too much trouble inserting all the various elements of your design and having them work together reasonably well. You can tie your elements together very simply by choosing a color palette at the beginning and then sticking to it, and if you alter the color palette, remember to alter it for everything. This does not mean that all key lights have to be the same color. It means that you pick your main colors, decide how far you are going to vary those colors through hue and value variations, then go with it. If you have decided to stick to earth tones, for example, and one scene is lit with purple and yellow, it is going to stick out. It won't belong to the scenes around it and will seem out of place. That's not to say that you can't make a scene appear out of place if you want. This is a great tool that can be used to keep your audience off balance and uncomfortable if that's what you wish.

Maintaining a thematic view is not going to be very difficult if you are working within a team. There are many other artists and designers working with you, discussing your ideas and offering their own. You are likely spending a great deal of time trying to sort out how to incorporate your own design ideas into the concepts of the other artists. This process is conducive to thematic work since a group of people all working together on the project are much less likely to go far off track than a single artist or a very small production team that doesn't meet often enough.

The main idea is that you should be thinking about making a pleasing picture — one that is pleasing to you because it conveys the messages and feelings that you want it to convey. It doesn't necessarily have to please your audience.

Art should not always be beautiful. Sometimes it should be ugly and horrible.

Saving and Reusing Lighting Rigs

Perhaps one of the most magnificent advantages of having your lights as nothing but a mess of pure data inside a conglomerate of plastic and metal is that you can save, copy, cut, and paste your lighting design together from previous designs as though you were copyediting a paragraph. I like to do this by stripping out all the objects in the scene, replacing any parent objects with nulls, making sure all the lights are parented to a main null, and then saving the scene as a lighting rig. When you want to use this rig again within your scene, simply choose Load Items From Scene and when you are asked if you wish to load lights as well as objects, respond "Yes." Of course, there are no objects (other than nulls) to be loaded, but the lights will load up nicely. You can manipulate the whole rig by grabbing the main null you added when creating the rig.

• • •

I have said it before and I'll say it again: "There are no rules!" If you are a new lighting designer, you can expect to have to gain some experience before you get some really great gigs. There is only one way to get experience: Get lighting! Think about light and observe light all the time. Every day is filled with uncountable opportunities to learn something that will help your lighting some day — maybe tomorrow. You can't learn lighting from a book. You must observe light in the real world and you must then attempt to simulate that light in the computer environment. Sooner or later you will gain an understanding of how light works. This understanding will make you a force among your peers. They will throw adulation and bottles of champagne in your direction, offer you ridiculous raises, and fall at your feet with gratitude for saving their show. Or at least they'll say, "Yeah, that looks pretty good. I could do that."

Chapter 23

Rendering Times

By the time you have finished this chapter, you should have several ideas on how to shorten your render times. These are but a few of the many, many tricks to get renders out under heavy time constraints. No doubt you will discover many more during the course of your career.

It's time for some big decisions. You know you want the lighting to be as accurate and as beautiful as possible. You would like to use some level of radiosity but know that you probably can't spare the render times. You might have time for area lights if you lower the quality and use Shading Noise Reduction. Or you may be so pressed for render time and the render farm may be so full of scenes from the other pesky animators that you have to abandon all your highbrow lighting plans and go for dirty, cheap tricks.

Whatever your final decision is, it will come down to simple math. How long does it take to render a single frame? How many processors are available to you? How much time do you have to deliver the final, rendered elements?

At one of the companies where I worked, there was a one-hour limit on render time for a single frame. Now, I think that is a good deal of time for a single frame, but I know animators who have worked in production environments with a five-minute limit. That seems awfully low to me and most certainly will be a strong determining factor in the final quality of the images. On the other hand, some very large, very complex work takes many hours per frame. Sometimes you simply can't justify sacrificing quality.

What it comes down to is a balance of image quality vs. available render time. Many battles have been won and lost over this very issue. Artists inevitably want to turn on every bell and whistle available to them to make their image sweeter. Supervisors try to calculate how many more processors they can afford to add to the render farm within the project's budget. Coordinators try to keep everything and everyone going at peak efficiency; otherwise there is no possible chance that delivery will be made on time. Directors are adding more shots but expecting delivery on the original date. Producers won't come up with any more money. And in the middle of this there is an artist trying to figure out if she can use an area light instead of a distant light.

It's a very large picture and you're likely to find yourself at the very end of a chain of discussions all influencing whether or not you can add that area light.

Well, I'm here to tell you that it's a battle and a conundrum you're likely to join at one time or another. Take heart. Sometimes you will be able to demonstrate how much better your image will be with your bells and whistles, and Those In Charge will look astonished and meekly say "OK." Other times, they won't care if it looks like a cheap cartoon. Choose your battles wisely. In the meantime, learn how to cheat, trick, connive, and deceive your way to lighting success.

Cheats and Tricks

When it comes down to the final render, physical accuracy doesn't matter. Using the "right" light type doesn't matter. The only thing that matters is whether or not the rendered image looks good. How you got there is completely irrelevant. There are many, many ways of shortening render times, some of which have already been discussed. A few of the most common and obvious tricks are mentioned in the following paragraphs.

Don't Tell Them

If any of my supervisors read this, I'll be in for it. Perhaps the greatest tool is the one that your supervisor doesn't know about. I recently completed a feature project in which I used Backdrop Only global illumination (radiosity) in every shot, just for the beautiful soft shadows. I had to be extremely careful not to use the word "radiosity"; otherwise I was told to turn it off, regardless of the quality. The issue is that many people are convinced radiosity results in extra hours per frame. It doesn't have to. In skilled hands, the extra time can be small. For us, it added between 5 and 15 minutes per frame, but for a full-aperture render (2048 x 1556) that's not too bad. The trick was, I had to call it Backdrop Only global illumination, and never, *ever* use the word "radiosity." Truth is, this mode isn't really radiosity because there are no light reflection calculations anyway. For a more detailed description of Backdrop Only GI, please see "Radiosity Setups" in Chapter 25.

Bear in mind that there is a stigma attached not only to radiosity but to other tools as well such as area lights, linear lights, and light arrays. If you can demonstrate the massive quality improvement without the massive render times, they'll be happy. What difference does it make if they don't know the exact tools you used?

Antialiasing Level

When I first started rendering images in LightWave, I was determined that Enhanced Medium antialiasing was the lowest acceptable AA quality. I had heard other artists claim that Enhanced Low was fine for many situations. Years of experience and thousands of rendered frames have convinced me that Enhanced Low is, indeed, fine for many situations, especially those without much motion blur.

All your antialiasing settings can be found on the Camera Properties panel.

Antialiasing smoothes out the "stairstepping" inherent in square pixels. If you have antialiasing set to Low or Enhanced Low, LightWave will make five separate passes, smoothing out the pixels five times. Medium does nine passes, High does 17 passes, and Extreme does 33 passes. You can also double the number of passes by changing Motion Blur to Dithered instead of Normal. Why are there very high settings? If you have an element with very fast motion through the frame, the separate passes will be obvious and visible if the antialiasing level is Low or Enhanced Low. The higher the antialiasing level, the smoother motion blur will appear. For more details on antialiasing level and motion blur, please see the LightWave manual.

Figure 23.1: The Camera Properties panel.

Figure 23.2: Ball with Enhanced Low antialiasing.

Sometimes you will find you must set your antialiasing levels higher to achieve an acceptable motion blur. Of course the problem with that is more render passes mean more render time. Going from Enhanced Low to Enhanced Medium nearly doubles your render time. Enhanced Medium with Dithered motion blur looks better but nearly quadruples render times from Enhanced Low with Normal motion blur.

Figure 23.3: Ball with Enhanced Medium antialiasing.

Figure 23.4: Ball with Enhanced Medium antialiasing
and Dithered motion blur.

Another way to allow you to keep your antialiasing lower is to make the
Blur Length lower. Blur Length is set to 50% by default. If you make it
more like 25% or 30%, the antialiasing passes will be closer together
and it will be harder to see the stepping.

The *blur length* represents the amount of translation an item will
have for all the motion blur passes. For instance, with a Blur Length of
50%, an item's "blur" will spread out the distance of half the distance
between the item's position in the current frame and the next. 50% is
chosen as the default to represent the look of motion blur on film. The
thing to keep in mind is that if your item travels a great distance
between frames, your "trails" will be spread out more than if it travels a
smaller distance, so you'd need to use a higher AA setting to get more
motion blur passes. Also, you can use blur lengths higher than 100% to
"shoot" past the next position or negative blurs to shoot out in the opposite direction.

Figure 23.5: Ball with Enhanced Medium antialiasing,
Normal motion blur, and 25% Blur Length.

You can also speed up your render times by enabling the Adaptive Sampling button directly below the Antialiasing drop-down, but be warned: Adaptive sampling antialiases edges. The overall quality of the antialiasing will suffer, and render times will be significantly increased in most cases. The threshold value determines how much of a difference between pixels in the "edge" before it is antialiased. You can tell how much is happening by watching the render progress window. The white area is what is being AA'd; you can adjust the threshold from there to do more or less.

Vector Blur

Vector Blur is a great tool that helps keep your antialiasing level as low as possible. Vector Blur is a post-process image filter that measures the vector, or direction and speed that the object is moving, then applies a blur in that direction for the object. This blur is applied after the render, which is why it is called a "post" process. This tool can make an Enhanced Low AA render look better than an Enhanced Medium AA render at just over half the rendering time.

This tool won't work for everything. There are issues with the way it shows objects behind the blurred item, as you can see in the shadow of Figure 23.6. It also is not applied to shadows, only the objects themselves.

Figure 23.6

Perhaps the main drawback to the Vector Blur tool is that, since it is a post-process, it does not see anything off the edge of the frame. So if you apply the blur to an object that is half out of frame, Vector Blur considers the edge of the frame to be the edge of the object and blurs it, creating transparency there.

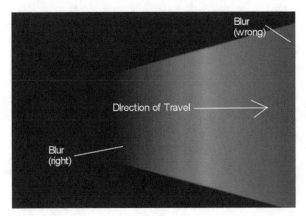

Figure 23.7

As you can see in the Low AA render in Figure 23.7, the box is moving quickly out of frame. The Vector Blur plug-in has been applied and does a good job of blurring the back end of the block, but it also blurs the block near the edge of the frame as though that were the other end of the block. The only way to get around this is to render the frame larger than you need it and then crop out the edge blur effect.

Limited Region Renders

No doubt you will eventually find yourself in the position (if you haven't already) of getting a note back on an element that you thought was finished. What's most irritating is that the note pertains to some small detail in the element. Most of the render is completely fine. Perhaps there is a dark area in the far lower left of an area and the director wants it lit a little brighter. You have to make that small adjustment and re-render your frames. Well, you don't have to. Thanks to limited region renders, you can isolate just the area you wish to correct, render only that small square, and then composite it back onto the original frames seamlessly (or better yet, have a compositor do it for you).

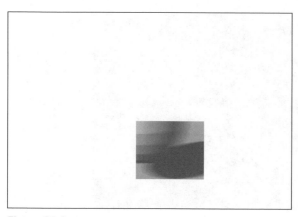

Figure 23.8

A limited region render will render proportionately faster than the whole frame. The limited region of the speeding ball in Figure 23.8 rendered in less than one-tenth the time of the original frame.

This is a massive time-saver, not only for final renders but also for making minor adjustments to specific areas of a shot. Why sit around and wait for the whole frame to render when you only need to see the adjustment in a corner?

As far as most-bang-for-the-buck, this tool has to be near the top of the list. It's incredibly simple to use; simply go to the Camera Properties panel in Layout, turn on Limited Region, and use the Adjust Region tool. Then render it. In the past, the rendered frames would be the same size of the limited region, meaning the rendered region would have to be carefully lined up in compositing. In LightWave 8, you now have the option of selecting limited region renders with or without a border.

If you render with a border, the limited region will be positioned correctly for composition back into the original render. If you render without borders, the frame will be rendered the same size of the limited region, like the old days.

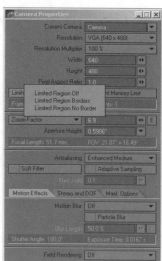

Figure 23.9

Baking Illumination

Baking illumination is a brilliant way of applying all sorts of fancy, expensive lighting conditions such as area lights and radiosity without having to put up with the three-hour-per-frame rendering times. The trick is to set up all the expensive lighting, use Surface Baker to create image maps of the final illumination data, and then reapply those maps to the surfaces so that you can achieve the lighting without using the lights. If that doesn't make sense, check out the Baking Radiosity tutorial in Chapter 25.

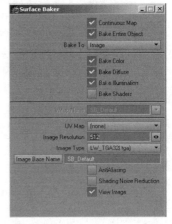

Figure 23.10

The only big drawback to baked illumination is that you only have illumination data for the single frame that you rendered, which means that the illumination in your scene will not change over time, even if you move stuff around. What it comes down to is that baking illumination is perfect for camera fly-throughs, but not great for scenes where a lot of objects or lights move around.

Of course, you always have the option of baking illumination from some surfaces and not others, then using LightWave's Light Exclusion to choose which surfaces get the heavy calculations and which don't.

• • •

I make jokes about render times. I hog the farm if anyone will let me get away with it. I use wildly ridiculous rendering times if I think nobody will notice, especially after hours and on the weekend when nobody else is around. It's like an addiction. I can't stop! But the fact is that most of the time, you can't get away with it and people will notice.

It is one of your primary jobs as a professional lighting artist to explore every possible technique for shaving time off your renders, for only rendering exactly what is necessary, and for dropping the quality as low as you think you can get away with. If the quality drops too low, somebody will almost certainly let you know about it. But you'll be amazed at what you can get away with, especially if there's a reasonable amount of motion blur in the scene.

So be cheap, use every crappy trick you can think of, and you will be admired the world over, and every choice job will be yours for the taking. Well, okay, I made that last bit up.

Hopefully you now understand some of the tricks and the spirit of reducing render times. There are many great hacks that you will discover on your own or from other artists. Some are great. Some go too far, affecting the overall quality too much. It is your job to judge how far to go with each shot. But there is no doubt that if you can render a frame in half the time of the guys sitting beside you, you're a more valuable asset.

Chapter 24

Identifying and Recreating Light Sources in a Plate

This chapter deals with a couple of simple examples about how to analyze the lighting in a photograph and recreate it in LightWave so that your CG elements will be lit appropriately on top of the background image. Analyzing and recreating lighting in this way is perhaps the single most crucial skill in creating 3D visual effects. By the time you have finished this chapter, you should have an idea how to go about this process.

About Photo-Real Lighting

There is nothing in the manual and no button or plug-in in LightWave or anywhere else that will create appropriate and photo-real lighting for your shot. The only thing that will do that is your understanding. Your understanding of the light types and properties, of the shadow types and properties, and of the lighting instruments, colors, and diffusion gels used on set is the only thing that will enable you to do a world-class job of lighting (or in this case relighting) the shot.

Further, it is crucial that you understand the textures and materials that you are lighting. You need to know the properties of those textures. Are they highly specular or matte in finish? Should they be highly reflective or glossy? Understanding how the textures *should* be reacting to your lights is a big indicator as to whether or not your lighting is appropriate or your textures are appropriate. If one or the other is too far off, either the element will be unsuccessful or the compositing artist will have a great deal of work to do to make it a success. As a lighting artist, you should take pride in providing lighting and shading that requires little compositing alteration. If nothing else, this makes you a valuable asset because you are saving your company money in compositing time.

About Plates and Light Sources

A *plate* is usually a photographic element (either a still or an image sequence) onto which we want to add some sort of computer-generated element. Take, for example, the dinosaurs in the movie *Jurassic Park*. The dinosaurs themselves, of course, were CG, but the background *plates* were filmed. This is what we mean when we talk about compositing a CG element onto a plate or background plate.

Now, how do we identify light sources? And how do we recreate them for CG elements that will be added to the plate?

First, learn how to look at light and shadow. Understand the qualities and properties of light. Know the color temperature, angle, size, and everything else about every light source. It is very helpful to understand the types of luminaries, or lighting instruments, gels, flags, and diffusion filters used by the lighting crew on set. Second, learn how to use the tools in LightWave. Know how to make a hard shadow and a soft one. Understand inverse square falloff and how to create real soft shadows and everything else there is to know about the lighting tools in LightWave. Part II of this book and the LightWave manual both deal extensively with how to use the toolset.

Probably the very easiest way to learn how to match CG lighting to a plate is simply to look at some photographs, identify the light sources, then proceed to set them up in LightWave, compositing the two at the end. We will look at a few different lighting scenarios.

After you have lit a few hundred CG elements to match plates, you will probably get a feel for the lighting just by looking at any old photo. But to begin, it may be beneficial to look at a couple of tools that can help you identify light sources, their direction, and other properties. Perhaps the most used lighting analysis tool is a matte ball. Just any old Styrofoam ball will do, although it should probably be at least 12" across to give you a good look at the lighting. Some prefer to use a gray ball. In this case, I managed to get my hands on an 18% gray ball used in a feature film and also a mirror ball (no, not the kind used in discos and high school dances), which we will discuss later.

If you need to light CG elements to a plate and you are lucky enough to have someone on set who will stick a ball in the shot and shoot a few frames in exactly the same lighting context, your life will be made easier. Rather than guessing at what the lighting might be, you will have a better visual reference. Of course, a well-organized shoot will include several feet of film containing nothing but the clean plate (empty set with no performers) and a gray or mirror ball. If the footage is shot through the same camera that is used to shoot the film, you'll be that much more likely to accurately match the lighting. Below is an image of a gray ball in a studio setting.

Figure 24.1

In this context, the direction and relative intensity of the key lighting source is completely obvious. We can see by the shadow on the ball that there is one key light source and that it is above the ball to the left and slightly closer to the camera than the ball. If the light source were behind the ball, more than half the ball would be in shadow. But more than half the ball is in the light, so we know that the light source is closer to the camera than the ball is, thereby illuminating more of the ball facing the camera.

Take a look at the next image and see if you can clearly identify the light source.

Figure 24.2

This time, it is easy to see that the light source is above and behind the ball. We know that a direct light source pointing at a spherical shape will illuminate half of it. If we see less than half of the ball illuminated, then the light source must be shining on the side of the ball that is facing away from us.

This is why using a ball is so simple for identifying light direction. If you choose to use a white ball, and you have the benefit of color images, you can also use the information in the ball photos to help you determine the color of the light sources as well. Be aware, however, that the colors on your computer monitor, your digital camera (if you are using one), and a television monitor are all likely to be quite different. While you may do your best to match colors in the plate with your CG lighting colors, the likelihood is that color adjustment will have to take place during final compositing. So while it is important to try to match the plate's light colors, to at least get in the ballpark, it is a waste of time trying to be completely precise, because the color palette is almost certainly going to be adjusted by someone with a different monitor calibration anyway. So get it close, but don't waste time trying to get it perfect. As a matter of fact, if all you are doing is spending time making slight adjustments to color, you should be using Worley Labs' G2 plug-in. Using this tool, you can make quick adjustments to scene lighting and color using G2's interactive preview. It will save you many long hours using the old (and now outdated) render-and-tweak method.

Replicating the Light Source

Let's take a look at one of our "ball in a studio" shots and see how easy it is to replicate within LightWave. The first thing we'll need is a ball. So open up Modeler, make a simple ball, and save it somewhere. Then send it to Layout if you use the Hub; otherwise, switch to Layout and load the ball object.

Once in Layout with the ball, open the Image Editor and load the background image Ball.tga. This image is available on the companion CD.

Now open up the Display Options panel by using the "d" key (assuming your keyboard is set to LightWave's default settings). Near the bottom of the panel, set the Camera View Background setting to Background Image. This will allow the camera view of Layout to show whatever image is selected for the background.

Figure 24.3

Figure 24.4

Next, open up the Compositing panel. This is a tab on the Effects panel. Once there, set the Background Image to the image you loaded, Ball.tga.

Figure 24.5

Now, when you switch to Camera View, you should see the Ball.tga image in the background with your ball in front of it. Move your ball a little to the side so you can make a comparison between the shadows in the background image and the shadows on your ball.

Figure 24.6

Two things are immediately obvious. First, we have to open the Surface Editor and turn on smoothing for our ball object. Second, the lighting direction is obviously completely wrong. So go ahead and open up the Surface Editor. At the bottom of the Basic tab, you will see the toggle box to turn smoothing on or off. Turn it on.

Figure 24.7

That looks much better. Now open up your Light Properties panel by selecting the Lights mode button at the bottom of the interface and clicking Properties or by hitting the "p" key.

Once this panel is open, click the Global Illumination button to open that panel, then set Ambient Intensity to 0%.

Figure 24.8

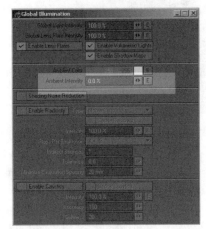

Figure 24.9

Having Ambient Intensity set to 0% will help us see the shadow terminator more easily.

Now, select your distant light and, using a number of different views, move the distant light so that it is visible in camera and is positioned above and just behind your ball, pointing toward it like in Figure 24.10.

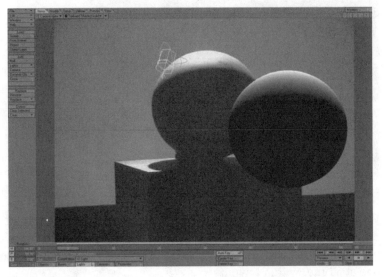

Figure 24.10

325

Now try a test render by hitting the F9 key and see how that looks.

Figure 24.11

Well, there is a pretty obvious specularity difference between the ball in the picture and our CG ball, but we're not looking at textures here as much as we are looking at the lighting properties. Nonetheless, let's open up the Surface Editor and tweak a little to see if we can achieve a superior result. I'm not going to offer you any data here; go ahead and try it on your own. Here's what I came up with:

Figure 24.12

Well, it certainly didn't take more than one or two minutes to sort that out. See how simple it is to recreate real lighting within LightWave? The trick is to recognize each individual light source and then build each one, one at a time, within Layout.

The Mirror Ball

Another way of analyzing light sources is to get a big shiny mirror ball and photograph it in the environment. You'll get a reasonably good look at the surrounding light sources, although I find this method tends to skew reality a little. Take a look at the following image and you'll see what I mean.

Figure 24.13

You can see most of the environment, but I find this method inferior to the gray (or preferably white) ball method. I prefer a white ball because you'll have a pure color mix. Using a gray ball affects the color saturation. I prefer a matte ball instead of a mirrored ball because a matte ball will have obvious shadows demonstrating the direction of the key light source. But that is not to say that the mirrored ball provides no useful information. As a second source of information, I'd use a mirrored ball so I could see the whole environment. If it is used on set, the mirror ball can give you valuable information about lighting placement, type, color, and intensity ratios. If you are having trouble identifying the light sources, this information could be quite valuable. But most of the time you should be able to get all the information you need from the matte ball. The gray ball has the advantage that it is not likely to look "blown out" if the illumination is too bright, which a white ball might. After you become experienced, you will find that you don't even need a ball anymore, as you can extract the lighting information from any old photo. But if you have the option, it's always wise to acquire as much data on set as possible. So if you have the option of getting mirror ball and matte ball photos, gray or white, under the lights and from the camera position, definitely do so. Ideally, the reference images will be taken with the same camera used for the principal photography, using the same lens,

under the same lighting conditions, and on the very day and at the time
of the shoot.

Let's look at an exterior photo with a matte ball.

Figure 24.14

As in the last section, let's add a ball to the scene and see if we can simulate the lighting in the photograph. The image is on the CD and is
called Ball2.tga. Load it up in the background as before. If you have the
previous tutorial scene open, you can simply replace the image.

Figure 24.15

The first and most obvious note is that our light type is definitely not soft enough for the task at hand. Since I took this photo, I know that the sky is overcast with clouds. If you take a look at the previous mirrored ball image, you will see the overcast sky as well. Since you have already read most of this book, you will know that an overcast sky means no direct sunlight, which means no hard shadows. The clouds are the only illumination source here. The best tool LightWave has to simulate an overcast sky is Backdrop Only global illumination. So let's turn off the distant light and enable Backdrop Only GI.

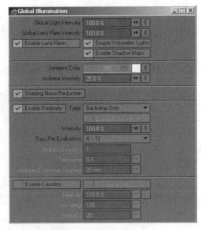

Figure 24.16

Backdrop Only GI is enabled in the Light Properties Global Illumination panel. Don't forget to turn on Shading Noise Reduction to improve shading quality.

Figure 24.17

In order for Backdrop Only GI to illuminate anything, the backdrop must be something other than black. In this case, I have used Textured Environment to place a gradient in the background that is white up to where the sky is and black down below where the ground is. This technique

329

lets me decide the direction the light comes from. After all, I don't want illumination from below, just from the sky above.

Now render out a frame and take a look.

Figure 24.18

That's not bad for a first kick at the cat. The only problem is that the shadow beneath the ball is missing. This makes the ball obviously added to the image. So here's a trick to add in the shadow.

First, you'll need to make a box in Modeler. It should be about the shape and size of the 2 x 6 lumber that the ball is sitting on. Once you have made your box, load it into Layout and move it around until it roughly lines up with the balcony rail in the photo.

Figure 24.19

Now in Layout, open Surface Editor and select the surface for your new box. Click on the color Texture button to open up the Texture Editor.

Next to Layer Type, select Image Map. Set Projection to Front and next to Image, select the Ball2.tga image we are using for our background.

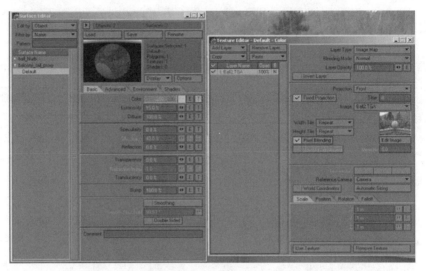

Figure 24.20

What you have just done is project the background image onto the box from the camera's point of view. This will make the box blend in with the image, so you won't actually see the box, except that now there is geometry to accept the shadow being cast by the ball. The box geometry may be a little too dark to correctly blend in with the background image. You can compensate for this by increasing the luminosity value of the box's surface in the Surface Editor

Figure 24.21

There, now it looks like there are two balls in the shot instead of one. All we used was Backdrop Only GI and no lights. The render took less than 5 seconds, which is quicker, if you can believe it, than an area light render, which took 13 seconds.

A More Complex Lighting Environment

Here's a photo of a typical sunny winter day in Vancouver. (Note the magnificent North Shore Mountains freshly dusted with snow — skiing just half an hour from the city core!)

Figure 24.22

Although this image is black and white, it demonstrates a lighting environment with three discrete lighting sources. The primary source, or *key*, is the sun. The two secondary, or *fill*, sources are the diffused skylight and the bright reflection from the wooden roof deck in the foreground. We can approximate the angle of the sunlight not only by the shadow terminator on the test ball but also by the direction of the shadows on the ground.

Recreating this lighting requires an understanding of the nature of each of these light sources. So what do we know about them?

We know that our key source, the sun, is the brightest of the three, produces the hardest shadows of the three, and is somewhere in the amber range of color. We know from our environment that this is a winter scene. We know that it's in the Northern Hemisphere above the 49th parallel, so the sun is fairly low in the sky. The length of the shadows on the ground confirms this. We know the mountains in the image are to the north of the city (hence "North Shore"); therefore the sun is in the west, indicating an afternoon timeframe. We know that the sky, one of our two fill sources, is very large and therefore creates very soft shadows. We know that the sky's color is somewhere in the blue range of the color spectrum. The second fill, the light that is being reflected off the wooden roof deck (this light is also known as a "bounce" light), is probably a light grayish or brownish color. It is also a fairly large diffused light source, although not nearly as large as the sky.

My first inclination is to use a distant light for the sun, even though the shadows will not be perfectly accurate, and two area lights, one for the sky fill and one for the bounce light. The sky fill light will be considerably larger than the bounce light.

Now there are a number of different ways I could approach this lighting problem using any number of lights and any number of combinations. There are methods that will render more quickly and there are methods that will render more slowly. (Believe me, there are always methods that will render more slowly!) I have selected this method as being a sort of "middle-of-the-road" solution. Quality is likely to be fairly high without monstrous render times.

First, let's take some object and throw it into the scene. Then load up the background image as we have done in previous sections. This image is called Vancouver.tga and can be found on the companion CD.

Figure 24.23

I've decided to throw an old Egyptian monolith into the scene. Never mind what an old Egyptian monolith is doing on a roof deck in Vancouver in the middle of winter.

We'll also need to add a ground plane so the monolith has something onto which to cast its shadows. Further, I'm going to replace the ball with a Gothic footsoldier's helmet that I have lying around. It's about the right shape and size to replace the ball.

Figure 24.24

Notice that there is a shadow object for both the monolith and the helmet. This piece of geometry serves the same purpose as the geometry we used in the previous example to catch the shadow of the ball. The monolith shadow object is at ground level, while the helmet shadow object is at table level. Without these objects, there would be nothing to receive the shadows.

When inserting objects into the image, it is very, very helpful to know the lens focal length and the focal distance. In this case, I snapped the photo without really thinking about either, then decided later to insert a CG element. This is often how it happens in production, so you may find yourself twiddling with things like lens, angle, and focal distance until you get the perspective lines in the CG elements to line up with the perspective lines in the image. Once this is accomplished, you can move on to lighting the elements. First, let's take our default distant light and aim it so that the shadows will fall in approximately the right direction.

Figure 24.25

Figure 24.26

That angle and length looks about right. But I already find the shadow too hard. I'm going to switch the distant light to a spotlight and use fuzzy shadow maps to get a little softness into the shadow.

Remember, when switching to a spotlight, the position of the spotlight becomes important, whereas a distant light can be anywhere and only its angle is important. You may also want to back the spotlight away and reduce the cone angle to make the light "rays" appear more parallel.

Figure 24.27

I used a shadow fuzziness of 5 here. It adds just a touch of softness that makes the shadow appear more like those in the plate.

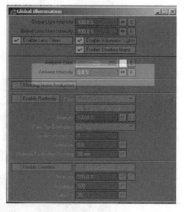

Now to add the fill lights. The first thing to do is open up your Light Properties panel, click on the Global Illumination button, and turn Ambient Intensity down to 0%. (If you don't know why we do this, you should go back and reread the previous chapters. I think I mention it at least 12 times.)

Next, add a new area light and position it over the CG element, being sure

Figure 24.28

that there is a wide margin around all sides. The skylight comes in from nearly 180 degrees so we want our skylight fill to be quite large.

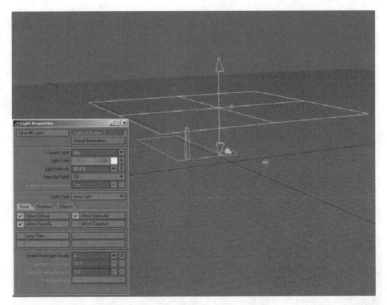

Figure 24.29

You'll notice that I set the intensity of the skylight to 50%. I generally start with a 2:1 key/fill ratio. It's not always right — as a matter of fact it seldom is perfect — but it's usually a good place to start. I'll render out a frame and see how that works.

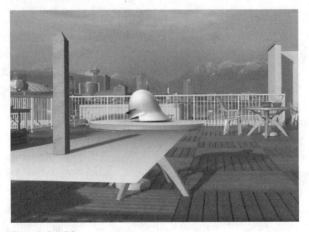

Figure 24.30

That added a nice intensity and soft shadows to the scene. The large area light only contributed a few seconds extra to each render pass.

The third light, our secondary fill, will be subtle and is meant just to fill in the darkest shadows, such as that one on the right-hand side of the monolith.

The easiest way to create this light is to clone your first area light, flip it upside down so it's now pointing upward, then lower it to ground level. Turn the intensity down to about 15%. You can also make the area light a little smaller. This will save on render times.

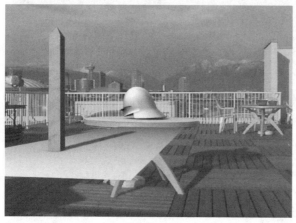

Figure 24.31

There, that's had the effect of lowering shadow density a little, and again with only a slight increase in render time. For an effect like this one, you could even use a light without shadows turned on, since the effect is just to lighten shadows. And, although it is a very fast solution and could be used, I would not encourage using ambient intensity for this purpose, as its lighting result is too even and perfect and tends to flatten out the lighting. The area light reduces shadow density while, at the same time, providing soft, natural shadows, which ambient intensity does not. On the other hand, if rendering time is crucial — more important than quality — ambient intensity might be the solution.

Now we need to get rid of the ugly shadow objects. To do this, open the Surface Editor, select the ground object, apply the background image, Vancouver.tga, as a front projection map, then turn Diffuse to 50% and Luminosity to 50%. This should make the polygon surface texture precisely match the background texture while still allowing a shadow to fall on the polygon. If not, fiddle with the Luminosity value until the shadow objects blend in better with the background plate. Bear in mind that you need some amount of Diffuse value in order for the shadow objects to pick up the shadows. Luminosity values may go as high as 100%.

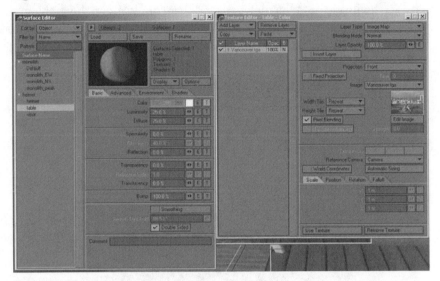

Figure 24.32

> **Note:** As a matter of fact, as long as the sum of the Diffuse and Luminosity settings equal 100%, the polygon should match the background plate pretty closely.

Now, do the same with the table polygon. Set Luminosity and Diffuse each to 50% (or whatever works best), then front project the background image onto the polygon. You should get a render that looks something like this:

Figure 24.33

That looks pretty good, but do you see the problem? The shadow from the monolith is falling on the front of the table. It shouldn't do that. To fix this we'll simply throw in a polygon where the table leg is, front project the image onto that polygon, and that should erase the problem. For a situation like this where we don't want any shadows to be cast upon the polygon, we can turn Luminosity up to 100% and turn Diffuse right down to 0%.

Figure 24.34

Figure 24.35

There are still one or two issues. The shadow, for example, is not quite dark enough. There are a number of ways to deal with that. First, if another artist will be compositing the shot, you will likely render out a separate shadow pass and the compositor will take care of the shadow darkness and match it up nicely so the question may be moot. Why spend time working on a perfect shadow if someone else is going to fiddle with it? If you are compositing the shot yourself in LightWave, you could always use Worley's Luminous Shadow Darkening tool. This tool was originally available in Worley's Gaffer. If you don't already own Gaffer, I recommend you get G2 instead. G2 has all of Gaffer's tools and many more.

Rendering the Element

We have been learning to match lighting by rendering our elements against the background plate and seeing how well they match up in the render. Under normal production circumstances, however, after you match up the lighting, you will almost certainly turn off the background and render the CG element by itself. This rendered sequence or still frame will then be handed off to a compositing station where another artist will import both the background plate and the CG element and marry them together. The compositing artist (or *compositor*) who does this marrying will be sure to very carefully match color. He will also add film grain if it is appropriate and soften, blur, sharpen, and adjust contrast, gamma, or color curves, or do whatever else might be necessary to make the CG element look like it really belongs in the image.

Getting the Color Perfect Is Not Your Job

Compositors and their tools are a critical part of the CG process. This is because computer-generated images almost always look CG straight out of the render. They need help such as blurs, grain, natural variations, and color correction. I don't believe the technology is yet mature enough to provide photo-real CG elements without compositing work. So when you are spending hours and hours trying to tweak the exact, precise color to match the plate, then the compositor imports it and changes everything anyway, remember this: Your light color will never be perfect simply because you are probably working with an uncalibrated monitor. Get the light shadows, distance, angle, and whatnot perfect, but get the color close. Trying to get the perfect color is a waste of time.

As a matter of fact, chances are the sequence will be color timed after leaving the compositor's station anyway. *Color timing* occurs when all the shots of the show are edited into proper sequence. Many different scenes shot on different days, using different lighting or even all-CG shots will be played back to back. This is when we discover the wild variation in color from one shot to the next. The color timer goes through all the shots to give them similar color values.

So you see, trying to make lighting color perfect is a big, fat waste of time.

Don't do it!

• • •

If you look through this chapter you will see a few simple examples of how to identify and replicate the lighting in a photographic plate. I chose simple examples, because the process really is simple. Select a single light source, identify its properties, then place an appropriate lighting tool in your LightWave environment to match it. Fiddle with the settings until you're happy. Select the next light source and repeat the previous steps. Once you've done this with all the light sources, your lighting will be complete.

It really is that simple.

If you don't already know how to identify a light source, then you haven't read this entire book. The beginning sections deal intensively with real-world light and lighting properties. Go and read them. When you come back, you will be one with the lighting.

Focus Power.

Chapter 25

Tips, Tricks 'n' Tutes

I have spent most of this book discussing theoretical issues, tool functions, design considerations, and esoteric concerns such as "what is the nature of art?" Now I know there are many artists who would rather just sit down with a bunch of tutorials and make their own discoveries by reverse-engineering the setups or by putting the scenes together step by step for those big "aha!" moments. This chapter is for you.

I don't advocate learning lighting only by example because I find specific tutorials teach only specific techniques for specific situations, and the key to being a good lighting artist is not employing a handful of specific techniques. The key to really good lighting lies in having a complete enough understanding of lighting and shading quality, of tools *and* techniques to design and implement your *own* techniques as you find situationally appropriate.

So here are some "paint-by-number" setups that will help you understand some practical implementations of the many techniques, properties, and principles I have discussed in the past pages starting with the historically original light, the sun.

Be aware that these tutorials will not make you a lighting god. They will not teach you The Ultimate Lighting Technique. They will not take the place of study and observation nor explain why lighting and shading works the way it does, but they will, hopefully, provide you with a practical understanding of the available tools so that you can design and implement your own techniques or combinations of other known techniques, as need be.

Some of the tutorials cover similar subjects. But rather than forcing you to go through every single tutorial to learn the principles herein described, I have taken the liberty of preparing tutorials on similar subjects but from different perspectives. You may page through the chapter and find a tutorial in the skylight section about creating a fill light using Background Only radiosity. There is also a tutorial in the radiosity section that describes the use of Background Only radiosity. Both employ similar techniques and both are important, but you shouldn't have to do every tutorial to learn every technique. So feel free to flip through, bypass techniques you already know, and skip to subjects that may be new to you.

The Sun and the Moon

The sun and the moon belong in the same category because, as far as lighting design and implementation are concerned, they have pretty similar properties. Both are distant light sources. Both are discs in the sky. Both provide the earth with a relatively similar spectrum of color. In fact, the only major difference for lighting considerations is illumination intensity. That's right; in case you hadn't noticed, the sun is way brighter than the moon. So we're going to look at a number of different ways to set up a big distant disc light source. We will then fiddle with some intensity settings to see what happens.

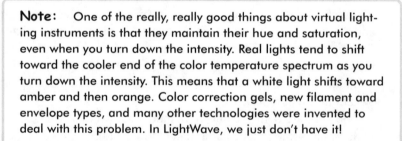

Note: One of the really, really good things about virtual lighting instruments is that they maintain their hue and saturation, even when you turn down the intensity. Real lights tend to shift toward the cooler end of the color temperature spectrum as you turn down the intensity. This means that a white light shifts toward amber and then orange. Color correction gels, new filament and envelope types, and many other technologies were invented to deal with this problem. In LightWave, we just don't have it!

Let's start by loading up a nice, fresh default LightWave Layout and adding a ground plane and a ...well... a sort of vulture guy playing bongos, courtesy of William "Proton" Vaughan. (This model is called Matt_MD.lwo and is available on the companion CD.) You can use any models you want. You don't even have to use anything from the companion CD. You can even throw the CD away if you feel like it or snip it up into pie shapes and tie it to your Christmas tree. There are lots of cool things on the CD, so you might want to back them up first.

In a default setup, there is a single distant light in the scene at an XYZ coordinate of –2m, 2m, –2m and at an HPB angle of 45.00, 35.00, 0.00.

If the camera isn't already there, move it so that it is overlooking the subject, slightly tilted down as in Figure 25.1, so you have a good view of the shadows on the ground plane.

The precise position and angle of the camera and lighting is not critical. A viewer will not likely be able to tell if your light is .05 degrees off as long as the scene looks good.

> **Note:**   I'm occasionally going to be giving you some coordinates in these tutorials, but now is a good time to start trusting your eye. Place things so that they look good. Start with the coordinates, but feel free to fool around with the positions and angles to suit yourself.

Open up your Camera Properties panel by clicking the Camera button at the bottom of the Layout interface, then clicking the Properties button just to its right. Once you have the Camera Properties panel up, set Antialiasing to Enhanced Low and deselect Adaptive Sampling. These two settings will give you a nicer image. Do a quick test render by hitting F9. You will see the object illuminated, but it looks pretty boring: just a default, white distant light at 100%, no shadows, and that usually awful ambient intensity at its default setting of 25%.

> **Note:**   Dear NewTek, can we please be allowed to change the default value of ambient intensity? Thanks.

Figure 25.1

Pretty boring. But we're going to spruce it up right quick. The first thing to do is open up the Light Properties panel by selecting Lights at the bottom of the Layout interface and then clicking the Properties button to its right (or press the "p" key).

Once you have the Light Properties panel open, click the Global Illumination button to open that panel.

Once in the Global Illumination panel, turn Ambient Intensity down to 0% either by clicking and dragging the slider arrow or by clicking on the number value and entering the new value manually.

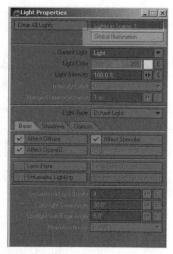

Figure 25.2

Figure 25.3

Once you have turned off ambient intensity, close the Global Illumination panel and the Light Properties panel, then try another test render. You should get something like Figure 25.4.

Still not very interesting, but don't go away; it's going to get much better. The first question you might ask is "Why, oh why, turn off ambient

Figure 25.4

intensity?" The answer is pretty simple: It's a very artificial illumination method. Ambient intensity adds exactly the same amount of illumination to every surface in the scene no matter where it is, no matter what direction it is facing. This is a very unnatural method of lighting, unless you're in a room with completely luminous walls, floor, and ceiling. Actually not even then, because ambient intensity also adds the same amount of illumination to areas that are in complete shadow, like the tonsils at the back of your mouth. It's pretty dark in there, but not when you add ambient intensity. It never happens in the real world, so ambient intensity, in most situations, is likely to leave your scene looking flat, clean, without form, and computer generated.

Now there are a number of good uses for ambient intensity and we'll get to those, so stay tuned. In general, if I'm going for a photo-real look, I never use ambient intensity unless I'm looking for a subtle boost or I'm using radiosity, in which case ambient intensity takes on a whole new purpose. So forget about that right now and let's go ahead and make our distant light into the sun.

Using a Distant Light

The first step to making your distant light setup look decent is to turn on ray-traced shadows. So go to the Render Options panel, click on the Rendering sub-tab if you are not already there, and click the box labeled Ray Trace Shadows.

Close the Render Options panel and hit F9 for a new render. It should look something like Figure 25.6.

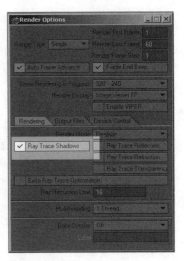

Figure 25.5

Figure 25.6

Now that's starting to behave a little like sunlight.

It looks pretty bland still, so let's increase the intensity to around 150% and render again.

347

> **Note:** Strangely, one of the hardest things for beginner lighting artists to get past is the concept that you can, and usually should, ramp lights up above 100%. 100% is just a number — *just a number* — just like any other number. It denotes nothing except some relative intensity that has no relationship to reality. Get over it!

There, that looks much more like sunlight. We are accustomed to direct sunlight being much brighter than indoor artificial lighting. Because of this, a default value of 100% is almost never enough to look like good, bright sunlight. If your image looks more like Figure 25.7, a little blown out in the whitest areas, the viewer is much more likely to accept it as sunlight without wondering what looks wrong with the picture.

Figure 25.7

If you are doing a lot of photo-real lighting, you will soon discover that this distant light method of creating sunlight doesn't exactly hold up to reality. There are several problems that we will address. The first is the shadows. Because a distant light is ray-traced along the edge of the shadow-casting subject, the shadows are completely hard-edged wherever they are cast. Real sunlight behaves differently than this, though, with the shadow edge appearing hard very near the subject and softening as the distance from the subject grows. This is because the sun is actually similar to an area light. It has size, which means that light is cast in all directions from every point on the sun's surface, very much like an area light. So if we wish to have realistic shadows for our sunlight (or moonlight for that matter) we should look into using an area light.

Note: Using an area light to create accurate shadows is only important if your CG element is casting shadows onto another CG element. If you have a single CG element that is being rendered for compositing over a plate, it is likely that it is not casting shadows onto anything other than itself, and therefore a distant light will do very nicely indeed.

Using an Area Light

The first thing you are likely to hear from a digital supervisor is that area lights are far too expensive to use. In other words, they are render intensive. They take much longer to calculate than their cheaper cousins, the distant light, the point light, and the spotlight. This is true — they do take longer to render — but they need not take an unreasonable time. Let's turn our distant light into an area light and then look at render times versus the improved quality of the shadow in the render.

First, open the Light Properties panel and switch the Light Type from Distant Light to Area Light.

You have probably noticed that your object has gone all black and that the light is not pointing exactly at your object. That's all right. Go into your Top View, select the light, and move it to a position something like in Figure 25.9.

Figure 25.8

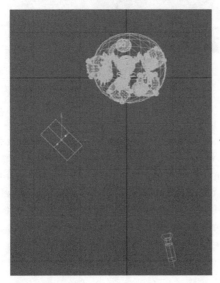

Figure 25.9

If you take a look through your Light View, it should look something like Figure 25.10.

Figure 25.10

Now hit the F9 button for another test render and you should get something looking like Figure 25.11.

Figure 25.11

The first thing I notice is that the image is blown out; in other words, the intensity of the sunlight is too high. The second thing I notice is that the shadows soften much too much to be sunlight. This is more like being beside an array of fluorescent tubes or a big neon sign. The sun is much farther away; therefore the shadows should soften very little over distance unless it is a very great distance. The shadow of a tree a hundred feet away from the base of the tree should be fairly soft. The shadow of a bongo-playing vulture three feet away should be just a little soft.

So how do we fix this? Well, we can move the light farther away or we can make it smaller. Also, let's remember to turn down the intensity a little.

I dialed the light intensity down to about 80% and moved the light much farther away until my Light View looked something like this:

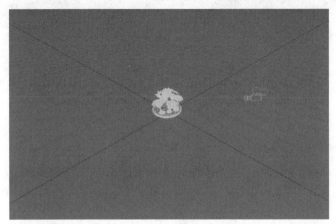

Figure 25.12

The actual coordinates of the light are now:

X	–12m	H	45.0
Y	14.3m	P	35.0
Z	–5.9m	B	0.0

If you render out another test image, you will see much more natural-looking shadows. These are soft, natural shadows that rendered for me on an Athlon XP1800 in about one minute. Granted this is not a complex scene, but it does demonstrate that using an area light in your scene does not have to be outrageously render intensive.

As a matter of fact, you can often improve render speed by decreasing the Linear/Area Light Quality setting without a noticeable loss in image quality.

One of the images in Figure 25.14 was rendered with an Area Light Quality setting of 4 and the other with an Area Light Quality setting of 3. The image set to a quality of 3 rendered in 38 seconds. That's a 37% speed improvement! See if you can tell which is which.

Figure 25.13

351

Figure 25.14

Using a Point Light

There are a couple of other methods for creating a sunlight source. Actually, there are as many as you can think of, but I'll discuss two here. First off, you can use a point light with ray tracing on. The results will be pretty similar to using a distant light. The shadow edges will be hard, but the render will be very fast. The only real difference between using a distant light and a point light is that the rays shot by distant lights are all parallel, while the rays from a point light originate from a single point in space and radiate outward. The practical result of this is that there will be some change to the shadow shape. Figure 25.15 is an image using a point light quite close to the subject.

Figure 25.15

You can see how the shadow is much larger than the subject because the light rays are diverging from the point light, which is very close to the subject.

Point Light

Figure 25.16

If we push the point light far away from the subject, however, the rays reaching the subject are much less divergent and much closer to parallel. It is difficult to tell that the light rays are divergent at all. This might just as well be a distant light.

This is how you turn a light source with divergent rays into a light source with almost-parallel rays. Remember this technique because it comes into play for a few of the techniques still to come in this chapter.

Figure 25.17

Using a Spotlight

The good thing about using a spotlight to create the sun is that you can switch the Shadow Type setting from Ray Trace to Shadow Map in the Light Properties panel.

This means a significant improvement in render times because shadow maps calculate much more quickly than ray-traced shadows. For example, the scene that took ten seconds with a point light using ray-traced shadows is now taking six seconds using shadow maps. A 40% time savings is good in anyone's book. Sure, it's only a few seconds now, but when you're doing a full-blown 2K render filled with complex models, textures, and lighting, a 40% savings can become huge. Another great thing about using spotlights, and especially shadow maps, is that you can fake soft shadows by increasing the fuzziness of the shadow.

Figure 25.18

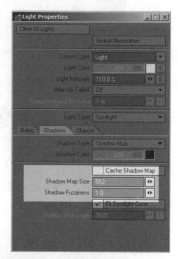

Figure 25.19

LightWave simply blurs the edge of the mapped shadow to soften it.

There is always a trade-off to these cheats, however. Remember that natural shadows are sharper or hard-edged near the object casting them and grow softer farther away. In contrast, fuzzy shadow-mapped shadows are blurry all the way around, whether they are near to the object or far away.

Figure 25.20

The main problem here is that the fuzzy shadows make objects near the ground appear to be floating. Of course you can adjust the shadow fuzziness lower so the problem is less apparent.

Figure 25.21

Now there is an even more obvious problem. The shadow appears blocky as though it is made of squares. That's because it *is* made of squares. If you look again on the Light Properties Shadows sub-tab you will see a Shadow Map Size setting. The default size of 512 means the shadow map is only 512 pixels square. The larger your area of illumination, the larger the pixelation problem will become. The simple answer is to increase the map size. This increases rendering time slightly, but provides a vastly superior shadow while still not coming close to ray-traced render times.

Figure 25.22

Figure 25.22 uses a Shadow Map Size of 2000, which is about average for an object at normal world scale, provided the spotlight cone angle isn't ridiculously large. Shadow Fuzziness is set to 1.0. The larger shadow map only added about one second to the render time. This is still much better than ray-traced times with a reasonably good soft shadow.

> **Note:** I have found that in most cases a Shadow Map Size setting in the range of 1000 to 2000 pixels does a fine job. I am just completing a feature film in which we rendered the entire project using a Shadow Map Size of 1000. Shadow fuzziness, motion blur, and good compositing also help keep the map size down.

Once again, though, we get into the problem that spotlights, like point lights, emit light from a single point, so the light rays are radiating from a point in space. Using the trick we learned in the last section, we can move the light pretty far away to make the light rays more parallel. In my opinion, this technique is far superior to using a distant light since it provides the option of shadow softness while providing a dramatically improved render time.

When using shadow-mapped spotlights, it is always best to try to optimize your shadow-mapped lights by only illuminating what is needed in the shot. For example, if you have a spotlight with a cone angle of 30 degrees, and the light is quite close to the subject, you might look through the Light View and see that the subject just fits inside the cone angle. This is an efficient use of the shadow-mapped light because the shadow map, which is by default 512 x 512 pixels in size, will be fairly smooth on the subject. If you see pixelation, you can increase the shadow map size a bit. If you then decide to back the light away, you will see through the Light View that the subject has become very small in the view and therefore most of the light from the spotlight is not illuminating the subject and most of the shadow map area is not even touching the subject. This means that only a small portion of the shadow map is now affecting the subject. The choppy pixel edges will become very apparent. When you back the light away, it is always best to then decrease the cone angle as small as possible so that as much of the shadow map as possible is used. This is an efficient use of shadow maps and the memory and calculation time they require.

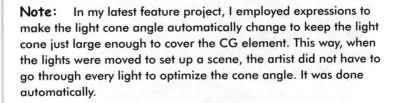

Note: In my latest feature project, I employed expressions to make the light cone angle automatically change to keep the light cone just large enough to cover the CG element. This way, when the lights were moved to set up a scene, the artist did not have to go through every light to optimize the cone angle. It was done automatically.

Adding a Skylight

Now that we've covered a bunch of different ways of making key sunlight or moonlight, it's time to throw in a secondary light source, a "fill" light as it were. Fill lights are so-named because they fill in the spaces where the key light does not illuminate. When there is sunlight in the sky (or moonlight for that matter), the most readily available fill light source is usually the sky. During the daytime, this often means a bright blue sky. During the night, it usually means barely perceptible starlight, but we'll deal with that later.

The main thing to understand about skylight is that it is, by nature, omnidirectional and soft. In other words, the shadows, if any, are very soft. This is because the entire sky is one big illumination source, so you have light approaching from all directions, wrapping around objects and causing very soft, sometimes imperceptible shadows.

So let's start with the simple, cheap tricks we can use to simulate skylight and then move gradually on to the more accurate and more expensive methods after that.

Using Ambient Intensity

By far the easiest, cheapest method of creating any fill light is by throwing in a little ambient intensity. I know, I just finished talking about how evil ambient intensity is, but, hey, we're looking for the cheapest method of creating a fill light. It doesn't have to be good, just cheap!

Ambient intensity is something that only exists in the CG world. LightWave just adds whatever percentage of illumination you choose to every surface in the scene. The net effect of high ambient intensity is that objects tend to look flat and fake. Figure 25.23 shows an image with an ambient intensity of 50%.

Figure 25.23

But used with subtlety, ambient intensity can help boost levels and provide a marginally acceptable, if not exactly accurate, fill light source. The problem, of course, is that since ambient intensity has no shadow provision, it does not produce the soft shadows with which skylight is associated.

Figure 25.24

Figure 25.24 has ambient intensity set at 10%. It is subtle but provides some illumination in areas that were otherwise black and completely unlit. This low-level ambient intensity suggests that there is another light source somewhere without providing any clues (such as shadows and therefore directionality) to its position.

Once again, this is a cheap, inaccurate solution, but it can work, especially in shots with a great deal of motion blur. (Did I mention that I don't like ambient intensity much?)

Using "No Shadows" Lights

This is an option that works something like ambient intensity. But where ambient intensity is omnidirectional with no source, this option allows you to define the position and direction of the light source. Hey, I know, let's call it "directional ambient." We use a light with the shadow options switched off in order to reduce render time and provide more even lighting (objects don't get in the way). The benefit to this over ambient intensity is that object self-shadowing still creates shadows on the polygons facing away from the light source.

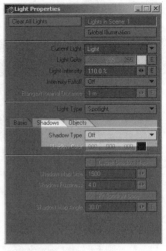

Figure 25.25

In the first example, I've added a distant light to our bongo-vulture scene, placed it directly above the object, and pointed it straight down. I left the light at its default intensity of 50% and turned shadows off for this light. See Figure 25.26. This technique is lightning fast because there are no shadows for the new fill light to trace, but a nice fill illumination is added, brightening up the darker areas of the floor and adding some intensity to the top of the object.

Figure 25.26

Of course, since the distant light is directional, it is only illuminating surfaces that are facing it. The underside of the object remains unlit. Also, to be really accurate, there would be soft shadows beneath the object. But because the distant light has its shadows turned off, there will be no shadows beneath the object. But that's OK, because if we turned shadows on, they would be ray-traced, hard-edged shadows, which are completely wrong in this instance and would look worse than having no shadows at all. Remember, there is only one sun in the sky at any given time on this planet in the current eon. It's unlikely that you can have two competing hard-edged shadows from natural light only.

Figure 25.27

So the moral of the story is, if you choose to use a "no shadows" fill option, remember to turn off the shadows.

You can use any light type you choose for this very simple and quick option. Point lights, spotlights, even area lights — they all work pretty much the same with shadows off. The only thing that changes is the direction that the light beams go. With a point light, it's all directions (omnidirectional) and diverging from the source. With a spotlight, it's in a cone (usually). Linear and area lights act like arrays of point lights. Fiddle with them if you wish. They all work for this trick.

Using an Area Light

Before global illumination came along, using an area light for a skylight fill was the only way to get a really accurate-looking soft shadow. There are those who will argue that the "spinning light" trick did this, or that fuzzy spotlights worked, or that any one of a thousand other techniques did the trick. All those techniques go some distance in creating the look by cheating, faking, and working around technology limitations, but, in my opinion, none of them quite reach it. Area lights have long been my lighting tool of choice for just about everything. Remember, just because it's an area light doesn't mean render times have to be outrageous. Smaller area lights render very quickly, and you can also change the quality setting to improve render times.

Note: If you want to get really tricky, and you are lucky enough to have G2 from Worley Labs, you can improve area light quality by improving the settings within G2. G2 uses its own rendering engine to calculate area light shadows. This adds a little extra time to the render but also seriously improves the shading quality. Your call.

Single Light Setup

So let's switch our newly added distant light to an area light on the Light Properties panel. To recap, we now have a spotlight as our key and an area light as our fill light. Once you have switched the distant light to an area light, hit the F9 button and take a look.

Figure 25.28

OK, that looks wrong! Where's the nice soft shadow? Well, take a look at the light size. The default area light is 1 meter square, and remember that we moved the light high up above the object. So the area light is a small light pretty far away from the subject. We know that the sky is much larger than 1 meter. We need to make our area light much larger to match. Let's size it up to about 15 meters square and bring it down so that it's about six meters off the ground. Remember, this area light should be pointing directly downward or have a pitch of 90 degrees. You could also make the pitch –90 degrees. Area lights work equally well in both directions.

Figure 25.29

Well, that certainly increased render times. This frame took 1:22 to render. But look at the beautiful soft shadows we are starting to get beneath the bongos.

> **Note:** Area lights and linear lights tend to create some "noise" that is especially apparent during animated sequences. Higher quality settings will reduce this noise, but you should always have Shading Noise Reduction enabled in the Global Illumination panel if you are using one of these light types. And don't forget the previous note about G2!!

> **Note:** Shading Noise Reduction works by blurring the diffuse channel of objects. Keep this in mind when using diffuse maps; they will become softer.

Figure 25.30

This is the same image as the previous one but with Shading Noise Reduction enabled. It adds only a few seconds to each pass of the render but really improves shadow quality by removing noise. If you closely compare this image with the previous one, you will find that the fuzziness of the shadow map is also softer and more pleasing.

Manual "Light Bowl" Setup

A single area light over the subject will often suffice as a soft sky fill source. But there are times when you need a sky fill that is shaped more like the sky. You can use global illumination, and we'll get to that later, but first let's look at a slightly cheaper (and slightly less beautiful) technique I call the *area light bowl*. It's a simple setup, really. You add two, three, four, five, or however many area lights you want in an inverted bowl shape to light your scene from more than one plane. Remember, the sky wraps around like an inverted bowl so this is more like a real sky than a single area light pointing downward. It's sort of a poor man's Backdrop Only global illumination. Bear in mind that as you add more area lights, your rendering times may increase dramatically, so try to get away with as few area lights as possible. Also keep in mind that as you add more area lights to your "light bowl," the light intensities will add up, so as you add more lights, you will need to proportionately decrease the intensity of every light in the "bowl."

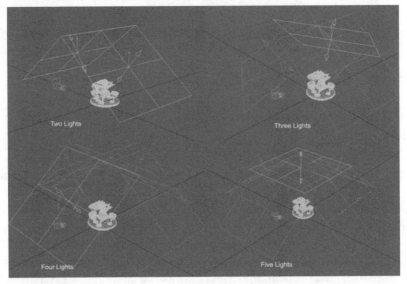

Figure 25.31

Here are the respective rendering times for each of the light bowl set-ups I used. The renders were done with Enhanced Medium antialiasing on a single-processor Athlon XP1800.

2 Lights	2:36
3 Lights	3:35
4 Lights	4:54
5 Lights	5:56

Figure 25.32 shows the final five-light "light bowl" area light setup. The shadows are beautiful and soft. And really, a render time under six minutes is not exactly outrageous. Obviously, the more area lights you add, the softer and more

Figure 25.32

pleasing the soft shadows will be. Since smaller area lights render more quickly than large ones, you might try adding an array of smaller area lights without too much of an increase from this time. But smaller area lights become more directional, creating harder shadows, so be careful. The nice thing is that you would have a more natural hemisphere shape instead of the blocky shape produced by the five-light setup. But it's a lot of work to set up a large array of lights in a hemisphere, isn't it? Not any more. Looks like a job for luxigons!

A "Light Bowl" Using Luxigons

Luxigons are an absolutely prime tool for exactly this type of setup. When you have a situation where you need to create a large array of lights in specific positions, the fact is LightWave's Modeler is so mature and robust that it is much easier to create, clone, and reposition polygons than lights. So do it. Make all your polygons in Modeler in the positions where you want lights. Import them into Layout and convert luxigons. Done.

First, open up a fresh Modeler. Now for an array of area lights, I'd like to have a nice, fairly even bowl of maybe 12 lights. More area lights than that are really not necessary since each area light already behaves like an array of point lights. As long as the coverage is even, the soft shadows will be very nice indeed.

I start by creating a ball using the Numeric panel. I make the ball have six sides and four segments.

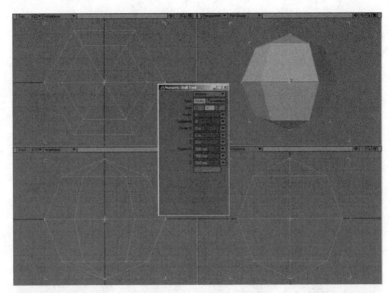

Figure 25.33

We're only going to use the top hemisphere for our luxigon array, so let's remove the bottom half.

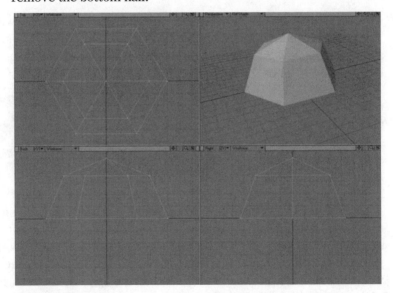

Figure 25.34

An important consideration when creating a luxigon array is the direction of the polygon normals. The initial rotation of the light will be whatever the direction of the normal is. We want all our lights pointing inward, so let's select all the polygons and flip them so that the normals are facing inward.

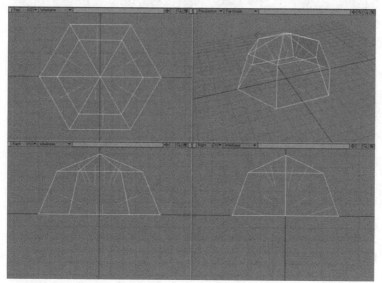

Figure 25.35

Now there are a couple of ways to define what the light settings will be. The first is done in Modeler, but the second method, done in Layout, allows you to include many more settings not available in Modeler. Let's look at both methods.

For the Modeler method, simply go to the Construct panel, click the Additional drop-down, and select the plug-in Add Luxigons. You will see the following panel appear.

Figure 25.36

Using the Attach Light to Polygon panel, you can define the lights' type, color, and intensity as well as whether shadows are on or off. If you are using a spotlight, you will also get the option to use either ray-traced shadows or shadow maps. I have set the light color to 6000 degrees Kelvin and set the intensity to 5%. Remember, the light intensities are additive, so 12 lights at 5% will produce sufficient illumination.

The second method of defining the light properties is to already have one light in Layout before loading in the luxigon object. When you convert luxigons in Layout, you will be presented with the option to clone any light in Layout. As you can see, this is a great way to set up very specific and detailed light settings for use with luxigons.

So now that we have our luxigon object set up, save it somewhere and send it to Layout or, if you don't use the Hub, switch to Layout and load the luxigon object you just created.

In Layout, make sure you have your luxigon object selected. Select your Generics drop-down in the Scene tab. There you will see the ConvertLuxigons command. Select ConvertLuxigons.

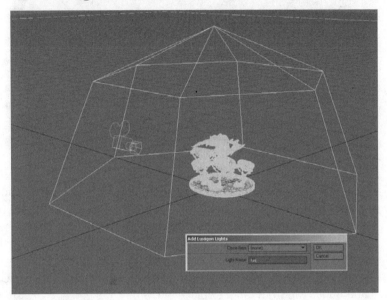

Figure 25.37

When the Add Luxigon Lights dialog box pops up, you have two options. You give all the lights a name and you can choose whether or not to clone an existing light in the scene. If you choose not to clone a light, the light settings from Modeler will be used for all the luxigon-generated lights. If, on the other hand, you prefer a more complex light setup, you can create a light in Layout and use that light as the template for all the luxigon light properties. Say you wanted a projection image in the light, or you wanted to specify object exclusion or perhaps a falloff option. You'd set up a light in Layout with all the settings you want, then when you convert luxigons, select that light as the clone object. All the luxigon-generated lights will now have the same settings as that first light you set up.

In this case, though, we're satisfied with the simple settings we were able to set in Modeler, so we'll just go ahead and hit OK. Let's see what we've come up with.

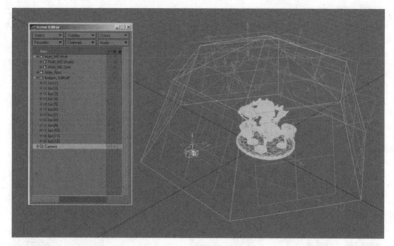

Figure 25.38

As you can see, there is an array of area lights coincident with the polygons of the light bowl luxigon object. If you look at the Scene Editor, you'll also see that all the lights are parented to the luxigon object, so you can move the whole array together by selecting and moving the object. But the object may become cumbersome. In order to remove the object, yet keep all the parenting info, it's easy to replace the object with a null under the Item tab's Replace button.

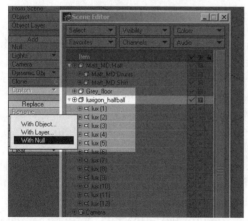

Figure 25.39

And now, a quick render to see how our luxigon setup worked.

Figure 25.40

OK, that wasn't exactly a quick render at 15:08, but the soft shadows sure look nice. Of course, you don't have to use 12 area lights either. This image doesn't show much better lighting quality than the five-light setup we did (which took a third of the time to render).

A Light Bowl Using Distant Lights

We know that ray-traced lights such as distant lights render much more quickly than area lights. We also know that an area light behaves like an array of ray-traced lights. So rather than creating an array of area lights, let's try an array of ray-traced lights. First, go back into Modeler and open up the luxigon object we created previously. Access the Add Luxigons plug-in and this time use the settings in Figure 25-41:

Figure 25.41

This will ensure that the lights are distant lights, with ray tracing on, an intensity of 5% each, and a light, sky blue color.

In Layout, load the light bowl object, and then convert luxigons, being sure not to clone any of the lights in the scene.

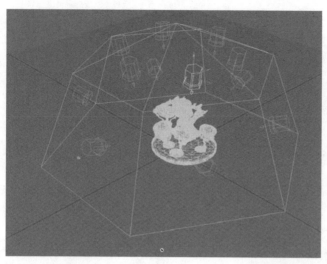

Figure 25.42

Don't forget to open up the Object Properties panel of the luxigon object and make sure it's unseen by cameras and rays, and does not cast, receive, or self shadow (or replace it with a null object).

Now let's take a look at the shadow quality.

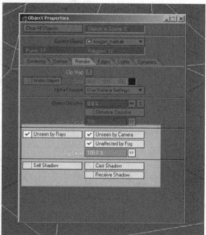

Figure 25.43

Figure 25.44

The shadows from the distant light array are pretty marginal. So let's use a variation of the "spinning light" trick to improve the quality of the soft shadows without increasing render times.

First, make sure the luxigon object has a keyframe at frame 0, with a heading of 0 degrees. Then, rotate the luxigon object on its heading 720 degrees on frame 1 and make a keyframe. Open up the Graph Editor, being sure the luxigon object is selected, and set Post Behavior to Repeat, which makes the object rotate twice per frame.

Next, we set Motion Blur to 50% and Antialiasing to Enhanced Low in our Camera Properties panel. This has the effect of spreading the motion blur passes over 50% of the motion from the previous frame (720 degrees). Now in every frame, the array will rotate 50% of 720 degrees each frame; in other words, 360 degrees. Render by pressing F9 and see what you get (see Figure 25.45).

Figure 25.45

That provided a slight improvement in image quality with no increase in render time. We can improve the shadow quality even more by increasing the anti-aliasing quality. Of course, that means more render passes, which means higher render times. But so far the render is under a minute, so let's see an image with Enhanced High dithered antialiasing.

Figure 25.46

The shadow quality is quite improved from Enhanced Low and the render was under 4 minutes. Not quite the quality of area lights, but definitely a time-saver. Of course, there are no shadows in Light-Wave superior to those created by LightWave's Global Illumination tool.

Global Illumination (Backdrop Only Radiosity)

Now we get to global illumination. Contrary to public belief, global illumination (and radiosity) does not necessarily have to signify outrageous render times. There are a number of settings you can alter to improve speed. In this case, we're going to try out LightWave's built-in solution to our "light bowl" setup, and that is radiosity in Backdrop Only mode.

The best argument for this type of solution for a skylight fill is that the shadows are very close to perfect. Global illumination in Background Only mode works like an *accessibility* plug-in. In other words, object surfaces are illuminated based on whether or not the sky backdrop can "see" them. So portions of the surfaces that face the sky will be fully illuminated with the radiosity intensity. Portions of the surfaces that are partly occluded from the sky backdrop will be partly illuminated and portions of the surface that are completely occluded from the sky backdrop will receive no illumination from it.

There are a number of ways to do a sky fill light using radiosity in Backdrop Only mode. Let's go ahead and turn radiosity on and set it to Backdrop Only. Open your Light Properties panel and click the Global Illumination button. In the Global Illumination panel, turn on Shading Noise Reduction and Enable Radiosity. Set Type to Backdrop Only, Intensity to 75%, and Rays Per Evaluation to 3 x 9. I find that having Shading Noise Reduction turned on often allows me to decrease the Rays per Evaluation to 3 x 9, thereby improving render times.

The next thing to do is to set up a backdrop. Open up your Backdrop panel.

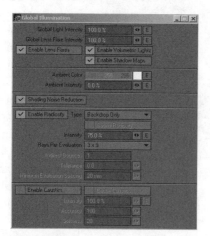

Figure 25.47

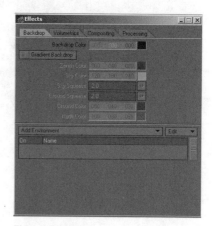

Figure 25.48

By default, LightWave sets the background to black, or 0, 0, 0. Black will emit no light for a radiosity setup, so if we expect to get some skylight illumination out of the backdrop we'll have to make some changes. First, let's change the color. Click on the color box next to Backdrop Color. When the LightWave color picker pops up, select the Kelvin tab.

> **Note:** To use the LightWave color picker instead of the default Windows color picker, open your General Options panel in Layout by hitting the "o" button, then next to Color Picker, change Default to LW_ColrPikr by clicking and dragging the drop-down.

I always use the Kelvin tab when selecting skylight, since skylight is usually measured in Kelvin degrees. On the Kelvin scale, skylight ranges between 10,000 and 20,000 degrees. Since LightWave's color picker only goes up to 11,000, I choose that number. So select 11,000 Kelvin as your color temperature and close the color picker. Now let's take a look at the render.

Now that is a fine-looking soft shadow in anyone's book. And at 3:20 it's not exactly a harsh render time. Granted, there are no textures and AA was set to Enhanced Low, but it's still not difficult to argue the benefit of such beautiful shadows for a reasonable increase in render time.

Figure 25.49

There are a couple of other background options to consider here as well. For one, you can use LightWave's built-in Gradient Backdrop tool.

The big advantage to using a gradient backdrop is that you can vary the background color. This is much more realistic since background radiosity comes from the ground as

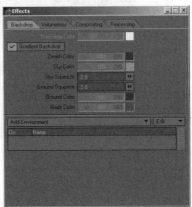

Figure 25.50

well as the sky. Also, you don't really want sky fill color coming from below in most cases. It would be nice to have blue above and green or brown below to imply dirt or greenery (or whatever is on the ground in the nearby environment). For details about setting up LightWave's built-in Gradient Backdrop, take a look through the manual.

As you can see, the one real disadvantage to the built-in Gradient Backdrop is that you don't have any control over where the ground meets the sky. If you are working on a scene in which the horizon is not visible, this is not a problem, and the built-in Gradient Backdrop is a very

Figure 25.51

quick backdrop solution. But if you want more control over your backdrop and especially over the position of the horizon, just look a little lower on the Backdrop panel.

Click on the Add Environment button and select Textured Environment from the drop-down.

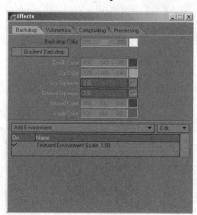

Figure 25.52

Now double-click on the plug-in and a small interface will open at the bottom of the panel.

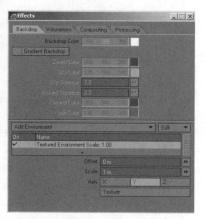

Figure 25.53

Select the Y axis and click on the Texture button to open a new interface.

In the Texture Editor, change Layer Type to Gradient and switch Input Parameter to Pitch. This ensures that your gradient will be applied so that the top of the gradient in this panel is at the top of the backdrop and the bottom of the gradient is at bottom of the backdrop. Now all you have to do is set some parameters in the gradient and choose the colors. I like to put two parameters where I want the horizon to be, then make a sky color and a ground color. Of course, this is a simple setup. You can make the gradient as complex as you like.

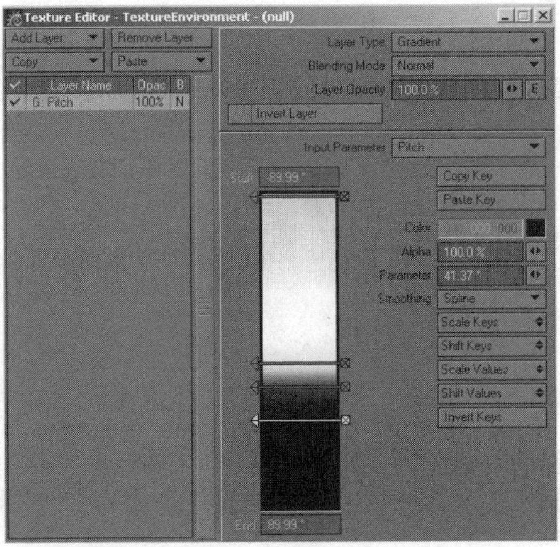

Figure 25.54

Because I have control over exactly where the horizon exists, I can make sure it is not visible above the ground plane polygon if I wish.

One of the really useful features of a gradient background is that you can alter the amount of illumination by using the Scale Values slider on the right of the gradient panel. If your render turns out too bright, simply scale the values down. If too dark, scale them up. Keep in mind that you can scale your color values above 255, which provides much more illumination than was possible in the past. Remember, we're dealing with floating-point colors now. We are no

Figure 25.55

longer limited to the 0 to 255 range. A value higher than 255 means increased illumination. This value scaling works as a multiplier to the radiosity intensity value you set in the Global Illumination panel.

Figure 25.56

As you can see in Figure 25.56, I have used a gradient backdrop but placed the horizon just below my polygon ground plane. The illumination is good; I scaled the values down a little, but I could have just as easily turned down the Intensity setting in the Global Illumination panel. The soft shadows are very nice.

Using Textured Environment is one of my favorite ways of creating a Backdrop Only radiosity setup.

Sky Fill Using an Image

Of course, when using Textured Environment, you have the option of using any textures available to you in the Surface Editor. That means not only gradient but procedural and image textures. If you want some real-istic-looking sky lighting, including variations in blue and white from clouds and atmospheric changes or perhaps reds and oranges from sunsets and whatnot, you can always add an image to Textured Environ-ment. You'd probably use a cylindrical or spherical map, maybe something like the following image.

Simply use an image instead of a gradient. For an image like this, I like to increase the Image Wrap setting to 3 so the image isn't so stretched. You don't have to use an HDRI image; any old image

Figure 25.57

will do. Background Only radiosity will use the background colors of the image to calculate.

Figure 25.58

Because this is not an HDRI image, the illumination range will not be as high. In other words, regular 8-bit RGB images are capable of only a certain level of illumination. This illumination level is clamped at the white point of the image. For more precise lighting, you will wish to use the HDRI method discussed later in this chapter. The nice thing about this method is that it gives you subtle color variations in the lighting, which are more natural than the smooth, homogeneous colors created by gradients.

It is possible, however, to squeeze more illumination out of a regular 8-bit background image, but this method comes at a price.

Open your Image Editor, select the background image, and select the Editing tab (Figure 25.59).

Notice you have slider control over brightness, contrast, hue, saturation, and gamma. By simply sliding the Brightness control to make the image brighter, the image will provide a higher level of illumination for a radiosity solution. I was able to achieve some interesting results by also fiddling with the saturation and contrast settings. Both saturation and contrast helped me maintain color in the image while brightening it.

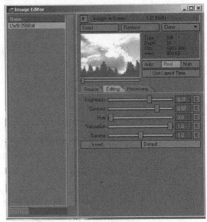

Figure 25.59

If you look at the quality of the background image, you will conclude that this technique is probably best used in a situation where the background is not visible in the shot.

Figure 25.60

Radiosity Setups

Radiosity is the best thing to come to CG lighting since the invention of ray-traced shadows. It embodies lighting that appears physically accurate and real. First, let's recall exactly what radiosity is.

Radiosity Recap

Radiosity, specularity, reflection, refraction, and caustics are all the redirection of light. The main difference is how we see that redirected light when it contacts a surface. In the case of radiosity, we are discussing a diffused reflection of light, usually from one surface onto another surface. Radiosity can reflect many times. This is known in LightWave as *multi-bounce* radiosity.

> **Note:** If you have ever looked at two mirrors that are facing each other, you have likely noticed how the image (and therefore the light reflected from the surface) bounced back and forth into infinity or until the light diffused enough that it became invisible. This is radiosity in action. Although LightWave makes a distinction between reflected images and reflected (bounced) light, they are the same in the real world.

Earlier versions of LightWave were capable only of one radiosity bounce. This kept calculations and render times relatively reasonable. Higher order bounces increase render times exponentially, although more bounces are more realistic and generally better looking. Here's our bald man again to demonstrate radiosity. Both images in Figure 25.61 use a single spotlight as the key light source. The only difference is that single-bounce radiosity is turned on for the image on the right.

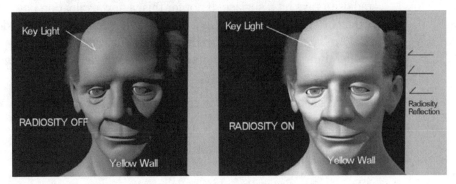

Figure 25.61

Radiosity generally distinguishes itself by the way it apparently "picks up" the color from a surface off which it reflects. Sunlight that is reflected off a yellow wall then becomes yellow reflected light. This is caused not by "picking up" color as it appears, but, in fact, by "dropping off" color. The yellow wall absorbs most of the blue wavelengths of the sunlight, leaving only the red and green to be reflected. Red and green light mix to make yellow.

Ambient Intensity and Radiosity

Ambient intensity has generally been viewed by lighting artists as a blight and a plague on lighting, something to be ignored, scoffed at, insulted, and spat upon except in the most extreme of time-constraint situations. Even then, ambient intensity would be added reluctantly, with dismay and disgust, sometimes forcing the artist to shower afterward to wash off the "ickiness" of the debasement he had just performed.

Perhaps I embroider the facts slightly, but ambient lighting is very unnatural and will make your lighting look flat. In a 3D environment, this is not considered desirable.

But with the addition of radiosity into LightWave a couple of years ago, ambient intensity has gained a new foothold in our lighting plans. This is because ambient intensity, when coupled with radiosity, takes on a new function that doesn't just wash out and flatten our images. It actually improves them and saves us render time. So you don't have to flip through the LightWave manual for this tidbit, here's a quote:

"Ambient light … is not directly added to surface points that are shaded with radiosity — where radiosity rays originate. However, it is added to points that are shaded without radiosity — where radiosity rays hit a surface. If not for this, a new evaluation point would be spawned at the hit points and render time would explode.

"Ambient light will still brighten every surface, but only indirectly, after bouncing off other surfaces. Thus it can simulate light that would have come from further radiosity bounces."

If this sounds confusing, bear with me. You'll see just what this means when we use ambient intensity with radiosity next.

Backdrop Only

LightWave's radiosity in Backdrop Only mode is an extremely useful feature. It is, perhaps, the most useful of all the radiosity modes. For one thing, it is the quickest-rendering of all the radiosity modes because it does not calculate any light bounces. Illumination from the background simply illuminates whatever surfaces are "visible" to the background. Calculations are much simpler and quicker than single-bounce or multi-bounce calculations. Further, the soft shadows created by Backdrop Only radiosity are vastly superior to any soft shadows created by any other method, technique, or "cheat" such as spinning lights, fuzzy shadow maps, and even area lights.

Creating a Backdrop Only radiosity setup in LightWave is a simple and straightforward process. Simply open your Light Properties panel, click on the Global Illumination button, select Enable Radiosity (and Shading Noise Reduction), and set the radiosity type to Backdrop Only.

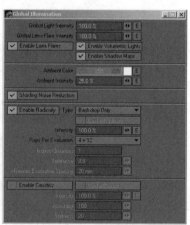

Figure 25.62

Now that we are using Backdrop Only mode, we'll need a backdrop to illuminate the scene. By default, LightWave's background is black. Black will definitely not produce any illumination for our scene. We have several options: We can use LightWave's built-in Gradient Backdrop, we can add LightWave's Textured Environment and add an image, gradient, or procedural texture as our backdrop (both of these methods are covered earlier in this chapter), or we can just change the backdrop color. For the simplest example of Backdrop Only radiosity, we'll just do that. Open up your Backdrop sub-tab in the Effects panel and select a nice color for your backdrop. It doesn't matter what color for the purposes of this tutorial, as long as the color is bright enough to illuminate the scene. I selected a color temperature of 11,000 from the Kelvin color picker.

Figure 25.63

By default, LightWave has one distant light in the scene at 100%. Turn that light off, and enable Ray Trace Shadows in your Render Options panel. Hit F9 and take a look at those beautiful soft shadows.

Figure 25.64

As the least "expensive" render of the radiosity modes, it's not too difficult to see why Backdrop Only mode might get used a great deal for photo-real work.

Monte Carlo

Monte Carlo is the Cadillac of radiosity modes in LightWave. With Monte Carlo you can specify multiple light bounces that dramatically improve the photo-realism of your lighting. There is no interpolation or estimation here. Naturally, a dramatic increase in render time comes with the dramatic improvement in visual quality. The big difference

381

between Backdrop Only mode and Monte Carlo mode is that light bounces are calculated in Monte Carlo. That's where the big rendering penalty comes in.

Setting up a Monte Carlo render is just the same as Backdrop Only, except that you select Monte Carlo mode as your radiosity type in the Global Illumination panel.

The radiosity results can be stunning. Unfortunately, until processors speed up considerably, Monte Carlo radiosity is most likely relegated to use in still images, as most production houses don't have enough render power to render full image sequences with Monte Carlo radiosity enabled.

Interpolated

Next to Monte Carlo radiosity mode, Interpolated is about the best thing. In addition to being gifted with multi-bounce radiosity, there are a couple of settings you can dial down to improve render times. Of course, faster render times come with a quality loss. But if you are careful and have Shading Noise Reduction turned on (as you always should when using any mode of radiosity), you will probably get away with some speed improvements with insignificant quality losses.

Interpolated mode provides you with Tolerance and Minimum Evaluation Spacing settings, both of which can be altered to improve render times.

Figure 25.65: Backdrop Only, 4:09

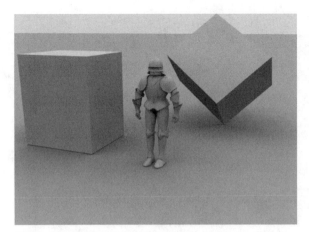

Figure 25.66: Interpolated 1 Bounce, 5:34

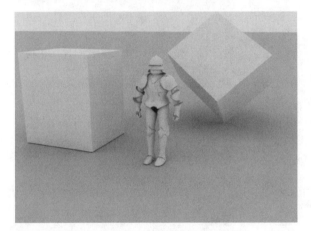

Figure 25.67: Interpolated 2 Bounces, 11:46

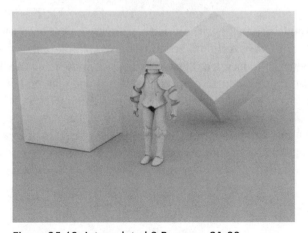

Figure 25.68: Interpolated 3 Bounces, 21:00

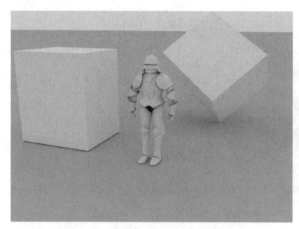

Figure 25.69: Interpolated 4 Bounces, 37:56

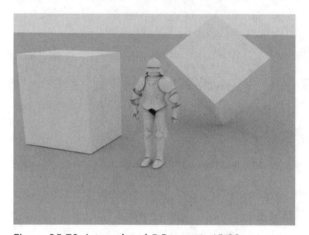

Figure 25.70: Interpolated 5 Bounces, 45:00

Interpolated mode seems to give rendering times equivalent to Monte Carlo mode if LightWave's default settings are used: Tolerance of 0.0 and Minimum Evaluation Spacing of 20mm. Of course, increasing the Tolerance or the Minimum Evaluation Spacing settings will give you faster renders but at a cost of lower quality. You are more likely to get away with lower quality if you are doing still images. If you are animating, though, be cautious about lowering the quality of your radiosity too much. Even Shading Noise Reduction can smooth over only so much noise.

Keeping Control of Render Times

I have seen many a digital supervisor pale when I used the evil "R" word. Radiosity strikes fear into the hearts of VFX producers and coordinators everywhere. Visions abound of 5-hour-per-frame renders and backed-up render queues, missed deadlines, and "oops, forgot to turn that on, better render the whole thing again."

When radiosity first came to us in LightWave version 6.0, there was plenty of reason for this sort of concern, mainly because processors were much less powerful and render farms were much more expensive than they are nowadays.

It is true, however, that an artist unfamiliar with the subtleties of radiosity setups can easily build monster scenes that hog farms and give supervisors coronaries. This is bad for the rest of us, because radiosity now has a bad name. It doesn't have to. It shouldn't. It's up to us to stand up and use our radiosity bravely. Just don't hog the farm.

With an eye to keeping render times within a reasonable limit, the following sections discuss a few of the settings you should be looking at to save yourself some render time.

Rays Per Evaluation

This is going to get a little theoretical, as we discuss how LightWave calculates radiosity. Don't get bored and flip pages; this is good stuff. It will give you a better understanding of exactly why your lighting looks the way it does and will give you clues as to whether or not you need to adjust your settings.

When LightWave determines that radiosity is being emitted from a surface, it creates the light rays by sticking a theoretical hemisphere on the surface and using the hemisphere's normals to generate new light rays. These "theoretical hemispheres," if you could see them, would look just like a half ball built in LightWave's Modeler.

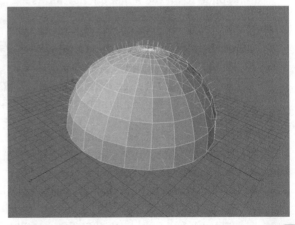

Figure 25.71

Each normal is now a new light ray radiating outward from the evaluation.

The Rays Per Evaluation setting is a set of numbers n x n that tells you how many segments and how many sides the hemisphere has. A very low Rays Per Evaluation setting like 1 x 3 will produce blotchy, uneven results in most cases, while a very high Rays Per Evaluation setting like 16 x 48 will produce very soft, even results. As usual, higher settings come with longer render times. You may have to experiment before you find the right balance of quality vs. render time. I usually set my Rays Per Evaluation setting to 3 x 9 automatically since I know that Shading Noise Reduction will smooth out most of the noise. Figure 25.72 gives visual examples of what the different RPE settings would look like.

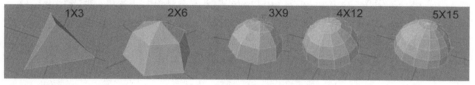

Figure 25.72

Cache Radiosity

If you are using Interpolated mode, you have the option to use a great feature called Cache Radiosity. If you check this box, the radiosity solution from the first rendered frame of the sequence will be held in memory and applied to all the subsequent frames so that the radiosity does not have to be recalculated for any frames other than the first. The obvious advantage to this is that you can have a very complex radiosity setup that takes five hours to render a frame, but after the first frame is rendered, radiosity will no longer be calculated and subsequent frames will render much more quickly.

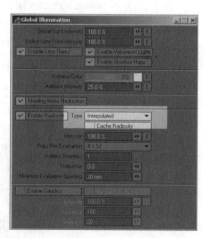

Figure 25.73

There are two main problems, however, that make Cache Radiosity not quite as useful as it otherwise might be. The first problem is understandable. If any objects (and therefore shadows) move in the scene, the radiosity will not be recalculated to reflect these changes. Therefore, the lighting will not be appropriate for any frames where objects and/or shadows have moved. Naturally, if things move in the scene, you would need to recalculate radiosity. With Cache Radiosity turned on, you are not doing those recalculations each frame. On the other hand, if the shot is a camera fly-through, then Cache Radiosity is a perfect solution since only the camera is moving, not any of the objects or shadows.

The second problem is that since the cached solution is held in memory and not in a file, it is not accessible to CPUs on a render farm. This means that any scenes that have Cache Radiosity enabled must be rendered locally. Rendering an entire shot on one single or dual proc machine can be time-consuming and may be impossible to accomplish. I like to set up these shots at night before I go home from work. In most cases, an average shot will be finished rendering by the time I return to work in the morning. In many production houses, however, everybody is expected to log their machine onto the render farm when they go home at night. If this is the case, then Cache Radiosity is useless to you.

Cache Radiosity can save you massive amounts of render time. For shots that can be rendered overnight (or if you have time to let it cook until it's done) and that have only a moving camera, Cache Radiosity is a very good way to get the most out of LightWave's awesome radiosity tools.

Indirect Bounces

The Indirect Bounces setting controls the number of times light bounces from one surface to another in the radiosity solution. One of the easiest ways to get radiosity render times out of control is to crank up the number of indirect bounces. Following are a number of render tests demonstrating the render time increase associated with an increase in the number of indirect bounces. Theoretically, high numbers of bounces will improve the photo-reality of the shot's lighting. This is because in the real world

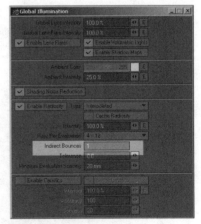

Figure 25.74

there is no limit to the number of indirect bounces. Remember the facing-mirrors example? Light just bounces and bounces until it is eventually completely absorbed, or sucked into a black hole or back into the universe's retracting core and regurgitated as a new sun following the next big bang, which, as you can imagine, could take millions of years. We don't have that much time to render, so best to keep your indirect bounces down. I have never been able to justify more than three indirect bounces, although in practical reality, I rarely use more than one or two. As you add more and more indirect bounces, the visible difference becomes negligible.

This is where ambient intensity is really useful. Because ambient intensity acts like higher order bounces when radiosity is turned on, it's best to leave Indirect Bounces at 1 and have Ambient Intensity on instead. This works very nicely and simulates multiple bounces very convincingly.

Here's what to do: First, add a ground plane and some object into your scene. You could add a bunch of objects if you like. The more you have in your scene, the better you'll see how the light bounces are working. Position the object(s) over the ground plane so you'll see the shadows and light reflections. Then add a gradient backdrop as discussed earlier in this chapter. It can be any color, any gradient, you like. It can even be an image or just a single color, as long as it is bright enough to provide some decent illumination. It doesn't matter; we're looking at low indirect bounces and ambient intensity.

Open the Light Properties panel and set the default light's intensity to 0%. That way we will only see the radiosity illumination.

In the Global Illumination panel, turn on Enable Radiosity and Shading Noise Reduction, set the radiosity type to Monte Carlo, and leave Indirect Bounces at 1. Make sure Ambient Intensity is at 0%; we'll add it later. Hit the old F9 button and see what you come up with. I set my antialiasing to Enhanced Low for this render, just to smooth out some of the lighting noise.

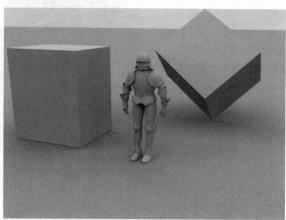

Monte Carlo 1 Bounce took 2:32 to render. The undersides of the objects are still fairly dark, although not as dark as if you used Backdrop Only mode, which is equivalent to 0 bounces.

Figure 25.75: Monte Carlo 1 Bounce, 2:32

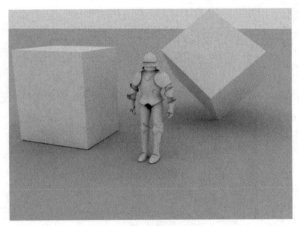

Figure 25.76: Monte Carlo 2 Bounces, 11:49.

Monte Carlo 2 Bounces took 11:49 to render. You can clearly see the additional illumination on the undersides of the objects. This second bounce really adds a lot to the lighting of this scene.

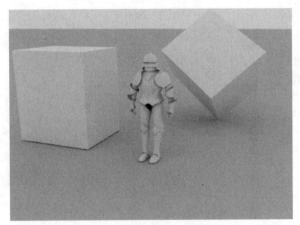

Figure 25.77: Monte Carlo 3 Bounces, 20:59.

Monte Carlo 3 Bounces took 20:59 to render. Render times are starting to get pretty hefty considering this took about 10 times as long as the one-bounce render. But if you look at the image, you can still see a significant illumination difference. We'll try one additional bounce before trying out the "single-bounce with ambient intensity" trick.

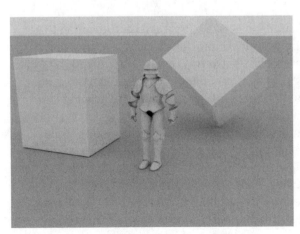

Figure 25.78: Monte Carlo 4 Bounces, 29:15.

Monte Carlo 4 Bounces took 29:15 to calculate. You can still see an increase in illumination with the additional bounce, but it's less significant and will become even less significant as more bounces are added.

Let's take a look now at a single bounce with Ambient Intensity turned on to about 75%. Bear in mind that under normal circumstances (i.e., without radiosity turned on), an Ambient Intensity of 75% would completely wash out and flatten the image.

As you can see in Figure 25.79, the image only took 5:36 to render, but I can't help noticing how similar it is to the three- and four-bounce renders we did that took much longer. Granted, the shadows are not quite as accurate, but it's a very, very good cheat.

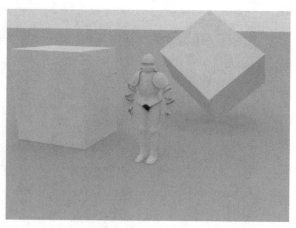

Figure 25.79: Single bounce, Ambient Intensity 75%.

Just so you have a really clear idea of what is different about using ambient intensity with radiosity turned on, Figure 25.80 shows what this render looks like with no radiosity and with the Ambient Intensity set to 75%.

That's a big difference, wouldn't you say?

Tolerance

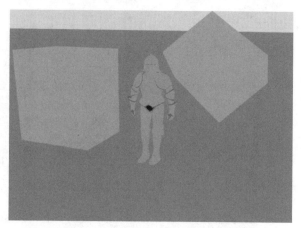

Figure 25.80: No radiosity, Ambient Intensity 75%.

If you are using Interpolated mode radiosity, you have the option to set the tolerance of evaluation recalculation. Tolerance is a setting that lets LightWave choose to interpolate between previously rendered radiosity evaluations. The higher the tolerance, the more often LightWave will use these stored values. With higher tolerances, LightWave will less often provide a new evaluation. If tolerance is set to 0, its lowest setting, LightWave will never interpolate and will always do complete evaluations. This is best if the lighting changes sharply in the scene. If, on the other hand, your lighting changes smoothly and gradually, a higher tolerance is usually allowed. To speed up render times, you should try to get away with as high a tolerance as possible, as it saves LightWave from recalculating evaluations and, therefore, speeds up rendering times.

Tolerance can be set as high as 1 (giving you a total range of 0.0 to 1.0), but be careful. If you set the tolerance too high, your radiosity illumination will become blotchy and unreliable. Following are some sample renders showing the Tolerance setting with render times.

Figure 25.81: Tolerance 0.0, 5:36.

Figure 25.81 was rendered using a tolerance of 0. It took 5:36 to render and there is no blotchiness.

Figure 25.82: Tolerance 0.1, 3:32.

For Figure 25.82, I set the tolerance to 0.1. The render took 3:32. You can definitely see the results of a Tolerance setting that is too high. There are blotchy shadows, especially in areas where the shadows change dramatically. Note, however, that the shading in the distance is still smooth.

Figure 25.83: Tolerance 0.2, 1:32.

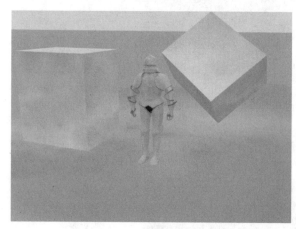

Figure 25.84: Tolerance 0.3, 1:03.

The shading problems are now very obvious in Figure 25.83. I set the tolerance to 0.2, and the render took 1:32. The shading is now so poor that there are hardly any shadows visible beneath the cube on its tip. Note that the shaded areas in the distance remain smooth.

Figure 25.84 had a tolerance of 0.3, and the render time dropped to 1.03. This shading is clearly unacceptable. A tolerance this high could only be used in scenes with very large, smoothly lit expanses. Further, the evaluations would be different for each frame so there would be a great deal of "noise" in the animated sequence. As a rule of thumb, more detail in the geometry requires smaller shaded areas. Smaller shaded areas require a higher tolerance, and therefore fewer interpolated evaluations.

I found that the best tolerance I could get away with in this example was 0.03. It's not much of a Tolerance setting, but even so, it shaved a few seconds off the render. When you're talking about rendering a lot of frames for a lot of shots, every shaved second counts!

Minimum Evaluation Spacing

Radiosity places hemispheres on the radiosity-shaded surface. These hemispheres then shoot "rays" of light to become the diffused lighting bounces. These hemispheres are referred to as "evaluations." LightWave places these evaluations all over the place to create as accurate a simulation of real lighting as possible. But the number of evaluations must be finite because our render time is finite. With this in mind, the brains at NewTek put in the Minimum Evaluation Spacing setting so that we can keep the number of evaluations under control.

LightWave will place more evaluations in corners and in areas where the lighting changes rapidly or dramatically in order to maintain an accurate simulation. Sometimes we can get away with fewer evaluations because corners may not be visible in the shot, or there may be motion blur, or any of a hundred other reasons. If this is the case, we can tell LightWave not to place evaluations any closer to each other than *xx* millimeters. This is what is meant by "minimum evaluation spacing." The evaluations will not be spaced any closer than we specify with this setting.

By increasing the Minimum Evaluation Spacing setting, we are able, once again, to decrease render times at the expense of quality.

Getting the right balance of quality vs. render speed can take a little experimenting, but after you've found the "sweet spot," you will find that your images have a higher quality with as short a render time as possible. When you combine the savings attainable by the careful adjustment of each of these settings, it doesn't become that difficult to justify using radiosity in everyday work, to one extent or another.

But even if you can't use "real" radiosity, there are other tricks and cheats. Read on and we'll discuss some of them a little later on in the chapter.

HDRI Setups

If you are picky about your lighting or if you want to achieve the best lighting possible within LightWave with the most natural intensity and color variations, you need look no further than HDRI lighting setups. For those who are new to HDRI or have not yet read about it in other chapters of this book, the following section provides a quick review of what HDRI really is.

HDRI Recap

Real-world lighting varies widely from pitch black, or no illumination at all, all the way to blinding illumination so bright it would damage the human retina, and even brighter. However, when we see lighting on a computer display, light ranges are limited to a range between black and white where white is the brightest and black is the darkest. In RGB values, we would consider a value of (0, 0, 0) to be complete darkness and a value of (255, 255, 255) to be maximum brightness.

Real-world illumination extends over a range much higher than computer monitors are capable of displaying. Real-world illumination also extends over a range much wider than is accessible by using regular RGB color values.

When lighting a scene using an image was first conceived, it was realized that conventional images did not contain enough data to accurately reflect the illumination values in the environment; therefore, HDRI (High Dynamic Range Images) was invented. These images contain all the same color values that regular images do. In addition, these images contain extra layers of illumination data for every pixel so that accurate illumination information can be encoded directly into the image. This is sometimes done by first photographing the image with 128 different exposures and then compiling all those images into a single HDR image containing all the exposure information. These images are also often taken as a 360-degree image by photographing a reflective ball. In this way, illumination from the entire global environment is captured and can be reapplied within LightWave as a spherical illumination map.

Figure 25.85: A 360-degree LightProbe image containing incidental illumination data.

With radiosity turned on, LightWave understands and utilizes the illumination data within the HDR image to illuminate the scene.

This is called *image-based lighting*. The illumination from this type of lighting is far more accurate, varied, and real than lighting applied in the traditional way using the simple lighting tools and instruments that come with LightWave. The trade-off, of course, is that radiosity renders take much more time to render than those using conventional lights. It is a decision you will want to make as often as you can. There really is nothing as good as image-based lighting.

Using Image World

Probably the best way to use HDR images in LightWave is to import them into your background using LightWave's built-in Image World plug-in.

Let's start, as we usually do, by adding a ground plane and some object in Layout. The ground plane is so we can see shadows and lighting changes created by the object. The object, conversely, is there to cast shadows on the ground plane. Amazing!

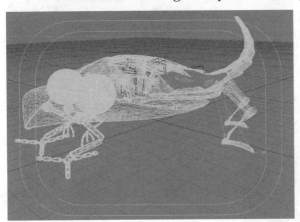

Next, we open up our Effects panel and click on the Backdrop tab.

Click on the Add Environment button and select Image World, which is probably at the top of the drop-down list; it will be added to your environments list. The Image World entry is reporting to you that there is no image in the Image World yet.

Figure 25.86

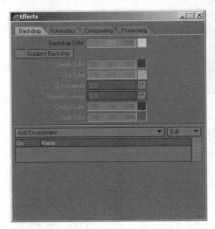

Figure 25.87

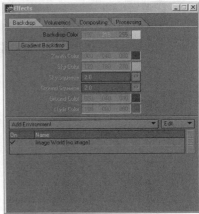

Figure 25.88

You're going to need a real HDR image for this next part. So take a look around the Internet. Search for "HDRI" or "High Dynamic Range," and you should soon have a number of sites where you can download free LightProbe images. Place one of them in your images directory, and then load it into LightWave in the normal way using your Image Editor. Once the image is loaded into LightWave, go back to your Effects panel Backdrop tab and double-click the Image World entry to open up the Image World interface.

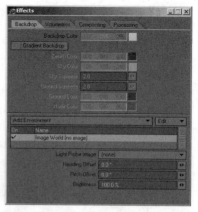

Click on the button beside Light Probe Image, and select the image you just loaded with your Image Editor. I chose to use the galileo_ probe.hdr image, which is freely available in Paul Debevec's Light Probe Image Gallery.

Figure 25.89

Once the image is loaded in, both the Image World text and the interface should change to reflect this image.

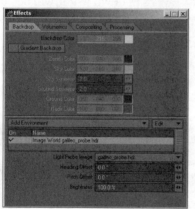

Figure 25.90

The rest of the Image World interface is straightforward. You have the option to change the pitch and heading of the image so that you may orient it as you please. For example, if the image has the sun at one side and the image loads with the sun on the wrong side for your scene, you could rotate all your geometry to match the image. Or you could simply add a heading offset to rotate the image within Image World.

There is also a brightness control that acts as a multiplier to the radiosity Intensity setting in the Global Illumination panel.

Now make sure any lights in your scene are off. If you started with a fresh default scene in Layout, there should only be a single distant light to deal with. Open the Light Properties panel and set its intensity to 0%.

Open the Global Illumination panel from the Light Properties panel and turn on Monte Carlo radiosity. I know, it's the most expensive render, but this is just a test, right? We want it to look nice for the book! After you see the results, you probably won't want to use any other settings either.

Figure 25.91

Now that's what I call fine lighting!

Textured Environment

Also in the LightWave Effects panel's Backdrop tab under the Add Environment drop-down is the option to use the Textured Environment plug-in instead of Image World. Textured Environment supports any of the usual image types that can be loaded into LightWave. The added advantage to Textured Environment is that you can use your HDR image as any of the standard projections, such as Spherical, Cylindrical, Planar, or Cubic, for example. You also have the option of using any axis to place the image just like in the Surface Editor.

These extra controls aside, Textured Environment produces the same illumination results as Image World, so whichever way you choose to set up your HDR images to illuminate your scene, it's going to look just as good.

For my money, Image World is a dead simple, very quick way to set up the environment for HDRI illumination. But if you need that extra control, just switch to Textured Environment.

Inverted Globe

This is a trick we used in the "old days" to add a global environment to our scene, but it's still valid today.

Let's take the scene with our object and ground plane and remove the backdrop Textured Environment or Image World plug-ins, if you have them active in the Backdrop tab.

397

Switch to Modeler and create a ball big enough to surround your object and ground plane, then flip the polygons so they all face inward. The resolution of the ball is not of great importance. Even the size doesn't matter, as you can scale it in Layout if you like.

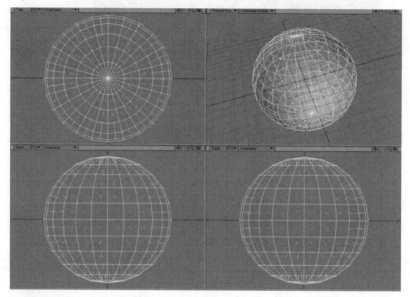

Figure 25.92

Save the ball object and send it to Layout if you use the Hub. If you don't, save the object and then load it in Layout. Make sure it's scaled so that it surrounds your scene.

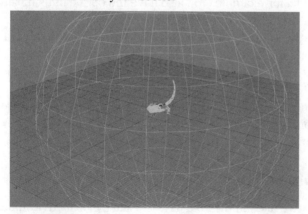

Figure 25.93

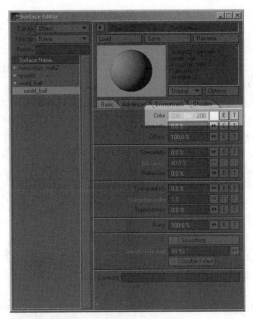

Figure 25.94

Next, open up your Surface Editor and open the ball's surface. Click the "T," or Texture button, beside the Color selection to open the Texture Editor.

This is where you add your image to your object surface.

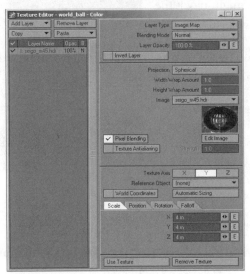

Figure 25.95

Note that I have selected Image Map as the Layer Type and Spherical as the Projection Type. I have also set the Texture Axis to Y; otherwise, the image will be on its side.

I prefer to turn off Texture Antialiasing as I find it softens the image data too much. As for Width and Height Wrap Amount, if you find that your image is stretched too long or squished too narrow, you can compensate for this with these settings. This usually matters if you are trying to wrap a regular photograph around an environment and it's stretching around the circumference of the scene. In those cases I usually set Width Wrap Amount to about 3, which usually

399

works well. But if you are using a LightProbe 360-degree image, as we are here, you can leave both of these settings at 1.

Once the HDR image is applied to the object's surface, save the object and render. You should see exactly the same results as you did when using Image World or Textured Environment.

Why use this method then? Well, that's simple. If you are working in a production house with a bunch of compositors and you find yourself rendering out a bunch of separate CG elements to be composited with each other or with live footage, the compositors always like you to render on a black background because their wicked, compositing voodoo needs blackness to survive. If you are using Image World or Textured Environment with an HDR image (or any image for that matter), the background will not be black. So if you use the inverted globe method, you can leave your background black and simply open the globe's Object Properties panel and enable Unseen by Camera. The camera will see the black background, but the illumination will still be coming from the inverted globe.

If you have other lights in the scene, you may also wish to turn off the shadow options as well (Cast Shadow, Receive Shadow, Self Shadow); otherwise it might block the ray tracing from a distant light or some other such nasty result, which will annoy you after you've spent 20 minutes trying to figure out what has gone wrong.

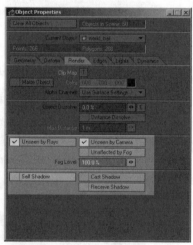

Figure 25.96

That way your scene will get the benefit of the HDRI illumination from the globe, but the globe will not be visible in the background, just black (assuming your backdrop is set to black!). The evil compositors will be happy, and you will have your HDRI lighting.

Creating Your Own HDRI Images Using HDRShop

HDRShop was developed at the University of Southern California's Institute for Creative Technologies. It is available free for academic and non-commercial use and can be licensed for commercial use. This software package allows you to build your own HDR images by compiling the illumination data from a series of photographs.

You can find this software, along with tutorials and a discussion forum, by doing a simple web search for "HDRShop." At publication, the web address for HDRShop was www.debevec.org/HDRShop/.

Faking Radiosity

Let's leave the dream world of Monte Carlo radiosity and HDRI illumination. Most of us don't have the render power to tackle this sort of lighting setup, so let's wake up and smell the coffee. Come on; snap out of it!

We always want that beautiful diffuse reflected light if we can get it. It makes our renders look great. Why? Because the world is full of diffuse reflected light. It may not be as obvious as direct lighting, but it's everywhere. The absence of this lighting is one of the things that really makes CG work stand out as fake. So let's find a way to add reflected light without having to use radiosity and HDRI, not because we don't want to, but because there will be a lynchin' if we do — ours!

There are tons of ways to fake diffuse reflected light. The first step is to understand the source of the diffuse reflection and grasp what the reflection should look like. For example, if a person is standing on some light gray concrete outside and it's a sunny day, we know that there will be a fairly bright reflection of light on the portions of the face that are normally in shadow. Light will reflect into areas such as the underside of the nose, the chin, and the eye socket. We also know that this is a *diffuse* reflection because the concrete is a very uneven surface and that means the shadows will be very soft. We also know that the light source is fairly large — as large as the area of concrete that is reflecting the sunlight.

If the shadows are very soft, we can't use ray-traced shadows from spotlights, distant lights, or point lights for that light because they result in very hard-edged shadows. If the light were reflected from a mirror, a glass office building, or even a pool of water, the shadows would be more hard-edged and we could use ray tracing then, but not in this case.

So now that we know what sort of lighting properties we are looking at, let's try out a few methods of tackling this particular problem.

Adding Lights for Reflections

Let's load up a head into Layout and use the default light, a distant light at 100% with ray-traced shadows, as our key light source. Nothing special to start with.

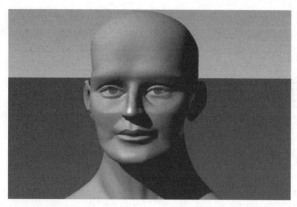

Figure 25.97

Using a Point Light

Now all we have to do in order to simulate a
radiosity reflection from the concrete in front of
the person is insert a light below the face and
turn it on; then we'll take a look at adjusting
settings. Let's start with a simple point light.
We can't use ray-traced shadows as we mentioned before, so after you add the point light,
open the Light Properties panel for that light,
click the Shadows sub-tab, and make sure
Shadow Type is set to Off. This works as though
it were a "directional ambient" light source.

Place the point light in front of and below
the head. Leave it at its default intensity of 50%
and its default color for now.

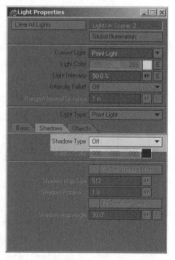

Figure 25.98

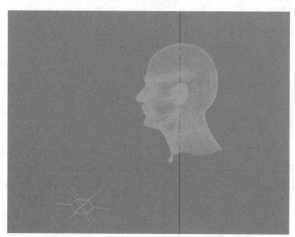

Figure 25.99

Make sure Ray Trace Shadows is turned on in your Render Options panel. Open up the Global Illumination panel from your Light Properties panel and check to make sure Ambient Intensity is set to 0%. This is not one of those occasions when we like Ambient Intensity. Now hit the F9 key and take a look at the results so far.

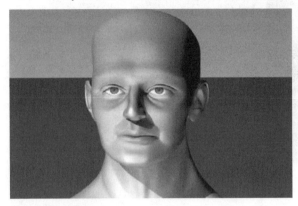

Can you see the subtle illumination on the underside portions of the face? The beauty of this method is this: Because we used a point light with no ray tracing, it cost us virtually nothing in render time to achieve this effect, although the results are fine, reasonably accurate, and subtle.

Figure 25.100

> **Note:** Subtlety is the key.
> There are as many different ways to do this as there are combinations of objects and lighting sources. Bear this one thing in mind: Subtlety is the key. If you make your diffuse reflection too bright, it may look very nice from an artistic perspective, but it might not necessarily look very real.
>
> So be subtle. Use real-world references to let you know just how far you can go. Done properly, this technique will provide you with ultra-realism in your CG work that is difficult to attain (or render intensive) any other way.

Using an Area Light

I've said it before, and I'll say it again: Area lights are my favorite lighting instrument in LightWave. This is because they most closely reproduce the illumination of lights in the real world. When you stop and think about it, all lights are like area lights. They all have some width, height, and depth to them, whether they are a tiny filament or a sun.

Let's get to it. We'll carry on where we left off with the point light in the last section. Select the point light, open the Light Properties panel, and switch the Light Type from Point Light to Area Light. Make sure you open the Shadows sub-tab and set Shadow Type to Ray Trace.

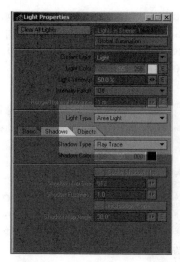

Figure 25.101

Now reorient the area light so that it is pointing upward toward the face. Of course we didn't have to do this with the point light because it is omnidirectional — it emits light in all directions. An area light, however, is not omnidirectional; therefore we have to point it in the direction we want the light to emit.

> **Note:** Area lights illuminate just the same pointing in either direction, but Layout's Light View will only show one of the directions.

There are a couple of ways to do this. But if you look at a side or perspective view, it's not immediately obvious which direction the area light is facing. I prefer to use the Light View in this case, then rotate it until it is looking upward toward the face.

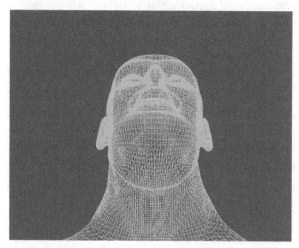

Figure 25.102

Simple enough. Let's not worry about color or intensity settings for now. Just hit the F9 button and take a look at the initial results.

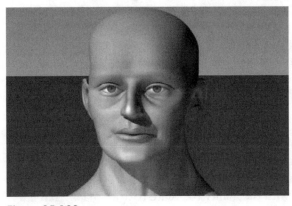

Figure 25.103

The advantage to using an area light is that there are shadows where there should be shadows. The shadows are very realistic looking, soft, and pleasing. With a point light with shadows off, areas will be illuminated that you may not necessarily want to be illuminated. It is a fairly subtle point, but if you compare Figures 25.100 and 25.103 closely, you will see the differences in the shadows and how much difference they make to the lighting.

As a last demonstration of this technique, let's crank up the intensity of the diffuse reflected light source (our area light) so we can get a really good look at exactly what it is doing to the scene's illumination.

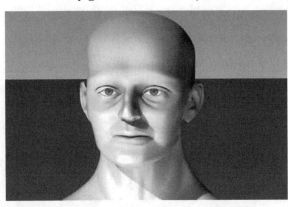

Figure 25.104

You can see clearly where the area light is doing the most lighting: on the portions that face downward.

You really can use any type of light you wish for this effect. If I had my choice, I would use an area light, but render times may be an issue. My second choice would be to use a spotlight with shadow-mapped shadows and a fairly high fuzziness to soften the shadows as much as possible. The main problem with most of LightWave's light types is that they originate from a point, whereas our light reflected off the concrete originates from an area. This is precisely why the area light is going to work the best if ultimate photo-reality is really an issue for you. The area light, unlike other light types, provides illumination from an "area"; therefore the illumination wraps around the object somewhat. This "wrap-around" effect does not occur with any of LightWave's "simple" light types.

405

As with all these lighting effects, you are going to have to make the choice between quality and render time. Find the balance that suits your artistic sensibilities but doesn't take 10 hours per frame to render. It's always a battle for balance when you wish to achieve photo-real lighting. You must know how far you can go, how far you have to go, and, especially, how much motion blur is in the shot to hide all your cheap, crappy tricks!

Baking Radiosity

Like a doughnut to a starving man, texture baking allows us to indulge in that oft-maligned lighting tool — radiosity. Baking Radiosity is the only current answer to Cache Radiosity's inability to render over a network. LightWave provides us with the ability to create texture maps from our renders that include the illumination data generated by the render. These maps are saved as image files and can be accessed by network renders.

Naturally there is a trade-off. If you create a luminosity map this way and apply that to your surface as the only illumination, you won't be able to light the surface with other lights, and you won't be able to have passing objects cast shadows. But we can get around this somewhat. Follow along and I'll show you.

The first thing to do is build a box in Modeler. This is going to be a room interior. A simple cube will do for now. Make sure the polygons are flipped inward (usually using the "f" key), then save the cube and send it to a freshly opened Layout. Once in Layout, select the distant light, open the Light Properties panel, and change the light to a point light. Place the point light inside the room near the top. You should now have a scene in Layout that looks something like Figure 25.105.

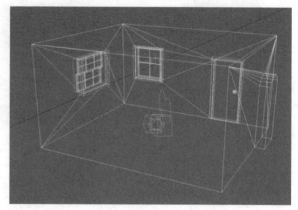

Figure 25.105

All right, I didn't exactly use a cube, but I had this room on hand so I used it. Sue me.

The next step is to open your cube (or room) object in Modeler and add a UV map. Make sure your object has no polygons with more than four vertices. The Surface Baker plug-in we are going to use doesn't like polys larger than that, so find any and triple them by choosing them from the Polygon Info window and then pressing the "t" key before making your UV map.

At the bottom right of the Modeler interface you will see five buttons labeled "W," "T," "M," "C," and "S" with a drop-down menu beside them which currently, most likely, says "(none)," indicating that no maps have been selected.

Figure 25.106

Click the "T" (for texture) button and click on the drop-down menu. You should be able to select "new" from the drop-down. Do that now to open up the Create UV Texture Map dialog.

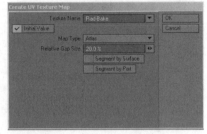

Figure 25.107

I set the name of the UV map to Rad-Bake and set Map Type to Atlas. I've left all the other settings at their default and clicked OK. Now when I switch one of my Modeler views to UV Texture I can see what the atlas projection of my room looks like.

Now save the object and let's head back to Layout.

Surface Baker allows us to bake all kinds of texture information together into a single map that we can then apply to the object's surfaces.

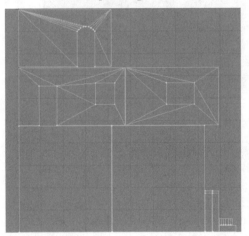

Figure 25.108

Say, for example, you had a complex layering of color maps, diffuse maps, bump maps, luminosity maps, and so forth. Sometimes these layers can grow out of proportion and take up too much memory, also taking a long time to load and calculate for renders. In such a case, it might be wise to bake all the surface information into a single UV map that is then applied to the surface instead of all those layers.

In our case, however, we are only interested in speeding up radiosity renders, so the only thing we're going to bake into our UV map is the illumination information in the scene.

Surface Baker is, coincidentally, a surface shader. You open up your Surface Editor, select your wall surface (mine's called kitchenwall;

yours is probably called default if you are using the cube you just made in Modeler), and click the Shaders tab. Click on the Add Shader drop-down and select Surface Baker from the list.

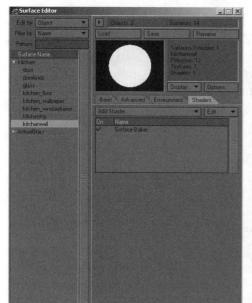

Once it's selected, double-click it to open the Surface Baker interface.

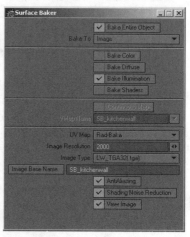

Figure 25.110

Figure 25.109

There are a lot of buttons here, and you might want to learn what each of them is for, but we're not going to go through them all here. For our purposes, it is sufficient to know that the only buttons we need for this procedure are Bake Entire Object, Bake Illumination, and Shading Noise Reduction. I like to turn on AntiAliasing as well to get the best possible shading. It takes longer in the initial render but will look superior and save you the hassle of redoing it later if the quality isn't high enough.

Under UV Map, I select the VMap Rad-Bake I created in Modeler. That way, Surface Baker knows how to lay out the render.

Next to Bake To we select Image so that the illumination data will be baked out to an image that we can apply later. By clicking on Image Base Name we can specify an image name and a save path for the new image we are about to create. You'll also need to select an image type or format. If you select a 32-bit image format (which contains an alpha channel), the resulting image you create will show the UV wireframe in the alpha channel. The alpha channel of the image allows you to control exactly where the image appears on surfaces. It acts as a "mask" that only allows desired portions of the image to appear on the surface.

Figure 25.111: An image of a UV map alpha channel.

Lastly, you'll need to decide what resolution you want the map to be. The Image Resolution setting sets the pixel height and width of the final image. The higher this setting, the more superior the quality of the final image but the longer the render time. In my experience, a larger image provides better results. You only have to render it once, so it's worth the extra time if you can afford it.

Once all your options are set, you need only hit the old F9 key and create a test render. Surface Baker will operate automatically and, if you have the image viewer turned on, you'll get to see both the new image map you've created and the original radiosity render. Make sure you have View Image selected in the Surface Baker panel.

Figure 25.112: The baked UV map.

Figure 25.113

Now that we have an illumination map to simulate our lighting, let's set it up. First, go into the Global Illumination panel and turn off radiosity. Won't need that anymore! Next, turn off any lights you have in the scene.

Open up the Surface Editor panel and click on the Texture Editor button (the T) next to Luminosity.

409

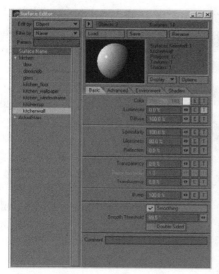

Figure 25.114

When you have the Texture Editor open, change Projection to UV and select the UV map you created in Modeler. Load up the image we just created with our Surface Baker and select it in the Image box.

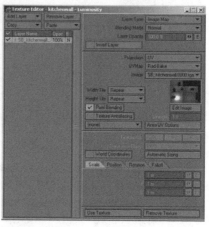

Figure 25.115

Set Luminosity of the surface to 100% and Diffuse to 0%. That will give illumination control exclusively to the luminosity map.

> **Note:** If you wanted to use this method but also have moving objects in the scene cast shadows onto the surfaces, you could retain some of the diffuse value of the surface, setting it to, perhaps, 50% instead of 0%.

IMPORTANT — Don't forget to open up the Surface Editor Shaders tab for the original wall surface and disable or remove Surface Baker. Now that we've baked the surface, we no longer need this plug-in, its render times, or its results.

Let's render the room and see what we have.

The most obvious difference is that the window and door frames are black in this render. That's because we didn't include them in the

Figure 25.116

surface bake and, since we turned all the lights off, they are not illuminated. The next thing we notice is that the illumination of the walls is
pretty similar to the illumination we originally rendered with radiosity
turned on. The big difference is that this render took about six seconds
instead of 22 minutes.

I'd say that's a time savings worth noticing.

Caching Radiosity

Caching radiosity is a simple concept also worthy of your attention. If
you are working on a scene in which only the camera moves and you
wish to use radiosity in your lighting setup, there are few tools superior
to Cache Radiosity. Why? Simply put, this tool allows you to use
radiosity on every frame but only calculates it on the first frame.

Cache Radiosity is also an extremely easy tool to use. Simply set up
your radiosity settings, open the Global Illumination panel from your
Light Properties panel, then click the Cache Radiosity button.

> **Note:** Cache Radiosity only works if you have radiosity enabled
> and are using Interpolated mode.

That's it. Now render.

There are two current drawbacks
to caching radiosity. We can't do anything about the first one; it's the
nature of cached information. Because
illumination from the first frame is
cached and used to illuminate the
remaining frames, anything that
moves around in the scene will not
reflect a change in radiosity. This
could look strange. The second drawback is that the cached data is not
stored in a file, but rather is held in
local memory. This means that if you

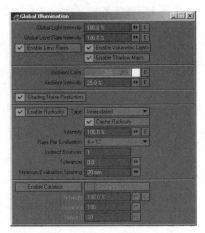

Figure 25.117

intend to render your scene on multiple processors over a network, the
networked processors will not have access to the caching solution;
therefore each processor will calculate its own cached radiosity. This will
result in flickering radiosity — not desirable at all. So if you want to render a sequence using Cache Radiosity, you have to do it all on one
machine where the processor(s) can access the cache.

Cache Radiosity would be a vastly more useful tool if the cached radiosity solution, instead of being held in local memory, were held in a file. That way, networked machines could access the information the same way networked machines access Particle FX solutions from a single file for particle renders. I'm sure if enough of us continue to make noise about this, NewTek will see fit to include it in the next great release of LightWave.

Faking Soft Shadows

No doubt about it, sometimes we just can't use radiosity to achieve those beautiful soft shadows we have come to know and love. The truth is, it is very difficult to fake that kind of quality, but there are many situations in which that level of quality is not necessary because there may be heavy motion blur in the shot or perhaps any soft shadows are not forefront in frame. If you come across a situation where the soft shadows are unimportant enough to fake, you should do it. There are literally dozens of way to fake soft shadows. Here are a couple of my favorite tricks. They're easy, quick, and provide reasonable results without major render power.

Using an Area Light

OK, using an area light isn't exactly what we'd call a quick render, but it's quicker than radiosity in most cases.

The first rule with area lights is to keep them as small as possible. The larger the area light, the more render time is required. Second, try to reduce Area Light Quality to 3 instead of the default 4. I have never been able to get away with less than 3 for a final render, although I have never had to go above 4 either. The maximum quality for area lights is 5.

Getting a soft shadow out of an area light is easy. Place it, turn up the intensity, and render. The larger the area light, the softer your shadows will be.

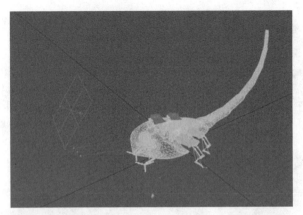

Figure 25.118

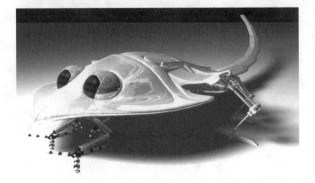

Figure 25.119

Using Spotlights and Shadow Maps

This is a favorite of mine because spotlights with shadow maps render very quickly and because spotlights with shadow-mapped shadows are the only light in LightWave other than area lights that provide a built-in soft shadow. These are also extremely easy to set up and, although the quality of the shadows is not nearly as good as area lights, it's a reasonable fake that's good enough to make it on the big screen.

Let's look at our mechanical bug scene and open up the Light Properties panel where we will change our area light into a spotlight. We'll turn on shadow-mapped shadows, select a nice high map resolution like 2000, and set the map fuzziness (blur) to 15 for a nice soft edge.

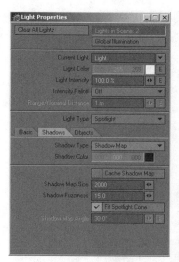

Figure 25.120

Now render it out and take a look at those soft shadows. Compare them with the shadows from the area light.

Make sure you place the spotlight where it will illuminate your whole object. I like to do this by using the Light View. Or, if you need the light to illuminate other things in your scene but only need the shadow for your object, make Shadow Map Angle smaller than the cone angle of your light, and make sure the object is contained within the square representing the shadow map angle.

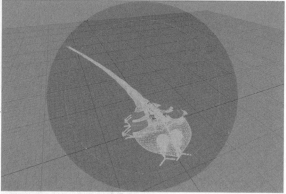

Figure 25.121

Figure 25.122

As you make your shadow softer, you will start to notice that the shadow stands away from the object casting it, giving the impression that the object is floating above the surface. This is a normal side effect of very fuzzy shadow maps. Since the "softness" of the shadow is nothing more than an edge blur, the shadows will blur evenly all around the edge, even where it is directly under the object. This sometimes makes it appear that the shadow is not contacting the object.

If this is a problem, simply decrease the fuzziness setting or select a different method of creating soft shadows.

Using the "Spinning Light" Trick

This lighting trick is an "oldie but a goodie." The spinning light trick has been attributed to many artists over the years, but it is generally accepted that this technique was first implemented in LightWave by Dave Jerrard, one of the original LightWave gurus — He Who Has Been Around A While — although it may have been independently discovered by other artists as well. Dave came up with it back in the mists of time when LightWave 3 was released. It's a very clever concept. Once you figure out how it works you will probably scratch your head and wonder how the dickens it was conceived in the first place.

It is a good trick for creating fairly accurate soft shadows in LightWave. Before area lights existed in LightWave, the spinning light trick was the *only* way of creating fairly accurate soft shadows in LightWave, since all the other light types are cheap approximations of real-world lights. Its whole premise is based on how LightWave calculates motion blur, so let's take a look at that first.

LightWave calculates motion blur by interpolating motion from the previous frame to the current frame multiplied by the Blur Length setting in the Camera Properties panel. For example, if you have low antialiasing on, LightWave will render the frame five times. For each of the five render passes, any objects in motion will be moved one-fifth of the Blur Length percentage further along in position from where the objects were in the previous frame to where they are in the current frame. All five render passes are then sandwiched together and the

edges appear as though they are blurred. If the motion is high enough, you can actually see the stepped edges of each render pass.

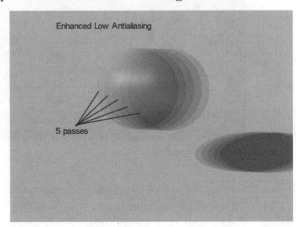

Figure 25.123

If the motion is high enough to make the stepping visible, then you have the option of setting your antialiasing to a higher level, in which case, LightWave will calculate more passes to make the steps closer together, hopefully fooling your eye into believing that it is real motion blur.

Naturally, since a moving object is motion blurred, and therefore has stepped antialiasing passes, its shadows must also be motion blurred and have stepped antialiasing passes. This is where we get into the territory of the spinning light trick.

The second thing we have to understand is how soft shadows work. We understand that even the softest shadows are hardest near the object casting them and softest farthest away. So if we have a whole bunch of lights pointing inward toward an object, we will get this soft shadow effect. That is, after all, essentially what the sky is — a huge array of lights all pointing inward toward the object.

The spinning light trick puts these concepts together.

Start by opening up a fresh Layout and loading in a ground plane and some object to cast shadows onto the plane. I'll stick with my metal bug.

In my scene, I position the default distant light over the object so you can see it. In reality, the position of a distant light is irrelevant since its rays are all parallel. Only the direction of the light will make any difference.

Now clone the distant light five times, and rotate four of them so that the rotations are evenly spaced.

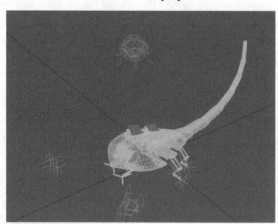

We end up with an array of distant lights all in one spot, all facing different directions. Since the position of distant lights is irrelevant, we can argue that this is just the same as placing a bunch of lights all around the perimeter of our scene pointing inward. Let's render a frame and take a look at the shadows.

Figure 25.124

Don't forget that since we now have five lights, we'll need to reduce the intensity on all the lights; otherwise our scene will probably be overilluminated. LightWave light intensities are additive.

Figure 25.125

See the shadow array created below the object? There are five distinct shadows. Now let's remove the four extra lights we added. Instead, we'll spin the one distant light with an Antialiasing setting of Enhanced Low. Don't forget to turn the light's intensity back up to 100% for this test.

Open your Camera Properties panel to set the antialiasing level. Make sure Motion Blur is set to Normal and Blur Length is set to 50% as well.

Now, set a keyframe for the distant light at frame 0. Set a second keyframe for the light at frame 1. With the distant light selected, open the Graph Editor and make the light's heading 0 degrees at frame 0 and 720 degrees at frame 1. Set Post Behavior to Repeat.

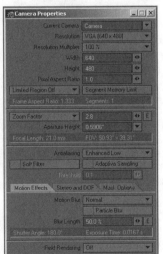

Figure 25.126

We make the light rotate 720 degrees, or two full rotations, on each frame because the motion blur is set to 50%. 50% of 720 degrees is 360 degrees. This means that for every frame, the distant light will rotate exactly once. If we set the antialiasing level to Low or Enhanced Low, then we expect there to be five distinct shadows beneath the object, just as there were when we had the five separate lights.

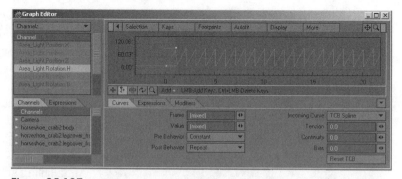

Figure 25.127

Let's have a render and see.

Figure 25.128

Figure 25.129

That's fairly similar to the render with five lights. Now let's try to smooth those shadows together a bit. We'll increase the antialiasing level to Enhanced Medium, which will give us nine passes. In addition, we'll turn on Dithered Motion Blur instead of Normal. That change will double our number of passes. The goal is to try to make the "stepping" invisible and blurred or unnoticeable to the casual viewer.

Now we could continue to smooth out the shadow by increasing the antialiasing level, but each level higher we go doubles the render time. So we can add more lights instead. Clone the distant light twice and parent both clones to the original light, but remove the motion keys from the clones. Rotate the first clone on its heading by 120 degrees, and rotate the second clone –120 degrees. Now the three lights' rotations should be evenly spaced. Run a test render. Adding the two extra lights will add a little time as LightWave now has to calculate ray tracing for three lights, but you get triple the number of shadows for just a little more render time.

Obviously, you can further improve the shadow softness by increasing either the number of lights or the number of antialiasing passes. Remember, though, as you add more lights, you need to proportionately reduce the intensity level of all the lights.

Figure 25.130

> **Note:** There are *many* variations on the spinning light trick. For instance, you can "wiggle" a light's heading a bit between two frames and then repeat the motion. We often use this for cheap soft edges. Another good one is to offset a light from a null a bit, target it to an object or another null, then spin the first null 360 degrees and repeat. This way you get a focused light at the target point and increased softness out from there. You have the spinning light, the moving light, the wiggling light, and a million other variations to soften hard shadows.

Faking Volumetrics

Volumetric lighting is that light you see in a smoky room. It's the rays of light shining out of the trees and through the fog, the "God" rays coming from those silver-lined clouds. In other words, volumetric lighting is simply light rays that are illuminating particulate matter in the air.

This fake volumetrics technique is the last trick in this chapter. It's another technique belonging in the "old but good" category as it is simple to set up and use and can save you major render time. This trick was also developed way back in the early days before LightWave was equipped with "real" volumetrics.

The Old Geometry Trick

One thing we know about volumetric lighting is that if you don't actually have to have the camera fly through it, it doesn't have to be an actual volume. This is one of the easiest and most obvious tricks in the LightWave arsenal. If you need a volumetric spotlight, just create a cone in Modeler, stick it in front of the light, and add some illumination and a nice transparency falloff to the cone. I'll use a gradient based on a weight map. So let's open up Modeler and make the cone.

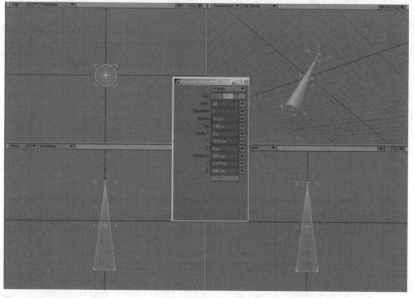

Figure 25.131

Now select the point at the top of the cone and create a weight map named Volumetric.

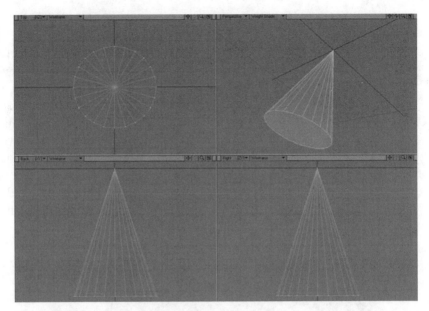

Figure 25.132

Save the object and send it to a fresh, default Layout. Once in Layout, change the default distant light to a spotlight, then parent the cone to the light. You may need to rotate the cone so that it aligns with the light's beam.

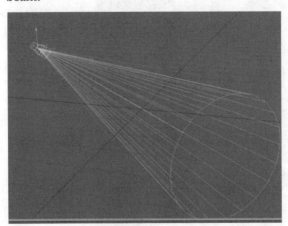

Figure 25.133

Open the Surface Editor and select the cone's surface. Open up the Luminosity Texture Editor. Set Layer Type to Gradient and proceed to set up the values shown in Figure 25.134.

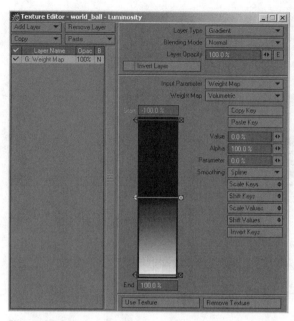

Figure 25.134

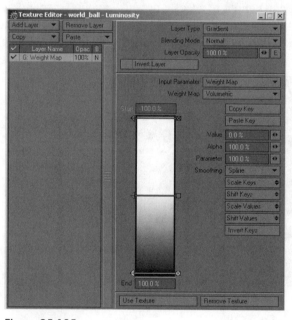

Figure 25.135

Or if you want to do it the way we used to in the old days, just create a black-to-white gradient image in your favorite paint program and apply it along the length of the cone so that the tip of the cone is brightest and the round end of the cone is dimmest.

Apply the same gradient to the transparency channel but with the values reversed.

This will make the cone less transparent near the light and more transparent farther away. You can fiddle with these settings until you are happy with them.

Feel free to throw in a procedural texture to break up the cone's even look a little.

Figure 25.136

Now hit the render button and have a look.

Figure 25.137

Granted, this trick won't work for everything, especially not if the camera passes directly in front of or through the volumetric, but for my money it's a cheap, quick technique, valuable in anyone's toolkit.

• • •

It is my sincere hope that by looking through these tutorials, you have gained some new knowledge that will help you light your scenes. Most of these tutorials have been designed to help you understand how to implement specific tricks and techniques, rather than teaching particular lighting setups or techniques.

For tutorial examples of a few of the infinitely variable lighting set-ups, please see the following chapter.

Chapter 26

Lighting Setup Examples

For those of you who prefer concrete examples of lighting setups, this chapter contains a number of such examples. Rather than providing a single setup technique for a sunny day or a room interior, however, I employ the various properties of the lighting tools to demonstrate a number of different techniques for dealing with each lighting scenario. The purpose of this is to demonstrate the flexibility of LightWave's lighting toolkit and to put into practice the lighting theory and tool descriptions found earlier in the book. I hope you find these short tutorials useful in describing the many uses of LightWave's lighting tools.

Exterior Sunny Day

This is a very common lighting scenario and a very good place to start since the lighting setup is very simple. If you find yourself in a situation where you must create a lighting setup for an exterior sunny, clear day, the first thing you should do is examine that environment and decide exactly how many light sources exist and what their position, angle, color, and size are.

Typically, exterior sunny days have two or three light sources, depending on the environment. The key light is the sun. It's a bright, slightly amber light source in the color temperature range of 5500 to 5700 Kelvin degrees. It is relatively small in the sky, but is not a point light.

The fill light is the sky. Since we know that the sky itself is luminous, we know that it is diffusing light from the sun and spreading it in all directions, some of which reach our subject. The skylight is very large, hemispherical in shape, and has quite a blue hue, in the range of 10,000 to 20,000 Kelvin.

A third light source, if there is one, is likely to be a reflected light from the ground. This is often called a "bounce" light and is usually diffuse, unless it is reflected off a highly specular surface such as water, polished marble, or glass. This third source may or may not be required. For one thing, there may not be a surface light enough to justify a bounce source. You will have to decide. Bear in mind that a subtle bounce will add a great deal of realism to your shot, but it doesn't have to increase your render times.

Let's take a look now at some ways of tackling this problem, beginning with the cheapest render solutions.

Distant Key, Ambient Fill

For super-fast renders where photo-real quality is not an issue, there are many options, most of which do not include shadows.

Start by loading your trusty ground plane object (just a single polygon will do) into a fresh Layout. After that, add an object. Any object will do, although we will be able to see the effects of our lighting better with slightly complex objects that have lots of places for shadows and highlights to fall.

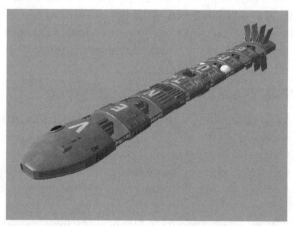

Figure 26.1

Now open your Light Properties panel. The default light is a distant light. We want to make its color more sun-like. Open up your LightWave color picker by clicking on the color square. Select the Kelvin tab to open up the color temperature color picker. Now select 5500 in the numeric box and hit OK.

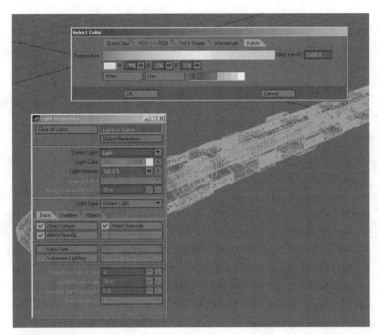

Figure 26.2

Note: If you are using the Windows default color picker instead of the LightWave color picker, I highly recommend you stop it immediately. Just open up your General Options in Layout and click the Color Picker drop-down to select LW_ColrPikr. You'll be glad you did.

Figure 26.3

Once you have set the sunlight to the right color, click the Global Illumination button on the Light Properties panel to get to the Ambient Color setting. Once again click the color square, open the Kelvin tab on the LightWave color picker, and this time select 11,000 as the color. Skylight usually varies in the 10,000 to 20,000 Kelvin range; however, the LightWave color picker is limited to 11,000 K.

Once you have selected the color of the blue fill, click OK on the color picker to close it. We now have a sunlight color and a skylight color. You can leave the ambient intensity around 25%.

The last thing to do is open the Render Options panel and make sure Ray Trace Shadows is enabled.

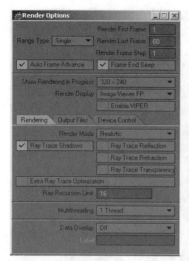

Figure 26.4

Under Camera Properties, set Antialiasing to Enhanced Low and turn off Adaptive Sampling. Now let's have a look at the render.

Figure 26.5

That's not too bad for a 22-second render. Granted, there are a lot of fine details not visible in the shadows that probably should be there, and the ambient intensity is too flat to be realistic. If you're in a hurry, this will do, especially if details can be hidden with motion blur or quick cuts. On the other hand, you can speed this render up even more if necessary. If, for example, there were no ground plane onto which the shadows fall,

Figure 26.6

you might even get away with having shadows turned off. The object will still be shaded on surfaces facing away from the light, so you might get by with an even quicker render.

Distant Key, Distant Fill

Here's another simple solution to the exterior sunny shot that places a distant light for the sky fill instead of ambient intensity. This method provides the artist with a little control over the direction of the skylight, where the ambient solution gives the artist no control.

Let's leave our distant key just as it is. Open up the Global Illumination panel and set Ambient Intensity at 0%.

Now add a second distant light and orient it so that its rotation is 0, 90, 0. This has the light pointing directly downward onto the scene. If you like, you can move the light above the subject, although with distant lights it doesn't matter where you place them.

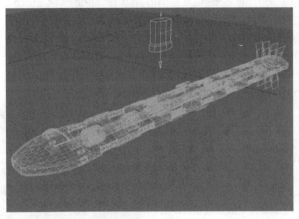

Open the Light Properties panel for this light, click the Shadows sub-tab, and set Shadow Type to Off. Leave the light at its default intensity of 50%, then click the color square to open the LightWave color picker. Once again, set the Kelvin color temperature to 11,000.

Figure 26.7

That's it. Now render out a frame and take a look.

Figure 26.8

Figure 26.9

At first glance the render is quite similar to the ambient fill render we did earlier. If you look carefully, though,

you will see that the surfaces facing away from the sky fill still remain unlit, creating darker shadows than the ambient solution. This is slightly more realistic and takes little additional render time because the sky fill light's shadows have been turned off so there is no ray tracing to calculate.

It's a subtle and simple change in technique that takes slightly longer to render than the ambient technique. If I had my choice, though, I'd select this method.

Distant Key, Spot Fill

Here's another technique for this common setup that provides yet more control and options. The advantage to using a distant light for the sky fill was the ability to control the direction of the light. If we use a spotlight instead of a distant light, we still get to control the direction, but we have the added bonus of being able to apply soft shadows. Naturally, this means using shadow maps instead of ray-traced shadows.

So, still working with the scene we used in the last tutorial, select your sky fill distant light and open the Light Properties panel. Switch Light Type from Distant Light to Spotlight. Then click on the Shadows sub-tab and switch Shadow Type to Shadow Map. Make Shadow Map Size 1000 and set Shadow Fuzziness to 5.

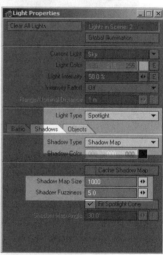

Figure 26.10

Now in Layout, switch to Light View and make sure the light is lining up with the object and completely covering it and any other areas around it you may want illuminated. One thing worth considering here is the cone angle. Because of the nature of a large, diffused light source like the sky, you probably want to get the spotlight's cone angle as narrow as possible so that the light "beams" appear to be parallel. What you don't want is a spotlight that's close to the object with a wide cone angle. This would result in a shadow that is obviously *not* from a sky-light source.

Figure 26.11

Notice that the soft shadow from the object is much larger than the object itself. This is because the light angle is very wide, ruining the illusion of a unidirectional light source.

Figure 26.12

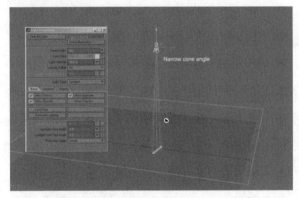

Figure 26.13

Figure 26.14

If this light were cast by a large source like the sky, the shadow should be smaller than the object, since the light is approaching from all directions. So the trick is to back the light away and keep the cone angle nice and narrow. It's a bit of a hack, but it works.

Another problem with having a very wide cone angle, as you can see in the previous render, is that the shadow map becomes pixelated. That's what is causing the stepped, or aliased, edges in the shadow. If you have a very wide cone angle, you are spreading out the shadow map, so a higher Shadow Map Size setting might be required. But in this case, we have made the cone angle nice and narrow. Let's render it out and take a look.

There are two main problems in this image. First, we can see the cone edge. Second, the shadows are much too hard for this type of effect. So, rather than make the cone angle larger, we'll just back the light away a little farther. Let's also ramp up the Shadow Fuzziness to 20 and see where that gets us.

That's a fine-looking soft shadow for a fuzzy spotlight, if I do say so myself.

Figure 26.15

Distant Key, Area Fill

Moving on, we keep our distant light as our sunlight key and get into some of the more render-intensive options for a fill light. As our lighting and shadows become more mission-critical, and as we have less motion blur and other artifacts to hide our cheats and tricks, we sometimes find ourselves forced down the road of more expensive lighting solutions. Area lights were originally considered unusable by most artists as the render time was intense. But code, quality options, and processing power has made the area light more and more of a daily tool.

Open up the Light Options panel and select the sky fill light from the previous tutorial. Switch Light Type from Spotlight to Area Light.

Now the first thing you will notice is that the area light is much, much too high, since we placed our spotlight high in the previous tutorial.

Bring the area light much closer to the object. From the Top View, make the area light about twice the size of the object. We want the area light to be larger than the object so that some light "wraps around" the object, creating a nice soft shadow.

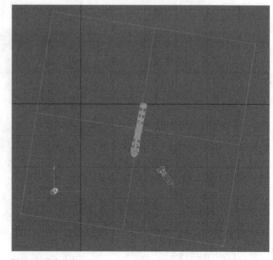

Figure 26.16

Figure 26.17

> **Note:** Try to keep the area light as small as possible. The larger the area light, the longer the rendering times.

Now make sure Ray Trace Shadows is turned on in your Render Options panel and render out a frame.

Figure 26.18

That render was pretty lengthy compared with the shadow-mapped spotlight technique, although the soft shadows are more accurate and nicer looking, especially among the complex shapes within the object. If you wish to speed up your render times using this area light technique, you have the option of reducing the Area Light Quality setting in the Light Properties panel.

Figure 26.19

Keeping Shading Noise Reduction on in the Global Illumination panel
will help hide some of the artifacting produced by lower quality area
lights; however, I have never been able to get a satisfactory result from
an area light quality lower than 3. You also have the option of increasing
the quality up to 5 if need be.

Distant Key, GI Fill

Stepping up the quality and render time one more notch, we always have
the option of using global illumination or radiosity to act as our fill skylight. Now don't go getting worried about horrendous render times. For
the purposes of this tutorial we will be using the Background Only mode
of radiosity, which in effect turns light bounces off. So there are no actual
bounces to calculate, only the illumination provided by the background.

First, open up your Light Properties panel, select the sky fill light
we have been playing with in these past few tutorials, and turn its intensity down to 0%. We won't need it for this technique.

In Layout, open up your Effects panel and click on the Backdrop
sub-tab. Click the color box beside Backdrop Color. When the LightWave
color picker opens, click on the Kelvin sub-tab and enter a value of
11000. That should provide us with a nice, soft sky blue color for our
background — perfect for a sky fill light source.

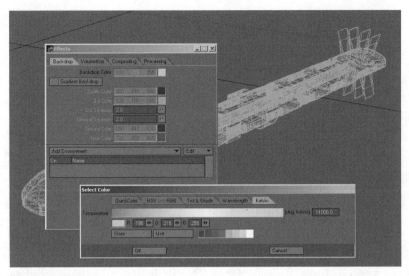

Figure 26.20

Click OK and close the Effects panel. Now open the Light Properties panel and click on the Global Illumination button. Select Shading Noise Reduction and Enable Radiosity. Using the drop-down next to Type, select Backdrop Only.

That's it. Now close the GI panel, close the Light Properties panel, and hit the F9 key for a test render.

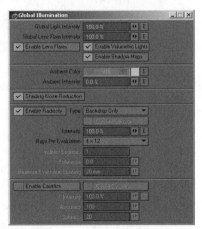

Figure 26.21

That's a nice-looking image with good soft shadows. As a matter of fact, this image is head and shoulders above the others in terms of lighting and shadow quality. But let's do a little math. Using Backdrop Only radiosity this took over 11 minutes to render. That's twice as long as the area light technique. This render

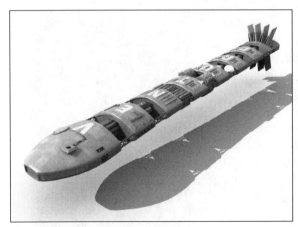

Figure 26.22

is superior to the fuzzy shadow map technique, but the spotlight technique took only a few seconds to render!

Spot Key, Spot Fill

There is one compelling reason to use a spotlight for your key sun light instead of a distant light. True, distant lights provide much wider coverage. You have to back your spotlight way, way off to get really wide coverage while maintaining close-to-parallel light beams. But spotlights have that nice shadow fuzziness that can never exist with distant lights. Because distant lights' shadows are ray-traced and parallel, they are hard-edged. They are hard-edged near the object casting the shadow and hard-edged far away from the object casting the shadow. This is a very unnatural and inaccurate way of making shadows. Why do they do it then? It's a simple calculation that doesn't take much time to calculate, where natural shadows that are hard-edged near an object and softer farther away require much more intensive calculations. We already know that we can cheat and get away with inaccurate shadows at times, especially when the cast shadow is not in frame, when motion blur obscures the true nature of the shadow, or if the shadow is very short and the softness might not be visible anyway. But there will be times when you simply must have soft shadows, but you don't have the render time to create realistic, accurate shadows. That's when this technique becomes most useful.

It's a very simple setup. We've messed around so much with our scene for the previous tutorials that we should start fresh. So clear Layout to get all the defaults back. Then load up some object and a ground plane onto which we can cast shadows.

Open the Light Properties panel and switch Light Type from Distant Light to Spotlight. Click on the Shadows sub-tab and change Shadow Type to Shadow Map.

Add a new spotlight to the scene. Place it directly above your object and pointing straight downward. Turn on Shadow Map, set Shadow Map Size to 2000, and set Shadow Fuzziness to 100.

Now, switch to Light View and line up both lights so that they completely cover your object.

Figure 26.23

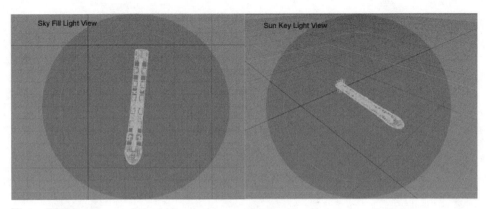

Figure 26.24

Choose a warm color for your key, around 5500 Kelvin degrees color temperature, and a cool color for your sky fill, around 11,000 Kelvin degrees color temperature. Those are fairly natural color temperatures for sunlight and skylight.

Now set your antialiasing level to Enhanced Low, turn off Adaptive Sampling, and hit the F9 key to produce a test render.

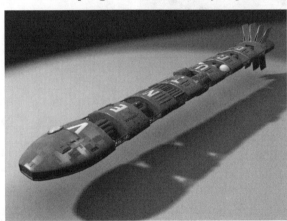

Figure 26.25

There are two immediately obvious problems with this render. The first one is that the spotlights are not large enough to fill the frame. This is a dead giveaway that our lights are neither sunlight nor skylight. Fortunately the fix is easy: Just back off the lights until the cone covers all areas within frame.

The second problem is not fixable. The problem is that the shadows are uniformly soft all the way around. That's the nature of fuzzy shadow maps. Just as ray-traced shadows are evenly hard-edged all the way around, fuzzy shadow maps are evenly soft-edged all the way around. You can't change it without using another technique. That means that this technique is only useful in situations where you do not necessarily see the shadow for a long distance, so you don't need to see it softening as it gets farther away from the object that is casting it.

437

Let's fix the first problem though and take a look at the improved render. Remember that as you move your key light farther away the light is spreading out wider, so you can reduce the shadow fuzziness. In this render, I reduced it to 35. Since I pushed the key light farther away, I also reduced its shadow fuzziness to 35.

> **Note:** Very high shadow fuzziness can result in unacceptable artifacts over an animation. You'll have to experiment to see what the tolerance is for your particular shot, but very high shadow fuzziness is best used for stills only.

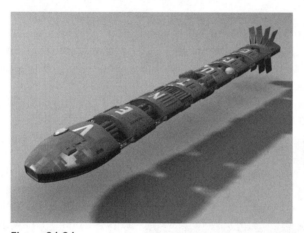

Figure 26.26

That's all there is to it. It's a very fast, very simple setup that you can get by with when render time is at a premium.

Spot Key, GI Fill

I've said it before and I'll say it again: There is nothing quite as beautiful and accurate as LightWave's global illumination. So scrap the sky fill light by opening its Light Properties panel and turning the intensity down to 0%. Or you could just delete the light from the scene if you like.

Now open your Effects panel and click on Gradient Backdrop to enable LightWave's built-in gradient backdrop.

Figure 26.27

Or if you like you could make your own gradient by selecting LightWave's Textured Environment from the drop-down menu. Or if you want to be ultra-simple about it, just select a single color for the back-drop and forget about gradients, image backdrops, and whatnot. It

doesn't matter, as long as your back-drop is light enough to produce the illumination you require once we turn on radiosity.

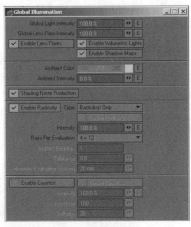

Figure 26.28

That's the second part of this setup. Open your Light Properties panel and click on Global Illumination to open that panel. Select Shading Noise Reduction and Enable Radiosity. Then change the radiosity type to Backdrop Only.

That's it. Now render out a test frame by hitting the F9 key.

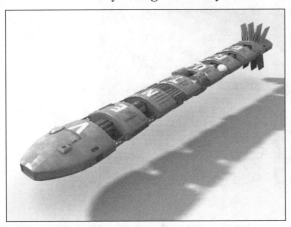

Figure 26.29

Using GI as a skylight fill source takes considerably longer to render than spotlights, distant lights, or area lights, but the soft shadows are second to none. You can even rationalize it by noting that your spotlight takes so little time to render that it offsets the render time of GI. Well, OK, maybe that won't fly, but you can always try it.

Area Key, Spot Fill

Here's a good technique. Global illumination and area lights are pretty heavy in the render department, especially when they have to be as huge as the sky. Remember, the larger the light, the longer the render time. But we now know that a fuzzy spotlight can make a fine skylight fill source. We can then change our key sun light source to an area light. "Wait!" you say. "Area lights take too long to render." In general that is true. This is where the real beauty of this technique comes in. If you see the sun up in the sky, does it look huge? Not really. It's a small disc tak-ing up a very small portion of the sky. So why use a huge area light?

For one thing, a very big area light would create inappropriately soft shadows. So instead let's use a *small* area light. We get quicker rendering times and better shadows.

First, open up your Light Properties panel, open the Global Illumination panel, and turn off radiosity. We won't need that render-sucking menace for this technique.

Next, open the Light Properties panel for the sky fill source we used earlier. Remember, we were using a spotlight pointing straight down at our object and it had shadow-mapped shadows enabled with a very high fuzziness. Make sure the light's intensity is 50%.

Now select the sun light. Open the Light Properties panel, if you don't already have it open, and switch Light Type to Area Light. Make sure Ray Trace is selected for Shadow Type under the Shadows sub-tab.

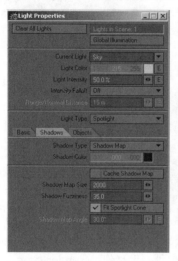

Figure 26.30

Figure 26.31

Now, in Layout's main interface, switch to Perspective View and rotate so that you have a good view of the new area light that you are using for your key. Size it so that it's roughly the size you imagine the sun might appear from earth. It should look something like Figure 26.32.

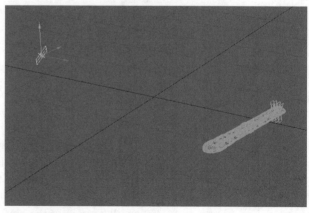

Figure 26.32

You can see that the area light is relatively small compared to the object. The last thing I'm going to do is stand my object up like a telephone pole so you can observe the difference in shadows near the object as compared to the shadows that have fallen farther away from the object. Now hit the F9 button to render out a test and see how things look.

Figure 26.33

This render took less time than either the GI skylight technique or the area light skylight technique, yet the results are comparable or better. Having a key light that produces natural-looking shadows can really sell your shot. You'll notice in this render that the shadows are harder nearest the subject and get softer farther away, just like the shadows from real sunlight in the real world.

Area Key, Area Fill

Moving on to more expensive techniques for the classic sunny day scenario, we get to use an area light for the key as well as for the fill. This is by no means a pie-in-the-skylighting solution. Once again, the accuracy you select for your lighting and shadows depends entirely on the need of the shot. If you are creating stills, that's all the more reason to crank up render times. If you're only rendering one frame, who cares if it takes all night for the final render? When you come to work in the morning, you'll have a shot with beautiful lighting. All that matters is that the shot looks good enough for whatever purpose you or your director or VFX supervisor has in mind.

Moving along from the previous tutorial, the setup is simple. Just keep your area light key as it is, open the Light Properties panel, and select the fill light. Now switch the Light Type to Area Light. Make the area light roughly twice the size of the object and drop it low enough that the width of the light will provide reason-able lighting coverage by reaching its light rays beneath the object. This is a cheap way of creating a "wraparound" sort of skylighting.

Figure 26.34

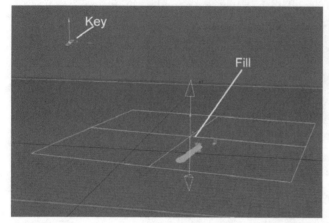

Figure 26.35

Check that the key-to-fill ratio is about 2:1. In other words, if the key light intensity is at about 100%, the fill light intensity should be at about 50%. This is a good rule of thumb for starting out when creating a key-fill relationship.

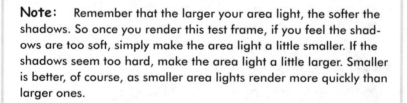

Note: Remember that the larger your area light, the softer the shadows. So once you render this test frame, if you feel the shadows are too soft, simply make the area light a little smaller. If the shadows seem too hard, make the area light a little larger. Smaller is better, of course, as smaller area lights render more quickly than larger ones.

Now render out a frame by hitting the F9 key.

That just about does it. The large area light for the fill added considerable time onto our render, but it was still cheaper than GI Backdrop Only mode. You now have another technique for your toolbox.

Figure 26.36

Area Key, GI Fill

And speaking of more expensive renders, we can add even more time onto our render by substituting a nice GI backdrop for our fill light instead of an area light. We'll keep the area light we're using for our key, but you can either delete the fill light or open up the Light Properties panel and turn its intensity down to 0%.

Now open up your Effects panel and select a backdrop color in your Kelvin color picker in the 10,000 to 11,000 K range. That's about right for skylight. Alternately, you can throw in a backdrop gradient with LightWave's Textured Environment or you can simply use LightWave's built-in Gradient Backdrop if you like. Either way, make sure there is a color light enough to provide sufficient illumination once we turn on Backdrop Only radiosity.

Now open the Light Properties panel and click on Global Illumination to open the Global Illumination panel. Click on Shading Noise Reduction and Enable Radiosity to turn them on if they are not on already. Now switch the radiosity type to Backdrop Only mode. That will turn off all radiosity bounces. This is, in effect, Monte Carlo radiosity with 0 bounces selected.

Now render out a test frame by hitting the F9 button.

Figure 26.37

Once again, global illumination is pretty hard to beat. There's nothing quite like the soft shadows and even, natural illumination of a GI backdrop. Well, except perhaps for a GI backdrop with some radiosity bounces enabled…

Area Key, GI Fill, Radiosity

We are getting near the end of our list of "a million and one ways to do a sunny day." Not that there are a million and one suggestions here, but I'm sure you can figure out the other ones. So let's have some fun. Simply using the scene as-is from the last tutorial, open up your Global Illumination panel by opening the Light Properties panel and clicking on the Global Illumination button. Now switch the radiosity type setting to Monte Carlo. Yes, there are cheaper rendering solutions, but we're having fun now, right? Set the number of bounces to 2. You'll get a nasty warning that the next Ice Age will be approaching before your render is finished. Ignore it — it's usually wrong. That's all there is to this little tutorial. Hit the F9 key and bask in the glory of multi-bounce radiosity.

Figure 26.38

That looks very nice, but the render time was through the roof — in the 40-minute range. Unless you are rendering still images or real bounced radiosity is mission-critical to your render, you probably won't be using this technique too often.

HDRI Only

This is our final look at the sunny day scenario. What is unique about this technique is the fact that it doesn't employ any lights at all. In fact, all the illumination, including sunlight, is interpreted from an HDRI photograph. With the sun in the photograph, the image contains enough information to closely recreate the lighting environment including most of the qualities and properties such as color, size, angle, and intensity. I have found the HDRI-only technique most useful for scenes that do not employ a direct source of light such as the sun. While HDR images provide a beautiful, varied illumination environment, I have yet to see them used effectively for more direct, bright illumination such as the sun. Nonetheless, here is our scene rendered with an HDR image in the backdrop using LightWave's Image World plug-in. The image used was a simple sunny exterior image from Paul Debevec's online Light Probe Image Gallery at http://athens.ict.usc.edu/Probes/.

Figure 26.39

If you have taken the time to work through, or at least to read through, most of these tutorials, you should realize by now that the purpose of this chapter is not to teach a particular technique for dealing with a particular lighting scenario. In fact, the purpose of these tutorial techniques is not to teach any techniques at all. It is to provide you, the reader, with practical understanding and experience of some of the myriad uses and combinations of LightWave's lighting tools. You may end up using actual techniques from this section. I know I do all the time. But that's not the purpose. Before we carry on with a completely new lighting scenario, let's take a look at a similar one.

Exterior Cloudy Day (Soft Shadows Only)

The next few pages deal with sky fill only. This means there is global illumination providing soft shadows, but there is no direct lighting. There is no sunlight, in other words. Let's look at the exterior cloudy day.

The primary lighting property of a cloudy exterior shot is that there is no direct light source and that shadows are very soft. This automatically rules out using distant lights or point lights due to their harsh, hard-edged shadows (unless you plan to employ the "spinning light" trick). I have never been that happy with the spinning light trick for really high quality soft shadows, especially where there is no key light and other lighting effects to obscure the shadows. When you are doing a cloudy day, that's all there is to look at so your shadows better be nice and soft with no stepping.

Spotlight

Probably the cheapest way to accomplish this is by using a simple spotlight with Shadow Map enabled instead of ray tracing and with a high Shadow Fuzziness setting.

Start with a fresh Layout and add a ground plane and an object to cast the shadows. Any object will do, although objects with higher complexity offer a better example of exactly what the shadows are doing. Next, open the Light Properties panel and change the default distant light to a spotlight. Under the Shadows sub-tab, switch Shadow Type from Ray Trace to Shadow Map. Set the fuzziness nice and high, somewhere around 15.

Now place the light directly above your object, nice and high with a narrow cone angle, and point the light directly downward so that it encompasses your object. Render out a test frame and have a look.

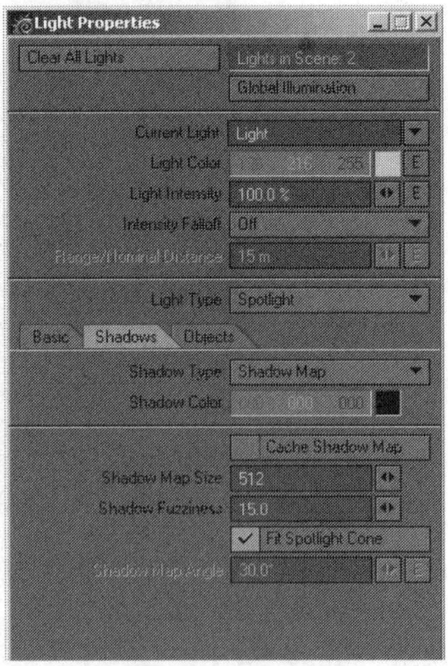

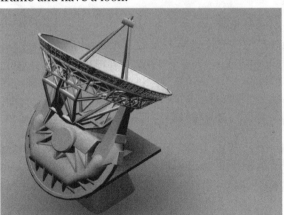

Figure 26.40

Well, the shadows are not exactly accurate, but they're soft. This technique will do in a pinch and is lightning-fast to render.

Figure 26.41

Area Light

For accurate, good-looking soft shadows, we really need to get into something like a light array. Fortunately NewTek has gifted us with area lights, which take the place of old point-light arrays.

Carrying on from where we left off in the last tutorial, simply open up your Light Properties panel and switch Light Type to Area Light. The Shadow Type will automatically switch to Ray Trace. Now looking from the Top View, make the area light about twice the size of the object you are illuminating.

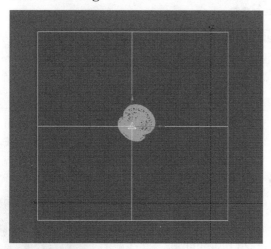

Figure 26.42

Render out a test frame.

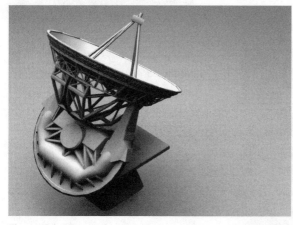

Figure 26.43

This is unquestionably a real improvement in both shadow quality and accuracy. It could be better though. For one thing, the default quality setting of an area light is 4. You can now set it as high as 5, which will help reduce some of the grainy artifacts that are inherent in lights of this type. No matter what, though, when using area lights or global illumination you should always make sure Shading

Noise Reduction is enabled in the Global Illumination panel to help smooth out those artifacts.

> **Note:**   If you happen to own Worley's G2, you can improve the quality of area lights past the quality setting of 5 without Shading Noise Reduction by applying the G2 shader to your surface and increasing the shadow quality in G2's master panel.

Global Illumination

For soft shadow quality, global illumination is your new best friend. For a soft-shadows-only setup like a cloudy day, you don't even need to have any lights active. Of course, LightWave insists that you have at least one light in the scene at all times, but you can always just set its intensity to 0% and forget about it. Let's do this, carrying on from the last tutorial.

First, open up the Light Properties panel, select the area light, set its intensity to 0%, and forget about it. You won't need it any more for this tutorial.

Now open your Effects panel and select a backdrop color that is something on the light gray side.

Now open the Light Properties panel, click on the Global Illumination button, and click on Shading Noise Reduction and Enable Radiosity. Be sure to select Background Only as the radiosity type.

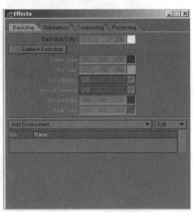

Figure 26.44

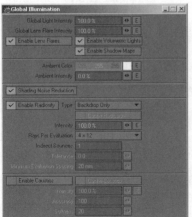

Figure 26.45

Now hit the F9 button to make a test render.

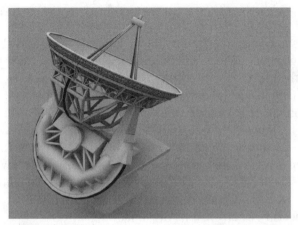

Switching from an area light to global illumination really cranked up the render time, but oh, the shadows. It's enough to make a lighting geek weep!

Figure 26.46

GI, Radiosity

As a last kick at this particular can, we're going to render this same shot with 2-bounce radiosity turned on. In your Global Illumination panel, simply change the radiosity type from Background Only to either Monte Carlo or Interpolated, then make the number of bounces 2.

Render out another frame and bask once again in the glory of multi-bounce radiosity. Sure it takes a long time, but it's nice to look at once in a while.

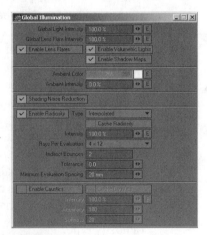

Figure 26.47

Figure 26.48

Exterior Night

Nighttime is usually characterized not by its light but by its lack thereof. So how do we go about lighting a dark scene? Well, the first thing to understand is that the human perception of illumination is relative. For example, if you are inside a room with no windows and someone turns a 1,000-watt lightbulb on in front of you, you will perceive that as being extremely bright. If you then walk outside into the sunlight, you will realize that the 1,000-watt lightbulb was actually comparatively dim. Your perception is relative to the environment and is based on how wide your pupils are dilated at the time. The wider your pupils, the more sensitive your eyes are to light. We can use this perception to our advantage in lighting, especially when creating night shots.

So we must create a scene that is illuminated enough to see the relevant details, yet is perceived as night.

Night shots usually have deep, dark shadows. Since there is no bright key light, there is very little radiosity to fill in shadows. The moon reflects some light, but it is infinitesimal compared to the light output of the sun.

Night lighting is usually very cool. This is because most of the light is reflected moonlight. Because the surface of the moon is a light gray color, most of the amber from the sunlight is absorbed. The remaining reflected light is cool. Further, just as in the daytime, most of the red wavelengths are absorbed by the atmosphere and most of the blue wavelengths pass through, making the light even cooler.

So we know that we need to create cool light with deep, dark shadows to simulate nighttime lighting.

This is one of the few lighting scenarios in which it is probably acceptable to get away without a fill light. We will try a couple of different techniques both with and without fill lights. In a night shot, fill should be very subtle indeed.

Distant Key, Ambient Fill

Here's a pretty typical technique for dealing with exterior, nighttime lighting. Considering that the fill light source (the starlight) is extremely low as to be almost imperceptible, we can get away with all sorts of rude tricks without worrying much about shadow quality.

First, open up a fresh Layout to return to the default settings. Load some sort of a ground plane and an object. For this example, I have chosen to load a street scene with a vehicle parked by the street.

Figure 26.49

Now open the Light Properties panel and click on the square beside Light Color. Enter the color values numerically as 75, 86, 149. Or you could click directly on the color numbers and slide them back and forth until you achieve a nice dark blue color.

Close the Light Properties panel and use the Light View to aim your default distant light at your subject so that the light is approaching the subject roughly perpendicular to the camera's view.

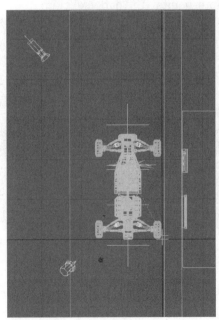

Now open the Light Properties panel and click on Global Illumination. When that panel is open, set Ambient Intensity to about 10% and make its color also a dark blue.

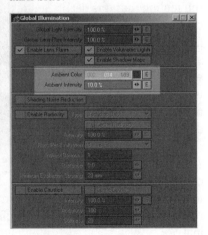

Figure 26.50

Figure 26.51

Now hit the F9 key for a test render. Let's see how it looks.

That's not too bad. By making the light blue, we give the perception of night-time. We also help that perception by keeping ambient light levels low and by creating deep, dark shadows.

Figure 26.52

Adding Some Interior Light

If we want to add a little more to that illusion, we could add some interior light from the windows as a counterpoint to the dark exterior.

Interior light is not usually seen during daylight, so even though this image is black and white, you get the feeling that it is dark outside because the light from the windows is highly visible. The addition of a warmer interior light spilling into the street also makes the exterior seem darker and colder.

This was accomplished simply by adding an amber colored point light to the interior. The light playing along the window panes and across the vehicle really helps with the illusion of night, even more so than the illuminated interior.

Figure 26.53

Adding a Streetlight

Adding a streetlight to this scene will also really help sell it. Simply placing a spotlight above the vehicle and having it fall somewhere within the camera's view will be enough. You can choose the color of your streetlight. The color varies widely and so does the softness. I have found that most streetlights cause fairly hard, harsh shadows, however, because they are relatively small.

This streetlamp light source also acts as a nice rim light so we can show off our nice car. Who said you can't do three-point lighting? Did I say that?

There are dozens of different ways of accomplishing this shot using a variety of different lighting instruments and techniques. If you have looked through the earlier portions of this chapter, however, you will probably already have figured out how to adapt those tutorials for this lighting scenario. If you can't figure it out, I recommend you go back and work through all the tutorials in this and the previous chapters. By the time you get back here again, you will have figured it out. If not, maybe it's time for a nice career canning fish.

Figure 26.54

Interior, Incandescent

Interior scenes are common in life and therefore are common in visual effects. If you are called on to provide a VFX element for an interior plate, there are several things you need to know.

First, incandescent light fixtures are usually relatively small, ranging from light-emitting diodes to lightbulbs a few inches across. This size can be mitigated by shades and diffusers that make the light source apparently larger, but usually not much larger than 12 inches or so.

Second, incandescent light sources are the result of heating a metal element (known as a filament) until it is hot enough to begin emitting light. This is called *incandescing*. We know by looking at the Kelvin color scale that a low color temperature is red. That is the temperature where a filament of metal will begin to incandesce. As more current is applied, the filament becomes hotter. The higher temperature makes the filament whiter. White-hot is much hotter than red-hot. At some point, the filament will melt and incandescence will cease because the circuit is broken.

What is important here is that incandescence occurs in the warm side of the Kelvin color temperature scale. For normal household lightbulbs, the Kelvin color temperature is usually in the 2800 to 2900 range. For tungsten-halogen bulbs, it's usually in the 3200 to 3600 K range. If you open your LightWave Color Picker and look under the Kelvin sub-tab, you will see that this range of color temperature is very orange indeed. This tells us that most of our household bulbs are actually burning relatively coolly.

So let's build a scene and experiment with incandescent lighting.

First, open a fresh Layout to make sure all of Layout's settings are at the default. Now, you'll need an interior scene. If you don't have one built, a cube will do to simulate a room interior. I'm using this kitchen scene I have on hand.

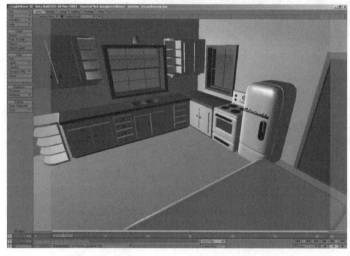

Figure 26.55

I look at this shot and immediately consider that there is probably a bare bulb or a diffused fixture in the middle of the ceiling of this room that provides a general light for the entire room. This would be an omnidirectional light source. So let's go ahead and use a point light. Open the Light Properties panel and switch the default distant light to a point light. Now place that light near the ceiling at about the center of the room.

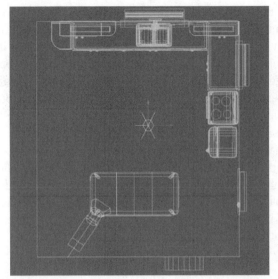

Under the Light Properties panel, click the colored square beside Light Color. When your LightWave Color Picker opens up, select the Kelvin sub-tab and enter a numeric value of 2900. This will give your light a natural incandescent color.

Figure 26.56

Figure 26.57

Render out a frame and see how that looks.

Figure 26.58

While this is technically a good color for this light type, I find it to be too orange. Remember, what looks and feels right is more important than what is technically correct. I know that incandescent lights burn in this range of color temperature, but it just feels wrong. I'm going to open my Kelvin color picker again and select a color more in the 5200 K range. This color just seems better to me. It might be the color calibration of my monitor or video card. It might be my perception. It might be that the relative intensity I have chosen for my light source has no connection to reality. What I know for sure is what *looks* right. This is the kind of judgment call you will have to make. Trust your instincts. The numbers may be scientifically correct, but this is a virtual environment. There are many factors at work that change the look of lights. Also, these are not real lights and they most often don't behave like real lights, so use your judgment.

Another thing that I find immediately wrong with the picture is that the illumination is much too even. This is because a real light has intensity falloff. In other words, as you get farther away from the light, the intensity spreads out and diminishes. So it is only natural for us to use intensity falloff as well.

Open your Light Properties panel and enable Intensity Falloff by opening the drop-down menu and selecting Inverse Distance ^ 2. This is also called *inverse square*. Inverse square is, in fact, the only physically correct model for the diminishment of light over distance. It works exactly the same as for the diminishment of sound over distance.

You also need to set the Range/Nominal Distance. When you have either of the inverse falloffs enabled, the nominal range changes function. It becomes the point at which falloff begins, whereas if you are using linear falloff the Range/Nominal Distance determines where the light falls off to 0%.

Set the nominal range by using the Top View in LightWave's Layout interface. You will see a dotted circle around the light source. Make it about half the size of the room.

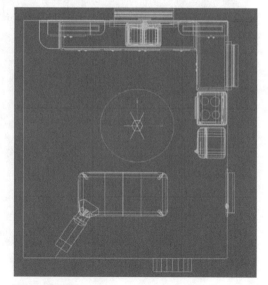

Figure 26.59

Because you are now causing your light to reduce in intensity relatively quickly, you will probably find that you need to increase your light's intensity. I'll set mine to 200% in the Light Properties panel. Now let's render a frame to see how it looks.

Figure 26.60

That is far superior to the original render. Notice how shadows fall off softly in the corners, how the lighting is even yet reaches items in the scene with different intensity depending on their distance from the light source. Light intensity falloff is crucial to this look.

Now let's add a little more detail to the lighting. I imagine that there is probably a light fixture of some sort hanging over the kitchen table. Perhaps that is on instead of the overhead light. And maybe there is a light fixture over the sink. I know there has been one in every kitchen I ever entered. Let's add those and see how this changes the scene.

Figure 26.61

There you have it — a completely different looking scene, just by moving a couple of lights around. In this case, I chose to use two spotlights, each with a fairly high spotlight soft edge angle of around 15 to 20 degrees.

Interior, Fluorescent, Night

We can use the scenic setup from the previous tutorial to continue on into fluorescent lighting. Kitchens often make use of fluorescent lights, and this one will be no exception. Let's try to find a more interesting position to place the lights, however. I have seen fluorescent lights placed beneath cabinets where they provide bright, unobstructed illumination of the counter working area. This is a particularly interesting place to position lights because it means the lighting will be reaching any people in the scene from below, which is a very unnatural and interesting lighting angle.

Before we build and place these lights, however, let's examine the qualities of fluorescent lights and other similar light types such as neon tubes.

First, we know that fluorescent lights generally burn much cooler than incandescent lights. That is meant both in terms of heat temperature and color temperature. Fluorescent lights are usually in the 7000 K range, often in the green range, while neon tubes can be any color ranging from subtle to wildly saturated.

Second, we know that these tube lights can be virtually any shape and size, but are almost always larger than household lightbulbs. Fluorescent tubes are most often long, straight tubes, but can also be bent into a variety of shapes, while neon tubes are usually used in sign-making and can therefore be any of an infinite variety of shapes and sizes.

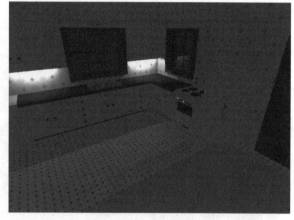

Figure 26.62

In this case, I chose to use two linear lights for the job. They are conveniently shaped roughly like fluorescent tubes and are relatively fast to render, although not as fast as point lights or spotlights. In lieu of a linear light, you could always make an array of point lights, which is what we used to do in the old days. Just parent a bunch of point lights together and string them out in a line. This is essentially how a linear light works anyway.

We can further enhance this scene by adding a third linear light on the ceiling to act as a main, room fluorescent light fixture.

Figure 26.63

Although it is difficult to see in a black and white image, the cool fluorescent lights tend to make the room look more stark and clean.

Interior, Radiosity

Naturally, there are few lighting effects in LightWave that look as good as radiosity. Let's apply some to our kitchen scene and see what the net lighting effect is, then we'll see if we can simulate that radiosity using other tricks.

First, open up your Light Properties panel and click on the Global Illumination button. Once that panel is open, click Enable Radiosity and Shading Noise Reduction, and set the radiosity type to Interpolated.

Now simply hit the F9 button to create a test render.

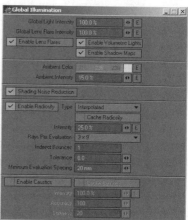

Figure 26.64

Figure 26.65

There are several problems with this render. First, it took over two hours to render a single frame with Enhanced Low radiosity. Second, the image is grainy and of poor quality. We could fix the grain by increasing the Rays Per Evaluation setting, but the render time is already out of control. So instead, we'll solve both of these problems by turning off radiosity and using a few tricks to simulate the radiosity bounces. So go ahead and disable radiosity in your Global Illumination panel.

Now, the trick is to add *bounce lights* wherever we think there should be a radiosity bounce. The purists will argue that every surface in the room produces a radiosity bounce, and that is technically correct. What we are interested in, however, is where the most apparent bounces will occur so that we can place lights there of the right color, shape, and intensity to simulate the radiosity bounce. To LightWave, this is just another light, so there will be no deadly radiosity calculations taking up your wee hours.

When I look at our kitchen scene with the two fluorescent tubes beneath the cabinets, I imagine that the most obvious place for a bounce light source is on the counter beneath the cabinets, directly under the bright light sources. I could use any light type I wish, but I know that a radiosity bounce is diffused, causing soft shadows. I also know that most radiosity bounces take place over a wide area. Therefore, I'm going to select area lights as our bounce lights. If this technique requires too much render time, we can always retreat to a spotlight if necessary, but that wouldn't be my first choice.

I'll place a pair of rectangular area lights facing upward just above the countertop, right beneath the fluorescent sources.

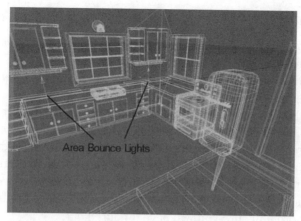

Figure 26.66

Although you can't tell from the black and white image, the countertops are green. Any bounce light will obey the laws of physics. The colored bounce surface will absorb most of the light wavelengths except those that are the color of the surface, in this case green. Our bounce lights should therefore be green.

Subtlety is the key with fake radiosity bounces. Set the lights' intensity fairly low, maybe around 20 to 25%. Turn on Linear falloff. Check the falloff Range/Nominal Distance to be sure that the light will reach the immediately surrounding geometry but not too much farther.

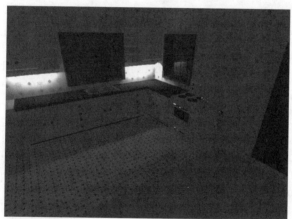

Figure 26.67

Adding two area lights to our scene only increased the render by a couple of minutes because they were fairly small. Remember, the larger the area light, the longer the render time.

Notice the gentle highlights along the bottom edges on the cabinet. There is also a nice soft illumination near the right window. Both of these indicate a very nice, subtle bounce lighting effect, and while using LightWave's built-in radiosity took over two hours to render a frame, this took just over four minutes and has a higher image quality. No tough decision here.

Exterior, Radiosity

Having now worked through a number of tutorials dealing both with exterior lighting situations and with the use of real and simulated radiosity, it should be easily apparent how to combine the two for effective lighting setups.

Once you have placed your key and fill light sources, you have the option of enabling LightWave's built-in radiosity solution. Or you can estimate where the most pronounced radiosity bounces might occur in the scene and place bounce lights at those locations yourself, therefore removing the need to use LightWave's radiosity. Try this out yourself. If you find it difficult, then work through all the tutorials again. By the time you get back here, I'm sure you will have it figured out.

Why am I not simply providing a detailed tutorial? Well, the purpose of this book is not to provide you with a handful of easy techniques to deal with all lighting scenarios. It is to teach you the tools so that you can develop your own techniques as needed. That is what makes a good lighting artist.

· · ·

My intention with this chapter was not to help you learn about specific lighting techniques, although many have been used here, but to help you learn about the lights themselves. I hope you have learned more about light and shadow and about the combinations of possibilities that lie at your command with the simple application of a little knowledge and imagination.

My suggestion is to try to use every light type for every type of application. There is usually some way to do it, although the quality and render times may vary greatly and may not be exactly what you had hoped for. Every time you learn some new way of doing something, even though it may not apply to your current project, it is yet another tool for you to file away in your toolkit. It may be the tool that saves your shot one day. It may be the tool that saves your job or gets you a new one. That may sound melodramatic, but consider how many work hours are spent every day by CG artists all over the world who struggle to attain simple, quality lighting. Many have no idea how to accomplish it and, therefore, waste many hours fruitlessly chasing a lighting setup they don't understand. You must realize that a skilled, knowledgeable lighting artist is going to be a valuable asset. The clever artist will now come up with his own numerous, subtle, and cheap techniques for creating the lighting environments described in this chapter.

Observe the world and learn the tools — that's all there is.

Chapter 27

Anatomy of a Production Lighting Rig

This chapter details the process, thinking, and problem solving used to create a production lighting rig that served the twin goals of output quality and acceptable render time.

Our job was to provide a number of shots in which live animal faces were replaced with talking, photo-real CG animal faces. This meant the lighting would have to be as photo-accurate as possible from our end. I was tasked with creating a multifunction lighting rig that was versatile, highly adjustable, feature-rich, and simple for all the artists to operate.

Initially, we examined the footage and concluded that most of the shots used soft lighting with occasional special directional or highlight lighting. In other words, the gaffer made extensive use of diffusion gel to soften and widen the light source. With this information in hand, it became clear that we would have to use soft, diffuse lighting with special highlights and directional lights in our renders to get our CG elements to match the plate. The plan was to begin with a four-point beauty lighting rig and a single area light or two. The area lights would provide the soft, wide lighting in positions where the gaffer had used large diffusion, providing wide specularity and soft shadows, while the four-point rig would be composed of spotlights with shadow fuzziness high enough to simulate lighting appropriate to each plate.

> **Note:** "Plate" is the term used to refer to the image sequence used as a background reference for the CG element. The CG element is rendered on a black background when it is complete, and then handed to a compositor who places the CG element over the background "plate," seamlessly marrying the two together.

> **Note:** For more information on four-point lighting, please see Chapter 6.

The challenges began when we started adding fur to our animals. Dogs and cats have widely varying fur. Some fur is short and closely groomed. Some is long, wild, and frizzy. Some droops, some stands up on end. Either way, all fur requires lighting that makes it fit seamlessly into the plate.

In this case, we used Worley's Sasquatch for our fur. Sasquatch is an extremely powerful tool with a wide range of lighting and shading tools that help improve both the rendering speed and the render quality. We were, however, limited by some of the ways Sasquatch tackles lighting and shading.

The first thing we discovered was that we had to learn Sasquatch front to back and top to bottom to be able to predictably achieve the results we desired. This is not a complaint; it is the double-edged sword of powerful software. It has so many controls that it is easy for the novice to quickly become buried in a quagmire of messed-up settings. On the other hand, it provides unparalleled power and flexibility to the knowledgeable user. It takes a while to fully understand the functionality of each of the many settings. As a matter of fact, I could write a big, thick chapter on lighting fur in Sasquatch, but that does not really lie within the scope of this book.

So we began with a simple rig containing five lights — four-point lighting for beauty renders (renders that will look good as temp renders without having to light to the plate) plus an area light. The intention was that this rig would be a starting template for all the shots. The template would be imported into a scene and then adjusted to match the plate lighting, or, for animation tests, simply import the lighting rig, render, and it will look pretty.

The initial setup looked like this:

Figure 27.1

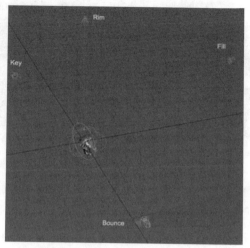

Figure 27.2

The first change we had to make came when we did some rendering tests and discovered that ray-tracing shadows from our area light, which normally takes quite a lot longer on geometry than fuzzy spotlights, would take a heinous chunk of time with the fur, which is volumetric. Imagine trying to calculate the rays from an area light through millions of fur fibers!

So we had to toss out our area light and come up with another solution. There was always Backdrop Only global illumination, but the same problem existed. The render times would be out of control.

I thought back to the days before area lights existed. What did they do then? How did they achieve soft shadows without area lights?

Light arrays! Back in the olden days, a lighting artist would build a rectangular array of point lights.

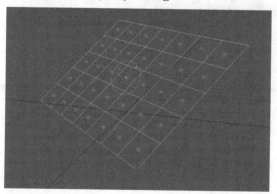

Figure 27.3

The point light array in Figure 27.3 was quickly created using luxigons. Boy, we sure could have used luxigons in the old days!

Not perfect, but not too bad for a 10-year-old lighting trick!

This is pretty much how an area light works anyway. But the problem with point lights again is ray tracing. Sasquatch uses its own engine to calculate shadows, but only with spotlights and only using shadow maps. So the immediate answer seemed to be an array made up of spotlights instead of point lights. This suited me fine, as I believed I could get away with fewer spotlights with higher shadow fuzziness. (Oh, what a fool I was!)

Figure 27.4

Note: I am washing over many details regarding Sasquatch as the exact particulars don't really apply here. For full details on the workings of Sasquatch, please see the Sasquatch manual.

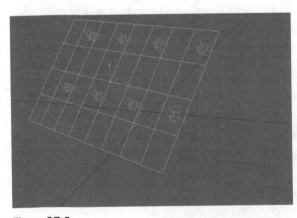

So I built an array of eight spotlights.

This seemed to work very well — so far. But when I rendered, I found lines of shadows created by the perfect geometry of the array. My solution to this was to offset half of the lights so that shadow lines would not be overlapping on the objects.

Figure 27.5

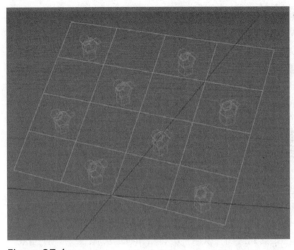

Figure 27.6

The next issue to be dealt with was that the animal heads would move around and rotate during a shot. Naturally, animals move their heads, just like people do. The head moves were carefully matchmoved, and we applied the finished motions to our geometry so that our CG heads would move in the same manner as the real animals' heads.

Note: Matchmoving is a grueling, brain-burning task involving taking geometrically imperfect geometry into Layout, loading up the plate, and making the geometry fit the animal on every single frame, one frame at a time. If you ever meet a matchmover, don't forget to give him cookies. It's a thankless job and has a rating of 11 on the tough-o-meter.

Our problem lay in that our spotlights have cone angles. In other words, there is a limited area where any given spotlight will illuminate something.

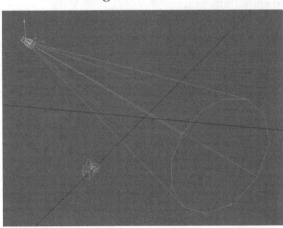

Figure 27.7

If the head is moving around, then either the cone has to be large enough to encompass the entire range of motion or the lights have to follow the head around as it moves. Both of these have their advantages and disadvantages.

467

If we make the light cones all large enough that we never have to move the lights, we never have to move the lights but we have a problem with shadow map resolution. We would have to crank up the shadow map resolution very high indeed so that the resolution was always high enough no matter where in the scene the object lay, and this would have a serious impact on render times. Remember, we're not talking about just one light calculating a shadow map; we're talking about eight array lights, a key light, a fill light, a rim light, and a bounce light. That's 12 lights with 12 shadow maps. So if we have to ramp up our shadow map resolution from 1000 to 4000 to cover the area of movement, that means it will take 16 times longer to calculate the shadow maps. We definitely needed a better solution than that! In addition, we wanted to keep the cone angle as narrow as possible so that the light "beams" were as parallel as possible, simulating a larger, more distant light source. If we had to make our lighting areas larger to encompass the range of motion we would have to back our lights off quite a distance to achieve the area of coverage we desired. This is not a huge problem, but when you are trying to get an overview of your lighting rig in the Perspective View and all your lights are a mile away, items get pretty tiny. You constantly have to ramp your world scale up and down to see things. It's a pain. There had to be a better way.

Of course, we could always target our spotlights to the CG animal head; that way each light would always illuminate the element, no matter how far it moved. But the problem with this is that the light angle would be changing relative to the object as it moved. It would look just like a bunch of follow-spots all aimed at the animal and following it around. Nope. We needed something better.

There was also the option of parenting all the lights to the animal head. This was not acceptable because the lights would always then maintain the same orientation to the head. As you know, when you turn your head in a lighting environment, the lights stay put and the orientation between head and lighting angle changes over time with your head rotation.

We needed all the good elements from each of these solutions with none of the bad ones. We needed a set of spotlights that would follow the head around without rotating. The most obvious solution to this was using expressions to make the light array maintain the same spatial position relative to the head but not rotate with the head. My first thought was to use LightWave's handy Follower plug-in.

Figure 27.8

With Follower, you can make one object follow another but only on the channels you desire.

So I parented all my lights on a null named Light_Main_Null. Then I applied Follower to the Light_Main_Null and opened its interface. In the Follower interface, I selected mm_Null as the object to follow, and told Follower to follow only the X,Y,Z channels.

I chose to use a null to apply Follower and parent the lights to the null rather than having all the lights follow the head object directly. That way, I could still independently move and rotate the lights relative to the head without affecting the following relationship.

Figure 27.9

> **Note:** The mm_Null ("matchmove" null) is where the animal's head rotation and motion information is applied. The actual head geometry is parented to the mm_Null. There are a ton of reasons why we did this, none of which are really related to lighting, so don't worry about it. Suffice it to say that since the motion and rotation were applied to a null object, the head, which was a child of the null object, moved just as it would if it had the motion and rotation applied directly to it.

Now that the lights follow the mm_Null but do not rotate, the spotlight cones always cover the geometry well just as we like. Our next step was to begin some rendering tests with fur enabled.

DISASTER STRIKES! During our tests we discovered that there is an issue between LightWave and Sasquatch which prevents Sasquatch from properly interpreting shadow fuzziness information from LightWave spotlights.

> **Note:** At the time of publication, it is not clear where the problem lies; however, both NewTek and Worley Labs are aware of the problem and are working to resolve it. We believe this problem will probably be resolved by the time you read this chapter; however, it didn't help us at the time of production!

The problem manifests itself in "crawling" fuzzy shadows. These artifacts were much too visible and obvious to allow use in a production environment. We were now tasked with creating soft shadows from spotlights with shadow maps, but we could not set our shadow fuzziness above 1.0 without the "crawling" artifact becoming visible. This meant that we either had to settle for hard-edged shadows or come up with another solution.

Fortunately, the old "spinning light" trick has been hanging around since the dawn of time, just waiting to save our bacon in a bad situation just like this one.

But the situation was a little more complex than a simple distant light rotating 360 degrees to make a big, soft shadow. We needed our lights to retain their directional qualities, to cast shadows, but simply to have those shadows soften at the edges.

We needed to create localized spinner setups for each of the four lights in our four-point rig, and we also needed a separate spinner that positionally spun the array without rotating it. I'll explain this in more detail later.

> **Note:** For details about just how and why the "spinning light" trick works, please see Chapter 25.

Adding a spinning light setup to each of the key, fill, rim, and bounce lights was not difficult. I started by adding a "Handle" null. This null is used to reposition the light. Beneath the Handle null I placed a

"Spinner" null. Beneath the Spinner null was the Offset null, and beneath the Offset null was the light itself.

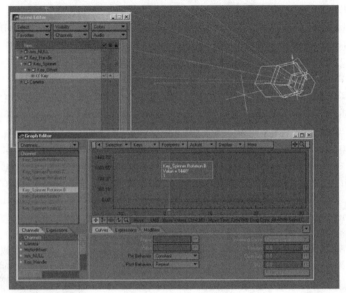

Figure 27.10

The handle is parented to the Light_Main null which is following the translation of the mm_ Null; therefore, all the spinning rigs will continue to maintain their spatial relationship with the head geometry.

Make sense so far? Not to worry, it gets much more complex.

Next, I had to set up a spinning rig for the array. But where you can simply spin a single light, you can't simply spin an array. Because the array is essentially a big, square fake area light, if you simply spin the whole thing, it will no longer behave like a rectangle but like a disc. You will lose shape control over your light. Furthermore, lights that are more distant from the rotation axis will cause softer shadows than those lights near the rotation axis. This is an undesired effect. This may be a moot and subtle point, but when you are dealing with as many variables as seemed to be creeping into this project, you want to minimize them as much as possible.

I placed a Handle null, Spinner null, Offset null, and Array Main null in parenting order. All eight array lights were parented to the Array Main null, while retaining their position in the array. To maintain the array's rotational orientation to the head geometry, I added an additional null in between the Offset null and the Array Main null called the Spin Corrector null. It works like this: Where the Spinner null rotates 1440 degrees for each frame (that's four complete rotations), the Spin

Corrector null rotates –1440 degrees for each frame. So while the entire array describes a circle around the spinner, at a distance set by the Offset null, the array itself does not rotate.

In addition to spinning lights, Sasquatch provided us with some tools to soften the shadows. Between the two, the shadows were looking quite good on the fur. But the geometry was another matter.

Due to heavy render times from the extremely dense fur we were using on our animals, we wanted to keep LightWave's AA level down to Enhanced Low. Often, you can set Sasquatch to render its antialiasing in one pass; however, the fur will then not be calculated in LightWave's motion blur. So we sometimes had to render the fur in each of Light-Wave's AA passes. The disadvantage to Enhanced Low AA is that the spinning light rigs now have only five passes to try to blend shadows into a soft shadow. While this looked good on the fur, the AA stepping became completely obvious where geometry was casting shadows onto itself.

The solution was to add a second set of lights. For example, instead of one key light, I would have two key lights, both the same color, intensity, angle, size, and everything, but one of them would only affect the fur and the other would only affect the geometry. The beauty of this solution was that I could turn shadow fuzziness back on for the geometry lights, thereby blurring the AA stepping. In the Object Properties panel, I excluded all the FUR lights from the geometry. In the Sasquatch pixel filter, I selected all the GEO lights as "Special Lights" and set the Special Light Strength to 0%, effectively excluding the GEO lights from Sasquatch and guaranteeing that all the GEO lights would not be used in the fur calculations.

All our problems seemed to be solved. Except now when I wanted to aim the key light, I had to aim two key lights. When I wanted to change the intensity of the rim light, I had to change the intensity of two rim lights. This quickly became cumbersome. I decided the quickest solution was to target both key lights to a Key Target null, both the fill lights to a Fill Target null, and so forth. The target nulls were parented to the mm_Null so that they would

Figure 27.11: You can see in the Scene Editor that there are now sets of lights exclusively for the geometry (GEO lights) and for the fur (FUR lights).

always maintain a spatial orientation to the geometry, and the lights would, therefore, always maintain their spatial and rotational orientation correctly. Each of the target nulls could be independently moved and keyframed, so aiming the light pairs would become very easy. This principle was also applied to the entire array, now 16 lights, so that all lights would be aimed wherever the Array Target was placed.

Imagine my horror, if you will, when I discovered that LightWave Targeting does not calculate properly if items are parented with expressions (i.e., Follower) instead of regular, hierarchical parenting. Suddenly all of the targeted lights were not aiming anywhere near the geometry. They were shooting out somewhere in space.

Once again, I was faced with a choice. I could eliminate the expressions in my lighting rig, which would mean the entire rig would no longer maintain its rotational orientation, or I could find another way of dealing with the expressions.

Enter Prem Subrahmanyam's Relativity 2.0.

I have used Relativity since version 1.0 was released several years ago. This plug-in has never failed me, and certainly did the job on this occasion as well. The main use of Relativity was to allow the Array_Main null (and therefore the light array) to match the position of the Spin Corrector null. No matter where the Spin Corrector null was located or oriented in the world, the Array_Main null had to occupy the same position. The Spin Corrector null was buried deep in a hierarchy of parenting and expressions. This made it impossible for LightWave's Follower plug-in to locate the correct position of this null.

Once I finally had everything moving, spinning, following, and targeting correctly, I got to work on a couple of workflow problems. One of the problems was that, although the light array was to be treated as a single light, it was in fact composed of 16 lights. Changing the intensity and color of 16 lights was definitely going to be a downer, not to mention the huge potential for pilot error once we started production. So I added a slider panel and included four channels, one for array intensity and one for each of the RGB channels.

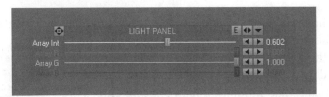

Figure 27.12

I then added a null called Array_Intensity and had the Array Intensity slider linked to the X channel of the null.

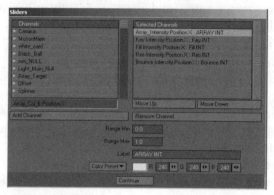

Figure 27.13

If the slider was at 0, then the Array_Intensity null was at X=0.0. If the slider was at 1.0, then the Array_Intensity null was at X=1. I then applied Relativity Channeler to the intensity channel of every array light in the Graph Editor under the Modifiers tab, linking the intensity to the X position of the Array_Intensity null.

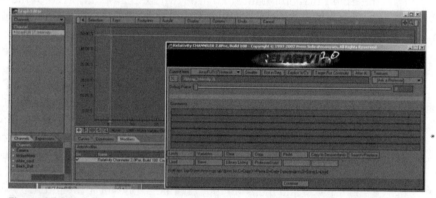

Figure 27.14

So now, when you moved the slider, the Array_Intensity null would move in the X channel. When the Array_Intensity null moved in the X channel, the intensity of every array light would go up or down. Having the Array_Intensity null also meant that intensity values could be entered numerically by entering the X value of the null in the numeric box.

Figure 27.15

I was also concerned that it would be time consuming to change the color of the array. With 16 lights, it would quickly become tedious to make even the smallest adjustment to hue or color temperature. So I applied the same thinking to the color channels that I had done to the intensity channel. I added one slider for each of the R, G, and B channels. I added a null for each, and I connected the red value of each light to the X value of each null, then controlled the null's X position with the slider.

Creating specific colors this way is not exactly easy. I ended up finding a color I liked using the color picker, recording the RGB values on paper, and then applying those values to the sliders to replicate the color I had chosen.

Since the key, fill, rim, and bounce lights were also arranged in GEO and FUR pairs, I decided to add four more sliders, one for each pair. My final slider panel had:

- Array Intensity
- Array Red Channel
- Array Green Channel
- Array Blue Channel
- Key Intensity
- Fill Intensity
- Rim Intensity
- Bounce Intensity

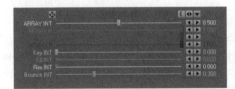

Figure 27.16

Since sliding the RGB channels is a pretty primitive method of selecting colors, and since each of the light pairs has only two lights, I decided not to add sliders for the RGB values of the key, fill, rim, and bounce lights, since it was simple enough to select a color and copy it to the second light. After all, LightWave's color picker has a sophisticated, full-featured set of color selection tools. Simply sliding RGB values actually kind of sucks.

Finally, since this lighting rig was developed under LightWave 7.5, we did not have the option of selecting which lights would illuminate OpenGL. In those days, only the first eight lights would illuminate

OpenGL. Since my key, fill, rim, and bounce lights were the first eight I had added to the scene, OpenGL would not illuminate at all if I only had the array turned on. So I had to add a special OpenGL light. I cloned the key light, renamed the original key light OpenGL, and parented it to the mm_Null, just to be sure the head geometry was illuminated at all times. Under Light Properties, I then disabled both Affect Diffuse and Affect Specular, leaving only Affect OpenGL enabled. This light was then set at 100%. Now animators would always have illumination in the OpenGL interface, regardless of the lighting setup, and that OpenGL lighting would never render. Perfect!

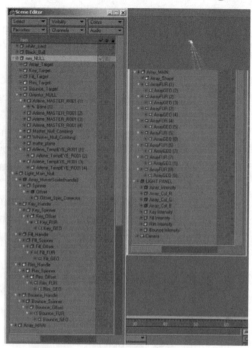

Figure 27.17

· · ·

It was a pretty complicated road that led to the development of this rig, but I hope I managed to describe not only the thinking process that was used to employ it but also the varied and unexpected production requirements that crop up, forcing you to rethink your methods and come up with solutions to seemingly unsolvable problems.

There is always a way to do it, if you just keep digging and thinking.

> **Note:** Since this chapter was written, the lighting rig went through a number of other changes to accommodate new information and new requirements. Chances are it will evolve until production is finished. But that's the fun part!

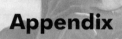

LightWave's "Full Precision" Renderer and You

mostly by Kenneth Woodruff, with contributions from
Arnie Cachelin and Allen Hastings

Reprinted with permission of NewTek, Inc.
The full, hyperlinked text is available at
http://www.lightwave3d.com/tutorials/fullprecision/index.html.

1. "Full precision"

A. What's it all about?

The human eye is capable of distinguishing massive ranges in brightness. Your eyes automatically adjust to lighting changes, and are capable of finding details lit by candlelight as well as the comparatively intense brightness of sunlight, all without any conscious effort on your part. Film captures a relatively small chunk of that range. Using the various controls and variables at his or her disposal, the photographer chooses which portion of the full brightness of the natural world to record to film. You, as a sort of photographer of your own scenes, can now exercise tremendous control over your renders, as well as use this range to apply realistic effects like film "bloom," caustics, and radiosity.

With LightWave® 6.0 came the powerful new rendering pipeline which renders with 128 bits of RGBA data throughout the rendering process (not including extra buffers!). This means that you get 32 bits of data for each color channel and the alpha channel. This flood of data traffic allows for very precise "floating-point," or decimal-based, values, as well as huge ranges of intensity — from previously impossibly low and subtle values to intensely high values. The most tangible example of a "high range" is a "high dynamic range" (HDR) image. An HDR image can contain intensity information with ranges many times greater than a normal RGB image. An HDR image contains a color range that is so wide that only a small portion of the image can be displayed in a normal 24-bit RGB color space (like your monitor). What you see when you render is a linear (flat and unadjusted) representation of that range of values. As in photography, the film's range can only record a portion of the range of lighting in the "real world," so the photographer has to choose which portion of the scene to capture. LightWave acts like a camera in this analogy, but automatically chooses a simple linear flattening of that range for display purposes. With tools like HDR Exposure and Virtual Darkroom, you can bias that compression however you'd like, effectively "exposing" the range that you'd like to extract from your piece of virtual film.

The practical effects of this technology, though transparent if you don't peek into or otherwise tweak your renders with the tools provided, range from subtle to astonishing. Every time a render is performed, you are given what amounts to a piece of film. The most basic use for this extra data is curve adjustments, which are given much more room for adjustment before the precision of the data contained in the image starts to break down. You can only adjust the gamma of a 24-bit render so much before you start seeing banding and stepping in your shading. A more extreme example involves exposing or "color correcting" the same rendered files as a completely different image without rendering again, going as far as turning day into night and near complete blackness into a day at the beach.

It's important to extend the camera analogy a bit further. Using traditional methods of lighting, surfacing, and rendering with LightWave is similar to using a "point-and-shoot" camera, in that most of the settings are determined for you, and you get what you expect just by setting up your shot and pressing the button. In the case of HDRI-based lighting, when delving into the higher intensity values for surfaces and internal lighting, and when activating radiosity rendering, you effectively change your point-and-shoot camera into a much more complex device (an "SLR," to further the analogy). In this state, you have many more choices to make, some of which can lead to conflicting results, easily confusing the goal and requiring more technical and/or practical knowledge of processes and terminology in order to bring out the desired image.

HDR/exposure/FP are not for everyone, and not for every situation. The FP pipeline was added to meet high-end needs, the benefits of which extend to whomever taps into them. The "SLR" technology is available to you, but it comes with responsibilities and its own share of setup complexities and issues. In many cases, you only want to simply capture an image. Following are some considerations, tips, and examples to help you understand what's going on, and how this immensely powerful system can help improve your output.

B. Where's the data?

Considering how much of this stuff is still mysterious and unexplored by most (which is like having a beefy sports car and just driving it around the block on occasion), this section serves to explain how to get to this FP goodness. Simply put, all you have to do is save the files. The entire pipeline is built to generate this data, but LightWave's defaults are set up to give you what you are accustomed to getting. The irony is that even though we've widened the highway, we're still pushing you through one lane at the end of your trip, by default. The data is only flattened into a non-FP range for display and saving purposes; it's only at this last step that any FP data is stripped away. The way to maintain this data is to simply save in an FP file format. If you are rendering directly to files, simply select an FP format instead of a "traditional" format and you'll get your FP data.

If you use an image viewer to view your renders and save files from inside the viewer, a distinction between Image Viewer FP and Image Viewer should be made. Image Viewer holds and displays data that has been squashed into 24 bits *before* being fed into the viewer. Image Viewer FP only flattens that data to display on your monitor, but it actually remembers much more information for that image. This is what makes the Exposure controls available in the Image Controls panel. Here you can perform some simple black and white point adjustments before saving. One caveat about Image Viewer FP is that it uses more RAM. If you are rendering at print resolutions, or are doing many test renders without closing the viewer, you might want to render directly to files.

For reference, the FP file formats included with LightWave are as follows: LightWave Flex (.flx), Radiance (.hdr), TIFF_LogLuv (.tif), CineonFP (.cin).

C. I don't use HDRI, or get into the fancy stuff, so why should I care?

The beauty of the FP pipeline is that even if you are not using HDRI, or pushing your ranges, you are always given a piece of film in the render. You are getting a precise render that can be adjusted and biased in a number of ways without being torn apart. If you set up a scene with almost imperceptible lighting, and your render turns to sludge, you can still squeeze some information out of the darkness, just like pushing a photographic negative during the printing process to milk it for more detail in the shadows. A scene built and rendered with this in mind can be adjusted in post without rendering again. This part is not new. What is new is the extent to which you can ruthlessly manipulate your images. The following images illustrate one of the advantages of post-adjusting images with a "full precision" range:

Images by Kenneth Woodruff

A. A raw LightWave render using an HDR reflection map. This is a collapsed (24-bit) version of a full-precision render.	B. A "re-exposed" version of the original render, with the white point set to ½ the original extreme and the black point set to 120% its original value.	C. This image has been "re-exposed" with the same settings, but the base image is the initial flattened, 24-bit render (image A). Notice that it is only more gray and there is no extra data. In a traditional pipeline, this information is completely lost.

2. Pre/post adjustment and exposure

A. Processing and adjusting your renders

Here's where it gets really interesting... The render that you see is not really the image that LightWave built for you. It appears to be the same as what you had been given in versions up to 5.6 (and in almost all other applications in use today). However, because of the limitations of modern displays, you initially see a flat, 24-bit version of the render. There is in fact a considerable amount of data that cannot be displayed on your monitor. A good way to get a sense of what you can pull off with your piece of digital film is to use Image Viewer FP. The Image Controls panel presents white and black point settings. To become more familiar with this process, you could set up a scene with some generic elements and use high intensity values in your lights, compensating for their effects in this panel. Even more adjustment power is available in the image filters included with LightWave.

If you've ever tinkered with gamma adjustment, channel mixing, histograms, or curve adjustment in a painting or compositing application, you probably understand the concepts of curves and histograms reasonably well. If not, the easiest way to explain what constitutes a curve is through example. In short, a curve represents a transition from the darkest to the lightest areas of the image. A cousin to the curve, the histogram represents the current levels of an image with vertical stacks of pixels that correspond to each value, spread out in a horizontal range from lowest to highest. This range is generally 0 to 255 (for a total of 256 possible values). In the case of FP data, this range is a value between two floating-point numbers. Regardless of the range of your image, the values in that image can still be represented in such a fashion; there's just more data (and more precise data) to represent. In a linear compression of FP values, white represents the brightest brights, or the highest highs of the image, and black the opposite. Having control over exposure adjustment allows you to focus on the areas of the image you'd like to represent more clearly, weighting portions of the curve based on the desired range, contrast, color variation, and tone.

To further illustrate the point, following is a progression of renders with post-adjustments, and fictitious representations of the curves involved in the adjustment. The yellow crosshairs represent a value that's sampled from the initial image (the range being represented by the horizontal arrow that runs along the bottom). The dot on the vertical line shows the value that the point is translated to on its way out:

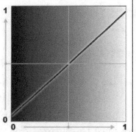

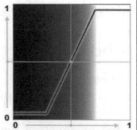

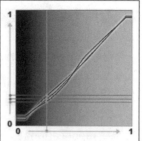

| I. Simple black-white gradient image. The sample point's value is the same going in and coming out. | II. Gradient image + HDR Exposure (with a lowered white point and a raised black point). The sample point value is the same, but the upper and lower limits (the white and black points) have been pushed towards the center, pushing contrast. The flat parts of this "curve" show areas that will be clipped. Sampling further along the curve would give you output values that are different from input values. | III. Gradient image + VDR color preset (gradient isn't smooth and colors are weighted according to the film's curves). In this case, the single curve is broken into different R, G, and B curves. Notice that the values on the output level (the line to the left) are staggered, indicating color variation for that sample point. |

B. Adjustment methods

I. More eloquence from Arnie regarding HDR Exposure: "The HDR Exposure filter can select how to spend the limited output dynamic range (typically 255:1) to best display the HDR data. Like gamma correction, this process can bring up detail in shaded areas. HDR Exposure rescales the image colors based on a black point, which is the highest level that will be black in the output. This is expressed as a percentage of the standard 24-bit black point (1/255). The white point is the lowest level that will be white. The default value, 1.0, usually maps to 255 in 24-bit imaging. Raising the white point brings detail out of the bright areas at the expense of the darker, while lowering the black point uses more colors in the darker areas." You can often achieve this type of detail extraction with a gamma adjustment (see 2BIII), without clipping your white and black extremes.

HDR Exposure provides options that are very similar to the Exposure settings in the Image Controls panel of the image viewer. This allows for manual and automatic assignment of the white and black points of the image. This can be used to bring the range of a render or HDR image into something that fits into 24-bit space. The simplest uses of this process would involve adjusting the black point to compensate for having used too much ambient light, or adjusting the white point to bring details out of a blown-out area. A more extreme example would involve using it to pull a manageable image out of a completely unruly HDRI map, as in some cases these images appear to only contain data in areas showing windows or light sources, when they in fact are hiding entire data in the dark areas. The following images demonstrate such a situation:

Source HDR courtesy of Paul Debevec and Jitendra Malik

| A. A raw HDR image, with little visible detail (initially). | B. The original image with a white point of 10.0. Notice that details are being pulled out of the blown-out areas. | C. The original image with a white point of 10.0 and a black point of 10% of the original black value. There's a real image in there! |

II. Regarding the Virtual Darkroom, here's more from our friend Arnie: "Making photographic prints from film also requires a restriction of an image's dynamic range. The original image, captured in the chemical emulsion on film, goes through two exposure processes that re-map the dynamic range. The first to create a negative, which is then used in the second pass to make a positive print. The Virtual Darkroom image filter simulates these two transformations using light response parameters from actual black and white or color film to match the results of photographic processing. This complex plug-in can be used to control the exposure of HDR images, while adding some film artifacts like grain and halo which may enhance the image's apparent naturalism."

The Virtual Darkroom (VDR) simulates the exposure and printing processes for different types of film and paper. It will introduce color shifting, representing the curves in the image in a way that more closely represents specific film types, going as far as applying sepia tones when the film stock has been designed to do so.

III. LightWave's gamma tends to be a bit darker than other renderers by default, due to its "linear" gamma curve. You can easily add a gamma adjustment as a post-processing image filter to adjust this gamma to your needs. Neither the included gamma adjustment filter or the Gamma slider in the Image Editor will flatten your ranges down into non-FP data, allowing you to save adjusted images into HDR file formats even after processing. We suggest processing the gamma of all of your output images, and that gamma adjustment is a good way to pull out seemingly imperceptible radiosity effects. Following is an example of that:

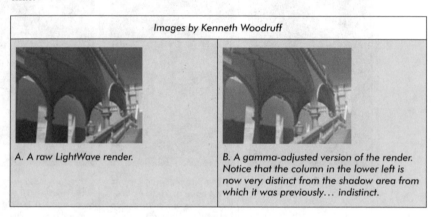

Images by Kenneth Woodruff

A. A raw LightWave render.

B. A gamma-adjusted version of the render. Notice that the column in the lower left is now very distinct from the shadow area from which it was previously... indistinct.

C. Should I post- or pre-adjust?

I. As with most situations, it depends. In some cases, you might want to pre-adjust an HDR image so that you can make other necessary adjustments to your scene without having to process the images just to see the effects of a change to your surfacing. Using straight HDR files, at times you may be confronted with an image that seems to be completely black with some bright spots, when it actually contains a wealth of detail. In this case, adjusting the range of the HDRI map to something that is easier to see without further tweaking may be in order. You may, however, want to maintain that huge range to allow for a wider range of possible final exposures. As for post-adjustments themselves, it's often best to render raw images and process them later, so that you do not waste time rendering images again just to make a slight adjustment, or if a client wants to see an image represented with a type of film that tends towards a darker tonal range. Also, while you may be a purist, preferring to tweak the lighting of a scene to perfection instead of relying on post-adjustment, in a production situation it's sometimes easier to run an image through a post-process and move on. Some studios render projects in HDR formats specifically so that they can reprocess the curves of the final image to accommodate client demands and to perform precision color corrections in compositing software without fear of clipping or other correction issues. That's powerful stuff.

II. In most cases, it is a great time-saver to render images into FP formats, then load the FP image for post operations like those mentioned above, producing a final image without damaging it in the initial render. This is a reasonable practice in other situations, like those involving post-glows and other post-processing filters.

3. Radiosity

Radiosity is the process of calculating lighting bounces from one object to another, and from the environment to the objects contained therein. It's a randomized process, using a high number of samples and generally taking more time than item-based lights. The complexity of the process has been simplified into just a few parameters, which determine the number of samples, the influence of the radiosity lighting, and various sampling settings.

A. The modes

I. Backdrop Only — Backdrop Only radiosity is similar to using an "accessibility" shader, like gMil or LightWave 5.6's Natural Shaders. Corners, nooks, and areas inaccessible to light are shaded according to how much light can reach them, which gives very natural shading, but this method is not as accurate as one that actually takes the environmental colors and light bounces into account. Backdrop Only is very useful for baking this accessibility information into image maps for layering with diffuse textures to improve shading realism, adding noise, pre-calculating global illumination, and rendering objects that are relatively isolated from other elements in an environment. Many outdoor situations can be generated without an extra bounce.

II. Monte Carlo — The catch-all for the average global illumination situation. Use this when you want stuff to actually bounce around — like indoor situations with a few light sources, when you have bright objects that would reflect their light and coloration onto surrounding elements.

III. Interpolated — By nature, this mode allows for more ray "tolerance" (basically, how much two adjacent rays can tolerate their different intensities). This is a mode that allows you to adjust more quality settings in order to tweak your render times. It uses a more visibly randomized process, so each frame of an animation can generate visibly different results — this is one reason that Monte Carlo is preferred. These settings can be fine-tuned for different situations however, so it can be used to generate faster renders than Monte Carlo, while providing a real bounce, unlike Backdrop Only.

IV. gMil — Though not radiosity, much less a radiosity mode, gMil should be mentioned in context with the other global illumination options available to you. gMil is a shader-based third-party solution (by Eric Soulvie) for generating global illumination effects. It is an "occlusion" shader, which means that it searches for how accessible to lighting the geometry might be. Its results are similar to the Backdrop Only radiosity mode, but it has specific controls for determining where the illumination effects are applied, as well as more options for determining what is affected. As it is a shader, it can be applied on a per-surface basis, which can save time when you do not need to generate radiosity for an entire scene.

Hydrant geometry courtesy of MeniThings			

I. Backdrop Only radiosity - Notice that there's no color "bleeding" between the objects in the scene.	II. A Monte Carlo render of the classic "Cornell box." There is no noise, but the render time was considerable when compared with the Interpolated version.	III. Interpolated Radiosity - The settings used for this scene cause it to render much faster than a Monte Carlo version, but the splotching has been retained to show the effects.	IV. gMil - This scene differs from image (I) only in that gMil was used for all shading. Notice that the darks are darker with default settings.

B. Ambient intensity and radiosity

This comes directly from Arnie Cachelin: "When Radiosity is enabled, the ambient light value is added only to the indirect diffuse lighting of surfaces, not to the direct lighting. This means that the ambient level functions as the sum of all the higher order diffuse light 'bounces.' This little-known solution provides adjustable levels of higher order lighting, which is generally a very subtle effect, while avoiding the exponential increase in the number of expensive ray-trace operations otherwise required by multi-bounce global illumination solutions. Contrary to your well-honed instinct for LW photo-realism, ambient intensity should NOT automatically be set to negligible levels for radiosity. In general, the ambient level will need to account for second and higher-order bounces from many directions. These bounces will tend to contribute more if there are very bright lights in the scene, or bright luminous objects or bright spots in HDR Image World environments. In these cases bumping up the ambient intensity will increase accuracy. It will also help smooth noisy artifacts of undersampling, and light nooks and crannies which may otherwise not sample enough of the environment. This is better than just a hack, because every level of bounce makes the lighting less directional, of far lower intensity, and more susceptible to undersampling. Subsuming these bounces into a uniform level takes advantage of these characteristics, and eliminates the extra sampling requirements."

It's important to interject that adding ambient to your radiosity-lit scenes will still lighten your darks. To compensate for this, you can post-adjust your renders, setting the black point higher, or compensate with gamma adjustment. It is also important to note that you may not need as much lighting as a raw render may lead you to believe. The linear gamma mentioned in 2BIII does cause the general tone of your radiosity renders to appear darker than they would be if the gamma were post-adjusted to compensate.

C. Multi-bounce radiosity

LightWave 7.5 came with quite a few new features, not the least of which is multi-bounce radiosity. This extends LightWave's radiosity capabilities tremendously, but comes at a price. Multi-bounce renders can be orders of magnitude more time-consuming than single-bounce. It is recommended that you exercise this feature with caution, and a lot of horsepower. Due to the render time considerations, this is definitely a good case for surface baking.

One of the most obvious uses of multi-bounce is in radiosity, lighting things like long halls. If you were to attempt to light this hall from one end using only one bounce, you'd have a reasonably lit area at one end of the hall and a void at the other end. Multi-bounce would transport those light rays well beyond their previous areas of influence. A more common use for this is achieving more realistic, and fuller, lighting in indoor situations. Using a single bounce often leads to inky shadows that would naturally be lit by the unfathomable number of bounces that real light makes. The following images show different levels of light influence,

beginning with a single point light and progressing through four
bounces.

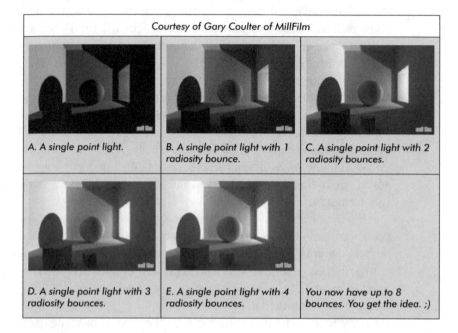

Courtesy of Gary Coulter of MillFilm		
A. A single point light.	*B. A single point light with 1 radiosity bounce.*	*C. A single point light with 2 radiosity bounces.*
D. A single point light with 3 radiosity bounces.	*E. A single point light with 4 radiosity bounces.*	*You now have up to 8 bounces. You get the idea. ;)*

D. Speed

I. Samples — The number of samples is your primary tool for adjustment of quality and speed. In general, you'll want to find the balance
between quality and render times, so some experimentation for each situation is in order. It's important to note that the effects of noise caused
by using too few samples is very much affected by antialiasing. Just like
bump maps (among other things), it's entirely possible for you to get
very different results with antialiased renders.

II. Shading Noise Reduction — Use of this option is highly recommended. It causes a blurring of the diffuse information in the scene,
which reduces splotchiness and softens radiosity calculations. With this
option, you can use fewer samples and still get soft shading. It is also
useful for reduction of noise in area/linear lights and caustics. The down-
side is that it sometimes blurs contrasting areas of your diffuse shading
that you would like to keep. For example, it may in some cases blur your
bump mapping more than you'd prefer or affect your mapped diffuse
channels. You can compensate by raising the bump value or using more
rays so that there's less to blur.

4. Global illumination with internal lighting, HDRI, and other methods

The ubiquity of the floating-point pipeline allows for HDR texturing and global illumination with HDRI maps, as well as the pushing of ranges using completely internal systems. For example, LightWave 7's Radiosity Intensity feature would allow for a setting such as 1000%. Adding an object to such a blinding environment would normally give you a render that is flat white (or deceptively speckled). Using exposure adjustment settings (in this example: white point set to 10.0 and black point set to 1000%) compresses that information down into a displayable bit depth, giving you an image very similar to one rendered with 100% radiosity. As mentioned in the section about curves above, the black point could then be pushed even higher, adjusting the tonal range of an image that was previously completely white.

A. Light is light (HDRI or not)

If you were to make an array of lights with the same placement, intensity values, and colors as individual areas of an environment-wrapped HDRI map, you could conceivably get results similar to radiosity renders — though the results might not be as convincing without a huge number of lights. Who has the time for that, and who has the patience to use as many "lights" as LightWave can generate automatically? You might be able to accurately represent a simpler environment with a few well-placed area lights, or you might need to capture all of the subtle coloration, shadow density, and shadow shaping that would be provided by using an HDRI map captured from a real location. You may even choose to combine the two. In this respect, each facet of the LightWave system allows you to choose where to expend your time. You do not have to use HDRI to take advantage of this data.

B. Mixing it up

I. Using familiar controls — LightWave's renderer is "full precision" at its core. Any surface can generate a 1000% luminous glow, for example, and lighting can range from tremendous subtlety to overpowering brightness. The resulting render can be adjusted by the same means mentioned above. Even Skytracer renders skies with FP ranges, so you can easily use it directly as a "light source" in your radiosity scenes, or "bake" the sky in an HDR file format so that you don't have to recalculate it for every frame.

II. Using images only — Thanks to LightWave's radiosity features, you can light a scene entirely with images. By surrounding your scene with an image map, the subtle colors and intensity values contained in the image map are used to trace light "sources" from their relative locations, as recorded in the map. This process — a subset of what is referred to as "global illumination" — is an accurate way to match CG elements with real environments, and imparts a range of hues and intensities into your scenes that is difficult to reproduce with internal lighting. These images can actually be any image that you produce, with any range of data, including any type of image that LightWave can load. You can use 24-bit images, but the range and precision of the color values will not be as great.

III. Combining images and internal stuff — LightWave provides the ability to "bake" radiosity calculations into image maps. You can choose to bake everything that you see (other than camera-relative properties like specularity and reflections) into image maps so that you do not have to recalculate the radiosity solution. In many cases, you can choose to bake only your diffuse shading into image maps, then combine the baked radiosity with rendered lighting to either provide the major lighting for the scene or augment the shading produced by the baked solution. You can also choose to use HDRI as the global light source, and place item lights in order to generate a more specific lighting direction, generate caustics, or provide different shadows than those which are based entirely on your maps. The following images show the same scene lit by different HDRI maps, one of which gets a nudge from a placed light source:

Images courtesy of Terrence Walker of Studio ArtFX	

A. Skull lit with a desert map and a strong light source to the right.	B. Skull lit entirely with an HDRI map and radiosity.

IV. Other methods — In addition to the many tools available inside LightWave, there are a few external options for adapting HDRI maps for use in LightWave. At the time of writing, there is only one solution for editing of HDR images, that being HDRShop. There is also a process involving a plug-in for HDRShop (LightGen) that converts illumination maps into an array of lights with appropriate coloration and intensity values. An LScript (LightGen2LW) is then used to convert this data to LightWave lights. This ends up being a sort of reversed global illumination process, which can sometimes give you equivalent results in less time. Unfortunately, also at the time of writing, these solutions are not available for the Macintosh.

5. Tips

- You can use radiosity to generate realistic lighting situations, then mimic the effect of the radiosity solution with LightWave lights to keep render times low.

- One way to help radiosity calculations when using very high-contrast images is to blur the environment image. Less contrasting values will be hit by adjacent rays, so there will be fewer sparkling and splotching problems.

- With very few exceptions, the only surface setting that should contain values greater than 100% is luminosity. No surface, even in a new limitless environment, will reflect more than 100% of any specific setting. Luminosity, being an emissive property, can be whatever it needs to be. The exceptions involve some exotic surfaces like dayglow materials and the occasional need to push a setting in order to compensate for some other deficiency or to "exaggerate" the effects of the physically accurate renders.

- Due to the removal of limits on brightness values, some conditions can lead to absurdly high values, resulting in speckling or completely blown-out areas. This is actually a result of the antialiasing being performed on the high-range image. An example of this sort of situation is the use of lights with inverse distance falloff. The logarithmic nature of this falloff can lead to exponentially higher values as objects are nearer to the light source. One way to counteract this problem, which you should only use if you cannot address the cause of the problem directly, is to use the Limit Dynamic Range function in the Image Processing panel. This will clamp the calculated output to 24-bit value ranges, thereby erasing the benefits and the pitfalls of these processes.

- A very blatant stair-stepping effect can occur when high-contrast ranges meet. This effect looks like a complete lack of antialiasing, but is really due to the range difference between two sharply contrasting pixels being too high to represent with only a few adjoining pixels. You can alleviate this by adjusting your setup to reduce these very high-contrast areas or by exposing the image to bring the black and white points closer together.

- A low radiosity sampling size can cause bright areas to be skipped. If your light source only covers a small amount of an image map, it could be skipped entirely by radiosity evaluation. For example, if only four rays are fired from a specific area, it's possible that as the rays travel away from the surface, they spread in such a way that they do not hit the area of your environment that represents the light source.

You've got it…USE IT!

Index

KEYFRAME
MAGAZINE

Keyframe Magazine has been published since January 1997, and has had a very strong readership with users of NewTek's LightWave 3D, Video Toaster, and other 2D/3D digital tools. These readers are using animation and visual effects media in their daily lives for photography, architecture, advertising, web sites, medicine, training, games and feature films. Keyframe is a magazine that provides a invaluable resource for them.

Here's your chance to have Keyframe, the industry favorite, delivered right to your door!

❏ USA 1 year (6 issues) $54

❏ USA 2 year (12 issues) $102

❏ Canada/Mexico 1 year (6 issues) $72

❏ Canada/Mexico 2 year (12 issues) $138

❏ All other countries 1 year (6 issues) $84

❏ All other countries 2 year (12 issues) $162

Name _____

Email _____

Phone _____ Fax _____

Company _____

Address _____

_____

_____

Credit Card # _____ Exp. _____

Signature _____

Free Subscriptions!

Get your
LightWave from us
and
we'll bundle a
free subscription
with it.

Go to our Online Store at
www.dmgpublishing.com

Save $$$
by Subscribing Online!

Save up to 70% on
our Magazine Bundle Offers

Go to our Online Store at
www.dmgpublishing.com

DMG Publishing
2756 N Green Valley Pkwy # 261
Henderson, NV 89014-2120 USA
Email: info@dmgpublishing.com
Tel: 1-702-990-8656 or 1-888-778-9283
Fax: 1-702-616-9647

LightWave 101
Interactive Training Course and Curriculum Guide™

LightWave 3D is one of the most powerful 3D graphics and animation programs on the market today. If you can dream it, you can build it in LightWave. Many of the awesome 3D graphics you see in movies, on TV, and in print were created with LightWave 3D. Yet with power comes complexity. **Beginners ask, "Where do I start?" The answer is - LightWave 101** - an Interactive Training Course and Curriculum Guide created by the artists and animators at the epic software group.

This CD-Based program contains everything you need to learn LightWave 3D. It takes a completely fresh approach to 3D training, and moves you through the program at a comfortable pace. The number of options available in LightWave can be intimidating to even a seasoned pro. LightWave 101 tames this 3D powerhouse by showing you how to do the right things, the right way, right from lesson one. Before you know it, you'll be creating 3D graphics that will astound both you and your friends.

Although LightWave 101 was originally created for 3D Instructors, we have expanded it to be a perfect learning tool for students, as well. There are six sections to this multimedia training guide:

Section 1 - 3D Interactive

Here you will learn all about the Animation Process. Multimedia demos are used to illustrate the concepts of 3D.

- Conceptualization
- Storyboards
- Character Design
- 3D Space
- Primitives
- Boolean
- Extrude
- Lathe
- Mirror
- Subdivision Surfaces

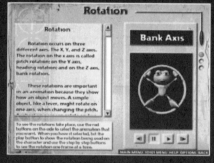

- Rotate
- Walk Cycles
- Bones
- Key Frames
- Lights
- Specularity
- Image Mapping
- Anti Aliasing
- Lip Syncing
- Demo Reels
- Glossary of 3D Terms

Section 2 - Curriculum Guide

Welcome to our virtual classroom where you'll find a full semester's curriculum. Easy to follow lessons make this curriculum guide perfect for both students and teachers.

Section 3 - Intermediate Tutorials

After you have mastered the basics in sections 1 and 2, get ready to put your knowledge to the test. There are over 20 tutorials to help you learn to create everything from animated logos to basic character modeling.

- Bones Made Simple
- Building 3D Interfaces
- Bumpy Textures with Bump Maps
- Creating Tileable Textures
- Displacement Map Basics
- Animate a Bouncing Logo
- Lasers and Energy Beams
- Layout Basics
- Magnification Using Refraction
- Character Modeling with Subdivision Surfaces

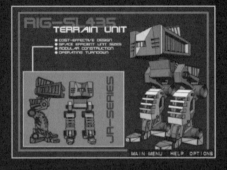

- Making Logos Come Alive in 3D
- Making the Most of Fractal Noise
- Modeling Basics
- Modeling Terrain
- Moving Multiple Objects Using Nulls
- Pipes and Banners
- Repeating Motion Paths
- Squashing 3D Into 2D
- Taking 2D Labels to a New Dimension
- Volumetric Lighting
- 3D Industrial Design

Section 4 - Lights, Camera, Action

Ever watch a blockbuster movie, see a special effect, and wonder - How did they do that? In this section, you'll learn the techniques of the digital cinematographer.

Section 5 - LightWave Resource Guide

This Resource Guide is complete with links to the most popular LightWave 3D web sites, LightWave 3D books, 3D model libraries, listing of popular LightWave plug-in's, texture sources, and so much more. You are always just a click away from anything LightWave, when you are in the Resource section of the program.

Section 6 - Bonus Section

In our Bonus Section, feast your eyes on a gallery of 3D graphics and animations to inspire you. An arcade, complete with 10 games (created with 3D graphics produced in LightWave), will entertain you. We have also included 100 free 3D models from the epic software group 3D model library, for you to use in your scenes.

Special offer for WordWare Customers:

LightWave 101 Interactive Training Course and Curriculum Guide™ is just **$59.95**, plus **$4.95** S&H (North America), **$8.95** (International) As a WordWare customer, you can save **20%** by ordering directly from the epic web site (www.epicsoftware.com) and entering discount code **WW-101**, or by calling epic directly at: 281-363-3742.

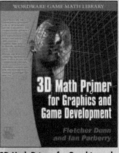

spinQuad
XYZ entertainment

spinQuad

www.spinquad.com
Your LightWave Community

Honor is Life

Filmmaking should be the domain
of every dedicated person who
dreams to "dream aloud..."

Timothy Albee --
Goldstream Valley, Alaska

KAZE
GHOST WARRIOR

This DVD contains the complete
22-minute film in region-free format,
plus bonus material.

Order your copy today!

For more information, please go to:
http://www.wordware.com/ghostwarrior

About the CD

The companion CD contains a number of illustrative images, objects, and scenes used in the book, including a 60-frame underwater image sequence discussed in Chapter 10, materials for the Overcaster tutorial in Chapter 16, and two LightWave models by William Vaughan. Additionally, all of the figures from the book are located in the Figures folder and are organized by chapter.

 Warning: By opening the CD package, you accept the terms and conditions of the CD/Source Code Usage License Agreement. Additionally, opening the CD package makes this book nonreturnable.

CD/Source Code Usage License Agreement

Please read the following CD/Source Code usage license agreement before opening the CD and using the contents therein:

1. By opening the accompanying software package, you are indicating that you have read and agree to be bound by all terms and conditions of this CD/Source Code usage license agreement.

2. The compilation of code and utilities contained on the CD and in the book are copyrighted and protected by both U.S. copyright law and international copyright treaties, and is owned by Wordware Publishing, Inc. Individual source code, example programs, help files, freeware, shareware, utilities, and evaluation packages, including their copyrights, are owned by the respective authors.

3. No part of the enclosed CD or this book, including all source code, help files, shareware, freeware, utilities, example programs, or evaluation programs, may be made available on a public forum (such as a World Wide Web page, FTP site, bulletin board, or Internet news group) without the express written permission of Wordware Publishing, Inc. or the author of the respective source code, help files, shareware, freeware, utilities, example programs, or evaluation programs.

4. You may not decompile, reverse engineer, disassemble, create a derivative work, or otherwise use the enclosed programs, help files, freeware, shareware, utilities, or evaluation programs except as stated in this agreement.

5. The software, contained on the CD and/or as source code in this book, is sold without warranty of any kind. Wordware Publishing, Inc. and the authors specifically disclaim all other warranties, express or implied, including but not limited to implied warranties of merchantability and fitness for a particular purpose with respect to defects in the disk, the program, source code, sample files, help files, freeware, shareware, utilities, and evaluation programs contained therein, and/or the techniques described in the book and implemented in the example programs. In no event shall Wordware Publishing, Inc., its dealers, its distributors, or the authors be liable or held responsible for any loss of profit or any other alleged or actual private or commercial damage, including but not limited to special, incidental, consequential, or other damages.

6. One (1) copy of the CD or any source code therein may be created for backup purposes. The CD and all accompanying source code, sample files, help files, freeware, shareware, utilities, and evaluation programs may be copied to your hard drive. With the exception of freeware and shareware programs, at no time can any part of the contents of this CD reside on more than one computer at one time. The contents of the CD can be copied to another computer, as long as the contents of the CD contained on the original computer are deleted.

7. You may not include any part of the CD contents, including all source code, example programs, shareware, freeware, help files, utilities, or evaluation programs in any compilation of source code, utilities, help files, example programs, freeware, shareware, or evaluation programs on any media, including but not limited to CD, disk, or Internet distribution, without the express written permission of Wordware Publishing, Inc. or the owner of the individual source code, utilities, help files, example programs, freeware, shareware, or evaluation programs.

8. You may use the source code, techniques, and example programs in your own commercial or private applications unless otherwise noted by additional usage agreements as found on the CD.

 Warning: By opening the CD package, you accept the terms and conditions of the CD/Source Code Usage License Agreement.
Additionally, opening the CD package makes this book nonreturnable.